CRITICAL   G$
VIOLENCE   H$

 in CULTURAL and MEDIA STUDIES

Series editor: Stuart Allan

Published titles:

CRITICAL READINGS: VIOLENCE AND THE MEDIA

Edited by
C. Kay Weaver and Cynthia Carter

OPEN UNIVERSITY PRESS

Maidenhead and New York

Open University Press
McGraw-Hill Education
McGraw-Hill House
Shoppenhangers Road
Maidenhead
Berkshire
England
SL6 2QL

email: enquiries@openup.co.uk
world wide web: www.openup.co.uk

and Two Penn Plaza, New York, NY 10121–2289, USA

First published 2006

A catalogue record of this book is available from the British Library

ISBN-10: 0 335 21805 9 (pb) 0 335 21806 7 (hb)
ISBN-13: 978 0 335 21805 9 (pb) 978 0 335 21806 6 (hb)

Library of Congress Cataloging-in-Publication Data
CIP data applied for

Typeset by RefineCatch Limited, Bungay, Suffolk
Printed in Poland by OZGraf S.A.
www.polskabook.pl

CONTENTS

SERIES EDITOR'S FOREWORD

The body count in prime-time television entertainment, anecdotal evidence would suggest, is on the increase. Leading the way are crime-oriented dramas, such as *CSI: Crime Scene Investigation*, *Law & Order* or *The Sopranos*, which are remarkably popular with audiences and critics alike. Meanwhile in the cinema, grisly films with chilling special effects regularly top the box office – some of the most gruesome of which end up being watched by viewers otherwise too young to see them, thanks to videos, DVDs and the internet in the home. Why, we may be tempted to ask, is this so? What is it about such material, with its gratuitous splatter of human misery, that makes it so compelling? More to the point perhaps, what is it about our everyday cultures that engenders the desire to welcome it so warmly into our lives in the first place?

Questions such as these are easy enough to pose, of course, yet satisfactory answers to them have proven surprisingly elusive over the years. In seeking to help identify ways forward, C. Kay Weaver and Cynthia Carter's *Critical Readings: Violence and the Media* highlights a number of important contributions to this area of investigation. The Reader is divided into four substantive sections, the first of which provides a broad introduction to some of the influential ideas that have inspired research over the past four decades. Together these essays elucidate several key concepts in the course of outlining the principal terms of debate within media violence research. The second section revolves around essays focusing on the dynamics of media institutions – emphasizing the significance of media ownership and regulation, among other factors – where the production of violent material is concerned. Essays in the third section examine media content, paying close attention to the ways in which violence is represented, and how such portrayals connect with society more widely. The fourth and final section presents essays exploring how audiences actively negotiate the contradictory meanings of media violence as part of their everyday lives. Across its breadth, then, this volume's alignment of such a rich array of topics and perspectives promises to help reinvigorate current thinking, pushing it forward in new and exciting directions.

The *Issues in Cultural and Media Studies* series aims to facilitate a diverse range of critical investigations into pressing questions considered to be central to current thinking and research. In light of the remarkable speed at which the conceptual agendas of cultural and media studies are changing, the series is committed to contributing to what is an ongoing process of re-evaluation and critique. Each of the books is intended to provide a lively, innovative and comprehensive introduction to a specific topical issue from a fresh perspective. The reader is offered a thorough grounding in the most salient debates indicative of the book's subject, as well as important insights into how new modes of enquiry may be established for future explorations. Taken as a whole, then, the series is designed to cover the core components of cultural and media studies courses in an imaginatively distinctive and engaging manner.

Stuart Allan

ACKNOWLEDGEMENTS

C. Kay Weaver would like to thank Cynthia Carter for her support, enthusiasm, good humour, and extraordinary energy over the years that we have worked together. A number of people have been very generous with, variously, their friendship, advice, sustenance and entertainment during the time that I have been involved with this book: Trena Marshall, Olive Jones, Ann Hardy, Michele and Mutzi Schoenberger-Orgad, Liz Lake, Juliet Roper, David McKie, Ted Zorn, Mary Simpson, Cheryl Cockburn-Wootten, and Debra Fraser. Thanks to you all. I would like to dedicate this Reader to Nan Seuffert, and thank her especially for her tolerance, sense of fun, and contagious capacity for adventure.

Cynthia Carter thanks Kay Weaver for cheerfully agreeing to work on a second book together. The 11-hour time difference between New Zealand and the UK, and our respective back to front semesters, made coordinating this project somewhat complicated at times. But, of course, the intellectual challenge of putting together this Reader and the fun that we had discussing its contents, scope, and potential contribution to media violence debates far outweighed whatever logistical difficulties we encountered. Thanks for being such a great co-editor, Kay. I am grateful to Geoffrey and Stuart for their love, support, and patience with me while I was working on this project. Thanks guys. I owe you.

We would both also like to thank Christopher Cudmore of Open University Press for his enthusiasm to follow up our co-authored book, *Violence and the Media*, with this accompanying Reader. Also at the Press, we're grateful to Hannah Cooper, Editorial Assistant, for dealing with all of our changing requests for different permissions. We would also like to thank all those authors whom we contacted to ask them if they would be willing to have their work reprinted in this volume. Regrettably, in the end, we were unable to include all the papers we would have liked due to the exigencies of constructing a broadly based Reader with only a limited number of words at our disposal. To those who kindly agreed to have their chapter included, and who worked with us to ensure that the redactions still reflected their main arguments and conclusions, we are grateful to you for your patience and graciousness. And, lastly, our warmest thanks to our Series Editor, Stuart Allan. His advice, encouragement, and commitment to this project certainly resulted in our producing a much more engaging Reader than the one we originally had in mind.

ORIGINAL REFERENCES AND ACKNOWLEDGEMENTS FOR READINGS

The authors and publishers wish to thank the following for permission to use copyright material:

Adam, A. 'Cyberstalking and Internet Pornography: Gender and the Gaze', in *Ethics and Information Technology*, Vol. 4, No. 2, pp. 133–42, © 2002, Kluwer Academic Publishers. Reproduced with kind permission from Springer Science and Business Media and the author.

Bandura, A., Ross, D. and Ross, S.A. 'Imitation of Film-mediated Aggressive Models', *Journal of Abnormal & Social Psychology*, Vol. 66, pp. 3–11, © 1963, American Psychological Association. Reproduced by permission of the American Psychological Association and the first author.

Barker, M. and Petley, J. 'Introduction: From Bad Research to Good – A Guide for the Perplexed', in *Ill Effects: The Media/Violence Debate* (2nd edn), Barker, M. and Petley, J. (eds), Routledge (2001). Reproduced by permission of the author. Originally published by Routledge in 2001.

Bruce, D.R. 'Notes Toward a Rhetoric of Animation: *The Road Runner* as Cultural Critique', in *Critical Studies in Media Communication*, Vol. 18, No. 2, pp. 229–45, © 2001, Routledge. Reproduced by permission of Routledge (http://www.tandf.co.uk/journals) and the author.

Buckingham, D. 'Children Viewing Violence', in *After the Death of Childhood*, Polity (2000). Reproduced by permission of Polity and the author.

Campbell, D. 'Horrific Blindness: Images of Death in Contemporary Media', *Journal for Cultural Research*, Vol. 88, No. 1, pp. 55–74, © 2004,

Initiative', in *Framing Abuse: Media Influence and Public Understanding of Sexual Violence Against Children*, Pluto (2004). Reproduced by permission of Pluto and the author.

Labre, M.P. and Duke, L. ' "Nothing Like a Brisk Walk and a Spot of Demon Slaughter to Make a Girl's Night": The Construction of the Female Hero in the Buffy Video Game', *Journal of Communication Inquiry*, Vol. 28, No. 2, pp. 138–56, © 2004, Sage. Reproduced by permission of Sage Publications and the authors.

Merskin, D. 'The Construction of Arabs as Enemies: Post-September 11 Discourse of George W. Bush', *Mass Communication & Society*, Vol. 7, No. 2, pp. 157–75, © 2004, Lawrence Erlbaum. Reproduced by permission of Lawrence Erlbaum and the author.

Ogle, J.P., Eckman, M. and Leslie, C.A. (2003) 'Appearance Cues and the Shootings at Columbine High: Construction of a Social Problem in the Print Media', *Sociological Inquiry*, Vol. 73, No. 1, pp. 1–27, © 2003, Blackwell. Reproduced by permission of Blackwell Publishing and the authors.

Palmer-Meta, V. and Hay, K. 'The Anti-gay Hate Crime Story Line in DC Comics' *Green Lantern*: An Analysis of Reader Responses', GLAAD: Center for the Study of Media and Society (2003). Reproduced by permission of the authors.

Piot, C. 'Heat on the Street: Video Violence in American Teen Culture', *Postcolonial Studies*, Vol. 6, No. 3, pp. 351–65, © 2003, Routledge. Reproduced by permission of Taylor & Francis Ltd (http://www.tandf.co.uk/journals) and the author.

Ramasubramanian, S. and Oliver, M.B. (2003) 'Portrayals of Sexual Violence in Popular Hindi Films, 1997–99', *Sex Roles: A Journal of Research*, Vol. 47, No. 7, pp. 327–36, © 2003, Kluwer Academic Publishers. Reproduced with kind permission from Springer Science and Business Media and the authors.

Semanti, M. 'Imagine the Terror', *Television and New Media*, Vol. 3, No. 2, pp. 213–18, © 2002, Sage. Reproduced by permission of Sage Publications and the author.

MEDIA VIOLENCE RESEARCH IN THE TWENTY-FIRST CENTURY
A CRITICAL INTERVENTION

C. Kay Weaver and Cynthia Carter

Why Study Violence and the Media?

Debates about the possible effects that media violence – from Hollywood cinema to Saturday morning cartoons – may have on audiences have long been hotly contested in media research and policy. The key issues have attracted attention well beyond the confines of research institutions and policy-making bodies, with questions about whether the media play a role in encouraging violent and criminal behaviour proving to be particularly vexing. Indeed, from the early days of the newspaper, to the invention of moving pictures, then radio, comic books, television and the internet, fears have been expressed about the potential risks associated with violent imagery. Expressions of concern about the harmful influence depictions of violence may have on children have been particularly salient (Anderson and Bushman 2001, 2002; Cantor 2002; Johnson *et al.* 2002; Starker 1989), even to the extent of encouraging moral panics (Critcher 2003).

Researchers who subscribe to 'effects theory' arguments tend to assume that there is a strong link between viewing violent media content and violent behaviour in individuals. As Geen (1994: 158) suggests, media violence can 'engender a complex of associations consisting of aggressive ideas, emotions related to violence, and [serve as] the impetus for aggressive acts'. **Fictional representations of violence** are considered of particular concern, especially where they are regarded to be glamorizing crime and violence or trivializing it by way of encouraging audiences to simply view such content as entertainment. It is claimed that by failing to ensure that the serious and harmful consequences of crime and violence are understood, and by often portraying those who commit acts of violence as heroes, the media are encouraging audiences to imitate aggressive and anti-social acts. Moreover, even if people are not affected by media violence in terms of behaving more aggressively than they otherwise might, it is often contended that the media's use of increasingly explicit and sensational violence to sustain ratings and increase revenue is **desensitizing** audiences' abilities to empathize with others when real violence occurs (Gunter 1994; Molitor and Hirsch 1994; Potter 2003; Wilson *et al.* 2002). With these and related assumptions in mind, then, researchers have sought to understand how specific media content might affect or cultivate audience attitudes towards violence, or document possible links between the viewing of violent media content and personal behaviour.

Other media commentators have taken a different stance on the issue of media representations of violence, claiming that such representations have **no causal effects** on audiences. They reject the implicit notion that people are largely passive recipients of powerful media messages and, therefore, susceptible to their influence. From this perspective, researchers have asserted that there is a need to appreciate the complex ways in which audiences engage with media portrayals of violence, and argue that such portrayals are never the single most important factor contributing to the development of personal aggression or violent behaviour. Those who argue this position claim that research studies that identify a direct cause–effect relationship between media representations of violence and aggressive or criminal behaviour in audiences are conceptually flawed in methodological design, as well as in terms of how conclusions about **media effects** are extrapolated from research data (Barker and Petley 2001; Gauntlett 1995; Heins 2002; Hill 1997). Advocates of the no effects position on media violence argue that depictions of violence need to be understood in the wider cultural context within which they are produced and distributed. It is only one of a *variety* of factors influencing public attitudes and social behaviour (Freedman 2002; Jones 2002; von Feilitzen 2001).[1] Furthermore, these researchers contend that audiences are very capable of differentiating between fictional and factual portrayals of violence, *and* appropriately responding to real incidents of violence when they occur.

The debate about the relative extent that media portrayals of violence may be affecting audience attitudes and behaviour has been extraordinarily polemical in nature, with powerful media effects and no effects advocates holding firm to their own positions, while seeking to refute the claims of alternative perspectives. It was in order to move beyond this unfruitful, binaristic game of oppositions that we argued for the need to rethink the media violence debate in our book, *Violence and the Media* (Carter and

Weaver 2003). We suggested that to cut a critically informed path between the two models requires an intellectual reorientation and a repoliticization of the entire field of study. This involves more than merely re-theorizing what we mean by 'media violence'. It also involves moving the debate about media violence beyond the argument about whether representations of individual acts of violence produce particular responses in individual readers or viewers. Successfully recasting of this field of enquiry, we argue, will include focusing on the extent to which everyday representations of violence in the media contribute to its normalization and legitimization. It also necessitates examining whose ideological (see **ideology**) and economic interests media violence might be serving (see Giroux in this volume). Consequently, we maintain that researchers ought to examine how media violence is implicated in the structural legitimization of the place and position of influential groups in society.

The need to reconsider how we theorize and research media representations of violence has become increasingly pressing in the post-**September 11, 2001** era. That day's tragic attacks on the World Trade Center and the US Pentagon witnessed an extraordinary merging of the fictional imagining of violence with the factual obliteration of thousands of people. Indeed, as Semanti (in this volume) argues, 'among the most pronounced reactions to the September 11 terrorist attacks in the United States was the degree to which press and public alike said that the events "looked like a movie" '. He goes on to suggest that 'the images of those airplanes deliberately flying into the twin towers of the World Trade Center and their subsequent implosion looked too fantastic to be real. There are, of course, good reasons why Hollywood images resonate with the horrors of September 11 in the public imagination. New York City has been a favourite disaster site for Hollywood'. Today there also is a pressing need to consider how factual media and content formats, such as news, current affairs, reality shows and documentaries use violence and often highly spectacular imagery in order to attract and maintain audiences, and why audiences want to read about and watch that violence. It may be, as Höijer's research suggests (in this volume), that factual violence serves to increase our compassion towards victims of real violence. There is equally the possibility that reporting about war, terror and conflict may increase compassion while also serving particular politics ends by soliciting public support for the US- and British-led invasion of Iraq, for example. We also need to examine how factual reporting and representations of violence might contribute to a public sense of inevitability around real violence, and increased tolerance for aggressive actions in everyday life. In light of these new violent realities, as well as the wars in Afghanistan and Iraq, and the bombings in Bali, Madrid, London,

Sharm el-Sheik and elsewhere, media scholars now urgently need to recast many old assumptions about differences between fictional and factual media violence.

In order to provide a more detailed appreciation of why the media's representation of violence has been a matter of such controversy and debate, we turn our attention in the next section of this introductory chapter to the question of precisely what types of representations have been defined as problematic, and by whom. We then offer a brief outline of research investigating some of the ways in which specific audiences have responded to violent media content. We end the chapter with a discussion of how major twenty-first-century events, particularly the attacks on September 11 and the ensuing US declaration of a '**war on terrorism**', are forcing a radical rethink in terms of how we debate and analyse media violence.

Identifying 'the Problem' of Media Violence

There have been many attempts to define precisely what constitutes 'the object' of media violence analysis for the purpose of identifying what type of material 'counts' in this debate. A commonly used definition is that a media representation of violence will contain 'the overt expression of physical force (with or without a weapon) against self or other, compelling action against one's will on pain of being hurt or killed, or actually hurting or killing' (Gerbner *et al.* 1980). There have been revisions to this definition to include, for example, violence against animals, inanimate objects, and verbally threatening behaviour (National Television Violence Study 1997). Such definitions have enabled the analysis of just how *much* violence is portrayed in the media. Yet, defining precisely what counts as a media representation of violence is perhaps less interesting than examining *why* certain types of depiction are deemed problematic. By exploring the debate from this perspective, interesting patterns in the identification of media violence as a 'problem' emerge.

Both the factual reporting and the fictional portrayal of violent crime have provided a central rallying point for anxieties about the potential 'effects' of media portrayals of violence for well over a century now. In many nineteenth-century Western countries, penny newspapers ('**dreadfuls**') became the target of attacks for their detailed coverage of crimes and disasters, often replete with images of violence. Criticism of this sensational reporting primarily came from the older, self-proclaimed 'respectable press' catering to middle-class readers (Goldberg 1998). Middle-class social reformers of the time were generally of the view that penny news-papers encouraged working-class readers to revel in the salacious detail of certain events – train crashes, steamboat explosions, industrial fires and violent crime. An additional concern was that others could use the detail in the reports, in relation to crime reporting, to plan further criminal acts (Goldberg 1998).

There is little doubt that crime reporting helped to sell newspapers then as now (Allan 2004). As early as the nineteenth century, explicit accounts and coloured artist impressions of serial killer Jack the Ripper's murders published by London's weekly penny comic, *Illustrated Police News*, were criticized by the middle-class press for exploiting and glamorizing the Rip-per's crimes (Frayling 1986). The illustrations featured on large hoardings to promote the paper were considered especially likely to provoke thoughts about violent and even murderous behaviour in people of 'unbalanced minds'. The claim that the relatively uneducated are intellectually and emo-tionally 'vulnerable', and are therefore more likely to be susceptible to cor-ruption by media representations of violence remains a principal rationale behind calls for **censorship** of media violence to this day. Sometimes coupled with this assertion are calls for media owners and producers to act responsibly with regard to the social values that they communicate in and through depictions of violence.

The widespread distribution of moving pictures from the 1920s onwards further added to middle-class fears about the influence of the mass media, and especially on the 'impressionable minds' of children and those with little by way of formal education. However, it is important to understand these concerns in relation to specific film content that was regarded as objectionable. In the United States, for example, members of the clergy, politicians and middle-class social reformers expressed concern about the fictional characterization of both the *perpetrators* and the *victims* of the violence. Early gangster movies were a particular target for attack (Spring-hall 1998). For example, *Little Caesar* portrayed working-class men secur-ing wealthy lifestyles through crime and violence at the expense of innocent hard-working citizens, while suggesting, in turn, that members of the police force and judiciary were corruptible. Such films were thought to undermine respect for the Protestant work ethic and law enforcement agencies, and as such became the focus of widespread public concern around their potential threat to 'decent' social moral values (Carter and Weaver 2003; Schaefer 1999; Yaquinto 1998).

Following the rise of the second wave of Western feminism in the 1960s, many women academics, writers and public commentators began to object to how both the mainstream media and **pornographic representation** depicted women as either willing victims of violence, or at least as soliciting their own victimization (Haskell 1987; Kuhn 1982; Modleski 1988). Since the very early days of cinema, women have been routinely portrayed as the victims of male violence, yet such violence is often *not* represented as being criminal. Indeed, portrayals of violence against women frequently operate as a means of representing a male character as particularly virulent (see Ramasubramanian and Oliver in this volume). For decades, this went largely unchallenged. However, second-wave feminists have argued that such representations are far from harmless, and form part of a wider cultural environment that includes actual violence against women, such as rape, assault and domestic violence (Caputi 1988; Carter and Weaver 2003; Michelle and Weaver 2003; Weaver, Carter and Stanko 2000). In challenging taken for granted assumptions about the harmlessness of images of violence against women, feminist critics have contested what they regard as the underlying sexism of the mass media. Ironically, feminist calls for media censorship as part of a response to media violence against women have sometimes aligned women's rights groups with moral and religious organizations who are unsupportive of gender equality in their politically conservative campaigns to 'clean up' media content.

Children and Media Violence

From the 1960s onwards, when ownership of television sets in the West became widespread, followed by the arrival of video recorders and video games in the early 1980s, the effects of images of violence on children again became a major focal point of public concern. Indeed, media representations of children are now at the centre of debates around the circulation and availability of media violence in society (Buckingham, and Barker and Petley in this volume; Davies 2001; Holland 2004). This is primarily the case for two reasons. Firstly, many adults regard children as less able to distinguish between fact and fiction. As such, they are considered more likely than adults are to be disturbed by images of violence. Secondly, models of child development promoted by social psychologists have tended to suggest that since children's moral frameworks are less developed than those of adults, children may be especially prone to imitating what they see on television, video, film and on computer screens (Buckingham 1996; Davies 1996; Gauntlett 1997). Particularly disturbing crimes, such as the killing of the British toddler **James Bulger** by two 10-year-old boys in 1993, and the initial – though later found to be spurious – linking of the killing with the boys' viewing of the video *Child's Play III*, added considerable strength to such claims during the 1990s (Barker 2001). More recently, examples of children who allegedly have been directly influenced to copy something they have seen in the media include:

- a Scottish teenager who, after watching the film *Braveheart*, attacked an English schoolboy because of his accent. The teenager copied his idol, William Wallace, by shouting the battle cry 'Freedom!' as he and two other teens punched and kicked the 15-year-old boy in the head (*Daily Record*, 19 August, 1997);
- a 13-year-old boy who poured gasoline on his feet and legs and lit himself on fire, imitating a stunt he'd seen on the MTV series *Jackass* (*New York Daily News*, 30 January, 2001);
- a 14-year-old Florida boy, Lionel Tate, was convicted of first-degree murder and given a life sentence without the possibility of parole for killing 6-year-old Tiffany Eunick. Tate imitated a wrestling hold he had seen on TV, bear-hugging the girl, lifting her, dropping her on the floor, which resulted in her death (*New York Times*, 26 January, 2001).

The protection of children has become a rallying point for assertions about the dangers posed by media violence. The market growth in children's computer games, music videos and CDs containing explicit language, sexual imagery and graphic violent content has fuelled the fires of public debate, and provided a whole new focus for 'effects' research (Anderson 2004; Anderson and Dill 2000; Gentile *et al.* 2004; Hoga and Bar-on 1996). The rapid development of new technologies and the ever-decreasing cost of existing ones make it increasingly likely that children will consume media violence in the private contexts of their bedrooms. Lupton (2000) suggests that, as a result, many parents are therefore less likely to be aware of, let alone monitor, the media content with which their children engage (Buckingham in this volume; Funk, Hagan and Schimming 1999; Gentile *et al.* 2004). An example of the perceived consequences of children's private interactions with violent media content came with the 1999 **Columbine High School shootings** in Littleton, Colorado, when two teenagers, Dylan Klebold and Eric Harris, shot and killed 12 of their fellow high school students and a teacher, and wounded 21 others, before committing suicide. Some US journalists reporting this event proposed that the killers' actions were directly influenced by their fascination with media violence and that the computer games both teenagers obsessively played may have even provided them with a means of rehearsing their attack (see Ogle, Eckman and Amoroso Leslie in this volume).

After the events at Columbine High School, many parents, teachers, politicians and journalists began to express openly concerns about the potentially negative influence of violent computer games on young people. A more recent public discussion around media violence is related to public worries that internet chat rooms and email may facilitate, for example, the activities of **paedophiles**, **cyberstalkers**, racists, and **fascists** (Adam in this volume; Attorney General 1999; Glaser, Dixit and Green in this volume; Spitzberg and Hoobler 2002).

The widespread use of mobile telephones – and with them digital videoing and text messaging – has raised a host of new anxieties around the possible use of digital media to violent ends. For example, bullying by text messaging has been widely reported among children (NCH 2005; Youngsters targeted by digital bullies 2002), as has the phenomenon of strangers photographing naked children in public changing rooms (Dubecki 2003; McLeod 2003). While the mobile phone photographing of images of the immediate aftermath of the 7 July 2005 London bombings was heralded as marking a new form of 'open source news', or **citizen journalism**, words of concern were quickly voiced by a number of journalists about the possible abuses of this news technology. Graham Lovelace, a former senior editor with both the BBC and ITN news, has cautioned that:

> The opportunity for individuals to see something awful happen in front of them and to record it is one thing. But the opportunity is then also there for the perpetrators of these awful crimes. If we have learned anything from the internet, it is that for every good, legitimate use, there is an infinite number of misleading abuses (cited in Smyth 2005).

Following up this point, *Scotsman* reporter Anna Smyth (2005) offers a specific example of recent mobile phone abuse in order to point to some of the possible dangers of unfettered citizen journalism:

> We have also seen evidence of a dark side to new technology with the beheading videos from Iraq which, for now, remain mercifully restricted to the internet. But with mobile phones establishing themselves as the reporting tool of choice, there is disturbing potential for a wash of repugnant, ready-to-film atrocities.

Just because mobile phone technology may be open to abuse is not sufficient reason to try to restrict the participation of citizens in newsmaking, since citizen journalism can be a source of empowerment for ordinary people, particularly those whose views do not typically feature in the mainstream news media (see 'Citizen journalism' 2005). Instead, as Lovelace suggests, 'We just need to manage it well, strike the right balance and be sure not to encourage those aspects which could ultimately lead to no good' (cited in Smyth 2005).

Given the considerable concerns raised about how the media represent violence, and how those representations might affect individual attitudes and behaviours, and the well-being of society more broadly, it is not surprising that these issues have been the subject of extensive academic research over the years. In the next section, we outline certain approaches to researching the relationship between media representations of violence and audiences.

How Has Media Violence Been Researched?

The first detailed studies of the 'effects' of engaging with portrayals of film violence were conducted in the USA in the late 1920s and early 1930s, through the **Payne Fund Studies** (Jowett, Jarvie and Fuller 1996; Lowery and DeFleur 1995). The research was varied in methodological approach, primarily drawing on **content analysis** and **longitudinal studies** that attempted to correlate viewing violent film content with 'deviant' behaviour, and self-reporting by young people on how they understood the relationship between violence in the movies and their own behaviour. Researchers found very limited connections between viewing such material and the development of 'delinquent' attitudes and behaviours. However, the research funders – a group of middle-class social reformers who sought proof that films contributed to juvenile delinquency – reported the findings so selectively that there appeared to be a direct correlation between watching violence and behaving violently or criminally (Jowett, Jarvie and Fuller 1996).

The rapid growth in television ownership from the early 1960s onwards in the US, alongside numerous examples of what appeared to be 'copycat' crimes mimicking scenes from films and television programmes, added to public demands to investigate possible connections between violent media content and viewer behaviour. One famous example of what some believed to be an act that directly imitated fictional media violence was the 1961 San Francisco knife attack on a boy, which some journalists claimed to closely resemble a scene from the movie *A Rebel without a Cause* which had broadcast on television the evening prior to the attack. Having already identified that children were extremely likely to imitate aggressive behaviour they witnessed from adult role models (Bandura, Ross and Ross 1961), certain psychologists turned to assess whether watching such aggressive behaviour on film and television had the same effect. Generally described as

behavioural effects research, and underpinned by **social learning theory**, this research was conducted in laboratory contexts where children watched films that portrayed adults behaving aggressively (Bandura, Ross and Ross in this volume). After children viewed several films, they were then deliberately frustrated by adults (by having toys removed from them) to see how the children responded under stress. The researchers found that children who had watched the screen-mediated acts of violence were more likely to respond aggressively than those who had not. However, they did question the extent to which the behaviour exhibited by the children in the experiments produced *genuine* aggression. This type of laboratory research is commonly critiqued on the grounds that the children involved may have felt safe in acting or playing aggressively as there were no negative consequences of their doing so – being chastised, or at risk of violent retaliation from their victim. Nevertheless, Bandura, Ross and Ross' experimental study has been replicated in many hundreds of similarly designed studies over the years (see Paik and Comstock 1994; Wood, Wong and Cachere 1991), and this research is frequently cited by substantial numbers of psychologists, paediatricians, mental health care professionals and media watch campaigners as evidence that viewing violent content can influence viewers to behave similarly.

Cultivation theory has been widely used over the past forty years to research media violence, producing findings that appear to lend considerable support to the 'effects thesis'. Developed by George Gerbner and colleagues at the Annenberg School of Communications, Pennsylvania, through their '**Cultural Indicators Project**', cultivation theory rests on the idea that media violence affects audience conceptions of social reality and who has power and who does not in that reality. To support this claim, cultivation researchers have undertaken extensive quantitative content analyses of US prime-time television programming. The aim of such research has been to identify how much violence appears, who are the victims, and who are the perpetrators. For example, Gerbner *et al.* (1978: 191) examined which character types are most likely to be portrayed as perpetrators or victims of violence and found that 'of the 20 most victimized groups . . . all but three are composed of women'. Some researchers further assert that television's repeated portrayal of certain groups as victims represents a symbolic expression of those victim types' impotence in society (Gerbner and Gross 1976: 182). In terms of the audience, such symbolic imagery is theorized as cultivating social conceptions about 'who are the aggressors and who are the victims' where 'there is a relationship between the roles of the violent and the victim. Both roles are there to be learned by viewers' (Gerbner *et al.* 1979: 180). The more heavily television is watched, the more vulnerable is the viewer to this learning (Gerbner and Gross 1976). More recently, Gerbner (1994) developed a thesis to describe what he refers to as the '**mean world syndrome**'. According to this thesis, heavy users of television tend to overestimate the occurrence of violence in society. As Gerbner (1994: 40) elaborates:

> [. . .] growing up from infancy with this unprecedented diet of violence has three consequences, which, in combination, I call the 'mean world syndrome.' What this means is that if you are growing up in a home where there is more than say three hours of television per day, for all practical purposes you live in a meaner world – and act accordingly – than your next-door neighbor who lives in the same world but watches less television. The programming reinforces the worst fears and apprehensions and paranoia of people.

As with all media effects theories, cultivation theory has been widely criticized (see, for example, Gauntlett in this volume). Its conclusions are indeed problematic given that they are largely based on content analyses of the media that make no distinction between the types of programmes in which violence is shown. Violence in children's cartoons, for example, is often equated with violence in realist drama and horror movies (Barker 2001; Cumberbatch 1989, 1995). A related concern is that cultivation research tends to overemphasize individualistic responses to media violence, thus under-assessing the significance of the ways in which representations of violence in the media contribute to the (re)production of structural social inequalities (see Linné and Wartella 1998; von Feilitzen 1998). As such, it tends to 'abstract the relationship of message content and individual perceptions from the historical, political, and economic conditions which influence both' (White 1983: 288). This clearly suggests a need to examine how factors outside of the media affect how audiences interpret media content.

In Europe and Australasia, where **critical theory, interpretivist, post-structuralist** and **post-modern** theories have had a longer history of academic influence than in the US, some sociologists, media studies and **cultural studies** scholars have ridiculed the **positivist science** methodologies that claim to establish causal connections between social phenomena (media content and audience attitudes and behaviour) as fundamentally flawed (Barker and Petley, and Gauntlett in this volume). Rather than focusing on the question of whether violent media content influences the behaviour of audiences, researchers informed by these theories ask questions about how the contexts of media production shape the selection, framing and characterization of both factual and fictional violent media content. For example, Schlesinger and Tumber (1994) have investigated how crime reporting represents women and argue that it often **stereotypes** them as sexually provocative and failing to take sufficient precautions against sexual attack. Other researchers have examined the phenomenon of crime reconstruction and 'reality' police programmes, and have argued that they tend to encourage fears around crime which encourage a discursive identification with law and order politics, and that the programmes fail to reflect how crime and violence are linked causally to structures such as poverty, racism and sexism (Anderson 1995; Cavender 1998).

Critical and interpretative researchers have also analysed **audience reception** of violent media content. Using qualitative research methods such as individual and focus group interviews, researchers have demonstrated the complex ways in which audiences interpret portrayals of violence (see Buckingham in this volume; Morrison *et al.* 1999; Tulloch and Tulloch 1993; Vares 2002). For example, Schlesinger *et al.*'s audience studies *Women Viewing Violence* (1992) and *Men Viewing Violence* (1998) both concluded that sexual, ethnic and class identities are often important variables shaping how women and men respond to media violence. One key difference between the two studies, researchers found, is that regardless of cultural background, most of the women in the first study expressed a concern about how media violence might affect men or children (see also Höijer in this volume), while in the second study, few men conveyed any worry about the ways in which media violence might influence women or children.

Some studies have found that viewers are less disturbed by fictional portrayals of violence than factual ones (Docherty 1990). The extremes of shock and horror that audiences feel when they are viewing fictional media violence occur in the safe environments of the movie theatre or the living room. When they are over, viewers return to everyday lives that are far removed from those implausibly violent worlds portrayed in the media (Hill 1997). Indeed, far from fuelling fears about the potential negative social and psychological consequences of violent content on audiences, some researchers argue that media violence may actually provide audiences with a positive means through which they can experience subjectivities, emotions, and behaviours considered to be socially inappropriate or which simply cannot occur in 'real life' (Alloway and Gilbert 1998; Labre and Duke in this volume). For example, Piot (in this volume) argues that many violent video games empower players by allowing them to experience operating as half-human, half-machine beings in a post-modern, post-human world that is unconstrained by national, geographic, temporal and moral boundaries.

While for some these experiences are seen to be a positive force in society that break down social inequalities, for others there is a concern that new technologies might be used to promote hostility or advocate violence toward persons identified by their ethnicity, sexuality, gender, religion or national origin (Bremer and Rauch 1998; Duffy 2003; Ferreday 2005; Williams and Skoric 2005; Zickmund 1997). For example, Glaser, Dixit and Green (in this volume) have researched how internet chat rooms sponsored by white supremacist groups are used to advocate race **hate crimes**. While finding that the internet can operate as a forum through which hate crimes are encouraged, the authors are nevertheless unable to verify the extent to which such encouragement has led to the actual perpetration of racist hate crimes.

When the issue of media violence is debated in public, there is a tendency for participants to fall into the polemical and fundamentally opposed positions of those who favour the psychological behavioural science arguments outlined above or those who advocate sociological, media and cultural studies approaches. Those who espouse the first position tend to argue that media violence can *directly* increase aggressive or violence inclinations, or even fear of violence, lend support to conservative values, politics and ideologies and calls for censorship. In contrast, critical research on media violence tends to suggest that it does not have any causal effects on human behaviour. Instead, representations and their interpretation by media audiences are intricately entwined in wider cultural **discourses** of identity and subjectivity. Advocates of this position on media violence tend to support liberal values, politics and ideologies that oppose censorship.

However, returning to the argument we made in *Violence and the Media*, rather than perpetuating the dualisms of the effects versus no effects debate on media violence, we believe that it is essential to expend greater research effort investigating who are the key beneficiaries of the existing system of production, representation and consumption of media violence. What is needed is a more nuanced and politically aware understanding of the complex ways in which the growing 'normalcy', 'banality' and 'everydayness' of media violence influences our relationships with each other in the world. The need for more critically informed research has become more urgent in the light of new trends in the mediation of violence in which the boundaries between factual and fictional media formats have become increasingly blurred.

De-Westernizing Media Violence

The new global realities around war, conflict and **terrorism** are having a profound influence on current debates on media violence. Such political developments should compel researchers to rethink the range of media content to be studied and the relationships that increasingly global audiences have with it. Now, perhaps more than ever, there is a growing need to examine **factual media violence** formats and audiences. The global circulation and increasing blurriness of the boundaries between factual and fictional media violence demand the development of new conceptual tools that will enable researchers to address some of the most pressing political questions that currently need to be asked. What are the social and political consequences of the media's sanitization of violence in both the reporting and dramatization of violent events? Under what conditions do audiences experience so-called '**compassion fatigue**', after repeated exposure to news about war, conflict and terrorism? What is the significance of such fatigue in terms of how the public evaluates and responds to the reality of violence? Might repeated coverage also encourage greater compassion for victims of violence, as well as a better grasp of the arguments made by those who justify the use of violence in order to achieve certain political objectives?

Definitions of violence typically encountered in media research have tended to emanate from Western points of view. In order to further de-Westernize, and thus enrich, public debates, there is a need for examination of a wider array of media cultures than currently exists.[2] As such, it is important to come to grips with how media violence is variously used in different cultural settings:

- for propaganda purposes;
- to resist oppressive political and cultural regimes;
- as an instrument of oppression of disadvantaged groups in society;
- for purposes of entertainment.

Many of these issues are taken up in the essays included in this Reader. In the next section of this introductory essay, we explain the rationale behind the decisions we have taken regarding the inclusion of the chapters selected. We also offer a brief outline of each of them so as to provide a better sense of the overall range and scope of the arguments, theories, methods and objects of analysis covered.

Structure and Aims of *Critical Readings: Violence and the Media*

In designing this Reader, we sought to reflect on the ways in which research into media violence has been centrally shaped by concerns about media effects. In our view, critical research is now contributing to the development of more innovative theorizing around the role that violent media content plays in the twenty-first century. A further aim was to bring together – as much as is possible within the confines of a single book – a range of writing on media violence in different parts of the world, covering a variety of media institutions, media genres and media audiences, and to consider some of the theoretical responses to claims made about the 'effects' of violent media content on audiences.[3]

The Reader begins in Part I, 'Conceptual approaches to media violence', with essays representing some of the leading communication models that have been developed to research and theorize media violence. As such, it provides a historical and contextual understanding of the development of the field of Western media violence research. The first chapter, Albert Bandura, Dorothea Ross and Sheila A. Ross's 'Imitation of film-mediated aggressive models' is widely regarded as one of the classic media effects studies in this field (sometimes referred to as the '**Bobo doll**' experiment). This study has been particularly influential in supporting the hypothesis that children are very likely to imitate media representations of aggressive and violent behaviour when the perpetrator of that behaviour is left unpunished.

George Gerbner's 'Television violence: at a time of turmoil and terror' outlines his pioneering work developing the media effects 'cultivation theory' as a framework for understanding media violence. That theory and its accompanying research are reviewed in this piece, which makes connections between the profit imperatives of the media industries, long-term exposure to violence on television and perceptions of the world as a 'mean and dangerous'.

From there, attention turns to David Gauntlett's 'Ten things wrong with the media "effects" model'. Gauntlett asserts that decades of effects research has failed to prove a direct link between audience exposure to media violence and real-life aggression. Thus, either there are no direct effects or media researchers have 'consistently taken the wrong approach to the mass media, its audiences, and society in general'. The rest of the chapter is devoted to detailing what Gauntlett believes to be the ten consistent flaws indicative of this research tradition.

Martin Barker and Julian Petley raise a number of related issues in their chapter 'From bad media violence research to good – a guide for the perplexed'. They begin by outlining how recent research has questioned effects definitions of violence, thereby shifting focus away from trying to determine the negative effects of watching media violence so as to examine how audiences differentially *interpret* that violence. Qualitative audience research, the authors suggest, might better enable scholars to understand how and under what circumstances the media can be influential.

Annette Hill's 'The social amplification of risk and the media violence debate' argues that campaigns to censor media violence typically construct it as posing a risk to the well-being of individuals and society. Drawing conceptual links between **moral panic theory** and media violence debates in the UK, Hill suggests that media, politicians and anti-violence campaign groups contribute to the symbolic and social amplification of risk, and in so doing attempt to shape public opinion in a manner that supports conservative family values and law and order politics.

Part I draws to a close with Henry A. Giroux's chapter, 'Private satisfactions and public disorders: *Fight Club*, patriarchy and the politics of masculine violence', on how **neoliberalism** has contributed to the growing commodification of US culture. In his examination of the film *Fight Club*, Giroux concludes that even though the film appears to challenge contemporary material relations of capitalist power, domination and exploitation, this message is undermined because the violence of capitalism is reinscribed as a personal attack on traditional (regressive) notions of masculinity that must ultimately end in a war against all that is feminine.

In Part II, 'Producing media violence', we have included examples of research that examine how media institutional structures, norms and values shape media content. Specific chapters examine how public policies on media violence, media economics and professional socialization within media organizations can influence the ways in which violence is represented. This section starts with Christine L. Kellow and H. Leslie Steeves' 'The role of radio in the Rwandan genocide', which looks at the role government-controlled radio played in inciting genocide through an analysis of its broadcasts and observational accounts by those working in radio at the time. Extreme **media dependency** in Rwanda set the stage for radio campaigns that in turn served as catalysts for ethnic hatred and fear. Media dependency and the generation of collective fear provide only part of an interpretation of the role of radio in the genocide. In-depth interviews, the authors contend, would yield important new insights on the extent to which audiences resisted or complied with the messages they heard on the radio.

The next chapter, 'Surviving violence: Hillsborough, Dunblane and the press', by Ann Jemphrey and Eileen Berrington, examines how the British press reported the **Hillsborough Disaster** in Liverpool, England, in 1989 and the shootings at **Dunblane Primary School**, Scotland, in 1996. In disaster reporting, journalists are under pressure to produce copy quickly and to dramatize and sensationalize what are already dramatic stories. In complying with these editorial demands, the rights and expectations of bereaved people and survivors are endangered, and sensitivity is sacrificed to the business and managerial imperatives of publishing. As long as there is a market for prurience, sensation and intrusion, newspapers will try to meet that public demand.

Turning from analyses of the news media to the music industry, Derek Iwamoto's 'Tupac Shakur: understanding the identity formation of hyper-masculinity of a popular hip-hop artist' engages with the assertion that all hip-hop and **gangsta-rap** promotes violence. The most significant – and often overlooked – factor perpetuating and reinforcing violent behaviour is the way that US culture defines and glorifies violent masculinity. Analysing rapper Tupac Shakur's music, his life and a music industry that exploited his position as a black man, Iwamoto provides evidence of the rapper's empathy for women, and his awareness of issues around the articulation of violence, 'race' and class oppression.

Next, we turn to consider the relationship between fictional Hollywood representations of violence and the factual violence of terrorist attacks in Medhi Semanti's 'Imagine the terror of September 11'. Addressing a widely stated comment that the two commercial jetliners that deliberately flew into each of the two twin towers of the World Trade Center in New York City the morning of September 11, 2001 'looked like a movie', Semanti explores the blurring of boundaries between media fact and fiction, reflecting on this possible political implications of this development. More specifically, he examines the relationship between the realities of current political violence in the Middle East with the ways in which the region is portrayed in Hollywood cinema.

From there, we turn to David Campbell's 'Horrific blindness: photographic images of death in contemporary media', which argues for the importance of understanding how the social and political context shapes photographic images of death. Far from there being too many of these images, Campbell contends that death is disappearing from factual media, thus contributing to a diminution in the power of photography to provoke. As such, the author suggests, it is becoming ever more difficult to develop an ethical politics needed to engage with the political realities upon which contemporary atrocities are founded and how such violence is represented in the media.

The final essay in this section is 'Cyberstalking and internet **pornography**: gendered violence' by Alison Adam, who argues for the need to develop feminist responses to the cyberethical issues of internet child pornography and **cyberstalking**. In Adam's view, these issues have a gendered dimension that is only rarely explored by media scholars. Because Western philosophy has tended to equate women with the bodily realm, feminist theories would enable scholars to address questions around the bodily invasions of privacy that occur online, where bodies are watched, looked at or subject to surveillance, or indeed where bodies are actually subject to violence and where this violence is watched on-line.

Attention turns in Part III, 'Representing media violence', to the examination of media violence across a range of media texts using quantitative content analysis and various types of qualitative textual analysis. We start with Douglas R. Bruce's 'Violence in children's cartoons: *The Road Runner* as mythical discourse', which seeks to develop a new approach to understanding violence in children's television programming. Bruce begins with an historical discussion examining developments in the field of animated short cartoons in the context of the post-World War II technological boom in the United States. Technology, Bruce suggests, is the source of most of the violence in the cartoon, and the violence is created by failures of technology. Examination of *The Road Runner*, for example, yields insights into the meanings of cartoon violence, into how media reproduce mythic structures, and into the potentially rich message systems of children's media.

Next is 'Portrayals of **sexual violence** in popular Hindi films' by Srividya Ramasubramanian and Mary Beth Oliver. Through their content analysis of nine recent Hindi box office hits, the authors demonstrate how what they categorize as 'moderate sexual violence' is portrayed as pleasurable and, as such, as an acceptable part of romantic love. Sexual violence committed by heroes is a common depiction, they suggest, particularly harassment, or '**eve-teasing**', of women with whom the heroes ultimately become romantically involved. While 'severe sexual violence' is portrayed as criminal and serious, 'moderate sexual violence' was treated as 'fun' and 'romantic'.

Jennifer Paff Ogle, Molly Eckman and Catherine Amoroso Leslie's 'Personal **appearance as a social problem**: newspaper coverage of the Columbine High School shootings' looks at the ways in which personal appearance became a central feature in news reporting of this event. Of particular interest to the authors is the process by which the US press constructed appearance as a social problem by linking school violence to personal styles in clothing. By constructing Columbine as an appearance-related problem with appearance-based solutions, the press ultimately undermined public debates that might have taken place which could have lead to concrete proposals for positive social change to prevent future school shootings.

From there, we turn to examine the relationship between gender empowerment, violence and video games in Magdala Peixoto Labre and Lisa Duke's 'Between feminine empowerment and subjugation: sexualizing the violent female hero in the *Buffy the Vampire Slayer* video game'. Here the authors argue that this video game exaggerates both the violent actions and sexual characteristics of its central hero, Buffy. As such, it creates a certain ambiguity between feminine empowerment and subjugation and lends support to the idea that female heroes can be powerful yet, at the same time, must also conform to traditional constructions of femininity.

The section ends with 'Constructing Arabs as enemies after September 11: an analysis of selected speeches by George W. Bush' by Debra Merskin. Bush's rhetoric in these speeches, from his public statements on September 11, 2001 to the January 29, 2002 State of the Union address were built on stereotypical words and images already established in more than 20 years of violent media and popular culture images of Arabs as evil, bloodthirsty, animalistic terrorists. The author's textual analysis of the speeches identifies the construction of a certain image of Arabs as 'the enemy', a finding that has important human rights implications, suggests Merskin, for Arab American citizens and non-citizens living in the US.

The chapters included in Part IV, 'Media violence audiences', ask the question of how audiences are actually making sense of the violence they encounter in their engagement with a wide range of media texts. Here, we start with David Buckingham's 'Children viewing violence' that offers a critical overview of various approaches that have been used over the years to study children's responses to media violence. Buckingham's research identifies the complexity involved in children's relationships with the media and their interpretations of both fictional and factual violent media content, as well as why they may be motivated to engage with this content in the first place.

Jack Glaser, Jay Dixit and Donald P. Green's chapter 'Internet research on hate crime: what makes racists advocate violence?' reports on their pioneering study based on online interviews with contributors to white supremacist internet chat rooms. Capitalizing on the anonymity and candour afforded by these sites, the authors were able to gather interview data from people openly calling for racist violence in response to what they perceived to be social threats posed by blacks – inter-racial marriage and blacks moving into white neighbourhoods. This study is particularly valuable in investigating how the internet can operate as a site for the expression of violent attitudes and ideologies in a way that is not possible via other media channels.

Attention then turns to the issue of **homophobia** in Valerie Palmer-Mehta and Kellie Hay's 'Reader responses to the anti-gay hate crime story line in DC Comics' *Green Lantern*'. Examining the hate crime story line in the *Green Lantern* comic books in relation to reader feedback provides an opportunity, suggest the authors, to make sense of contemporary cultural perceptions in the US regarding the gay, lesbian, bisexual and transgender community. The authors found that most readers hold positive views about addressing homophobia – many believing that violence is never justified just because someone is gay and that the anti-gay hate crime portrayed in *Green Lantern* comics was handled thoughtfully and progressively.

Charles Piot's 'Revelling in the gore in the room next door: video game violence and US teen culture' asks why spectacular displays of bodily violence in many video games are so compelling for large numbers of teens today. Why have video arcades, often situated in suburban malls, become popular spaces for dystopic, end-of-the-world scenarios that are played out on video screens and in the imaginations of these teens? The commodity form, Piot suggests, depends on and inscribes alienation, violence and exclusion. The commodity is embodied violence, and the shopping mall is a product of that violence. Thus the popularity of such games might lie in their ability to allow young people to re-imagine their identities and bodies outside consumerism in ways that are exciting and empowering.

The next chapter is Jenny Kitzinger's 'Zero Tolerance: public responses to a feminist anti-sexual violence advertising campaign', in which the author examines audience reactions to a Scottish local government advertising campaign aimed at tackling sexual violence. Most people understood and agreed with the central message of the ZT campaign, which was to challenge the mainstream media's misleading focus on stranger-danger in order to prioritize the issue of sexual abuse by men known to, and trusted by, their victims. Many, however, were resistant to the campaign's attempt to re-frame sexual violence debates in feminist terms, highlighting questions around gender and power. Even so, the degree of positive support for the campaign and the extent to which it encouraged people to think about the issues were testimony to its success.

This section, and the Reader as a whole, wind up with Birgitta Höijer's 'Global discourses of compassion: audience reactions to news reports of human suffering', in which the author asks the question 'how do people react to the emotional engagement that media offer by focusing on innocent victims of political conflicts, war and other violence?' The media offer pictures of distant victims of civil wars, genocide, massacres and other violence, thereby playing an important role in making audiences aware of human suffering around the world. Her detailed audience research refutes the claim that media representations of this suffering necessarily and always result in 'compassion fatigue'. Instead, images of suffering can also enable audiences to experience moral compassion at a distance.

It should be clear from this introductory chapter that the Reader that we have constructed is politically critical in its orientation. We use the term 'critical' here to denote an approach to media research that has socially progressive aims: the promotion of democracy, social justice, equality, and social tolerance. In other words, one of the central aims of this Reader is to contribute to the field of research that seeks to understand why, and to what extent, unequal relations of power in society are reproduced via the media, but also how and when these power relations are challenged. It is our hope that it might play a positive role in the ongoing development of critical research and teaching on media violence.[4]

Notes

1. See Cumberbatch (1995) for a useful historical overview of media violence research and its policy implications.
2. See James Curran and Myung-Jin Park (2000) (eds) *De-Westernizing Media Studies*, London: Routledge, which engages in more detail with the issue of challenging the Eurocentrism of media studies.
3. Students, teachers and researchers may use this Reader as a stand-alone intro-duction to the study of media violence or as a companion volume to *Violence and the Media* (Carter and Weaver 2003). The latter outlines a distinctive critical framework through which we intervene in the media violence debate so as to try to encourage a movement beyond the binaristic arguments around media effects. The rest of the book employs that framework to make sense of a wide range of media forms, including news, Hollywood cinema, television, pornography, advertising, video games and the internet.
4. There are a number of video resources that are useful for researching and teaching media violence. These include: *Dreamworlds 3: Desire, Sex & Power in Music Video* (2006, Media Education Foundation, 55 mins); *Game Over: Gender, Race & Violence in Video Games* (2000, Media Education Foundation, 41 mins); *Tough Guise: Violence, Media & the Crisis in Masculinity* (1999, Media Education Foundation, 82 mins, 57 abridged); *Wrestling with Manhood: Boys, Bullying & Battering* (2002, Media Education Foundation, 60 mins); *Peace, Propaganda & the Promised Land: U.S. Media & the Israeli-Palestinian Conflict* (2004, Media Education Foundation, 80 mins); *Beyond Good & Evil: Children, Media & Violent Times* (2003, Media Education Foundation, 39 mins); *The Myth of 'The Clash of Civilizations'*, with Edward Said (1998, Media Education Foundation, 40 mins); *The Killing Screens: Media & the Culture of Violence*, with George Gerbner (1994, Media Education Foundation,

37 mins); *Understanding America's Terrorist Crisis: What Should Be Done?*, with Gore Vidal (2003, Media Education Foundation, 70 mins); *Class Dismissed: How TV Frames the Working Class* (2005, Media Education Foundation, 50 mins).

References

Allan, S. (2004) *News Culture*, 2nd edn. Maidenhead and New York: Open University Press.

Alloway, N. and Gilbert, P. (1998) Video game culture: playing with masculinity, violence and pleasure, in S. Howard (ed.) *Wired Up: Young People and the Electronic Media*. London: UCL.

Anderson, C. A. (2004) An update on the effects of playing violence video games. *Journal of Adolescence*, 27: 113–122.

Anderson, C. A. and Bushman, B. J. (2001) Effects of violent video games on aggressive behavior, aggressive cognition, aggressive affect, physiological arousal, and prosocial behavior: a meta-analytic review of the scientific literature. *Psychological Science*, 12(5): 353–359.

Anderson, C. A. and Bushman, B. J. (2002) The effects of media violence on society. *Science*, 295(5564): 2377–2379.

Anderson, C. A. and Dill, K. E. (2000) Video games and aggressive thoughts, feelings and behaviour in the laboratory and in life. *Journal of Personality and Social Psychology*, 78: 772–790.

Anderson, R. (1995) *Consumer Culture and TV Programming*. Boulder, CO: Westview Press.

Attorney General (1999) Report on Cyberstalking: A New Challenge for Law Enforcement and industry. A Report from Attorney General to the Vice President, August 1999. http://www.usdoj.gov/criminal/cybercrime/cyberstalking.htm (accessed 1 Aug. 2005)

Barker, M. (2001) The Newson Report: a case study in 'common sense', in M. Barker and J. Petley (eds) *Ill Effects: The Media/Violence Debate*, 2nd edn. London: Routledge.

Barker, M. and Petley, J. (2001) (eds) *Ill Effects: The Media/Violence Debate*, 2nd edn. London: Routledge.

Bandura, A., Ross, D. and Ross, S. A. (1961) Transmission of aggression through imitation of aggressive models. *Journal of Abnormal Psychology*, 63: 575–582.

Bremer, J. and Rauch, P. K. (1998) Children and computers: risks and benefits. *Journal of the American Academy of Child & Adolescent Psychiatry*, 37(5): 559–560.

Buckingham, D. (1996) *Moving Images: Understanding Children's Emotional Responses to Television*. Manchester: Manchester University Press.

Cantor, J. (2002) Fright reactions to mass media, in J. Bryant and D. Zillmann (eds) *Media Effects: Advances in Theory and Research*. Mahwah, NJ: Erlbaum.

Caputi, J. (1988) *The Age of Sex Crime*. London: The Women's Press.

Carter, C. and Weaver, C. K. (2003) *Violence and the Media*. Buckingham and Philadelphia: Open University Press.

Cavender, G. (1998) In 'the shadow of shadows': television reality crime programming, in M. Fishman and G. Cavender (eds) *Entertaining Crime: Television Reality Programmes*. New York: Aldine de Gruyter.

Citizen journalism (2005) *Wikipedia*. http://en.wikipedia.org/wiki/Citizen_journalism (accessed 6 October 2005).

Critcher, C. (2003) *Moral Panics and the Media*. Buckingham and New York: Open University Press.

Cumberbatch, G. (1989) Violence and the mass media: the research evidence, in G. Cumberbatch and D. Howitt (eds), *A Measure of Uncertainty: The Effects of the Mass Media*. London and Paris: John Libbey.

Cumberbatch, G. (1995) *Media Violence: Research Evidence and Policy Implications*. Report prepared for The Council of Europe Directorate of Human Rights, The Communications Research Group, Ashton University, Strasbourg, The Council of Europe. http://www.academicarmageddon.co.uk/library/EURO.htm (accessed 26 July 2005).

Curran, J. and Park, M. (eds) (2000) *De-westernizing Media Studies*. London: Routledge.

Davies, M. M. (1996) *Fact, Fake and Fantasy: Children's Interpretations of Television Reality*. Mahwah, NJ: Lawrence Erlbaum.

Davies. M. M. (2001) *'Dear BBC': Children, Television Story-telling and the Public Sphere*. Cambridge: Cambridge University Press.

Docherty, D. (1990) *Violence in Television Fiction*. London: John Libbey.

Dubecki, L. (2003) Privacy fears on phone cameras. *The Age*, 12 June.

Duffy, M. (2003) Web of hate: a fantasy theme analysis of the rhetorical vision of hate groups online. *Journal of Communication Inquiry*, 27(3): 291–312.

Ferreday, D. (2005) Bad communities: virtual community and hate speech. *M/C Journal*, 8(1). http://journal.media-culture.org.au/0502/07-ferreday.php (accessed 1 Aug. 2005).

Frayling, C. (1986) The house that Jack built: some stereotypes of the rapist in the history of popular culture, in S. Tomaselli and R. Porter (eds) *Rape*. Oxford: Basil Blackwell.

Freedman, J. L. (2002) *Media Violence and Its Effects on Aggression: Assessing the Scientific Evidence*. Toronto, ON: University of Toronto Press.

Funk, J., Hagan, J. and Schimming, J. (1999) Children and electronic games. a comparison of parents' and children's perceptions of children's habit and preferences in a United States sample. *Psychological Reports*, 85: 883–888.

Gauntlett, D. (1995) *Moving Experiences: Understanding Television's Influences and Effects*. London: John Libbey.

Gauntlett, D. (1997) *Video Critical: Children, the Environment and Media Power*. London: John Libbey Media.

Geen, R. G. (1994) Television and aggression: recent developments in research and theory, in D. Zillman, J. Bryant and A. C. Huston (eds) *Media, Children and the Family*. Hillsdale, NJ: Lawrence Erlbaum.

Gentile, D. A., Lynch, P. J., Linder, J. R. and Walsh, D. A. (2004) The effects of violent video games habits on adolescent hostility, aggressive behaviours, and school performance. *Journal of Adolescence*, 27: 5–22.

Gerbner, G. (1994) Reclaiming our cultural mythology: television's global marketing strategy creates a damaging and alienated window on the world. *The Ecology of Justice*, 38: 40. http://www.context.org/ICLIB/IC38/Gerbner.htm (accessed online 6 October 2005).

Gerbner, G. and Gross, L. (1976) Living with television: the violence profile. *Journal of Communication*, 26(2): 173–199.

Gerbner, G., Gross, L., Jackson-Beeck, M., Jeffries-Fox, S. and Signorielli, N. (1978) Cultural indicators: violence profile no. 9. *Journal of Communication*, 28(3): 176–207.

Gerbner, G., Gross, L., Morgan, M. and Signorielli, N. (1980) The mainstreaming of America: violence profile No 11. *Journal of Communication*, 30(3): 10–29.

Gerbner, G., Gross, L., Signorielli, N., Morgan, M. and Jackson-Beeck, M. (1979) The demonstration of power: violence profile no. 10. *Journal of Communication*, 29(3): 177–196.

Goldberg, V. (1998) Death takes a holiday, sort of, in J. Goldstein (ed.) *Why We Watch: The Attractions of Violent Entertainment*. Oxford: Oxford University Press.

Gunter, B. (1994) The question of media violence, in J. Bryant and D. Zillman (eds) *Media Effects: Advances in Theory and Research*. Hillsdale, N.J: Lawrence Erlbaum.

Haskell, M. (1987) *From Reverence to Rape: The Treatment of Women in the Movies*, 2nd edn. Chicago: The University of Chicago Press.

Heins, M. (2002) *Not in Front of the Children: Indecency, Censorship, and the Innocence of Youth*. New York: Hill and Wang.

Hill, A. (1997) *Shocking Entertainment: Viewer Response to Violence*. Luton: University of Luton Press.

Hoga, M. and Bar-on, M. (1996) Impact of music lyrics and music videos on children and youth. *Paediatrics*, 98(6): 1219–1221.

Holland, P. (2004) *Picturing Childhood: The Myth of Childhood in Popular Imagery*, London: IB Taurus.

Johnson, J. G., Cohen, P., Smailes, E. M., Kasen, S. and Brook, J. S. (2002) Television viewing and aggressive behaviour during adolescence and adulthood. *Science*, 295(5564): 2468–2471.

Jones, G. (2002) *Killing Monsters: Why Children Need Fantasy, Super Heroes, and Make-Believe Violence*. New York: Basic Books.

Jowett, G. S., Jarvie, I. C. and Fuller, K. H. (1996) *Children and the Movies: Media Influence and the Payne Fund Controversy*. Cambridge: Cambridge University Press.

Kuhn, A. (1982) *Women's Pictures: Feminism and Cinema*. London: Routledge and Kegan Paul.

Linné, O. and Wartella, E. (1998) Research about violence in the media: different traditions and changing paradigms, in R. Dickinson, R. Harindranath and O. Linné (eds) *Approaches to Audiences: A Reader*. London, New York, Sydney and Auckland: Arnold.

Lowery, S. A and DeFleur, M. L. (1995) *Milestones in Mass Communication: Media Effects*, 3rd edn. London: Longman.

Lupton, D. (2000) The embodied computer/user, in D. Bell and B. M. Kennedy (eds) *The Cybercultures Reader*. London and New York: Routledge.

McLeod, C. (2003) Sneaky Cameras. Australian Press Council News. http://www.presscouncil.org.au/pcsite/apcnews/aug03/cameras.html (accessed 1 August 2005).

Michelle, C. and Weaver, C. K. (2003) Discursive manoeuvres and hegemonic recuperations in New Zealand documentary representations of domestic violence. *Feminist Media Studies*, 3(3): 283–299.

Modleski, T. (1988) *The Women Who Knew Too Much*. London: Methuen.

Molitor, F. and Hirsch, K. W. (1994) Children's tolerance of real-life aggression after exposure to media violence: a replication of the Drabman and Thomas studies. *Child Study Journal*, 24(3): 191–207.

Morrison, D. E. with MacGregor, B., Svennevig, M. and Firmstone, J. (1999) *Defining Violence*. Luton: University of Luton Press.

National Television Violence Study (1997) *National Television Violence Study*, vol. 1. Thousand Oaks, CA: Sage.

NCH (2005) Putting U in the Picture: Mobile Bullying Survey 2005. http://www.nch.org.uk/information/index.php?i=237 (accessed 1 August 2005).

Paik, H. and Comstock, G. (1994) The effects of television: a meta-analysis. *Communications Research* 21: 516–546.

Potter, J. (2003) *The 11 Myths of Media Violence*. Thousand Oaks and London: Sage.

Schaefer, E. (1999) *Bold! Daring! Shocking! True! A History of Exploitation Films, 1919–1959*. Durham, NC: Duke University Press.

Schlesinger, P., Dobash, R. E., Dobash, R. and Weaver, C. K. (1992) *Women Viewing Violence*. London: British Film Institute.

Schlesinger, P., Haynes, R., Boyle, R., McNair, B., Dobash, R. E. and Dobash, R. (1998) *Men Viewing Violence*. London: Broadcasting Standards Council.

Schlesinger, P. and Tumber, H. (1994) *Reporting Crime: The Media Politics of Criminal Justice*. Oxford: Clarendon Press.

Smyth, A. (2005) Answering the call. *The Scotsman*. 12 July. http://thescotsman.scotsman.com/s2.cfm?id=785792005. (accessed 6 October 2005).

Spitzberg, B.H. and Hoobler, G. (2002) Cyberstalking and the technologies of interpersonal terrorism. *New Media & Society* 4(1): 71–92.

Springhall, J. (1998) *Youth, Popular Culture and Moral Panics: Penny Gaffs to Gangster-Rap, 1830–1996*. London: Macmillan.

Starker, S. (1989) *Evil Influences: Crusades Against the Mass Media*. New Brunswick, NJ and London: Transaction Publishers.

Tulloch, J. and Tulloch, M. (1993) Understanding TV violence: a multifaceted cultural analysis, in G. Turner (ed.) *Nation, Culture, Text: Australian Cultural and Media Studies*. London: Routledge.

Vares, T. (2002) Framing 'killer women' films: audience use of genre, *Feminist Media Studies*, 2(2): 213–229.

von Feilitzen, C.V. (1998) Media violence – four research perspectives, in R. Dickinson, R. Harindranath and O. Linné (eds) *Approaches to Audiences: A Reader*. London, New York, Sydney and Auckland: Arnold.

von Feilitzen, C.V. (2001) *Influences of Media Violence: A Brief Research Summary*. Göteborg, Sweden: Nordicom, Göteborg University.

Weaver C. K., Carter, C., and Stanko, B. (2000) The female body at risk: the media, sexual violence and the gendering of public environments, in S. Allan, B. Adam and C. Carter (eds) *Environmental Risks and the Media*. London and New York: Routledge.

White, R.A. (1983) Mass communication and culture: transition to a new paradigm, in special *Ferment in the Field* issue of *Journal of Communication*, 33(3): 279–301.

Williams, D. and Skoric, M. (2005) Internet fantasy violence: a test of aggression in an online game. *Communication Monographs* 72(2): 217–233.

Wilson, B. J., Stacy L., Smith, W., Potter, J., Kunkel, D., Linz, D., Colvin, C. M. and Donnerstein, E. (2002) Violence in children's television programming: assessing the risks. *Journal of Communication*, 52(1): 5–35.

Wood, W., Wong, F. and Cachere, J. (1991) Effects of media violence on viewers' aggression in unconstrained social interaction. *Psychological Bulletin*, 109: 371–383.

Yaquinto, M. (1998) *Pump 'em Full of Lead: A Look at Gangsters on Film*. New York: Twayne.

Youngsters targeted by digital bullies. (2002) http://news.bbc.co.uk/1/hi/uk/1929944.stm (accessed 1 Aug. 2005).

Zickmund, S. (1997) Approaching the radical other: the discursive culture of cyberhate, in S. G. Jones (ed.) *Virtual Culture: Identity and Communication in Cybersociety*. London: Sage.

CONCEPTUAL APPROACHES TO MEDIA VIOLENCE

A range of conceptual approaches has been used in both the analysis and theorizing of media violence. These vary from psychological science-based behavioural effects studies, to quantitative and qualitative textual content studies, audience reception research, and political economy analyses. In this section we have selected readings that illustrate the dominant approaches to the research and theorizing of the 'effects' of media representations of violence, including work from those scholars highly critical of claims that violent media content has any 'effect' on audiences. Our aim in this section has been to provide readers with an opportunity to directly engage with the writing of those scholars who have been especially influential in contributing to media violence research, theorizing, and the media violence debate more broadly.

The first reading in this section, by Albert Bandura, Dorothea Ross and Sheila A. Ross, is a classic example of early US-based media effects research. The reading illustrates how researchers grounded in social learning theory devised laboratory experiments to investigate the effect of viewing acts of aggression on children. The study involved 96 children (48 boys and 48 girls) ranging from just under 3 to 5 years in age. In a laboratory setting the children individually watched either a physically present person behaving both verbally and physically aggressively and violently toward a large inflated doll (named a 'Bobo doll'), a 10-minute colour film recording of identical behaviour, or the television screening of a fantasy cartoon cat character also exhibiting such behaviour with accompanying cartoon music and sound effects. A fourth 'control group' was not witness to any aggressive behavior. After the viewing, the children were deliberately frustrated by having toys removed from them to see how they responded under stress. The study found that 'exposure to humans on film portraying aggression was the most influential in eliciting and shaping behavior'. Boys were also found to exhibit more aggression than girls in the experiment. It is commonly claimed that these findings provide proof for behavioural media effects theories by demonstrating how, especially the visual media communicate symbolic models for appropriate behavioural conduct to children.

The next reading in this section is by George Gerbner, whose cultivation theory also lends considerable support to the media effects arguments. Basing his conclusions on the content analysis of fictional television programmes in the US, Gerbner argues that the sheer quantity of dramatic violent material watched by television audiences cultivates beliefs that the world is a mean and dangerous place. Depending on our gender, ethnicity, class and sexual identities, etc., media images of violence teach us about the 'pecking order' in society. Furthermore, the socially powerful position of middle-class white males and their acts of violence are legitimated by media, whereas ethnic minorities, women and children are cast as weak, and their use of violence typically portrayed as inappropriate or criminal. The more heavily we watch television, the more prone we are to the cultivation of such views.

From there, attention turns to David Gauntlett's chapter, which provides a critique of the media effects tradition of research. Promoting a critical, sociological perspective in the media violence debate, Gauntlett decries effects research theories as underpinned by the ill-conceived research methodologies and informed by conservative moral ideologies. He argues that these ideologies are unable to consider aggressive and violent behaviour as a caused by the social structures of class, poverty, racism, unemployment, and the failures of the education system. Furthermore, drawing on theories of the active critical media viewer, Gauntlett contends that media audiences are in fact discerning in how they interact with, make sense of, and respond to violent media content.

The reading by Martin Barker and Julian Petley builds on the critical perspective advanced by Gauntlett. Like Gauntlett, Barker and Petley largely advocate a no-effects perspective on media violence. Yet, in an effort to move the media violence debate beyond the polarized theoretical 'effects' versus 'no-effects' positions, they advocate alternative **framings** for media violence. Encouraged by qualitative audience reception studies that investigate viewers' interpretations of representations of media violence and how those interpretations relate to and impact on their social self-perceptions, Barker and Petley present a case for the ongoing research of the social 'purpose and meanings' of media portrayals of violence. Additionally, they emphasize the need to investigate the pleasures and expression of social political subjectivities that such portrayals might afford.

Annette Hill's essay is also highly critical of effects theories of media violence, arguing that they reflect particular social and moral agendas. She demonstrates how moral campaigners rhetorically co-opt discourses of risk to amplify beliefs about the morally degenerative 'hazards' posed to society by media representations of violence. In these terms, Hill theorizes organizations that deliberately stimulate moral panics about the possible effects of media violence as 'social amplification stations'. Using the British examples of the 1980s 'video nasty' controversy, the murder of the toddler James Bulger in 1993, the 1996 massacre of 16 school children at Dunblane Primary School in Scotland, and the banning of the film *Crash*, Hill demonstrates how organized social amplification of risk informs media reporting, public debate, and policy regulation of violent media content.

Where Hill's reading is highly critical of those advocating particular social and moral concerns about the effects of mediated violence, Henry Giroux's chapter urges a consideration of the representational politics of Hollywood films featuring highly explicit and spectacular images of violence. Giroux emphasizes the importance of investigating what violent movies teach audiences – as 'public pedagogies' – about social and political relations. In a detailed textual analysis of *Fight Club*, he highlights how the film promotes the politics of **hypermasculinity** and extreme neo-liberal individualism. The film encourages identification with violence as a glamorous and legitimate form of masculine personal and political expression. For Giroux, the significance of the identity politics constructed by many Hollywood films goes well beyond the cinematic context of viewing, contributing to the shaping of the public imagination of the nature of social relations, human suffering and about how to effect social change.

2 | IMITATION OF FILM-MEDIATED AGGRESSIVE MODELS

Albert Bandura, Dorothea Ross and Sheila A. Ross

[. . .]

A recent incident (San Francisco Chronicle, 1961) in which a boy was seriously knifed during a re-enactment of a switchblade knife fight the boys had seen the previous evening on a televised rerun of the James Dean movie, *Rebel Without a Cause*, is a dramatic illustration of the possible imitative influence of film stimulation. Indeed, anecdotal data suggest that portrayal of aggression through pictorial media may be more influential in shaping the form aggression will take when a person is instigated on later occasions, than in altering the level of instigation to aggression.

In an earlier experiment (Bandura & Huston, 1961), it was shown that children readily imitated aggressive behavior exhibited by a model in the presence of the model. A succeeding investigation (Bandura, Ross, & Ross, 1961), demonstrated that children exposed to aggressive models generalized aggressive responses to a new setting in which the model was absent. The present study sought to determine the extent to which film-mediated aggressive models may serve as an important source of imitative behavior.

Aggressive models can be ordered on a reality-fictional stimulus dimension with real-life models located at the reality end of the continuum, non-human cartoon characters at the fictional end, and films portraying human models occupying an intermediate position. It was predicted, on the basis of saliency and similarity of cues, that the more remote the model was from reality, the weaker would be the tendency for subjects to imitate the behavior of the model.

Source: *Journal of Abnormal and Social Psychology*, 66, 1963, 3–11.

Of the various interpretations of **imitative learning**, the sensory feedback theory of imitation recently proposed by Mowrer (1960) is elaborated in greatest detail. According to this theory, if certain responses have been repeatedly positively reinforced, proprioceptive stimuli associated with these responses acquire secondary reinforcing properties and thus the individual is predisposed to perform the behavior for the positive feedback. Similarly, if responses have been negatively reinforced, response correlated stimuli acquire the capacity to arouse anxiety which, in turn, inhibit the occurrence of the negatively valenced behavior. On the basis of these considerations, it was predicted subjects who manifest high aggression anxiety would perform significantly less imitative and nonimitative aggression than subjects who display little anxiety over aggression. Since aggression is generally considered female inappropriate behavior, and therefore likely to be negatively reinforced in girls (Sears, Maccoby, & Levin, 1957), it was also predicted that male subjects would be more imitative of aggression than females.

To the extent that observation of adults displaying aggression conveys a certain degree of permissiveness for aggressive behavior, it may be assumed that such exposure not only facilitates the learning of new aggressive responses but also weakens competing inhibitory responses in subjects and thereby increases the probability of occurrence of previously learned patterns of aggression. It was predicted, therefore, that subjects who observed aggressive models would display significantly more aggression when subsequently frustrated than subjects who were equally frustrated but who had no prior exposure to models exhibiting aggression.

Method

Subjects

The subjects were 48 boys and 48 girls enrolled in the Stanford University Nursery School. They ranged in age from 35 to 69 months, with a mean age of 52 months.

Two adults, a male and a female, served in the role of models both in the real-life and the human film-aggression condition, and one female experimenter conducted the study for all 96 children.

General procedure

Subjects were divided into three experimental groups and one control group of 24 subjects each. One group of experimental subjects observed real-life aggressive models, a second group observed these same models portraying aggression on film, while a third group viewed a film depicting an aggressive cartoon character. The experimental groups were further subdivided into male and female subjects so that half the subjects in the two conditions involving human models were exposed to same-sex models, while the remaining subjects viewed models of the opposite sex.

Following the exposure experience, subjects were tested for the amount of imitative and nonimitative aggression in a different experimental setting in the absence of the models.

The control group subjects had no exposure to the aggressive models and were tested only in the generalization situation.

Subjects in the experimental and control groups were matched individually on the basis of ratings of their aggressive behavior in social interactions in the nursery school. The experiment and a nursery school teacher rated the subjects on four five-point rating scales which measured the extent to which subjects displayed physical aggression, verbal aggression, aggression toward inanimate objects, and aggression inhibition. The latter scale, which dealt with the subjects' tendency to inhibit aggressive reactions in the face of high instigation, provided the measure of aggression anxiety. Seventy-one percent of the subjects were rated independently by both judges so as to permit an assessment of interrater agreement. The reliability of the composite aggression score, estimated by means of the Pearson product-moment correlation, was .80.

[. . .]

Experimental conditions

Subjects in the Real-Life Aggressive condition were brought individually by the experimenter to the experimental room and the model, who was in the hallway outside the room, was invited by the experimenter to come and join in the game. The subject was then escorted to one corner of the room and seated at a small table which contained potato prints, multi-color picture stickers, and colored paper. After demonstrating how the subject could design pictures with the materials provided, the experimenter escorted the model to the opposite corner of the room which contained a small table and chair, a tinker toy set, a mallet, and a 5-foot inflated Bobo doll. The experimenter explained that this was the model's play area and after the model was seated, the experimenter left the experimental room.

The model began the session by assembling the tinker toys but after approximately a minute had elapsed, the model turned to the Bobo doll and spent the remainder of the period aggressing toward it with highly novel responses which are unlikely to be performed by children independently of the observation of the model's behavior. Thus, in addition to punching the Bobo doll, the model exhibited the following distinctive aggressive acts which were to be scored as imitative responses:

The model sat on the Bobo doll and punched it repeatedly in the nose.

The model then raised the Bobo doll and pommeled it on the head with a mallet.

Following the mallet aggression, the model tossed the doll up in the air aggressively and kicked it about the room. This sequence of physically aggressive acts was repeated approximately three times, interspersed with verbally aggressive responses such as, "Sock him in the nose . . .," "Hit him down . . .," "Throw him in the air . . .," "Kick him . . .," and "Pow."

Subjects in the Human Film-Aggression condition were brought by the experimenter to the semi-darkened experimental room, introduced to the picture materials, and informed that while the subjects worked on potato prints, a movie would be shown on a screen, positioned approximately 6 feet from the subject's table. The movie projector was located in a distant corner of the room and was screened from the subject's view by large wooden panels.

The color movie and a tape recording of the sound track was begun by a male projectionist as soon as the experimenter left the experimental room and was shown for a duration of 10 minutes. The models in the film presentations were the same adult males and females who participated in the Real-Life condition of the experiment. Similarly, the aggressive behavior they portrayed in the film was identical with their real-life performances.

For subjects in the Cartoon Film-Aggression condition, after seating the subject at the table with the picture construction material, the experimenter walked over to a television console approximately 3 feet in front of the subject's table, remarked, "I guess I'll turn on the color TV", and ostensibly tuned in a cartoon program. The experimenter then left the experimental room. The cartoon was shown on a glass lens screen in the television set by means of a rear projection arrangement screened from the subject's view by large panels.

The sequence of aggressive acts in the cartoon was performed by the female model costumed as a black cat similar to the many cartoon cats. In order to heighten the level of irreality of the cartoon, the floor area was covered with artificial grass and the walls forming the backdrop were adorned with brightly colored trees, birds, and butterflies creating a fantasy-land setting. The cartoon began with a close-up of a stage on which the curtains were slowly drawn revealing a picture of a cartoon cat along with the title, *Herman the Cat*. The remainder of the film showed the cat pommeling the Bobo doll on the head with a mallet, sitting on the doll and punching it in the nose, tossing the doll in the air, and kicking it about the room in a manner identical with the performance in the other experimental conditions except that the cat's movements were characteristically feline. To induce further a cartoon set, the program was introduced and concluded with appropriate cartoon music, and the cat's verbal aggression was repeated in a high-pitched, animated voice.

In both film conditions, at the conclusion of the movie the experimenter entered the room and then escorted the subject to the test room.

Aggression instigation

In order to differentiate clearly the exposure and test situations subjects were tested for the amount of imitative learning in a different experimental room which was set off from the main nursery school building.

The degree to which a child has learned aggressive patterns of behavior through imitation becomes most evident when the child is instigated to aggression on later occasions. Thus, for example, the effects of viewing the movie, *Rebel Without a Cause*, were not evident until the boys were instigated to aggression the following day, at which time they re-enacted the televised switchblade knife fight in considerable detail. For this reason, the children in the experiment, both those in the control group, and those who were exposed to the aggressive models, were mildly frustrated before they were brought to the test room.

Following the exposure experience, the experimenter brought the subject to an anteroom which contained a varied array of highly attractive toys. The experimenter explained that the toys were for the subject to play with, but, as soon as the subject became sufficiently involved with the play material, the experimenter remarked that these were her very best toys, that she did not let just anyone play with them, and that she had decided to reserve these toys for some other children. However, the subject could play with any of the toys in the next room. The experimenter and the subject then entered the adjoining experimental room.

It was necessary for the experimenter to remain in the room during the experimental session; otherwise, a number of the children would either refuse to remain alone or would leave before the termination of the session. In order to minimize any influence her presence might have on the subject's behavior, the experimenter remained as inconspicuous as possible by busying herself with paper work at a desk in the far corner of the room and avoiding any interaction with the child.

Test for delayed imitation

The experimental room contained a variety of toys, some of which could be used in imitative or nonimitative agression, and others which tended to elicit predominantly nonaggressive forms of behavior. The aggressive toys included a 3-foot Bobo doll, a mallet and peg board, two dart guns, and a tether ball with a face painted on it which hung from the ceiling. The non-aggressive toys, on the other hand, included a tea set, crayons and coloring paper, a ball, two dolls, three bears, cars and trucks, and plastic farm animals.

In order to eliminate any variation in behavior due to mere placement of the toys in the room, the play material was arranged in a fixed order for each of the sessions.

The subject spent 20 minutes in the experimental room during which time his behavior was rated in terms of predetermined response categories by judges who observed the session through a one-way mirror in an adjoining observation room. The 20-minute session was divided in 5-second intervals by means of an electric interval timer, thus yielding a total number of 240 response units for each subject.

The male model scored the experimental sessions for all subjects. In order to provide an estimate of interjudge agreement, the performances of 40% of the subjects were scored independently by a second observer. The responses scored involved highly specific concrete classes of behavior, and yielded high interscorer reliabilities, the product-moment coefficients being in the .90s.

Response measures

The following response measures were obtained:

Imitative aggression. This category included acts of striking the Bobo doll with the mallet, sitting on the doll and punching it in the nose, kicking the doll, tossing it in the air, and the verbally aggressive responses, "Sock him," "Hit him down," "Kick him," "Throw him in the air," and "Pow."

Partially imitative responses. A number of subjects imitated the essential components of the model's behavior but did not perform the complete act, or they directed the imitative aggressive response to some object other than the Bobo doll. Two responses of this type were scored and were interpreted as partially imitative behavior:

Mallet aggression. The subject strikes objects other than the Bobo doll aggressively with the mallet.

Sits on Bobo doll. The subject lays the Bobo doll on its side and sits on it, but does not aggress toward it.

Nonimitative aggression. This category included acts of punching, slapping, or pushing the doll, physically aggressive acts directed toward objects other than the Bobo doll, and any hostile remarks except for those in the verbal imitation category; for example, "Shoot the Bobo," "Cut him," "Stupid ball," "Knock over people," "Horses fighting, biting."

Aggressive gun play. The subject shoots darts or aims the guns and fires imaginary shots at objects in the room.

Ratings were also made of the number of behavior units in which subjects played nonaggressively or sat quietly and did not play with any of the material at all.

Results

The mean imitative and nonimitative aggression scores for subjects in the various experimental and control groups are presented in Table 1.

Since the distributions of scores departed from normality and the assumption of homogeneity of variance could not be made for most of the measures, the Freidman two-way analysis of variance by ranks was employed for testing the significance of the obtained differences.

Total aggression

The mean total aggression scores for subjects in the real-life, human film, cartoon film, and the control groups are 83, 92, 99, and 54, respectively. The results of the analysis of variance performed on these scores reveal that the main effect of treatment conditions is significant ($\chi r^2 = 9.06$, $p < .05$), confirming the prediction that exposure of subjects to aggressive models increases the probability that subjects will respond aggressively when instigated on later occasions. Further analyses of pairs of scores by means of the Wilcoxon matched-pairs signed-ranks test show that subjects who viewed the real-life models and the film-mediated models do not differ from each other in total aggressiveness but all three experimental groups expressed significantly more aggressive behavior than the control subjects (Table 2).

Imitative aggressive responses

The Freidman analysis reveals that exposure of subjects to aggressive models is also a highly effective method for shaping subjects' aggressive responses ($\chi r^2 = 23.88$, $p < .001$). Comparisons of treatment conditions by the Wilcoxon test reveal that subjects who observed the real-life models

Table 1 Mean aggression scores for subgroups of experimental and control subjects

Response category	Real-life aggressive		Human film-aggressive		Cartoon film-aggressive	Control group
	F Model	M Model	F Model	M Model		
Total aggression						
Girls	65.8	57.3	87.0	79.5	80.9	36.4
Boys	76.8	131.8	114.5	85.0	117.2	72.2
Imitative aggression						
Girls	19.2	9.2	10.0	8.0	7.8	1.8
Boys	18.4	38.4	34.3	13.3	16.2	3.9
Mallet aggression						
Girls	17.2	18.7	49.2	19.5	36.8	13.1
Boys	15.5	28.8	20.5	16.3	12.5	13.5
Sits on Bobo doll[a]						
Girls	10.4	5.6	10.3	4.5	15.3	3.3
Boys	1.3	0.7	7.7	0.0	5.6	0.6
Nonimitative aggression						
Girls	27.6	24.9	24.0	34.3	27.5	17.8
Boys	35.5	48.6	46.8	31.8	71.8	40.4
Aggressive gun play						
Girls	1.8	4.5	3.8	17.6	8.8	3.7
Boys	7.3	15.9	12.8	23.7	16.6	14.3

[a] This response category was not included in the total aggression score.

and the film-mediated models, relative to subjects in the control group, performed considerably more imitative physical and verbal aggression (Table 2). [. . .]

The prediction that imitation is positively related to the reality cues of the model was only partially supported. While subjects who observed the real-life aggressive models exhibited significantly more imitative aggression than subjects who viewed the cartoon model, no significant differences were found between the live and film, and the film and cartoon conditions, nor did the three experimental groups differ significantly in total aggression or in the performances of partially imitative behavior (Table 2). Indeed, the available data suggest that, of the three experimental conditions, exposure to humans on film portraying aggression was the most influential in eliciting

Table 2 Significance of the differences between experimental and control groups in the expression of aggression

Response category	χ^2	p	Comparison of treatment conditions[a]					
			Live vs. Film p	Live vs. Cartoon p	Film vs. Cartoon p	Live vs. Control p	Film vs. Control p	Cartoon vs. Control p
Total aggression	9.06	< .05	ns	ns	ns	< .01	< .01	< .005
Imitative aggression	23.88	< .001	ns	< .05	ns	< .001	< .001	< .005
Partial imitation								
Mallet aggression	7.36	.10 > p > .05						
Sits on Bobo doll	8.05	< .05	ns	ns	ns	ns	< .05	< .005
Nonimitative aggression	7.28	.10 > p > .05						
Agressive gun play	8.06	< .05	<.01[b]	ns	ns	ns	< .05	ns

[a] The probability values are based on the Wilcoxon test.
[b] This probability value is based on a two-tailed test of significance.

and shaping aggressive behavior. Subjects in this condition, in relation to the control subjects, exhibited more total aggression, more imitative aggression, more partially imitative behavior, such as sitting on the Bobo doll and mallet aggression, and they engaged in significantly more aggressive gun play. In addition, they performed significantly more aggressive gun play than did subjects who were exposed to the real-life aggressive models (Table 2).

Influence of sex of model and sex of child

In order to determine the influence of sex of model and sex of child on the expression of imitative and nonimitative aggression, the data from the experimental groups were combined and the significance of the differences between groups was assessed by t tests for uncorrelated means. In statistical comparisons involving relatively skewed distributions of scores the Mann-Whitney U test was employed.

Sex of subjects had a highly significant effect on both the learning and the performance of aggression. Boys, in relation to girls, exhibited significantly more total aggression ($t = 2.69$, $p < .01$), more imitative aggression ($t = 2.82$, $p < .005$), more aggressive gun play ($z = 3.38$, $p < .001$), and more nonimitative aggressive behavior ($t = 2.98$, $p < .005$). Girls, on the other hand, were more inclined than boys to sit on the Bobo doll but refrained from punching it ($z = 3.47$, $p < .001$).

The analyses also disclosed some influences of the sex of the model. Subjects exposed to the male model, as compared to the female model, expressed significantly more aggressive gun play ($z = 2.83$, $p < .005$). The most marked differences in aggressive gun play ($U = 9.5$, $p = .001$), however, were found between girls exposed to the female model ($M = 2.9$) and males who observed the male model ($M = 19.8$). Although the overall model difference in partially imitative behavior, Sits on Bobo, was not significant, Sex × Model subgroup comparisons yielded some interesting results. Boys who observed the aggressive female model, for example, were more likely to sit on the Bobo doll without punching it than boys who viewed the male model ($U = 33$, $p < .05$). Girls reproduced the nonaggressive component of the male model's aggressive pattern of behavior (i.e., sat on the doll without punching it) with considerably higher frequency than did boys who observed the same model ($U = 21.5$, $p < .02$). The highest incidence of partially imitative responses was yielded by the group of girls who viewed the aggressive female model ($M = 10.4$), and the lowest values by the boys who were exposed to the male model ($M = 0.3$). This difference was significant beyond the .05 significance level. These findings, along with the sex of child and sex of model differences reported in the preceding sections, provide further support for the view that the influence of models in promoting social learning is determined, in part, by the sex appropriateness of the model's behavior (Bandura et al., 1961).

Aggressive predisposition and imitation

Since the correlations between ratings of aggression and the measures of imitative and total aggressive behavior, calculated separately for boys and girls in each of the experimental conditions, did not differ significantly, the data were combined. The correlational analyses performed on these pooled data failed to yield any significant relationships between ratings of aggression anxiety, frequency of aggressive behavior, and the experimental aggression measures. In fact, the array means suggested nonlinear regressions although the departures from linearity were not of sufficient magnitude to be statistically significant.

Discussion

The results of the present study provide strong evidence that exposure to filmed aggression heightens aggressive reactions in children. Subjects who viewed the aggressive human and cartoon models on film exhibited nearly twice as much aggression than did subjects in the control group who were not exposed to the aggressive film content.

In the experimental design typically employed for testing the possible cathartic function of vicarious aggression, subjects are first frustrated, then provided with an opportunity to view an aggressive film following which their overt or fantasy aggression is measured. While this procedure yields some information on the immediate influence of film-mediated aggression, the full effects of such exposure may not be revealed until subjects are instigated to aggression on a later occasion. Thus, the present study, and one recently reported by Lövaas (1961), both utilizing a design in which subjects first observed filmed aggression and then were frustrated, clearly reveal that observation of models portraying aggression on film substantially increases rather than decreases the probability of aggressive reactions to subsequent frustrations.

Filmed aggression not only facilitated the expression of aggression, but also effectively shaped the form of the subjects' aggressive behavior. The finding that children modeled their behavior to some extent after the film characters suggests that pictorial mass media, particularly television, may serve as an important source of social behavior. In fact, a possible general-ization of responses originally learned in the television situation to the experimental film may account for the significantly greater amount of aggressive gun play displayed by subjects in the film condition as compared to subjects in the real-life and control groups. It is unfortunate that the qualitative features of the gun behavior were not scored since subjects in the film condition, unlike those in the other two groups, developed inter-esting elaborations in gun play (for example, stalking the imaginary oppon-ent, quick drawing, and rapid firing), characteristic of the Western gun fighter.

The view that the social learning of aggression through exposure to aggressive film content is confined to deviant children (Schramm, Lyle, & Parker, 1961), finds little support in our data. The children who participated in the experiment are by no means a deviant sample, nevertheless, 88% of the subjects in the Real-Life and in the Human Film condition, and 79% of the subjects in the Cartoon Film condition, exhibited varying degrees of imitative aggression. In assessing the possible influence of televised stimula-tion on viewers' behavior, however, it is important to distinguish between learning and overt performance. Although the results of the present experiment demonstrate that the vast majority of children *learn* patterns of social behavior through pictorial stimulation, nevertheless, informal obser-vation suggests that children do not, as a rule, *perform* indiscriminately the behavior of televised characters, even those they regard as highly attractive models. The replies of parents whose children participated in the present study to an open-end questionnaire item concerning their handling of imi-tative behavior suggest that this may be in part a function of negative reinforcement, as most parents were quick to discourage their children's overt imitation of television characters by prohibiting certain programs or by labeling the imitative behavior in a disapproving manner. From our knowledge of the effects of punishment on behavior, the responses in ques-tion would be expected to retain their original strength and could reappear on later occasions in the presence of appropriate eliciting stimuli, particu-larly if instigation is high, the instruments for aggression are available, and the threat of noxious consequences is reduced.

The absence of any relationships between ratings of the children's pre-disposition to aggression and their aggressive behavior in the experimental setting may simply reflect the inadequacy of the predictor measures. It may be pointed out, however, that the reliability of the ratings was relatively high. While this does not assure validity of the measures, it does at least indicate there was consistency in the raters' estimates of the children's aggressive tendencies.

A second, and perhaps more probable, explanation is that proprioceptive feedback alone is not sufficient to account for response inhibition or facilitation. For example, the proprioceptive cues arising from hitting responses directed toward parents and toward peers may differ little, if any; nevertheless, tendencies to aggress toward parents are apt to be strongly inhibited while peer aggression may be readily expressed (Bandura, 1960; Bandura & Walters, 1959). In most social interaction sequences, proprioceptive cues make up only a small part of the total stimulus complex and, therefore, it is necessary to take into consideration additional stimulus components, for the most part external, which probably serve as important discriminative cues for the expression of aggression. Consequently, prediction of the occurrence or inhibition of specific classes of responses would be expected to depend upon the presence of a certain pattern of proprioceptive or introceptive stimulation together with relevant discriminative external stimuli.

According to this line of reasoning, failure to obtain the expected positive relationships between the measures of aggression may be due primarily to the fact that permissiveness for aggression, conveyed by situational cues in the form of aggressive film content and play material, was sufficient to override the influence of internal stimuli generated by the commission of aggressive responses. If, in fact, the behavior of young children, as compared to that of adults, is less likely to be under internal stimulus control, one might expect environmental cues to play a relatively important role in eliciting or inhibiting aggressive behavior.

A question may be raised as to whether the aggressive acts studied in the present experiment constitute 'genuine' aggressive responses. Aggression is typically defined as behavior, the goal or intent of which is injury to a person, or destruction of an object (Bandura & Walters, 1959; Dollard, Doob, Miller, Mowrer, & Sears, 1939; Sears, Maccoby, & Levin, 1957). Since intentionality is not a property of behavior but primarily an inference concerning antecedent events, the categorization of an act as 'aggressive' involves a consideration of both stimulus and mediating or terminal response events.

According to a social learning theory of aggression [. . .] proposed by Bandura and Walters (in press), most of the responses utilized to hurt or to injure others (for example, striking, kicking, and other responses of high magnitude), are probably learned for prosocial purposes under nonfrustration conditions. Since frustration generally elicits responses of high magnitude, the latter classes of responses, once acquired, may be called out in social interactions for the purpose of injuring others. On the basis of this theory it would be predicted that the aggressive responses acquired imitatively, while not necessarily mediating aggressive goals in the experimental situation, would be utilized to serve such purposes in other social settings with higher frequency by children in the experimental conditions than by children in the control group.

The present study involved primarily vicarious or empathic learning (Mowrer, 1960) in that subjects acquired a relatively complex repertoire of aggressive responses by the mere sight of a model's behavior. It has been generally assumed that the necessary conditions for the occurrence of such learning is that the model perform certain responses followed by positive reinforcement to the model (Hill, 1960; Mowrer, 1960). According to this theory, to the extent that the observer experiences the model's reinforcement vicariously, the observer will be prone to reproduce the model's behavior. While there is some evidence from experiments involving both human (Lewis & Duncan, 1958; McBrearty, Marston, & Kanfer, 1961; Sechrest, 1961) and animal subjects (Darby & Riopelle, 1959; Warden, Fjeld, & Koch, 1940), that vicarious reinforcement may in fact increase the probability of the behavior in question, it is apparent from the results of the experiment reported in this paper that a good deal of human imitative learning can occur without any reinforcers delivered either to the model or to the observer.

[. . .]

References

Bandura, A. Relationship of family patterns to child behavior disorders. Progress Report, 1960, Stanford University, Project No. M-1734, United States Public Health Service.

Bandura, A., and Huston, Aletha C. Identification as a process of incidental learning. *J. Abnorm. Soc. Psychol.*, 1961, 63, 311–318.

Bandura, A., Ross, Dorothea, and Ross, Sheila A. Transmission of aggression through imitation of aggressive models. *J. Abnorm. Soc. Psychol.*, 1961, 63, 575–582.

Bandura, A., and Walters, R. H. *Adolescent Aggression*. New York: Ronald, 1959.

Bandura, A., and Walters, R. H. *The Social Learning of Deviant Behavior: A Behavioristic Approach to Socialization*. New York: Holt, Rinehart, & Winston, in press.

Darby, C. L., and Riopelle, A. J. Observational learning in the Rhesus monkey. *J. Comp. Physiol. Psychol.*, 1959, 52, 94–98.

Dollard, J., Doob, L. W., Miller, N. E., Mowrer, O. H., and Sears, R. R. *Frustration and Aggression*. New Haven: Yale University Press, 1939.

Hill, W. F. Learning theory and the acquisition of values. *Psychol. Rev.*, 1960, 67, 317–331.

Lewis, D. J., and Duncan, C. P. Vicarious experience and partial reinforcement *J. Abnorm. Soc. Psychol.*, 1958, 57, 321–326.

Lövaas, O. J. Effect of exposure to symbolic aggression on aggressive behavior. *Child Develpm.*, 1961, 32, 37–44.

McBrearty, J. F., Marston, A. R., and Kanfer, F. H. Conditioning a verbal operant in a group setting: Direct vs. vicarious reinforcement. *Amer. Psychologist*, 1961, 16, 425. (Abstract)

Mowrer, O. H. *Learning Theory and the Symbolic Processes*. New York: Wiley, 1960.

San Francisco Chronicle. "James Dean" knifing in South City. *San Francisco Chron.*, March 1, 1961, 6.

Schramm, W., Lyle, J., and Parker, E. B. *Television in the Lives of Our Children*. Stanford: Stanford University Press, 1961.

Sears, R. R., Maccoby, Eleanor E., and Levin, H. *Patterns of Child Rearing*. Evanston: Row, Peterson, 1957.

Sechrest, L. Vicarious reinforcement of responses. *Amer. Psychologist*, 1961, 16, 356. (Abstract)

Warden, C. J., Fjeld, H. A., and Koch, A. M. Imitative behavior in cebus and Rhesus monkeys. *J. Genet. Psychol.*, 1940, 56, 311–322.

3 | TELEVISION VIOLENCE
AT A TIME OF TURMOIL AND TERROR

George Gerbner

[...]

The New Cultural Environment

Nielsen figures show that an American child today is born into a home in which television is on an average of more than 7 hours a day. For the first time in human history, most of the stories about people, life, and values are told not by parents, schools, churches, or others in the community who have something to tell, but by a group of distant conglomerates that have something to sell.

Television, the mainstream of the new cultural environment, has brought about a radical change in the way children grow up, learn, and live in our society. Television is a relatively nonselectively used ritual; children are its captive audience. Most people watch by the clock and not by the program. The television audience depends on the time of the day and the day of the week more than on the program. Other media require literacy, growing up, going out, and selection based on some previously acquired tastes, values, predispositions. Traditional media research assumed such selectivity. But there are no 'previously acquired tastes, values, predispositions' with television. Viewing starts in infancy and continues throughout life.

Television helps to shape from the outset the predispositions and selections that govern the use of other media. Unlike other media, television requires little or no attention; its repetitive patterns are absorbed in the course of living. They become part and parcel of the family's style of life, but they neither stem from nor respond to its particular and selective needs and wants. It is television itself that cultivates the tastes, values, and predisposition that guide future selection of other media. That is why television had a major impact on what movies, magazines, newspapers, and books can be sold best in the new cultural environment.

The roles children grow into are no longer homemade, handcrafted, community-inspired. They are products of a complex, integrated, and globalized manufacturing and marketing system. Television violence, defined as overt physical action that hurts or kills (or threatens to do so), is an integral part of that system. A study titled *The Limits of Selective Viewing* (Sun, 1989) found that, on the whole, prime-time television presents a relatively small set of common themes, and violence pervades most of them.

Of course, representations of violence are not necessarily undesirable. There is blood in fairy tales, gore in mythology, murder in Shakespeare. Not all violence is alike. In some contexts, violence can be a legitimate and even necessary cultural expression. Individually crafted, historically inspired, sparingly and selectively used expressions of symbolic violence can indicate the tragic costs of deadly compulsions. However, such tragic sense of violence has been swamped by 'happy violence' produced on the dramatic assembly line. This happy violence is cool, swift, painless, and often spectacular, even thrilling, but usually sanitized. It always leads to a happy ending. After all, it is designed to entertain and not to upset; it must deliver the audience to the next commercial in a receptive mood.

The majority of network viewers have little choice of thematic context or cast of character types, and virtually no chance of avoiding violence. Nor has the proliferation of channels led to greater diversity of actual viewing (see, e.g., Gerbner, 1993; Gerbner et al., 1993; Morgan & Shanahan, 1991). If anything, the dominant dramatic patterns penetrate more deeply into viewer choices through more outlets managed by fewer owners airing programs produced by fewer creative sources.

Message System Analysis

My conclusions are based on the findings of our Cultural Indicators project (CI) that began in 1967.[1] CI is a cumulative database and an ongoing research project that relates recurrent features of the world of television to media policy and viewer conceptions of reality. Its computer archive contain observations on over 3,000 programs and 35,000 characters coded according to many thematic, demographic, and action categories.

CI is a three-pronged research effort. '**Message system analysis**' is the annual monitoring of television program content; 'institutional policy analysis' looks at the economic and political bases of media decision making; '**cultivation analysis**' is an assessment of the long-range consequences of exposure to television's systems of messages.

Message system analysis is the study of the content of television programs. It includes every dramatic (fictional) program in each annual sample. It provides an unusual view of familiar territory. It is not a view of individual programs but an aggregate picture of the world of television, a bird's-eye view of what large communities of viewers absorb over long periods of time.

The role of violence in that world can be seen in our analysis of prime-time network programs and characters. Casting and fate, the demography of that world, are the important building blocks of the story-telling process. They have presented a stable pattern over the almost 30 years of monitoring network television drama and coding every speaking character in each year's sample. Middle-class white male characters dominate in numbers and power. Women play one out of three characters. Young people comprise one third and old one fifth of their actual proportions of the population. Most other minorities are even more underrepresented. That cast sets the stage for stories of conflict, violence, and the projection of white male prime-of-life power. Most of those who are underrepresented are also those who, when portrayed, suffer the worst fate.

The average viewer of prime-time television drama (serious as well as comedic) sees in a typical week an average of 21 criminals arrayed against an army of 41 public and private law enforcers. There are 14 doctors, 6 nurses, 6 lawyers, and 2 judges to handle them. An average of 150 acts of violence and about 15 murders entertain them and their children every week, and that does not count cartoons and the news. Those who watch more than 3 hours a day (more than half of all viewers) absorb much more.

About one out of three (31%) of all characters and more than half (52%) of major characters are involved in violence either as victims or as victimizers (or both) in any given week. The ratio of violence to victimization defines the price to be paid for committing violence. When one group can commit violence with relative impunity, the price it pays for violence is relatively low. When another group suffers more violence than it commits, the price is high.

In the total cast of prime-time characters, defined as all speaking parts regardless of the importance of the role, the average 'risk ratio' (number of victims per 10 violents) is 12. Violence is an effective victimizer–and characterizer. Its distribution is not random; the calculus of risk is not evenly distributed. Women, children, poorer, and older people and some minorities pay a higher price for violence than do males in the prime of life. The price paid in victims for every 10 violents is 15 for boys, 16 for girls, 17 for young women, 18.5 for lower-class characters, and more than 20 for elderly characters.

Violence takes on an even more defining role for major characters. It involves more than half of all major characters (58% of men and 41% of women). Most likely to be involved either as perpetrators or victims, or both, are characters portrayed as mentally ill (84%), characters with mental or other disability (70%), young adult males (69%), and Latino/Hispanic Americans (64%). Children, lower class and mentally ill or otherwise disabled characters, pay the highest price – 13 to 16 victims for every 10 perpetrators.

Lethal victimization further extends the pattern. About 5% of all characters and 10% of major characters are involved in killing (kill or get killed or both). Being Latino/Hispanic or lower class means bad trouble: they are the most likely to kill and be killed. Being poor, old, Hispanic, or a woman of color means double trouble, a disproportionate chance of being killed; they pay the highest relative price for taking another's life.

Among major characters, for every 10 'good' (positively valued) men who kill, about 4 are killed. But for every 10 'good' women who kill, 6 women are killed, and for every 10 women of color who kill, 17 women are killed. Older women characters get involved in violence only to be killed.

We calculated a violence 'pecking order' by ranking the risk ratios of the different groups. Women, children, young people, lower class, disabled, and Asian Americans are at the bottom of the heap. When it comes to killing, older and Latino/Hispanic characters also pay a higher than average price. In other words, hurting and killing by most majority groups extracts a tooth for a tooth. But minority groups tend to pay a higher price for their show of force. That imbalance of power is, in fact, what makes them minorities even when, as women, they are a numerical majority.

Cultivation Analysis: the 'Lessons' of Television

What are the consequences? These representations are not the sole or necessarily even the main determinants of what people think or do. But they are the most pervasive, inescapable, and policy-directed common and stable cultural contributions to what large communities absorb over long periods of time. We use the term *cultivation* to distinguish the long-term cultivation of assumptions about life and values from short-term 'effects' that are usually assessed by measuring change as a consequence of exposure to certain messages. With television, one cannot take a measure before exposure and rarely without exposure. Television tends to cultivate and confirm stable conceptions about life.

Cultivation analysis measures these 'lessons' as it explores whether those who spend more time with television are more likely than comparable groups of lighter viewers to perceive the real world in ways that reflect the most common and repetitive features of the television world. (See Morgan & Signorielli, 1990, for a detailed discussion of the theoretical assumptions and methodological procedures of cultivation analysis.)

The systemic patterns in television content that we observe through message system analysis provide the basis for formulating survey questions about people's conceptions of social reality. These questions form the basis of surveys administered to large and representative national samples of respondents. The surveys include questions about fear of crime, trusting other people, walking at night in one's own neighborhood, chances of victimization, inclination to aggression, and so on. Respondents in each sample are divided into those who watch the most television, those who watch a moderate amount, and those who watch the least. Cultivation is assessed by comparing patterns of responses in the three viewing groups (light, medium, and heavy) while controlling for important demographic and other characteristics such as education, age, income, gender, newspaper reading, neighborhood, and so forth.

These surveys indicate that long-term regular exposure to violence-laden television tends to make an independent contribution (i.e., in addition to all other factors) to the feeling of living in a mean and gloomy world. The 'lessons' range from aggression to desensitization and to a sense of vulnerability and dependence.

The symbolic overkill takes its toll on all viewers. However, heavier viewers in every subgroup express a greater sense of apprehension than do light viewers in the same groups. They are more likely than comparable groups of light viewers to overestimate their chances of involvement in violence; to believe that their neighborhoods are unsafe; to state that fear of crime is a very serious personal problem and to assume that crime is rising, regardless of the facts of the case. Heavy viewers are also more likely to buy new locks, watchdogs, and guns 'for protection.' It makes no difference what they watch because only light viewers watch more selectively; heavy viewers watch more of everything that is on the air. Our studies show that they cannot escape watching violence (see, e.g., Gerbner et al., 1993; Sun, 1989).

Moreover, viewers who see members of their own group under-represented but over-victimized seem to develop a greater sense of apprehension, mistrust, and alienation, what we call the 'mean world syndrome.' Insecure, angry people may be prone to violence but are even more likely to be dependent on authority and susceptible to deceptively simple, strong, hard-line postures. They may accept and even welcome repressive measures such as more jails, capital punishment, harsher sentences – measures that have never reduced crime but never fail to get votes – if that promises to relieve their anxieties. That is the deeper dilemma of violence-laden television.

The Structural Basis of Television Violence

Formula-driven violence in entertainment and news is not an expression of freedom, viewer preference, or even crime statistics. The frequency of violence in the media seldom, if ever, reflects the actual occurrence of crime in a community. It is, rather, the product of a complex manufacturing and marketing machine.

Mergers, consolidation, conglomeratization, and **globalization** speed the machine. 'Studios are clipping productions and consolidating operations, closing off gateways for newcomers,' notes the trade paper *Variety* on the front page of its August 2, 1993, issue. The number of major studios declines while their share of domestic and global markets rises. Channels proliferate while investment in new talent drops, gateways close, and creative sources shrink.

Concentration brings denial of access to new entries and alternative perspectives. It places greater emphasis on dramatic ingredients most suitable for aggressive international promotion. Having fewer buyers for their products forces program producers into deficit financing. That means that most producers cannot break even on the license fees they receive for domestic airings. They are forced into syndication and foreign sales to make a profit. They need dramatic ingredients that require no translation, 'speak action' in any language, and fit any culture. That ingredient is violence and mayhem. The events of September 11 were a striking example. (Sex is second but, ironically, it runs into more inhibitions and restrictions.)

Syndicators demand 'action' (the code word for violence) because it 'travels well around the world,' said the producer of *Die Hard 2* (which killed 264 compared to 18 in *Die Hard 1*). 'Everyone understands an action movie. If I tell a joke, you may not get it but if a bullet goes through the window, we all know how to hit the floor, no matter the language' (quoted in Auletta, 1993).

Our analysis shows that violence dominates U.S. exports. We compared 250 U.S. programs exported to 10 countries with 111 programs shown in the United States during the same year. Violence was the main theme of 40% of home-shown and 49% of exported programs. Crime/action series comprised 17% of home-shown and 46% of exported programs.

The rationalization for all that is that violence 'sells.' But what does it sell to whom, and at what price? There is no evidence that, other factors being equal, violence per se is giving most viewers, countries, and citizens 'what they want.' The most highly rated programs are usually not violent. The trade paper *Broadcasting & Cable* (Editorial, 1993) editorialized that 'the most popular programming is hardly violent as anyone with a passing knowledge of Nielsen ratings will tell you.' The editorial added that 'action hours and movies have been the most popular exports for years' – that is, with the exporters, not the audiences. In other words, violence may help sell programs cheaply to broadcasters in many countries despite the dislike of their audiences. But television audiences do not buy programs, and advertisers, who do, pay for reaching the available audience at the least cost.

We compared data from more than 100 violent and the same number of nonviolent prime-time programs stored in the CI database. The average Nielsen rating of the violent sample was 11.1; the same for the nonviolent sample was 13.8. The share of viewing households in the violent and nonviolent samples was 18.9 and 22.5, respectively. The amount and consistency of violence in a series further increased the gap. Furthermore, the nonviolent sample was more highly rated than the violent sample for each of the five seasons studied.

However, despite their low average popularity, what violent programs lose on general domestic audiences they more than make up by grabbing younger viewers the advertisers want to reach and by extending their reach to the global market hungry for a cheap product. Even though these imports are typically also less popular abroad than quality shows produced at home, their extremely low cost, compared to local production, makes them attractive to the broadcasters who buy them.

Of course, some violent movies, videos, video games, and other spectacles do attract sizable audiences. But those audiences are small compared to the home audience for television. They are the selective retail buyers of what television dispenses wholesale. If only a small proportion of television viewers growing up with the violent overkill become addicted to it, they can make many movies and games spectacularly successful.

Public Response and Action

Most television viewers suffer the violence daily inflicted on them with diminishing tolerance. Organizations of creative workers in media, health professionals, law enforcement agencies, and virtually all other media-oriented professional and citizen groups have come out against 'gratuitous' television violence. A March 1985 Harris survey showed that 78% disapprove of violence they see on television. A Gallup poll of October 1990 found 79% in favor of 'regulating' objectionable content in television. A Times-Mirror national poll in 1993 showed that Americans who said they were 'personally bothered' by violence in entertainment shows jumped to 59% from 44% in 1983. Furthermore, 80% said entertainment violence was 'harmful' to society, compared with 64% in 1983.

Local broadcasters, legally responsible for what goes on the air, also oppose the overkill and complain about loss of control. *Electronic Media* reported on August 2, 1993, the results of its own survey of 100 general managers across all regions and in all market sizes. Three out of four said there is too much needless violence on television; 57% would like to have 'more input on program content decisions.'

The Hollywood Caucus of Producers, Writers and Directors, speaking for the creative community, said in a statement issued in August 1993: 'We stand today at a point in time when the country's dissatisfaction with the quality of television is at an all time high, while our own feelings of helplessness and lack of power, in not only choosing material that seeks to enrich, but also in our ability to execute to the best of our ability, is at an all-time low.'

Far from reflecting creative freedom, the marketing of formula violence restricts freedom and chills originality. The violence formula is, in fact, a de facto censorship extending the dynamics of domination, intimidation, and repression domestically and globally. Much of the typical political and legislative response exploits the anxieties violence itself generates and offers remedies ranging from labeling and advisories to even more censorship.

There is a liberating alternative. It exists in various forms in most other democratic countries. It is public participation in making decisions about cultural investment and cultural policy. Independent grassroots citizen organization and action can provide the broad support needed for loosening the global marketing noose around the necks of producers, writers, directors, actors, and journalists.[2]

More freedom from violent and other inequitable and intimidating formulas, not more censorship, is the effective and acceptable way to increase diversity and reduce the dependence of program producers on the violence formula, and to reduce television violence to its legitimate role and proportion. The role of Congress, if any, is to turn its antitrust and civil rights oversight on the centralized and globalized industrial structures and marketing strategies that impose violence on creative people and foist it on the children and adults of the world. It is high time to develop a vision of the right of children to be born into a reasonably free, fair, diverse, and nonthreatening cultural environment. It is time for citizen involvement in cultural decisions that shape our lives and the lives of our children.

Notes

1. The study is conducted at the University of Pennsylvania's Annenberg School for Communication in collaboration with Michael Morgan at the University of Massachusetts at Amherst and Nancy Signorielli at the University of Delaware. Thanks for research assistance are due to Maria Elena Bartesaghi, Cynthia Kandra, Robin Kim, Brian Linson, Amy Nyman, and Nejat Ozyegin.
2. One such alternative is the Cultural Environment Movement (CEM). CEM is a nonprofit educational corporation, an umbrella coalition of independent media, professional, labor, religious, health-related, women's, and minority groups opposed to private corporate as well as government censorship. CEM is working for freedom from stereotyped formulas and for investing in a freer and more diverse cultural environment. It can be reached by writing to Cultural Environment Movement, P.O. Box 31847, Philadelphia, PA 19104.

References

[Editorial]. (1993, September 20). *Broadcasting & Cable*, p. 66.

Auletta, K. (1993, May 17). What won't they do? *The New Yorker*, pp. 45–46.

Gerbner, G. (1993). 'Miracles' of communication technology: Powerful audiences, diverse choices and other fairy tales. In J. Wasko (ed.), *Illuminating the blind spots*. New York: Ablex.

Gerbner, G., Gross, L., Morgan, M., and Signorielli, N. (1993). Growing up with television: The cultivation perspective. In J. Bryant and D. Zillmann (eds.), *Media Effects: Advances in Theory and Research*. Hillsdale, NJ: Lawrence Erlbaum.

Morgan, M., and Shanahan, J. (1991). Do VCRs change the TV picture? VCRs and the cultivation process. *American Behavioral Scientist*, 35(2), 122–135.

Morgan, M., and Signorielli, N. (1990). Cultivation analysis: Conceptualization and methodology. In N. Signorielli and M. Morgan (eds.), *Cultivation analysis: New directions in media effects research* (pp. 13–33). Newbury Park, CA: Sage.

Sun, L. (1989). *The limits of selective viewing: An analysis of 'diversity' in dramatic programming*. Unpublished master's thesis, Annenberg School for Communication, University of Pennsylvania, Philadelphia.

4 | TEN THINGS WRONG WITH THE MEDIA 'EFFECTS' MODEL

David Gauntlett[1]

It has become something of a cliché to observe that despite many decades of research and hundreds of studies, the connections between people's consumption of the mass media and their subsequent behaviour have remained persistently elusive. Indeed, researchers have enjoyed an unusual degree of patience from both their scholarly and more public audiences. But a time must come when we must take a step back from this murky lack of consensus and ask – why? Why are there no clear answers on media effects?

There is, as I see it, a choice of two conclusions which can be drawn from any detailed analysis of the research. The first is that if, after over 60 years of a considerable amount of research effort, direct effects of media upon behaviour have not been clearly identified, then we should conclude that they are simply *not there to be found*. Since I have argued this case, broadly speaking, elsewhere (Gauntlett, 1995), I will here explore the second possibility: that the media effects research has quite consistently taken the *wrong approach* to the mass media, its audiences, and society in general. This

---

[1] This article was first published as 'Ten things wrong with the "effects model"' in *Approaches to Audiences*, edited by Roger Dickinson, Ramaswani Harindranath and Olga Linné (Arnold, 1998). A different version appeared as part of the chapter 'The worrying influence of "media effects" studies', in *Ill Effects: The Media/Violence Debate (Second Edition)*, edited by Martin Barker and Julian Petley (Routledge, 2001). The version that appears here is basically a version that I produced for inclusion in *Media Studies: The Essential Resource*, edited by Philip Rayner, Peter Wall and Stephen Kruger (Routledge, 2004), and is an 'optimum mix' of both previous versions, but is mostly similar to the first one. The article, and much more material on media effects research, also appears in my book *Moving Experiences, Second Edition: Media Effects and Beyond* (John Libbey, 2005). Readers will be reassured – or perhaps appalled – to note that little has changed in the field of media effects studies since the piece was first written.

misdirection has taken a number of forms; for the purposes of this chapter, I will impose an unwarranted coherence upon the claims of all those who argue or purport to have found that the mass media will routinely have direct and reasonably predictable effects upon the behaviour of their fellow human beings, calling this body of thought, simply, the 'effects model'. Rather than taking apart each study individually, I will consider the mountain of studies – and the associated claims about media effects made by commentators – as a whole, and outline ten fundamental flaws in their approach.

1. The Effects Model Tackles Social Problems 'Backwards'

To explain the problem of violence in society, researchers should begin with that social problem and seek to explain it with reference, quite obviously, to those who engage in it: their background, lifestyles, character profiles, and so on. The 'media effects' approach, in this sense, comes at the problem *backwards*, by starting with the media and then trying to lasso connections from there on to social beings, rather than the other way around.

This is an important distinction. Criminologists, in their professional attempts to explain crime and violence, consistently turn for explanations not to the mass media but to social factors such as poverty, unemployment, housing, and the behaviour of family and peers. In a study which *did* start at what I would recognise as the correct end – by interviewing 78 violent teenage offenders and then tracing their behaviour back towards media usage, in comparison with a group of over 500 'ordinary' school pupils of the same age – Hagell & Newburn (1994) found only that the young offenders watched *less* television and video than their counterparts, had less access to the technology in the first place, had no unusual interest in specifically violent programmes, and either enjoyed the same material as non-offending teenagers or were simply *uninterested*. This point was demonstrated very clearly when the offenders were asked, 'If you had the chance to be someone who appears on television, who would you choose to be?':

> The offenders felt particularly uncomfortable with this question and appeared to have difficulty in understanding why one might want to be such a person ... In several interviews, the offenders had already stated that they watched little television, could not remember their favourite programmes and, consequently, could not think of anyone to be. In these cases, their obvious failure to identify with any television characters seemed to be part of a general lack of engagement with television (p. 30).

Thus we can see that studies which begin by looking at the perpetrators of actual violence, rather than at the media and its audiences, come to rather different conclusions (and there is certainly a need for more such research).[2] The fact that effects studies take the media as their starting point, however, should not be taken to suggest that they involve sensitive examinations of the mass media. As will be noted below, the studies have typically taken a stereotyped, almost parodic view of media content.

In more general terms, the 'backwards' approach involves the mistake of looking at individuals, rather than society, in relation to the mass media. The narrowly individualistic approach of some psychologists leads them to argue that, because of their belief that particular individuals at certain times in specific circumstances may be negatively affected by one bit of media, the removal of such media from society would be a positive step. This approach is rather like arguing that the solution to the number of road traffic accidents in Britain would be to lock away one famously poor driver from Cornwall; that is, a blinkered approach which tackles a real problem from the wrong end, involves cosmetic rather than relevant changes, and fails to look at the 'bigger picture'.

2. The Effects Model Treats Children as Inadequate

The individualism of the psychological discipline has also had a significant impact on the way in which children are regarded in effects research. Whilst sociology in recent decades has typically regarded childhood as a social construction, demarcated by attitudes, traditions and rituals which vary between different societies and different time periods (Ariés, 1962; Jenks, 1982, 1996), the psychology of childhood – developmental psychology – has remained more tied to the idea of a universal individual who must develop through particular stages before reaching adult maturity, as established by Piaget (e.g. 1926, 1929). The developmental stages are arranged as a hier-archy, from incompetent childhood through to rational, logical adulthood, and progression through these stages is characterised by an 'achievement ethic' (Jenks, 1996, p. 24).

---

[2] Another study of the viewing preferences of young offenders was commissioned in the UK (Browne & Pennell, 1998), but this made the 'backwards' mistake of showing violent videos to the offenders – putting violent media content onto the agenda from the start – rather than discussing the offenders' everyday viewing choices. (The study, which had some methodological flaws (see Gauntlett, 2001), was only able to hint that some violent individuals may enjoy watching violent material more than non-violent people do, if you actually sit the participants down, and show them the videos. Of course such a study is unable to tell us anything about 'media effects'.)

In psychology, then, children are often considered not so much in terms of what they *can* do, as what they (apparently) cannot. Negatively defined as non-adults, the research subjects are regarded as the 'other', a strange breed whose failure to match generally middle-class adult norms must be charted and discussed. Most laboratory studies of children and the media presume, for example, that their findings apply only to children, but fail to run parallel studies with adult groups to confirm this. We might speculate that this is because if adults were found to respond to laboratory pressures in the same way as children, the 'common sense' validity of the experiments would be undermined.

In her valuable examination of the way in which academic studies have constructed and maintained a particular perspective on childhood, Christine Griffin (1993) has recorded the ways in which studies produced by psychologists, in particular, have tended to 'blame the victim', to represent social problems as the consequence of the deficiencies or inadequacies of young people, and to 'psychologize inequalities, obscuring structural relations of domination behind a focus on individual "deficient" working-class young people and/or young people of colour, their families or cultural backgrounds' (p. 199). Problems such as unemployment and the failure of education systems are thereby traced to individual psychology traits. The same kinds of approach are readily observed in media effects studies, the production of which has undoubtedly been dominated by psychologically-oriented researchers, who – whilst, one imagines, having nothing other than benevolent intentions – have carefully exposed the full range of ways in which young media users can be seen as the inept victims of products which, whilst obviously puerile and transparent to adults, can trick children into all kinds of ill-advised behaviour.

This situation is clearly exposed by research which seeks to establish what children can and do understand about and from the mass media. Such projects have shown that children can talk intelligently and indeed cynically about the mass media (Buckingham, 1993, 1996), and that children as young as seven can make thoughtful, critical and 'media literate' video productions themselves (Gauntlett, 1997, 2005).

3. Assumptions Within the Effects Model Are Characterized by Barely Concealed Conservative Ideology

The systematic derision of children's resistant capacities can be seen as part of a broader conservative project to position the more contemporary and challenging aspects of the mass media, rather than other social factors, as the major threat to social stability today. Effects studies from the USA, in particular, tend to assume a level of television violence which is simply not applicable in Canada, Europe or elsewhere, and which is based on content analysis methods which count all kinds of 'aggression' seen in the media and come up with a correspondingly high number. George Gerbner's view, for example, that 'We are awash in a tide of violent representations unlike any the world has ever seen . . . drenching every home with graphic scenes of expertly choreographed brutality' (1994, p. 133), both reflects his hyperbolic view of the media in the US and the extent to which findings cannot be simplistically transferred across the Atlantic. Whilst it is certainly possible that gratuitous depictions of violence might reach a level in US screen media which could be seen as unpleasant and unnecessary, it cannot always be assumed that violence is shown for 'bad' reasons or in an uncritical light. Even the most 'gratuitous' acts of violence, such as those committed by Beavis and Butt-Head in their eponymous MTV series, can be interpreted as rationally resistant reactions to an oppressive world which has little to offer them (see Gauntlett, 1997). The way in which media effects researchers talk about the *amount* of violence in the media encourages the view that it is not important to consider the *meaning* of the scenes involving violence which appear on screen.

Critics of screen violence, furthermore, often reveal themselves to be worried about challenges to the status quo which they feel that some movies present (even though most European film critics see most popular Hollywood films as being ridiculously status quo-friendly). For example, Michael Medved, author of the successful *Hollywood vs. America: Popular Culture and the War on Traditional Values* (1992) finds worrying and potentially influential displays of 'disrespect for authority' and 'anti-patriotic attitudes' in films like *Top Gun* – a movie which others find embarrassingly jingoistic. The opportunistic mixing of concerns about the roots of violence with political reservations about the content of screen media is a lazy form of propaganda. Media effects studies and TV violence content analyses help to sustain this approach by maintaining the notion that 'antisocial' behaviour is an objective category which can be measured, which is common to numerous programmes, and which will negatively affect those children who see it portrayed.

4. The Effects Model Inadequately Defines its Own Objects of Study

The flaws numbered four to six in this list are more straightforwardly methodological, although they are connected to the previous and subsequent points. The first of these is that effects studies have generally taken for granted the definitions of media material, such as 'antisocial' and 'prosocial' programming, as well as characterisations of behaviour in the real world, such as 'antisocial' and 'prosocial' action. The point has already been made that these can be ideological value judgements; throwing down a book in disgust, sabotaging a nuclear missile, or smashing cages to set animals free, will always be interpreted in effects studies as 'antisocial', not 'prosocial'.

Furthermore, actions such as verbal aggression or hitting an inanimate object are recorded as acts of violence, just as TV murders are, leading to terrifically (and irretrievably) murky data. It is usually impossible to discern whether very minor or extremely serious acts of 'violence' depicted in the media are being said to have led to quite severe or merely trivial acts in the real world. More significant, perhaps, is the fact that this is rarely seen as a problem: in the media effects field, dodgy 'findings' are accepted with an uncommon hospitality.

5. The Effects Model Is Often Based on Artificial Elements and Assumptions Within Studies

Since careful sociological studies of media effects require amounts of time and money which limit their abundance, they are heavily outnumbered by simpler studies which are usually characterised by elements of artificiality. Such studies typically take place in a laboratory, or in a 'natural' setting such as a classroom but where a researcher has conspicuously shown up and instigated activities, neither of which are typical environments. Instead of a full and naturally-viewed television diet, research subjects are likely to be shown selected or specially-recorded clips which lack the narrative meaning inherent in everyday TV productions. They may then be observed in simulations of real life presented to them as a game, in relation to inanimate objects such as Bandura's famous 'bobo' doll, or as they respond to questionnaires, all of which are unlike interpersonal interaction, cannot be equated with it, and are likely to be associated with the previous viewing experience in the mind of the subject, rendering the study invalid.

Such studies also rely on the idea that subjects will not alter their behaviour or stated attitudes as a response to being observed or questioned. This naive belief has been shown to be false by researchers such as Borden (1975) who have demonstrated that the presence, appearance and gender of an observer can radically affect children's behaviour.

6. The Effects Model Is Often Based on Studies with Misapplied Methodology

Many of the studies which do not rely on an experimental method, and so may evade the flaws mentioned in the previous point, fall down instead by applying a methodological procedure wrongly, or by drawing inappropriate conclusions from particular methods. The widely-cited longitudinal panel study[3] by Huesmann, Eron and colleagues (Lefkowitz, Eron, Walder & Huesmann, 1972, 1977), for example, has been less famously slated for failing to keep to the procedures, such as assessing aggressivity or TV viewing with the same measures at different points in time, which are necessary for their statistical findings to have any validity (Chaffee, 1972; Kenny, 1972). The same researchers have also failed to adequately account for why the findings of this study and those of another of their own studies (Huesmann, Lagerspetz & Eron, 1984) absolutely contradict each other, with the former concluding that the media has a marginal effect on boys but no effect on girls, and the latter arguing the exact opposite (no effect on boys, but a small effect for girls). They also seem to ignore that fact that their own follow-up of their original set of subjects 22 years later suggested that a number of biological, developmental and environmental factors contributed to levels of aggression, whilst the mass media was not even given a mention (Huesmann, Eron, Lefkowitz & Walder, 1984). These astounding inconsistencies, unapologetically presented by perhaps the best-known researchers in this area, must be cause for considerable unease about the effects model. More careful use of similar methods, such as in the three-year panel study involving over 3,000 young people conducted by Milavsky, Kessler, Stipp & Rubens (1982a, 1982b), has only indicated that significant media effects are not to be found.

Perhaps the most frequent and misleading abuse of methodology occurs when studies which are simply *unable* to show that one thing causes another are treated as if they have done so. Such is the case with correlation studies, which can easily find that a particular personality type is also the kind of person who enjoys a certain kind of media – for example, that violent people like to watch 'violent films' – but are quite unable to show that the media use has *produced* that character. Nevertheless psychologists such as Van Evra (1990) and Browne (1999) have assumed that this is probably the case. There is a logical coherence to the idea that children whose behaviour is antisocial and disruptional will also have a greater interest in the more

---

[3] A longitudinal panel study is one in which the same group of people (the panel) are surveyed and/or observed at a number of points over a period of time.

violent and noisy television programmes, whereas the idea that the behaviour is a *consequence* of these programmes lacks both this rational consistency, and the support of the studies.

7. The Effects Model Is Selective in its Criticisms of Media Depictions of Violence

In addition to the point that 'antisocial' acts are ideologically defined in effects studies (as noted in item three above), we can also note that the media depictions of 'violence' which the effects model typically condemns are limited to fictional productions. The acts of violence which appear on a daily basis on news and serious factual programmes are seen as somehow exempt. The point here is not that depictions of violence in the news should necessarily be condemned in just the same, blinkered way, but rather to draw attention to another philosophical inconsistency which the model cannot account for. If the antisocial acts shown in drama series and films are expected to have an effect on the behaviour of viewers, even though such acts are almost always ultimately punished or have other negative consequences for the perpetrator, there is no obvious reason why the antisocial activities which are always in the news, and which frequently do *not* have such apparent consequences for their agents, should not have similar effects.

8. The Effects Model Assumes Superiority to the Masses

Surveys typically show that whilst a certain proportion of the public feel that the media may cause other people to engage in antisocial behaviour, almost no-one ever says that they have been affected in that way themselves. This view is taken to extremes by researchers and campaigners whose work brings them into regular contact with the supposedly corrupting material, but who are unconcerned for their own well-being as they implicitly 'know' that the effects could only be on others. Insofar as these others are defined as children or 'unstable' individuals, their approach may seem not unreasonable; it is fair enough that such questions should be explored. Nonetheless, the idea that it is unruly 'others' who will be affected – the uneducated? the working class? – remains at the heart of the effects paradigm, and is reflected in its texts (as well, presumably, as in the researchers' overenthusiastic interpretation of weak or flawed data, as discussed above).

George Gerbner and his colleagues, for example, write about 'heavy' television viewers as if this media consumption has necessarily had the opposite effect on the weightiness of their brains. Such people are assumed to have no selectivity or critical skills, and their habits are explicitly contrasted with preferred activities: 'Most viewers watch by the clock and either do not know what they will watch when they turn on the set, or follow established routines rather than choose each program as they would choose a book, a movie or an article' (Gerbner, Gross, Morgan & Signorielli, 1986, p. 19). This view – which knowingly makes inappropriate comparisons by ignoring the serial nature of many TV programmes, and which is unable to account for the widespread use of TV guides and digital or video recorders with which audiences plan and arrange their viewing – reveals the kind of elitism and snobbishness which often seems to underpin such research. The point here is not that the content of the mass media must not be criticised, but rather that the mass audience themselves are not well served by studies which are willing to treat them as potential savages or actual fools.

9. The Effects Model Makes no Attempt to Understand Meanings of the Media

A further fundamental flaw, hinted at in points three and four above, is that the effects model *necessarily* rests on a base of reductive assumptions and unjustified stereotypes regarding media content. To assert that, say, 'media violence' will bring negative consequences is not only to presume that depictions of violence in the media will always be promoting antisocial behaviour, and that such a category exists and makes sense, as noted above, but also assumes that the medium holds a singular message which will be carried unproblematically to the audience. The effects model therefore performs the double deception of presuming (a) that the media presents a singular and clear-cut 'message', and (b) that the proponents of the effects model are in a position to identify what that message is.

The meanings of media content are ignored in the simple sense that assumptions are made based on the appearance of elements removed from their context (for example, woman hitting man equals violence equals bad), and in the more sophisticated sense that even *in* context the meanings may be different for different viewers (woman hitting man equals an unpleasant act of aggression, *or* appropriate self-defence, *or* a triumphant act of revenge, *or* a refreshing change, *or* is simply uninteresting, *or* any of many further alternative readings). In-depth qualitative studies have unsurprisingly given support to the view that media audiences routinely arrive at their own, often heterogeneous, interpretations of everyday media texts (e.g. Buckingham, 1993, 1996; Hill, 1997; Schlesinger, Dobash, Dobash & Weaver, 1992; Gray, 1992; Palmer, 1986). Since the effects model rides roughshod over both the meanings that actions have for characters in dramas *and* the meanings which those depicted acts may have for the audience members, it can retain little credibility with those who consider popular entertainment to be more than just a set of very basic propaganda messages flashed at the audience in the simplest possible terms.

10. The Effects Model Is Not Grounded in Theory

Finally, and underlying many of the points made above, is the fundamental problem that the entire argument of the 'effects model' is not substantiated with any theoretical reasoning beyond the bald assertions that particular kinds of effects will be produced by the media. The basic question of *why* the media should induce people to imitate its content has never been adequately tackled, beyond the simple idea that particular actions are 'glamorised'. (However, antisocial actions are shown really *positively* so infrequently that this is an inadequate explanation.) Similarly, the question of how merely seeing an activity in the media would be translated into an actual *motive* which would prompt an individual to behave in a particular way is just as unresolved. The lack of firm theory has led to the effects model being rooted in the set of questionable assumptions outlined above – that the mass media (rather than people) should be the unproblematic starting-point for research; that children will be unable to 'cope' with the media; that the categories of 'violence' or 'antisocial behaviour' are clear and self-evident; that the model's predictions can be verified by scientific research; that screen fictions are of concern, whilst news pictures are not; that researchers have the unique capacity to observe and classify social behaviour and its meanings, but that those researchers need not attend to the various possible meanings which media content may have for the audience. Each of these very substantial problems has its roots in the failure of media effects commentators to found their model in any coherent theory.

So What Future for Research on Media Influences?

The effects model, we have seen, has remarkably little going for it as an explanation of human behaviour, or of the media's role in society. Whilst any challenging or apparently illogical theory or model reserves the right to demonstrate its validity through empirical data, the effects model has failed also in that respect. Its continued survival is indefensible and unfortunate. However, the failure of this particular *model* does not mean that the impact of the mass media can no longer be considered or investigated. Indeed, there are many fascinating questions to be explored about the influence of the media upon our perceptions, and ways of thinking and being in the world (Gauntlett, 2002), which simply get ignored whilst the research funding and attention are going to shoddy effects studies.

It is worrying to note the numbers of psychologists (and others) who conduct research according to traditional methodological recipes, despite the many well-known flaws with those procedures, when it is so easy to imagine alternative research methods and processes. (For example, see the website www.artlab.org.uk, and Gauntlett (2005), for information about the 'new creative audience studies' in which participants are invited to make media and artistic artefacts *themselves*, as a way of exploring their relation-ships with mass media.) The discourses about 'media effects' from politi-cians and the popular press are often laughably simplistic. Needless to say, academics shouldn't encourage them.

References

Ariés, Phillippe (1962), *Centuries of Childhood*, translated by Robert Baldick, Jonathan Cape, London.

Borden, Richard J. (1975), 'Witnessed Aggression: Influence of an Observer's Sex and Values on Aggressive Responding', in *Journal of Personality and Social Psychology*, vol. 31, no. 3, pp. 567–573.

Browne, Kevin (1999), 'Violence in the Media Causes Crime: Myth or Reality', Inaugural Lecture, 3 June 1999, University of Birmingham.

Browne, Kevin, & Pennell, Amanda (1998), 'Effects of Video Violence on Young Offenders', Home Office Research and Statistics Directorate Research Findings No. 65.

Buckingham, David (1993), *Children Talking Television: The Making of Television Literacy*, The Falmer Press, London.

Buckingham, David (1996), *Moving Images: Understanding Children's Emotional Responses to Television*, Manchester University Press, Manchester.

Chaffee, S. H. (1972), 'The interpersonal context of mass communication', in F. G. Kline and P. J. Tichenor (eds) *Current Perspectives in Mass Communication Research*, Beverly Hills, CA: Sage.

Gauntlett, David (1995), *Moving Experiences: Understanding Television's Influences and Effects*, John Libbey, London.

Gauntlett, David (1997), *Video Critical: Children, the Environment and Media Power*, John Libbey Media, Luton.

Gauntlett, David (2001), 'The worrying influence of "media effects" studies', in Barker, Martin & Petley, Julian, eds, *Ill Effects: The Media/Violence Debate* (Second Edition), Routledge, London & New York.

Gauntlett, David (2002), *Media, Gender and Identity: An Introduction*, Routledge, London.

Gauntlett, David (2005), *Moving Experiences, Second Edition: Media Effects and Beyond*, John Libbey, London.

Gerbner, George (1994), 'The Politics of Media Violence: Some Reflections', in Linné, Olga, & Hamelink, Cees J., eds, *Mass Communication Research: On Problems and Policies: The Art of Asking the Right Questions*, Ablex Publishing, Norwood, New Jersey.

Gerbner, George, Gross, Larry, Morgan, Michael, & Signorielli, Nancy (1986), 'Living with Television: The Dynamics of the Cultivation Process', in Bryant, Jennings, & Zillmann, Dolf, eds, *Perspectives on Media Effects*, Lawrence Erlbaum Associates, Hillsdale, New Jersey.

Gray, Ann (1992), *Video Playtime: The Gendering of a Leisure Technology*, Routledge, London.

Griffin, Christine (1993), *Representations of Youth: The Study of Youth and Adolescence in Britain and America*, Polity Press, Cambridge.

Hagell, Ann, & Newburn, Tim (1994), *Young Offenders and the Media: Viewing Habits and Preferences*, Policy Studies Institute, London.

Hill, Annette (1997), *Shocking Entertainment: Viewer Response to Violent Movies*, John Libbey Media, Luton.

Huesmann, L. Rowell, Eron, Leonard D., Lefkowitz, Monroe M., & Walder, Leopold O. (1984), 'Stability of Aggression Over Time and Generations', in *Developmental Psychology*, vol. 20, no. 6, pp. 1120–1134.

Jenks, Chris (1982), 'Introduction: Constituting the Child', in Jenks, Chris, ed., *The Sociology of Childhood*, Batsford, London.

Jenks, Chris (1996), *Childhood*, Routledge, London.

Kenny, D. A. (1972) 'Threats to the internal validity of cross-lagged panel inference, as related to "Television violence and child aggression: A follow-up study"', in Comstock, George A., & Rubinstein, Eli A., eds, *Television and Social behavior*, National Institute of Mental Health, Maryland.

Lefkowitz, Monroe M., Eron, Leonard D., Walder, Leopold O., & Huesmann, L. Rowell (1972), 'Television Violence and Child Aggression: A Follow-up Study', in Comstock, George A., & Rubinstein, Eli A., eds, *Television and Social Behavior: Reports and Papers, Volume III: Television and Adolescent Aggressiveness*, National Institute of Mental Health, Maryland.

Lefkowitz, Monroe M., Eron, Leonard D., Walder, Leopold O., & Huesmann, L. Rowell (1977), *Growing Up To Be Violent: A Longitudinal Study of the Development of Aggression*, Pergamon Press, New York.

Medved, Michael (1992), *Hollywood vs. America: Popular Culture and the War on Traditional Values*, HarperCollins, London.

Milavsky, J. Ronald, Kessler, Ronald C., Stipp, Horst H., & Rubens, William

S. (1982a), *Television and Aggression: A Panel Study*, Academic Press, New York.

Milavsky, J. Ronald; Kessler, Ronald; Stipp, Horst, & Rubens, William S. (1982b), 'Television and Aggression: Results of a Panel Study', in Pearl, David; Bouthilet, Lorraine, & Lazar, Joyce, eds, *Television and Behavior: Ten Years of Scientific Progress and Implications for the Eighties, Volume 2: Technical Reviews*, National Institute of Mental Health, Maryland.

Palmer, Patricia (1986), *The Lively Audience: A Study of Children Around the TV Set*, Allen & Unwin, Sydney.

Piaget, Jean (1926), *The Language and Thought of the Child*, Harcourt Brace & Company, New York.

Piaget, Jean (1929), *The Child's Conception of the World*, Routledge, London.

Schlesinger, Philip; Dobash, R. Emerson; Dobash, Russell P., & Weaver, C. Kay (1992), *Women Viewing Violence*, British Film Institute Publishing, London.

Van Evra, Judith (1990), *Television and Child Development*, Lawrence Erlbaum Associates, Hillsdale, New Jersey.

FROM BAD MEDIA VIOLENCE RESEARCH TO GOOD - A GUIDE FOR THE PERPLEXED

5

Martin Barker and Julian Petley

Undoing the Category 'Violence'

[. . .]

We begin at the heart of the beast. A small but growing number of studies has begun to question the status of that central term 'violence', each in different ways showing that for real viewers, as against 'effects' researchers and moral campaigners, 'violence' is not some singular 'thing' which might grow cumulatively like poison inside people.

One of the earliest studies to explore the dimensions of 'violence' was Schlesinger et al.'s *Women Viewing Violence* (1992), which was undertaken for the Broadcasting Standards Council. The research focused on women's responses to four very different kinds of programme. One was *Crimewatch UK*, the BBC programme in which viewers are invited to call in with information to help solve current cases, focusing on an episode dealing with the rape and murder of a young hitchhiker. Second was *EastEnders*, the popular soap opera, and in particular a story-line about domestic violence. Third was a hard-hitting drama, *Closing Ranks*, also dealing directly with violence in the home, this time centred on a policeman's family. Finally, the 1989 feature film *The Accused*, which explored the difficulties of proving 'rape' in a case in which men claimed that a woman had been behaving provocatively; the film ends by showing the rape. Schlesinger et al.'s research is particularly useful for the range of women interviewed, and its mix of research methods. They recruited women across a wide range of class, age and ethnic backgrounds, and distinguished those with and without personal experience of violence. Their research combined questionnaires giving a picture of the social positions of their respondents, and close interviewing of the women in order to gain access to the detailed patterns of their responses.

Their findings reveal many things. They show, for instance, that for many women there is an important distinction between finding something *disturbing* and nonetheless *wanting it to be shown*. The responses to *East-Enders* proved complicated, in that the violence involved a white man and a black woman, and the black women in the research tended to assess the events in terms of their *racial* significance rather than in terms of domestic violence. Again, in the responses to the *Crimewatch* hitchhiker story, wider cultural attitudes concerning women going out on their own cut across women's assessment of the programme. *The Accused* aroused strong feelings across almost all participants, with close identification with Jodie Foster's victim-character. But only in a few cases did these strong feelings result in demands for censorship. Rather, it brought forth discussion of 'men' as viewers, and of what might be done to control their ways of watching programmes containing violence against women. Here is perhaps their most important conclusion:

> The issue is not whether depictions of violence increase the likelihood of similar violence among potential perpetrators, but the feelings and reactions that it creates among those who are the actual or potential victims of violence. Are women likely to feel more vulnerable, less safe or less valued members of our society if, as a category, they are with some frequency depicted as those who are subjected to abuse? If so, the portrayal of violence against women may be seen as negative, even if women viewers have never experienced such violence and/or its likelihood is not increased. (p.170)

These are not comfortable findings, and they challenge us all to a proper democratic debate about these issues. But comfortable or not, they change the terms in which that debate will need to take place. For it is not the sheer fact of the presence of violence that is the issue: it is its purpose and meanings, both within individual media items and the wider circuits and currents of feelings and ideas that accompany it, that have to be examined.

In 1998 Schlesinger et al. followed up this first investigation with a study of the ways in which groups of men perceived, understood and judged different kinds of media violence. They recognise that they are explicitly challenging the traditional 'effects' agenda: '[T]he present study, like its predecessor, is not a simplistic "effects" or "no effects" piece of research. Both studies represent attempts to move the research agenda away from this narrow debate onto more productive and relevant ground' (1998: 4).

The study used 88 men aged between 18–75, with a deliberate mix of class, ethnic memberships and sexual preferences, and showed them various combinations of: an episode of *EastEnders* featuring alcoholism leading to domestic violence; *Trip Trap*, a quality TV drama addressing issues of sexual violence; a documentary about street fighting; and two Hollywood box office successes, *Basic Instinct* and *Under Siege*. There was as much variety in the specific responses as there had been among their women interviewees, but even more strongly than the women, the men's perceptions and judgements of violent media were based on the *rules and standards of the groups and communities to which they belonged*. So, the street-fighting was judged 'ordinary' and in fact exciting by those men whose lives included the kinds of relationships and risks that fairly easily lead to such fights.

But even more strongly than in the case of the women, a line was drawn between 'realistic' violence – which could make you stop and think – and 'unrealistic' violence such as the two Hollywood films. These were assessed not against 'life' but against other movies – their meaning for men such as these was in terms of a world of entertainment.

Yet again, therefore, research that listens to the operative ideas of people, rather than encasing them in psychologistic language, finds people always responding to 'violent media' through their social and historical worlds, through shared understandings, and with (whether we like or approve of them or not) complicated moral codes.[1]

Finally, we want to draw attention to *Defining Violence* (1999), by David Morrison and others. This research, which was commissioned by all the major broadcasters and carried out at Leeds University, set out to discover 'the subjective meaning of violence. How, in other words, did people classify acts as violent and other acts, although ostensibly violent, as not really violent? Did people, furthermore, have a common definition of violence, or were there many different definitions?' (p. vii). To answer these questions, the researchers recruited a wide range of people who might be expected to have different experiences of and attitudes to violence both in real life and on screen: policemen; young men and women drawn from cultural groups familiar with violence; women who had a heightened fear of, but no personal experience of, violence; women with small children; men with small children, and so on. The groups were shown a wide variety of visual material and, in a significant methodological move, were given the chance during discussions actually to re-edit the footage as a means of clarifying what they meant by 'violence'.

What the research showed was that it is not particular acts which make a programme seem violent, but the context in which they occur, a finding which clearly backs up the work of Schlesinger et al. (1992, 1998). The Leeds researchers were able to distinguish several different kinds of fictional screen violence:

> *Playful violence* is clearly acted violence, and is seen as unreal. The violence looks staged, and has little significance beyond its entertainment value. It is invariably seen as violence with a little v. A lot of violent action may be involved, but it is not graphic and does not assault the sensibilities.
>
> *Depicted violence* is violence that is characterised by 'realism'. It attempts to depict violence as it would appear in real life. It often includes close-up shots of injury, and is very graphic. This can indeed assault the sensibilities, and is invariably defined as violence with a big V.
>
> *Authentic violence* is violence set in a world that the viewer can recognise. A classic case would be domestic violence. Violence in a pub or shopping precinct might be other examples. It is closer to the life of the viewer than other forms of violence. It might be seen as violence with a little v, depending on how the scene is played, although it does have the potential to be big V, and even massive V. In other words, it has the possibility of assaulting the senses very strongly indeed. (Morrison, 1999: 4–5)

These categories helped them to determine how their group members distinguished between violent scenes, but they still left a central question: what causes something to be perceived as violent? Group discussions revealed two determining factors: the *nature and quality* of the violence portrayed, which is a moral factor, and the *way in which* it was portrayed, which is an aesthetic one. The elements which make up the first factor the researchers called the *primary definers* of violence, those which contribute to the second factor the *secondary definers*. Together these determine the definition of violence. The primary definers are 'drawn from real life, and what is deemed violent on screen is the same as what is deemed violent in real life. An act is defined as violent in real life if it breaks a recognised and mutually agreed code of conduct' (ibid: 6). Thus, for example, for some groups a punch thrown in a pub is not judged to be violent in any serious sense, whereas 'glassing' somebody in the same situation would universally be regarded as a violent act. The researchers also found that the most prevalent general rule seems to be that behaviour which is judged to be appropriate, fair and justified – even when overtly violent – is not usually seen to be seriously or 'really' violent.

Once the primary definers have come into play, the secondary ones establish and grade the *degree* of violence perceived by the viewer:

The secondary definers categorise a scene of violence if it looks 'real' – as the viewer imagines it would if witnessed in real life. Close-up shots of an injury, and splattering blood, both make violence look 'real'. So does the manner in which an injury is delivered, and how it is portrayed. Each of these elements helps to produce a greater sense of violence once the primary definers have established the scene to be violent in the first place. (ibid: 7)

From their work with these groups, the researchers finally arrived at the following definition of violence:

Screen violence is any act that is seen or unequivocally signalled which would be considered an act of violence in real life, because the violence was considered unjustified either in the degree or nature of the force used, or that the injured party was undeserving of the violence. The degree of violence is defined by how realistic the violence is considered to be, and made even stronger if the violence inflicted is considered unfair. (ibid: 9)

This is valuable research with a great deal to teach, but here we simply draw attention to one of their central propositions, namely that in order to understand the meaning of 'violence' in the media, you have to understand the moral codes that different audiences bring to bear as they watch.

Positive Pleasures

One limitation of Schlesinger et al.'s first study was that many of its women respondents would not normally have watched, or certainly not watched with enjoyment, some of the materials about which they were asked to comment. In this, in fact, the research fits a little too comfortably with a stereotypical image that 'violent programming' is enjoyed only by men, not women. One recent piece of research by Annette Hill (1997) has begun to unpick this. Hill's study investigates in detail the kinds of pleasure that both men and women have taken in the crop of films that, post-Tarantino and *Pulp Fiction*, have generally been regarded by the media as upping the stakes in 'levels of violence'. According to Hill, consumers of violent movies possess 'portfolios of interpretation', a concept which she uses to catch hold of the ways people become *experienced* and *knowledge-able* in their ways of understanding violent movies. These 'portfolios' include:

• a conscious awareness that violent movies test viewers in various ways.

- anticipation and preparation as an essential aspect of the enjoyment of viewing violent movies.
- building relationships and engaging with certain screen characters, whilst establishing a safe distance from others.
- bringing into play a variety of methods to self-censor violence.
- utilising violent images as a means of testing personal boundaries and as a safe way (within a clearly fictional setting) of interpreting and thinking about violence.
- actively differentiating between real-life violence and fictional violence.

Hill also draws attention to the fact that the process of viewing violent films is very much a social activity, arguing that 'part of the enjoyment of viewing violence is to monitor audience reactions, as the films themselves provoke reaction. Individual response is part of a much wider awareness of the variety of responses available to consumers of violent movies' (ibid: 105–6).

Understanding how its actual audiences respond to a film all too easily dismissed as simply 'violent' was part of a project into the reception of action-adventure movies by Martin Barker and Kate Brooks (1998). In particular, they were interested in the ways in which fans talked about how they used and enjoyed the film, which led them to analyse what they called the fans' 'vocabularies of involvement and pleasure'. These revealed a series of practices of pleasure which included: physical satisfaction; being part of a crowd; creating imaginative worlds; game-playing and role-playing; taking risks; rule-breaking and defying convention; confirming membership of communities of response; and critical appreciation. A key point about these practices of pleasure is that they all:

> involve some kind of preparation, and therefore have a pattern of involvement which extends beyond the moments of pleasure, on which in significant ways the pleasures depend. Crudely, there are things we have to do, and to know, and to prepare for in advance if any of these pleasures are to be gained. (ibid: 145)

In relation to their target film *Judge Dredd*, Barker and Brooks identified a number of distinct patterns of expectation revealed by their interviewees, each expressing in its own 'language' a particular relation to the film and cinema-going, and providing a basis for distinct ways of being involved. According to Barker and Brooks, each vocabulary of involvement and pleasure represents a culturally-generated SPACE (standing for Site for the Production of Active Cinematic Experiences) into which an individual can move. There were six such SPACES:

- The Action-Adventure SPACE, for those aiming to become involved in the film at a sensuous, physical level, treating it as a roller-coaster experience.

- The Future-Fantastic SPACE, for those anticipating a physical experience too, but also getting ready to respond to spectacular technologies and demonstrations of new cinematic skills.
- The 2000AD-Follower SPACE, for those already familiar with the Judge Dredd world and who are hoping to see a huge character made as big and as public as he deserves and requires.
- The Film-Follower SPACE, for those committed to cinema as a medium and wanting the film to contribute to some aspect of 'cinematic magic'.
- The Stallone-Follower SPACE, for those wanting to see what the film adds to Stallone's career and his screen persona.
- The Culture-Belonging SPACE, for those who choose to raid a film for information, jokes, stories, catch-phrases which can contribute to their on-going membership of local groups.

Barker and Brooks are particularly interested in those respondents who combine two SPACES: Action-Adventure and Future-Fantastic. What they point to is an intriguing parallel between the filmic pleasures sought by young working class audiences – just the kind of young males who feature strongly in scares about 'dangerous' media – and the world view of those early Utopians, the medieval Chiliasts described by Karl Mannheim in *Ideology and Utopia* (1960). The Chiliasts, who tended to be drawn from the 'oppressed strata of society', sought their Utopia not in some far distant future, rather:

> The Chiliast expects a union with the immediate present. Hence he is not preoccupied in his daily life with optimistic hopes for the future or romantic reminiscences . . . He is not actually concerned with the millennium that is to come; what is important for him is that it has happened here and now, and that it arose from mundane existence, as a sudden swing over into another kind of existence. (ibid: 195)

In other words, what Chiliasm offered was a way of experiencing *in the present* the qualities of a transformed world, a process in which 'spiritual fermentation and physical excitement' (ibid: 192) played its part and in which 'sensual experience is present in all its robustness' (ibid: 194). In short: 'for the real Chiliast, the present becomes the breach through which what was previously inward bursts out suddenly, takes hold of the outer world and transforms it' (ibid: 193).

The parallels with action movie fans' love of cinema's sensuous qualities, its orgiastic excess and its possibilities for envisioning other worlds are thought-provoking. Furthermore, just as Mannheim points out that 'the utopian vision aroused a contrary vision' (ibid: 192), so action films such as *Judge Dredd* have been misrepresented and condemned as 'gratuitously violent' and so on. The significance of Barker and Brooks' findings is that what is condemned as 'gratuitous' and 'immoral' is actually experienced by its key fans as *political*.

One other piece of research acknowledges its small scale but still points up some important issues for us. John Fiske and Robert Dawson (1996) report on the way a group of homeless American men watch violent movies, in particular *Die Hard*. As part of a much wider **ethnographic** investigation of the world of the homeless, centred on a church shelter, they gained the chance to observe how a group of men responded as they watched this film which they had selected on video. The findings, albeit based on one group, are very suggestive.

They observed, for instance, that the men shifted in who they favoured as the movie progressed. At the start, they cheered and commented on the terrorists who invade and seize a corporate building and kill its chief executive. But when the film's hero begins his lone action against the terrorists, the fact that he does it alone, outside the law and at some cost to himself made him also attractive to these viewers. But once he began to side overtly with the police, and to become in effect their agent, they not only lost interest in him, they went so far as to turn the video off. Fiske and Dawson interpret their actions as an expression of their alienation and anger:

> Another favoured scene was that in which the terrorists easily repelled the police's attempt to retake the building. The climax of the scene occurred when an armoured car attempting to batter its way in was disabled by a rocket launched by the terrorists. The hero, from his hidden vantage point, can see them preparing to fire another rocket, whose purpose is not to save the building from attack, but to complete the tactically unnecessary destruction of the machine and the men in it. In voice-over he begs them not to. They do, and as the camera lingers on the apparently pointless destruction and death, the homeless men cheer enthusiastically. (p.306)

The men refused the 'lawful' positioning, and enjoyed their own refusal, Fiske and Dawson argue. What is interesting here is not just the demonstration of a political way of relating to the film, but that to make sense of it, Fiske and Dawson have to relate the men's behaviour to the detailed narrative workings of the film – something which moral campaigners simply don't understand how to do.

Children and the Media

At the heart of the 'effects' tradition stands the figure of the 'child': inno-cent, vulnerable, corruptible. A small but growing group of researchers have undertaken the difficult task of learning how to investigate children's own views and understandings of the media. The results have been distinctly productive.

A good early example of such productive and challenging work is Robert Hodge and David Tripp's (1986) Australian study of children's responses to a television mock-horror cartoon *Fangface*. With an eye directly on the kinds of claim made about children and cartoons (too much violence, anti-educational because too undemanding, perhaps leading to confusions between fantasy and reality), Hodge and Tripp carried out a series of experiments with children aged 10–14. The experiments were aimed at opening up children's own understandings of such cartoons. Beginning with a careful **semiotic** examination of the episode of *Fangface* which they used centrally in their research, and showing through this its potential for raising complex issues such as the nature of good and evil, they go on to explore how children make sense of characters, action and narrative. All this is done by using a careful, and semi-structured set of ways of listening symptom-atically to the way the children talk, drawing out the categories they are implicitly using, the distinctions they are drawing and the connections they are making.

Hodge and Tripp's findings show that a series of changes take place, as children are growing up, in the ways in which they learn to 'manage' the distinction between fantasy and reality, or how they learn how to make 'modality-judgements'. Children, they show, have a very compli-cated understanding, in which their judgements of 'reality' will for instance make distinctions between their parents (who is more 'real' can depend on who buys your clothes for you), and their friends and pets. So, 'reality' is not some simple category of 'true things versus fictional things'. But children learn over time to make sophisticated judgements – and one of the ways in which they learn this is precisely by engaging with story-forms. Cartoons and such equivalent materials are important to children *because* they simplify. They enable children to try out and develop complex conceptual connections, at the same time as they move from seeing stories as just composed of elements in a ('paratactic') series to perceiving and operating with the idea of a ('hypotactic') story-structure. Far from being 'harmful', Hodge and Tripp have shown ways in which these kinds of frequently damned materials are *necessary* to full human development.

Some of the most valuable work on children and television to have emerged in recent years has been carried out by David Buckingham, most notably in *Children Talking Television* (1993) and *Moving Images* (1996). Buckingham's focus is upon the development of television literacy in children. His own qualitative researches lead him to this conclusion:

> Children respond to and make sense of television in the light of what they know about its formal codes and conventions, about genre and narrative, and about the production process. In these respects, they are much more active and sophisticated users of the medium than they are often assumed to be. (1996: 7)

Buckingham's work is too wide to be adequately summarised here, but among his more specific conclusions are the following:

- most parents and children challenged the view that television on its own was a sufficient cause of violent behaviour. Parents were more likely to express concern about the possible 'effects' of television on other people's children than on their own, whilst the children themselves displaced such concerns onto younger children. Parents were more concerned that their children might be frightened or traumatised by violence on television than that they might try to imitate it.
- children had negative responses, such as fright, disgust, sadness or worry, not only to the more predictable genres such as horror, but also to a surprisingly wide and apparently innocuous range of programmes, including those specifically aimed at children. Negative responses are common amongst children, though they are rarely severe or long-lasting.
- children clearly distinguished between factual and fictional material on television, and found it easier to distance themselves from the latter than from the former. However, even where factual material, such as news coverage of wars and disasters, was described as upsetting it was also regarded by many as being important to watch, in that it provided necessary information about the real world.
- the main concern of children who watched horror films or true crime programmes was that they might become victims of violence. There was little sense of vicarious 'identification' with the monster or the perpetrator of violence.
- children had a wide range of strategies to protect themselves from or deal with negative responses. These ran the gamut from partial or total avoidance of potentially upsetting programmes to actively denying their reality status ('it's only a movie').
- children who watched fictional violence might become habituated to

watching more fictional violence, but this did not 'desensitise' their perceptions of real-life violence, whether mediated by television or not.

Buckingham's work challenges many of the assumptions that underpin the 'figure' of the child which is so essential to media moral scares. It shows the ways in which even young children are already making complex moral decisions about what they should watch, and for whom particular kinds of materials are appropriate. It also shows that children themselves know about, and indeed are influenced by, those scares – a point of greater weight than has so far been acknowledged.

Symbolic Politics

There is a strong tendency for press, politicians and pundits to 'name' something as 'violence', to judge it in simplistic moral terms, and thus to warrant searches for simple 'causes' (such as 'violent media') of events which happen for a whole variety of complex social and political reasons. An important example of just this kind is explored in Darnell Hunt's (1997) study of responses to the television coverage of the 1992 Los Angeles 'riots', which followed the initial Not Guilty verdict for the police who had been filmed beating up black motorist Rodney King. An important study in much wider ways than concern this book, Hunt's work has much to say that is relevant to our argument. Hunt investigated the responses to the television coverage of white, Latino and black LA viewers, and shows the different ways in which these audiences understood the events, the key players, and the 'violent acts' committed according not simply to their 'colour' but to their sense of the communities to which they belong.

Hunt argues that people responded to the TV coverage in the light of their 'raced subjectivity', that is, their sense of who they are and what groups they belong to in the wider world. This strongly affected not only their responses to the particular coverage, but also their wider sense of which media and which spokespeople they will trust. But perhaps most interestingly for our purposes, Hunt uncovered the way people acknowledged or denied a 'racial' component:

> When one surveys intergroup patterns . . ., evidence begins to mount
> for what I have referred to as 'raced ways of seeing'. Black-raced and
> Latino-raced study groups were quite animated during the screening
> of the KTTV text, while white-raced study groups watched quietly.
> For black-raced informants, in particular, raced subjectivity was
> clearly an important lens through which the events and the text were

viewed. . . . [W]hile white-raced and Latino-raced informants were *less* likely than their black-raced counterparts to talk about themselves in raced terms, they were *more* likely than black-raced informants to condemn the looting and fires and to support the arrests. (p.141)

Hunt is arguing that *everyone* responded via their sense of their 'racial' community, but that this was most clearly *acknowledged* in the case of black viewers. For white and Latino viewers, in ducking this, represented their responses through the seemingly 'neutral' categories of 'violence' and 'law and order'. The echoes for our own experiences of attitudes towards 'violence' are clear and audible.

In this connection, it is also worth considering the research reported in an essay by John Gabriel (1996), who explored the ways in which the film *Falling Down* was received in Britain. As with Fiske and Dawson, Gabriel starts by recognising the complicated meanings of this film, which tracks a white middle-class defence worker (played by Michael Douglas), known mainly through his car plates 'tag', D-Fens, who, finding his world going to pieces as he loses his job and is mugged and cheated by various ethnic groups, fights back violently, and is eventually killed. When the film was released in America, a series of press stories reported that white male audiences had cheered on Douglas' character, apparently identifying with his assertion that 'whiteness' has become minority in contemporary America.

Gabriel explores in detail the responses of 16 viewers, of whom a number were non-white. He found some real complexities in their responses, based on people at times giving and at others withholding their assent to D-Fens' actions and values. So, his black interviewees could join in and cheer when D-Fens confronts, as they felt on the basis of class, some rich golfers who seek to exclude him. But when he faces down a group of Latino muggers, they recognise a racist potential in him which leads them to distance themselves from him. So, although Gabriel's reading of the film indicates that it is centrally organised around ideas of 'whiteness', he concludes that 'whiteness' is not a singular thing, but something conveyed and understood in complicated ways:

Ironically, D-Fens was arguably at his most popular with his audience not in the Korean shop or the wasteland with the Latino gang members, but on the golf course when he confronted another version of white masculinity. In this scene, the golfers were more conspicuously white than D-Fens himself, not just because their whiter-than-white outfits outshone D-Fens' battle-dress, but also because their whiteness was associated with the affluence and exclusivity of the golf-course setting. (ibid: 150)

But D-Fens' seeming racism could be 'written out' by audiences who could see him as flawed and driven to extremes by his frustrations – and who could thus see his death as redeeming him. As with Fiske and Dawson, Gabriel reveals complexities of both attention and symbolic response which can be grasped only by methods of research which hear their audiences in complex ways. Both pieces of research, crucially, remind us that 'violence' too easily becomes a coded term hiding all sorts of political factors and preferences.

[. . .]

'Effects' and Beyond

It should by now be abundantly clear that a good deal of work on how audiences respond to media portrayals of violence of one kind or another has moved far beyond the crudities of the 'effects' paradigm. However, as David Buckingham points out:

> There are, of course, other effects which have been addressed within media research – effects which might broadly be termed 'ideological'. For example, the extensive debates about media representations of women or of ethnic minority groups are clearly premised on assumptions about their potential influence on public attitudes. (1996: 310)

We agree. Anyone with half an eye on the recent *News of the World* campaign to 'name and shame' paedophiles couldn't help but see real 'effects' of media output. Vigilantism, attacks on innocent people, at times escalating to near-riots: all fed by the ways in which the media, and especially the tabloid press, covered the murder of Sarah Payne, 'informed' their readers and gave vent to the most brutish of feelings in their editorial columns. But the example is apposite. No one 'copied'. No direct 'message' was involved. There was no 'cumulative' influence. The issue of *how* the media can be influential must now move centre-stage. The trouble is, the word 'effects' has come to be burdened with such a mighty load of negative, judgmental and censorious connotations that we need virtually a new language in order to delineate the impacts which Buckingham rightly calls 'ideological'.

Some particularly useful work in this area has emerged from *Seeing and Believing* (1990) by Greg Philo, which is based on a study of responses to television coverage of the 1984–5 coal dispute. Here, foreshadowing the study by Morrison and others (1999) described earlier, groups of people were asked not simply to comment on the news broadcasts which the researchers showed them, but also to write their own. As Philo explains:

> This would show what they thought the content of the news to be on a

given issue. It might then be possible to compare this with what they actually believed to be true and to examine why they either accepted or rejected the media account. The approach made members of the public temporarily into journalists and became the basis for the study. (1990: 8)

Philo was interested in the differences within the audience (including gender, regional location, class position, political culture and so on), and the consequences these might have for the way in which information from the media is received. Investigation of the complex interactions of media messages and their readers thus enabled the researchers to investigate 'long-term processes of belief, understanding and memory'.

What the researchers found was that in many cases there were 'extraordinary similarities' between the actual news programmes which their groups had watched and the news reports which they themselves subsequently wrote. In particular the groups tended strongly to reproduce the themes of the 'drift back to work' and of 'escalating violence' (especially by striking miners) which so heavily dominated media coverage of the dispute. To quote Philo: 'it was remarkable how closely some of the group stories reflected not only the thematic content of the news but also the structure of actual headlines. One of the surprises in this research was the clarity with which the groups were able to reproduce themes from the news. It also surprised group members' (ibid: 260).

The researchers also found remarkable the number of people who believed that the violent images of picketing which they saw on television accurately represented the everyday reality of picketing during the dispute. In all, 54 per cent of the general sample believed that the picketing was mostly violent, and the source for these beliefs was overwhelmingly given as the media, with the emphasis on television because of its immediate quality. However, Philo warns:

> It would be wrong to see people as being totally dependent on such messages, as if they were simply empty vessels which are being filled up by *News at Ten*. To accept and believe what is seen on television is as much a cultural act as the rejection of it. Both acceptance and rejection are conditioned by our beliefs, history and experience. (ibid: 260)

What emerged here was that beliefs about how much violence occurred on picket lines, and about how accurately television reflected actual daily life on the lines, differed greatly according to how much specialist knowledge and direct experience of the strike group members possessed. In short, the more knowledge they possessed, the less likely they were to believe that the picketing was mostly violent and that the television pictures of violence accurately represented the daily reality of the strike. But perhaps the most interesting finding came from a 'wild card' in the research. Respondents had been given a set of stills from news broadcasts which they were asked to put in order and then to write an accompanying news commentary. Among the stills was a shot of a gun (in fact, from a news item about a working miner threatening to defend himself). Such was the force of the news 'template' of picket line violence that even those who were most suspicious of the television coverage tended to associate the gun with the strikers or with 'militant outsiders'. Either way, even a year after the events, critics of the coverage and supporters of the striking miners still had to *defend themselves* against the perceived force of the news' claims.

[. . .]

The great strength of the recent rise of qualitative media audience research has been in the impetus which it has given to replacing figures of 'the audience' with detailed pictures of different kinds of audiences. This research, utilising increasingly sophisticated methodology, works from how those audiences themselves talk about or in other ways express their feelings about, responses to and relationships with different media.

This kind of research is not easy to conduct, but we badly need more it, because now we are beginning to understand a number of important processes in the ways that the media can persuade particular groups of readers and viewers under particular circumstances.

Note

1. An interesting small test. Schlesinger et al. include the following sentence from one man, reporting his feelings about films such as *Under Siege*: 'you do desensitise from it . . . 'cos you know it's not real'. The complexities of categorisation, self-evaluation and recognition of social discourses indicated in this one sentence are beyond understanding by the crudities of traditional psychological theory.

References

Barker, Martin and Kate Brooks (1998), *Knowing Audiences:* Judge Dredd, *Its Friends, Fans and Foes*, Luton: University of Luton Press.

Buckingham, David (1993), *Children Talking Television: The Making of Television Literacy*, London: Falmer Press.

Buckingham, David (1996), *Moving Images: Understanding Children's Emotional Responses to Television*, Manchester: Manchester University Press.

Fiske, John and Robert Dawson (1996), 'Audiencing violence: watching homeless men watch *Die Hard*', in Grossberg, Lawrence and Ellen Wartella, eds., *The Audience and its Landscape*, Boulder, CO: Westview Press.

Gabriel, John (1996), 'What do you do when minority means you? *Falling Down* and the construction of "whiteness" ', *Screen*, 37:2, 129–51.

Hill, Annette (1997), *Shocking Entertainment: Viewer Response to Violent Movies*, Luton: University of Luton Press.

Hodge, Robert and David Tripp (1986), *Children and Television: A Semiotic Approach*, Cambridge: Polity Press.

Hunt, Darnell M (1997), *Screening the Los Angeles 'Riots'*, New York: Cambridge University Press.

Mannheim, Karl (1960), *Ideology and Utopia*, London: Routledge and Kegan Paul.

Morrison, David E (1999), *Defining Violence: The Search for Understanding*, Luton: University of Luton Press.

Philo, Greg (1990), *Seeing and Believing: The Influence of Television*, London: Routledge.

Schlesinger, Philip, R Emerson Dobash, Russell P Dobash & C. Kay Weaver (1992), *Women Viewing Violence*, London: British Film Institute (in association with the Broadcasting Standards Council).

Schlesinger, Philip, Richard Haynes, Raymond Boyle, Brian McNair, R Emerson Dobash & Russell P Dobash (1998), *Men Viewing Violence*, London: Broadcasting Standards Council.

THE SOCIAL AMPLIFICATION OF RISK AND THE MEDIA VIOLENCE DEBATE

6

Annette Hill

Introduction

[...]

The alleged negative effects of media violence operate on physical and moral levels. The physical effects of media violence, such as copycat violence, or cultivation effects, have been well documented by academics in the field of social sciences (see Gerbner *et al.*, 1980, 1986; Cumberbatch and Howitt, 1989; Van Evra, 1990; Gauntlett, 1995; Buckingham and Allerton, 1996 amongst others), but the moral effects of media violence have received little serious attention. It is my intention to examine the connections between the physical and moral 'risks' of media violence. This demarcation is based upon scientific and moral discourses. The physical 'risks' of media violence originate in the scientific 'cause-effect' model, and therefore such effects as copycat violence, or desensitization, are tested, usually under laboratory conditions, in an attempt to prove a direct causal relationship exists between either fictional representations of violence, or factual mediated images of violence, and real acts of violence (Van Evra, 1990; Gauntlett, 1995). The moral 'risks' of media violence do not directly relate to the cause-effect model. Concern about the moral risks of media violence are framed in relation to the moral and ethical issues of family life, law and order, safety in the home and the community, and religious values (see Barker and Petley, 1997; Hill, 1999). It is the scientific and moral discourses of media violence which will be analysed in this article in relation to environmentalism.

The interpretive strategies used by professional groups, direct action groups, and religious groups to campaign against media violence are shaped by the discourse of environmental hazards (Gamson and Modigliani, 1989; Eder, 1996). The application of the discourse of environmentalism to the media violence debate is best understood by using the conceptual framework of the social amplification of risk (Kasperson *et al.*, 1988; Kasperson, 1992; Kasperson and Kasperson, 1996). The aim of this article is to examine the flow of communication after a media violence controversy, and consider how the model of the social amplification of risk can illuminate the way in which particular individual and social amplification stations amplify the alleged physical and moral risks of media violence. This research contributes to a wider understanding of social theories of risk by illuminating the application of the masterframe of environmental discourse to a non-risk arena.

[. . .]

Analysis of the social amplification of the physical and moral risks of media violence will reveal how the main individual and social amplification agents in this debate reinvent the symbol of risk in order to manipulate channels of communication concerning media violence. Thus, my argument draws upon suggestions made by Rip (1988: 195), in his review of the social amplification of risk framework, that researchers consider the way 'hazard signals' can be adopted and transformed by social groups. As media violence is commonly perceived as a 'stigmatized' form of popular culture by social commentators (see Kasperson and Kasperson, 1996: 99; Barker and Petley, 1997), horror, crime and action movies in particular receive much criticism for their alleged physical risks. However, this criticism becomes all the more powerful and dramatic if it is associated with the moralization of risk (Eder, 1996). It is my intention to show how the moral risks of media violence provide professional groups and direct action groups with a **rhetorical** framework within which to argue for a 'safer' moral environment.

The Emergence of Media Risks

A brief overview of the connections between nineteenth century discourses concerning nature and media violence [. . .] reveal the constant borrowing that has taken place between the construction of environmentalism and media violence controversies. Szerszynski (1993) and MacNaughton and Urry (1998) have argued that early representations of nature as a moral concern and moral source contributed to the postwar construction of nature as an 'environmental crisis'. Szerszynski (1993: 3–16) traced the development of Victorian representations of nature as threatened (e.g. nature as an 'exhaustible resource', or as a 'healthy body threatened by pollution') and nature as a moral source (e.g. nature as 'recreational space', or as an 'ecosystem'). Szerszynski (1993: 9) highlighted the class agenda of campaigns to ban cruelty to animals: 'The Royal Society for the Prevention of Cruelty to Animals (RSPCA), founded in 1824, repeatedly showed a predilection for attempting to outlaw cruel sports practised by the working classes, rather than those favoured by the elites'. The other function of the RSPCA and the National Society for the Prevention of Cruelty to Children (NSPCC) was to 'sanction the imposition of moral discipline and social order on a supposedly degenerate population' (Szerzynski, 1993: 9).

This class agenda was also apparent in early representations of 'media effects' and working-class popular entertainment (Pearson, 1983; Petley, 1997). As early as the 1850s, the popular press and social commentators expressed concern over media violence (Pearson, 1983). Concerts and theatres were seen to corrupt the young and new popular media were described by one professor in 1904 as having the same kind of 'evil effects as syphilis or leprosy' (Murdock, 1997: 77). As Murdock (1997: 68) points out: 'Commentators were quick to see [media violence] as both a potent symptom of moral decline and a powerful new incitement to anti-social behaviour.'

[. . .]

Physical and Moral Risks

The alleged negative 'effects' of media violence form part of the amplification spiral for media violence controversies and moral panics. The physical risks to watching media violence are outlined by the National Television Violence Study (NTVS). NTVS is a recent American study that was commissioned by the National Cable and Television Association to provide the largest content analysis of media violence ever undertaken. An executive summary of the NTVS for 1994–95 claims the following key finding: 'The context in which most violence is presented on television poses risks for viewers' (NTVS, 1995: ix). NTVS (1995: ix) explains the links between media violence and risk as follows:

The risks of viewing the most common depictions of televised violence include learning to behave violently, becoming more desensitized to the harmful consequences of violence, and becoming more fearful of being attacked. The contextual patterns . . . are found consistently across most channels, program types, and times of day. Thus, there are substantial risks of harmful effects from viewing violence throughout the television environment.

To substantiate the claim that there are substantial risks to viewing violence, NTVS (1995: 3) examined 2,693 programmes on 23 different channels, analysing over 18,000 violent interactions on television. The findings indicate that 'The majority of programs on television contain violence (57%), and roughly one third of violent programs contain nine or more violent interactions' (NTVS, 1995: 25). These statistics are presented as scientific proof that violence on television is not within 'acceptable levels' of exposure: if 57% of television programmes contain violent content then this is over half of all US television viewing.

[. . .]

[C]riticism and research which counteracts the claims of 'effects' researchers are rarely given a public hearing. [. . .] [S]uch information is not featured in press coverage of the alleged negative effects of media violence, nor is it given proper hearing in public discussion surrounding a risk event. In part, this is because newspapers and news bulletins are less interested in pro-social items and feature a predominance of 'bad news', especially crime stories. (Glasgow University Media Group, 1976, 1980)

It is also the case that media violence is perceived as a stigmatized form of popular culture, in a similar way as nuclear energy is an example of stigmatized technology (Gamson and Modigliani, 1989; Kasperson and Kasperson, 1996: 101). The physical risks of media violence remain steadfast in the public's mind, despite the existence of conflicting scientific information (Kasperson and Kasperson, 1996: 99). However, another reason why media violence is subject to intensely negative media coverage is because of the social construction of media violence as physically *and* morally hazardous.

Moral 'risks' are difficult to define, but through analysis of academic, political, popular press and campaign discourses certain patterns emerge which suggest key institutional and public concerns regarding moral issues and the regulation and control of media violence (see for example, Medved, 1992; Newson, 1994; Home Office Affairs Committee, 1994). There is not space in this article to analyse these discourses in detail, but I will briefly outline two interlocking rhetorical frameworks used by professional groups, direct action groups, and religious groups. First, television is primarily perceived to be a medium for family entertainment and thus, it is argued, media violence is unsuitable material for television programmes (see Gauntlett and Hill, 1999). Texts which contain fictional representations of violence, such as action cartoons, are criticized for their amoral 'glorification' of violence (see Chambers *et al.*, 1998). The moral risks of media violence are constructed as pollutants or drugs, potentially harmful for everyone. Dr Robert Coles, a Harvard child psychiatrist, believes: 'We're now going after the tobacco companies and saying "Don't poison people". It seems to me, the minds of children are being poisoned all the time by the networks' (see *Variety*, 1996). David Buckingham (1996: 25) noted the proliferation of drug-related language in coverage of the James Bulger case in 1993: 'Young people are "saturated", "hooked" and "corrupted": their "impressionable minds" are "bombarded" and "warped". The videos themselves are described as "an addictive pollutant".' Thus, the moral risks of media violence are related to the corruption of innocent children in the home environment.

Second, media violence is perceived as symptomatic of a general lack of moral values in the entertainment industry, and in contemporary society (see Medved, 1992; Laurence, 1994; Lisle, 1995; Hellen and Ruffurd 1997 for examples). Media violence is commonly perceived as a symptom of the erosion of traditional family life which uses the teachings of the bible as a foundation for ethical and moral values in the home, and the community. Mary Whitehouse (1996: 61), the founding member of NVALA [**National Viewers and Listeners Association**], argues that film-makers are responsible for the 'health and welfare of the whole of our society, but especially, for pity's sake, the welfare of the children who are the future'. Thus, concern about the moral 'risks' of media violence in academic, popular press, public, political and campaign discourses repeatedly links the alleged hazards of media violence in relation to the moral issues of family life, law and order, safety in the home and the community, and religious values (see Barker and Petley, 1997; Hill, 1999).

It is this use of the moral risks of media violence that is most relevant to the social amplification of media violence by politicians, the popular press, and citizen's groups. The moralization of risk is a means to amplify the real and symbolic risks of media violence. Levels of violence in the media and society are amplified so that the issue of media violence becomes one of law and order and social welfare. In the next section, the conceptual framework of the social amplification of risk will be applied to the media violence debate. This conceptual framework illuminates how the media risk repertoire flows through multiple communication networks; social and political groups, such as non-governmental organizations and professional groups, transform a 'hazard signal' in order to adopt and reinvent the risk event for their own political and social gain (Rip, 1988: 195).

The Social Amplification of Risk and Media Violence

The conceptual framework of the social amplification of risk, as outlined by Kasperson *et al.* (1988), is a framework that links technical assessment of risk with socio-cultural perspectives of risk and risk-related behaviour. The framework considers the amplification and attenuation of public and official response to risk. Kasperson *et al.* (1988: 180) draw upon the communications model of the source-receiver to explain how hazard signals from a risk event are received by individual and social groups. These hazard signals become part of the societal experience of risk, and can be used to amplify or attenuate the nature and magnitude of a risk event. The social amplification of risk model focuses on channels of communication, both in terms of information given about a risk event, and the response mechanisms of society (Kasperson *et al.*, 1988: 184). Individual and social amplification stations amplify or attenuate risks signals, and can generate secondary impacts, such as: enduring mental perceptions, images and attitudes towards risk; political and social pressure; changes in risk monitoring and regulation; repercussions on other technologies and social institutions. Kasperson *et al.* (1988: 182) use the analogy of dropping a stone into a pond to explain the secondary effects, and how they spread outwards from the victims of a risk event, to institutional and social arenas. It is this aspect of the social amplification of risk framework that is most applicable to the media violence debate and the control and dissemination of knowledge regarding the physical and moral risks of media violence.

[. . .]

The example of the James Bulger case in Britain [. . .] illustrate[s] the primary and secondary processes in the social amplification of the risks of media violence. James Bulger was murdered by two 10-year-old boys, Robert Thompson and Jon Venables, in Liverpool, in February 1993. The event characteristics of the James Bulger case were clearly interpreted from an early stage as a connection between media violence, law and order and social welfare. Before the murder trial, the then Conservative Prime Minister and Home Secretary made speeches about unacceptable levels of television violence, the **British Board of Film Classification** commissioned research in the viewing habits of young offenders, and the National Viewers and Listeners Association made alarmist pronouncements about television violence, and produced a report: 'Did he die in vain?' linking the death of James Bulger to the risks of media violence (Buckingham, 1996: 21). When the Honourable Mr Justice Moreland, in his summing up of the trial, suggested violent video films may have been in part responsible for the death of James Bulger, the flow of information about this risk event specifically focused on the physical and moral risks of media violence in contemporary society. One film in particular, *Child's Play* 3, was associated with the trial: the film had been rented by the father of Jon Venables, and although neither child claimed to have seen the film, it was suggested that there were similarities between the murder of James Bulger and representations of murder in this film. The interpretation and response by the popular press, television current affairs programmes, academics, public agencies, interest groups and government sources were widespread and alarmist, and can be related to other high profile risk events such as Brent Spa, and successful environmental campaigns against stigmatized risks (Kasperson, 1992; MacNaughton and Urry, 1998). The use of condensing symbols, such as the image of Chucky the demon doll from *Child's Play* 3 and the phrase 'video nasty', specifically highlighted the links between media violence and physical and moral risk. The spread of the impact of the James Bulger case suggested links between the risks to individual people; in this instance, James Bulger, his family, and viewers of horror movies; to institutions, such as entertainment industries, and to social and political arenas, such as the safety of local communities, the innocence of children, and the threat posed by media violence to law and order and family values.

[. . .]

The socio-cultural impact of this risk event reveals the ripple effect in relation to media violence. The popular press called for a wholesale ban on 'video nasties' which was a return to the alarmist **rhetoric** used in the 'video nasties' scare in the early 1980s (Barker, 1984), and served to create enduring mental perceptions of media violence as a physical and moral risk, especially to children. Local video chains burned their stocks of *Child's Play* 3, and the satellite company BSkyB banned the film, which was scheduled to be shown on satellite television. The film was temporarily withdrawn from video release by the distributors, and a report, commissioned by the Movement for Christian Democracy (MCD), conducted by a child development psychologist Elizabeth Newson, summarized existing research and anecdotal evidence on the negative effects of media violence, and claimed that video violence was a form of electronic child abuse (Newson, 1994). The report received extensive coverage in the popular press in April 1994 (see Barker and Petley, 1997), and was used as a political tool by David Alton, a leading member of the MCD, and then a Liberal Democrat MP, to campaign for an amendment to the Criminal Justice and Public Order Bill, requiring that the British Board of Film Classification pay particular attention to films which may potentially harm children as a result of watching degrading or gratuitously violent scenes (Home Office Affairs Committee, 1994). As a result of this, the Video Recordings Act was amended, to place greater emphasis on portrayals of violent or horrific behaviour, criminality, drug use and sexual behaviour, and potential harm to children.

[. . .]

As Horlick-Jones (1995) and Wynne (1992a, b) point out, risk perception is linked to social identity and lifestyle choices. In the case of the moral risks of media violence, non-governmental organizations amplify and reinvent risk signals in order to stigmatize and dramatize the physical and moral risks of media violence (Palmlund, 1992; Barker and Petley, 1997). These social amplification stations work together to generate public and government hearings, research reports, and campaign for amendments to existing media law in Britain.

The most vocal British anti-violence campaign groups are the NVALA, CARE [Cooperative for Assistance and Relief Everywhere] and the Movement for Christian Democracy (MCD). [. . .] What the NVALA, CARE and the MCD have in common is a shared belief that contemporary society has lost touch with religious morality. These associations do not only campaign to reduce levels of media violence. As Barratt (1997: 1) points out:

> These groups are engaged in a political struggle over the lifestyle choices of society: attacks on television, cinema and video form only one front in the battle against 'permissive society' which stands opposed to the fundamentalist Christian ideal. Both CARE and MCD actively campaign against homosexuality, abortion, euthanasia, genetic engineering, and single-parenthood in their support of 'traditional' family life underpinned by Christian morality.

Such shared religious and cultural beliefs have a significant impact on the adoption and re-invention of risk signals in media violence controversies. These social amplification stations construct media violence as a physical and moral risk, and yet at the same time organizations such as MCD do not wish to associate the risks of media violence within a specifically religious framework. For example, at the time of the James Bulger case, David Alton wrote: 'the MCD should be very careful with the media. We could and ourselves being caricatured as a worthy but eccentric God-squad and that would damage us in the future. We have to go way beyond the Christian constituency in order to win some of these arguments' (cited in Barratt, 1997: 1). The hypothesis by Rip (1988) that social organizations may re-invent risk signals is particularly appropriate to anti-violence campaign groups, who are sensitive to the unpopularity of religious morality, and adopt a more secular approach when discussing media violence controversies. The effects of media violence are interpreted as physical and moral risks, and 'moral risks' are defined as risks to innocent children, the breakdown of family values, and issues of law and order, rather than a religious morality that is based on Christian fundamentalist ideals.

For these religious campaign groups, the risks of media violence are amplified by secular political, economic and social organizations. NVALA, CARE and MCD believe the general public are corrupted by films and television programmes that contain scenes of violence or sexuality, or push boundaries of taste and decency. Non-Christians, in particular, children, have been taught by entertainment industries to desire 'risky' entertainment, such as action cartoons. Machlis and Rosa (1989) applied the social amplification of risk framework to desired risk, and risk recreational activities, such as hang gliding or mountain climbing. They found the amplification of the risks of these leisure activities could serve to heighten interest, and suggested revision of the social amplification of risk model to allow for variations in signal reception and behavioural responses (1989: 165). In relation to the issue of media violence, it can be argued that media consumers may benefit from the amplification of the risks of media violence. Hill (1997) conducted research in active consumers of violent movies and found that some people are attracted to watching notorious violent films because of media hype. Thus, it could be argued films such as *Natural Born Killers* (Oliver Stone, US, 1994) or *Crash* (David Cronenberg, Canada, 1996) have benefited from the social amplification of the risks of media violence, as more people would be likely to see these films on cinema release. However, loss of sales in video retail and rental, and the social stigma attached to the production and distribution companies of such 'risky' entertainment ensure the benefits of amplifying the risks of media violence are minimal. The moral stigmatization of media violence, and the widespread use of the rhetoric of risk in the media violence debate mean that consumers who wish to engage in 'risky' entertainment are viewed with suspicion and in turn stigmatized for their tastes in popular culture (Hill, 1997). The type of information flow and social group mobilization surrounding a media violence controversy ensures that behavioural responses which indicate anti-censorship attitudes, or desire to watch violent movies are interpreted as deviant forms of behaviour rather than acceptable examples of risk recreation (Barker and Petley, 1997).

The social processing of risk signals in relation to media violence controversies, reveals an imbalance of information. The amplification of the risks of media violence are channelled by religious campaign groups in order to creatively interpret and dramatize the alleged negative effects of media violence as physical and moral risks (Renn, 1992; Palmlund, 1992). Alternative behavioural responses and research in media violence are not given sufficient attention in cultural and political arenas. The extent to which media violence, in association with law and order, has become an important issue in political campaigns means that disputes about the risks of media violence outlive single controversies, and become templates for debates about censorship and regulation in Britain (Kasperson and Kasperson, 1996: 99; Barker and Petley, 1997).

Conclusion

[. . .]

The main findings of this article can be summarized as follows:

(1) The conceptual framework of the social amplification of risk can be applied successfully to non-risk arenas, in this instance media violence controversies.
(2) The social amplification of risk model illuminates the symbolic framing of media violence as an environmental risk.
(3) Professional groups and direct action groups use scientific, moral and environmental discourses to argue for the control and regulation of media risks.
(4) Social stations can reinvent the physical and moral risks of media violence to further social, political, religious and cultural beliefs.
(5) Anti-violence campaign groups play a role in shaping the societal experience of media violence, and the societal impact of media violence controversies on media law in Britain.

References

Barker, M. (ed.) (1984) *The Video Nasties: Freedom and Censorship in the Media*, London: Pluto.

Barker, M. and Petley, J. (eds) (1997) *Ill Effects: The Media Violence Debate*, London: Routledge.

Barratt, J.A.B. (1997) Faith over reason (unpublished), available on web site http://www.users.dircon.co.uk/~ajbb/response.html.

Buckingham, D. (1996) *Moving Images: Understanding Children's Emotional Responses to Television*, Manchester: Manchester University Press.

Buckingham, D. and Allerton, M. (1996) A review of research on children's 'negative' emotional responses to television, Research Working Paper 12, London: Broadcasting Standards Council.

Chambers, S., Karet, N. and Samson, N. (1998) *Cartoon Crazy? Children's Perceptions of Action Cartoons*, London: Independent Television Commission.

Cumberbatch, G. and Howitt, D. (1989) *A Measure of Uncertainty: The Effects of the Mass Media*, London: Libbey.

Eder, K. (1996) The institutionalisation of environmentalism: sociological discourse and the second transformation of the public sphere, in S. Lash, B. Szerszynski and B. Wynne (eds), *Risk, Environment and Modernity: Towards a New Ecology*, pp. 203–23, London: Sage.

Gamson, W.A. and Modigliani, A. (1989) Media discourse and public opinion on nuclear power: a constructionist approach, *American Journal of Sociology 95*, 1–37.

Gauntlett, D. (1995) *Moving Experiences: Understanding Television's Influences and Effects*, London: Libbey.

Gauntlett, D. and Hill, A. (1999) *TV Living: Television, Culture and Everyday Life*. London: Routledge.

Gerbner, G., Gross, L., Morgan, M. and Signorielli, N. (1980) The 'mainstreaming' of America: violence profile No. 11, *Journal of Communication 30*, 10–29.

Gerbner, G., Gross, L., Morgan, M. and Signorielli, N. (1986) Living with television: the dynamics of the cultivation process, in J. Bryant and D. Zillman (eds), *Perspectives on Media Effects*, Hillsdale, NJ: Erlbaum.

Glasgow University Media Group (1976) *Bad News*, London: Routledge & Kegan Paul.

Glasgow University Media Group (1980) *More Bad News*, London: Routledge & Kegan Paul.

Hellen, N. and Rufford, N. (1997) Official: violent videos cause crime, *The Sunday Times* 17 August, 1.

Hill, A. (1997) *Shocking Entertainment: Viewer Response to Violent Movies*, Luton: John Libbey Media.

Hill, A. (1999) A social drama: anti-violence campaign groups and media violence, in D. Berry (ed.), *Media Ethics: Practices and Representations*, London: Butterworth-Heinemann.

Home Office Affairs Committee. (1994) *Video, Violence and Young Offenders*, London: HMSO.

Horlick-Jones, T. (1995) Modern disasters as outrage and betrayal, *International Journal of Mass Emergencies and Disasters 13*, 305–15.

Kasperson, R.E. (1992) The social amplification of risk: progress in developing an integrative framework, in S. Krimsky and D. Golding (eds), *Social Theories of Risk*, pp. 153–78, Westport, CT: Praeger.

Kasperson, R.E. and Kasperson, J.X. (1996) The social amplification and attenuation of risk, *Annals of the American Academy of Political and Social Science 545*, 95–105.

Kasperson, R.E., Renn, O., Slovic, P., Brown, H.S., Emel, J., Goble, R., Kasperson, J.X. and Ratick, S. (1988) The social amplification of risk: a conceptual framework, *Risk Analysis 8*, 177–87.

Laurence, C. (1994) Our worst nightmare, *Daily Telegraph* 28 October, 27.

Lisle, L. de (1995) An unhealthy intimacy with violence, *Independent on Sunday* 11 June, 27.

Machlis, G.E. and Rosa, E.A. (1989) Desired risk and the social amplification of risk framework, *Risk Analysis* 10, 161–8.

MacNaughton, P. and Urry, J. (1998) *Contested Natures*, London: Sage.

Medved, M. (1992) *Hollywood vs. America: Popular Culture and the War on Traditional Values*, New York: HarperCollins.

Murdock, G. (1997) Reservoirs of dogma: an archaeology of popular anxieties, in M. Barker and J. Petley (eds), *Ill Effects: The Media Violence Debate*, pp. 67–86, London: Routledge.

Newson, E. (1994) Video violence and the protection of children, mimeo, University of Nottingham: Child Development Research Unit.

NTVS (The National Television Violence Study) (1995) *Executive Summary 1994–1995*, Mediascope, Inc.

Palmlund, I. (1992) Social drama and risk evaluation, in S. Krimsky and D. Golding (eds), *Social Theories of Risk*, pp. 197–214, Westport, CT: Praeger.

Pearson, G. (1983) *Hooligan: A History of Respectable Fears*, London: Macmillan.

Petley, J. (1997) Us and them, in M. Barker and J. Petley (eds), *Ill Effects: The Media Violence Debate*, London: Routledge.

Renn, O. (1992) The social arena concept of risk debates, in S. Krimsky and D. Golding (eds), *Social Theories of Risk*, pp. 179–96, Westport, CT: Praeger.

Rip, A. (1988) Should social amplification of risk be counteracted?, *Risk Analysis* 8, 193–8.

Szerszynski, B. (1993) Uncommon ground: moral discourse, foundationalism and the environmental movement, PhD thesis, Lancaster University.

Van Evra, J. (1990) *Television and Child Development*, Hillsdale, NJ: Erlbaum.

Variety (1996) Censors to the networks; gotcha, 19–25 February, 1, 61–2.

Whitehouse, M. (1996) Time to face responsibility, in K. French (ed.), *Screen Violence*, pp. 52–61, London: Bloomsbury.

Wynne, B. (1992a) Misunderstanding misunderstandings: social identities and public uptake of science, *Public Understanding of Science* 1, 281–304.

Wynne, B. (1992b) Risk and social learning: reification to engagement, in S. Krimsky and D. Golding (eds), *Social Theories of Risk*, pp. 21–9, Westport, CT: Praeger.

PRIVATE SATISFACTIONS AND PUBLIC DISORDERS
FIGHT CLUB, PATRIARCHY AND THE POLITICS OF MASCULINE VIOLENCE

Henry A. Giroux

> The 'public' has been emptied of its own separate contents; it has been left with no agenda of its own – it is now but an agglomeration of private troubles, worries and problems.
>
> Zygmunt Bauman[1]

Introduction

In the epigraph above, Zygmunt Bauman gives voice to a troubling feature of American society. Amidst the growing privatization of everyday life, the greatest danger to human freedom and democracy no longer appears to come from the power of the over-zealous state eager to stamp out individual freedom and critical inquiry in the interest of loyalty and patriotism. Authoritarianism no longer breeds a contempt for the virtues of individualism, all things private, and the dynamics of self-interest. On the contrary, totalitarianism now resides in a thorough dislike for all things social, public, and collective. Under the growing influence of the politics, ideology, and culture of neoliberalism, 'the individual has been set free to construe her or his own fears, to baptize them with privately chosen names and to come with them on her or his own.'[2] Agency has now been privatized and personal liberty atomized and removed from broader considerations about the ethical and political responsibility of citizens to defend those vital institutions that expand the rights and services central to a meaningful democracy. Stripped of its political possibilities and social underpinnings, freedom finds few opportunities for translating private worries into public concerns or individual discontent into collective struggle. Utopia is now conjured up as the privatized space of the shopping mall, intellectual effort is reduced to an instrument of the entrepreneurial self, and social visions are dismissed as hopelessly out of date. Public space is portrayed exclusively as an investment opportunity, and the public good increasingly becomes a metaphor for public disorder. As the public sphere is consistently removed from social consideration and notions of the public good are replaced by an utterly privatized model of citizenship and the good life, the collapse of public imagination and a vibrant political culture is celebrated by neoliberal warriors rather than perceived as a dangerous state of affairs that Americans should be both contemptuous of and ashamed to support.

Within the discourse of neoliberalism, issues regarding persistent poverty, inadequate health care, racial apartheid in the inner cities, and the growing inequalities between the rich and the poor have been either removed from the inventory of public discourse and public policy or factored into talk show spectacles that highlight private woes bearing little relationship either to public life or to potential remedies that demand collective action. Within this growing marketization and privatization of everyday life, democratic principles are either scorned as holdovers of an outmoded sixties radicalism or equated entirely with the imperatives of capitalism.

As Robert W. McChesney points out, Milton Friedman, the reigning guru of neoliberalism, both perfectly captures and legitimates this sentiment in *Capitalism and Freedom* arguing unabashedly that 'because profit-making is the essence of democracy, any government that pursues antimarket policies is being antidemocratic, no matter how much informed popular support they might enjoy. Therefore it is best to restrict governments to the job of protecting private property and enforcing contracts, and to limit political debate to minor issues.'[3] Within neoliberal discourse, freedom is negatively reduced to the freedom from government restraint and the rights of citizenship translate into the freedom to consume as one chooses. The state, in this instance, becomes a threat to freedom, particularly the freedom of the market, as its role as guardian of the public interests is actively disassembled, though its powers are still invoked by dominant interests to insure their own privileges, such as free trade agreements, government subsidies for business, and strike 'negotiations'. But as Pierre Bourdieu points out, while neoliberals highlight the threat the state poses to the freedom of the market, the real threat comes from a state, which under the control of neoliberal ideology, is increasingly transformed into a repressive apparatus aimed at those individuals and groups who get caught in its ever-expanding policing interventions.[4]

[. . .]

The ascendancy of neoliberalism and corporate culture into every aspect of American life not only consolidates economic power in the hands of the few, it also aggressively attempts to break the power of unions, decouple income from productivity, subordinate the needs of society to the market, and deem public services and amenities an unconscionable luxury. But it does more. It thrives on a culture of cynicism, boredom, and despair. Americans are now convinced that they have little to hope for – and gain from – the government, non-profit public spheres, democratic associations, or other non-governmental social forces.

[. . .]

It is against this ongoing assault on the public, and the growing preponderance of a free market economy and corporate culture that turns everything it touches into an object of consumption that David Fincher's [1999] film, *Fight Club*, must be critically engaged. Ostensibly, *Fight Club* appears to offer a critique of late capitalist society and the misfortunes it generates out of its obsessive concern with profits, consumption, and the commercial values that underline its market-driven ethos. But *Fight Club* is less interested in attacking the broader material relations of power and strategies of domination and exploitation associated with neoliberal capitalism than it is in rebelling against a consumerist culture that dissolves the bonds of male sociality and puts into place an enervating notion of male identity and agency. Contrary to the onslaught of reviews accompanying the film's premier that celebrated it as a daring social critique,[5] [. . .] *Fight Club* has nothing to say about the **structural violence** of unemployment, job insecurity, cuts in public spending, and the destruction of institutions capable of defending social provisions and the public good. On the contrary, *Fight Club* defines the violence of capitalism almost exclusively in terms of an attack on traditional (if not to say regressive) notions of masculinity, and in doing so reinscribes white, heterosexuality within a dominant logic of stylized brutality and male bonding that appears predicated on the need to denigrate and wage war against all that is feminine. In this instance, the crisis of capitalism is reduced to the crisis of masculinity, and the nature of the crisis lies less in the economic, political, and social conditions of capitalism itself than in the rise of a culture of consumption in which men are allegedly domesticated, rendered passive, soft and emasculated.

Fight Club, along with films such as *Pulp Fiction*, *Rogue Trader*, *American Psycho*, *Boiler Room*, and *Croupier*, inaugurates a new sub-genre of cult-film that combines a fascination with the spectacle of violence, enlivened through tired narratives about the crisis of masculinity, along with a superficial gesture toward social critique designed to offer the tease of a serious independent/art film. While appearing to address important social issues, these films end up reproducing the very problems they attempt to address. Rather than turning a critical light on crucial social problems, such films often trivialize them within a stylized aesthetics that revels in irony, cynicism, and excessive violence. Violence in these films is reduced to acts of senseless brutality, pathology, and an indifference to human suffering. Reproducing such hackneyed representations of violence ('senseless,' 'random'), they conclude where engaged political commentary should begin. Yet, I am less interested in moralizing about the politics of Fincher's film than I am in reading it as a form of public pedagogy that offers an opportunity to engage and understand its politics of representation as part of broader commentary on the intersection of consumerism, masculinity, violence, politics, and gender relations. Moreover, *Fight Club* signifies the role that Hollywood films play as teaching machines. A far cry from simple entertainment, such films function as public pedagogies by articulating knowledge to effects, purposely attempting to influence how and what knowledge and identities can be produced within a limited range of social relations. At the same time, I recognize that such texts 'are radically indeterminate with respect to their meaning, [and] any reading of a text must be determined by factors not prescribed by the text itself.'[6]

[. . .]

In taking up these issues, [. . .] I address critically the representational politics that structure *Fight Club* – especially its deeply conventional views of violence, gender relations, and masculinity – and how such representations work in conjunction with a deeply entrenched culture of cynicism. [. . .] I argue that such cynicism far from being innocent works in tandem with broader public discourses to undermine the faith of individuals and groups to engage in the possibility of a politics designed to struggle against the rising tide of anti-democratic forces and movements that threaten the already weakened fabric of democracy. Obviously, I am not arguing that Hollywood films such as *Fight Club* are a cause of these problems, but are symptomatic of a wider symbolic and institutional culture of cynicism and senseless violence that exerts a powerful pedagogical influence on shaping the public imagination.

[. . .]

Fight Club and the Crisis of Everyday Life

White, heterosexual men in America have not fared well in the nineties. Not only have they been attacked by feminists, gays, lesbians, and various subaltern groups for a variety of ideological and material offenses, they have also had to endure a rewriting of the very meaning of masculinity. [. . .] As Homi Bhabha has recently stated, the manifest destiny of masculinity with its hard-boiled, tough image of manliness has been disturbed, and its blocked reflexivity has been harshly unsettled.[7] [. . .] Moreover, as white, heterosexual working-class and middle-class men face a life of increasing uncertainty and insecurity, they no longer have easy access to those communities in which they can inhabit a form of masculinity that defines itself in opposition to femininity. In simple terms, the new millennium offers white, heterosexual men nothing less than a life in which ennui and domestication define their everyday existence.

[B]ased on a novel by Chuck Palahniuk, [*Fight Club*] attempts to critically engage the boredom, shallowness, and emptiness of a stifling consumer culture, redefine what it might mean for men to resist compromising their masculinity [. . .], and explore the possibilities for creating a sense of community in which men can reclaim their virility and power. The film opens with an inside shot of Jack's (played by Edward Norton) brain, tracking a surge of adrenalin that quickly finds an opening in Jack's mouth and then exits up the barrel of a gun. Jack then proceeds to lead the audience into the nature of his predicament and in doing so narrates his journey out of corporate America [. . .].

As a recall coordinator, Jack travels around the country investigating accidents for a major auto company [. . .]. Alienated from his job [. . .], Jack's principal relief comes from an unsatiable urge for flipping through and shopping from consumer catalogues. [. . .] But Jack's [. . .] consumerist urges only seem to reinforce [. . .] the emptiness of his daily life and [. . .] near terminable insomnia, Jack visits his doctor claiming he is in real pain. His thirty-something doctor refuses to give him drugs and tells him that if he really wants to see pain to visit a local testicular cancer survivor group. Jack [. . .] discovers that the group offers him a sense of comfort and community and in an ironic twist he becomes a support group junkie. At his first meeting of the Remaining Men Together survival group, Jack meets Bob [. . .] a former weightlifter who has enormous breasts (described as 'bitch tits') as a result of hormonal treatments. The group allows Jack to participate in a form of male bonding that offers him an opportunity to release his pent-up emotions and provides a cure for his insomnia. Bob becomes a not too subtle symbol in the film, personifying how masculinity is both degraded (he has breasts like a woman) and used in a culture that relies upon the 'feminine' qualities of support and empathy rather than 'masculine' attributes of strength and virility to bring men together. When Bob hugs Jack and tells him 'You can cry now,' *Fight Club* does more than mock new age therapy for men, it is also satirizing and condemning the 'weepy' process of femininization that such therapies sanction and put into place.

Jack eventually meets Marla (Helena Bonham Carter), [. . .] slumming in the same group therapy sessions as Jack. Jack views Marla as a tourist – addicted only to the spectacle of the meetings. Marla reminds him of his own phoniness and so upsets him that his insomnia returns [. . .]. In the voice over, Jack claims that 'if he had a tumor he would name it Marla.' Once again, repressed white masculinity is thrown into a crisis by the eruption of an ultra-conservative version of post-60s femininity that signifies both the antithesis of domestic security, comfort and sexual passivity – offering only neurosis and blame in their place. [. . .]

On the heels of this loss, Jack meets Tyler Durden (Brad Pitt) on an airplane. [. . .] If Jack is a model of packaged conformity and yuppie depthlessness, Tyler is a no-holds-barred charismatic rebel who as a part-time movie projectionist offers his own attack on family values by splicing frames of pornography into kiddie films, or when working as a banquet waiter in a luxurious hotel urinates into the soup to be served to high paying yuppie customers. Tyler also creatively affirms his disgust for women by making high-priced soaps from liposuctioned human fat and proudly telling Jack that he is 'selling rich ladies their own fat asses back to them at $20.00 a bar.' [. . .] Mesmerized by Tyler's high octane talk and sense of subversion, Jack exchanges phone numbers with him.

When Jack returns home, he finds that his apartment has been mysteriously blown to bits. He calls Tyler who meets him at a local bar and tells him that things could be worse: 'a woman could cut off your penis while you are sleeping and toss it out the window of a moving car.' Tyler then launches into a five minute cliché-ridden tirade against the pitfalls of bourgeois life [. . .]. As they leave the bar, Tyler offers Jack the opportunity to move in with him in what turns out to be a dilapidated, abandoned house near a toxic dump.

Then the magic happens. Before they go back to Tyler's place, Tyler asks Jack to hit him, which Jack does and then Tyler returns the favor. Pain leads to exhilaration and they sit exhausted, bloodied and blissful after their brute encounter. Soon Tyler and Jack start fighting repeatedly in a bar parking lot, eventually drawing a crowd of men who want to participate in brutally pummeling each other. Hence, Fight Club, a new religion and secret society open only to males is born. [. . .] For Tyler, physical violence becomes the necessary foundation for masculinity and collective terrorism the basis for politics itself. In other words, the only way Tyler's followers can become agents in a society that has deadened them is to get in touch with the primal instincts for competition and violence [. . .].

Eventually [. . .] Jack has second thoughts about his homoerotic attraction to Tyler as a self-styled anti-hero when [. . .] Tyler ups the stakes of Fight Club by turning it into Project Mayhem, a nationwide organization of terrorist graduates of the fight clubs, whose aim is to wage war against the rich and powerful. [. . .]

In a psychic meltdown that is long over-due, Jack realizes that he and Tyler are the same person, signaling a shift in the drama from the realm of the sociological to the psychological. Jack discovers that Tyler has planned a series of bombings around the [. . .] city and goes to the police to turn himself in. But the cops are members of Project Mayhem and attempt to cut off his testicles because of his betrayal. Once more Jack rescues his manhood by escaping and eventually confronting Tyler [. . .]. Jack fares badly in his fight with Tyler and ends up [. . .] with a gun in his mouth. Jack finally realizes that he has the power to take control of the gun and has to shoot himself in order to kill Tyler. He puts the gun in his mouth and pulls the trigger. Tyler dies on the spot and Jack mysteriously survives. [. . .]

Consumerism, Cynicism, and Hollywood Resistance

[. . .]

[C]entral to *Fight Club* is the interrelated critique of late capitalism and the politics of masculinity. The central protagonists, Jack and Tyler, represent two opposing registers that link consumerism and masculinity. Jack is representative of a generation of men condemned to corporate peonage whose emotional lives and investments are mediated through the allure of commodities and goods. No longer a producer of goods, Jack exemplifies a form of domesticated masculinity – passive, alienated, and without ambition. On the other hand, Tyler represents an embodied masculinity that refuses the seductions of consumerism, while fetishizing forms of production – from soaps to explosives – the ultimate negative expression of which is chaos and destruction. [. . .] If Jack represents the crisis of capitalism repackaged as the crisis of a domesticated masculinity, Tyler represents the redemption of masculinity repackaged as the promise of violence in the interests of social and political anarchy.

[. . .]

Consumerism in *Fight Club* is criticized primarily as an ideological force and existential experience that weakens and domesticates men, robbing them of their primary role as producers whose bodies affirm and legitimate their sense of agency and control. The importance of agency is not lost on director David Fincher, but it is restricted to a narrowly defined notion of masculinity that is as self-absorbed as it is patriarchal.[8] Fincher is less interested in fighting oppressive forms of power than he is in exploring the ways in which men yield to it. Freedom in *Fight Club* is not simply preoccupied with the de-politicized self, it also lacks a language for translating private troubles into public rage, and, as such, succumbs to the cult of immediate sensations in which freedom degenerates into collective impotence. [. . .] In *Fight Club*, the body is no longer the privileged space of social citizenship or political agency, but becomes 'the location of violence, crime, and [aggression].'[9] What changes in *Fight Club* is the context enabling men to assault each other, but the outside world remains the same, unaffected by the celebration of a hyper-masculinity and violence that provides the only basis for solidarity.

Fight Club's critique of consumerism suffers from a number of absences that need to be addressed. First, the film depicts capitalism and the ideology of consumerism as sutured, impenetrable, and totalizing, offering few if any possibilities for resistance or struggle, except by the heroic few. There is no sense of how people critically mediate the power of capitalism and the logic of consumerism, turn it against itself, and in doing so offer up daily possibilities for resistance, survival, and democratic struggles. [. . .] No space exists within *Fight Club* for appropriations that might offer critical engagements, political understanding, and enlightened forms of social change. Moreover, consumerism, for David Fincher, can only function with the libidinal economy of repression, particularly as it rearticulates the male body away from the visceral experiences of pain, coercion, and violence to the more 'feminized' notions of empathy, compassion, and trust. Hence, masculinity is defined in opposition to both femininity and consumerism while simultaneously refusing to take up either in a dialectical and critical way.

[. . .]

Second, *Fight Club* functions less as a critique of capitalism than as a defense of authoritarian masculinity wedded to the immediacy of pleasure sustained through violence and abuse. Once again, *Fight Club* becomes complicitous with the very system of commodification it denounces since both rely upon a notion of agency largely constructed within the immediacy of pleasure, the cult of hyper competitiveness, and the market-driven desire of winning and exercising power over others. Third, *Fight Club* resurrects a notion of freedom tied to a Hobbesian world in which cynicism replaces hope, and the 'survival of the fittest' becomes literalized in the form of a clarion call for legitimating dehumanizing forms of violence as a source of pleasure and sociality. Pleasure in this context has little to do with justice, equality, and freedom than with hyper modes of competition mediated through the fantasy of violence. More specifically, this particular rendering of pleasure is predicated on legitimating the relationship between oppression and **misogyny**, and masculinity gains its force through a celebration of both brutality and the denigration of the feminine. [. . .] In other words *Fight Club*'s vision of liberation and politics relies on gendered and sexist hierarchies that flow directly from the consumer culture it claims to be criticizing.

Violence and the Politics of Masculinity

Unlike a number of Hollywood films in which violence is largely formulaic and superficially visceral, designed primarily to shock, titillate, and celebrate the sensational, *Fight Club* uses violence as both a form of voyeuristic identification and a pedagogical tool. Although *Fight Club* offers up a gruesome and relentless spectacle of bare-knuckled brutality, blood-curling, and stylistic gore, violence becomes more than ritualistic kitsch. It also provides audiences with an ideologically loaded context and mode of articulation for legitimating a particular understanding of masculinity and its relationship to important issues regarding subjective agency, gender, and politics. Violence in *Fight Club* is treated as a sport, a crucial component that lets men connect with each other through the overcoming of fear, pain, and fatigue, while reveling in the illusions of a paramilitary culture. For example, in one vivid scene, Tyler initiates Jack into the higher reaches of homoerotically charged sadism by pouring corrosive lye on his hand, watching as the skin bubbles and curls. Violence in this instance signals its crucial function in both affirming the natural 'fierceness' of men and in providing them with a concrete experience that allows them to connect at some primal level. As grotesque as this act appears, Fincher does not engage it – or similar representations in the film – as expressions of pathology. On the contrary, such senseless brutality becomes crucial to a form of male bonding, glorified for its cathartic and cleansing properties. By maximizing the pleasures of bodies, pain, and violence, *Fight Club* comes dangerously close to giving violence a glamorous and fascist edge. As a packaged representation of masculine crisis, *Fight Club* reduces the body to a receptacle for pain parading as pleasure, and in doing so fails to understand how the very society it attempts to critique uses an affirmative notion of the body and its pleasures to create consuming subjects.

[. . .]

What are the limits of romanticizing violence in the face of those ongoing instances of abuse and violence that people involuntarily experience every day because of their sexual orientation, the color of their skin, their gender, or their class status? There is no sense in *Fight Club* of the complex connections between the operations of power, agency, and violence, or how some forms of violence function to oppress, infantalize, and demean human life. [. . .] Nor is there any incentive – given the way violence is sutured to primal masculinity-to consider how violence can be resisted, alleviated, and challenged through alternative institutional forms and social practices. It is this lack of discrimination among diverse forms of violence and the conditions for their emergence, use, and consequences coupled with a moral indifference to how violence produces human suffering that positions *Fight Club* as a morally bankrupt and politically reactionary film.[10] Representations of violence, masculinity, and gender in *Fight Club* seem all too willing to mirror the pathology of individual and institutional violence that informs the American landscape, extending from all manner of hate crimes to the far right's celebration of paramilitary and proto fascist subcultures.

[. . .] The message here is entirely consistent with the cynical politics that inform the film – violence is the ultimate language, referent, and state of affairs through which to understand all human events and there is no way of stopping it. This ideology becomes even more disheartening given the film's attempt to homogenize violence under the mutually determining forces of pleasure and masculine identity formation, as it strategically restricts not only our understanding of the complexity of violence, but also, as Susan Sontag has suggested [. . .] 'dissolves politics into pathology.'[11]

The pathology at issue, and one which is central to *Fight Club*, is its intensely **misogynist** representation of women, and its intimation that violence is the only means through which men can be cleansed of the dire effect women have on the shaping of their identities. From the first scene of *Fight Club* to the last, women are cast as the binary opposite of masculinity. Women are both the other and a form of pathology. [. . .] By constructing masculinity on an imaginary terrain in which women are foregrounded as the other, the flight from the feminine becomes synonymous with sanctioning violence against women as it works simultaneously to eliminate different and opposing definitions of masculinity. Male violence offers men a performative basis on which to construct masculine identity, and it provides the basis for abusing and battering an increasing number of women. According to the *National Center for Victims of Crime*, an estimated six million women are assaulted by a male partner each year in the United States and of these, 1.8 million are severely assaulted.[12] Affirming stereotypical notions of male violence while remaining silent about how such violence works to serve male power in subordinating and abusing women both legitimates and creates the pedagogical conditions for such violence to occur. *Fight Club* provides no understanding of how gendered hierarchies mediated by a misogynist psychic economy encourages male violence against women. In short, male violence in this film appears directly linked to fostering those ideological conditions that justify abuse towards women by linking masculinity exclusively to expressions of violence and defining male identity against everything that is feminine.

Fight Club as Public Pedagogy

[...]

In opposition to films such as *Fight Club*, progressives need to consider developing pedagogies of disruption that unsettle the commonsensical assumptions and ways of thinking that inform films and other cultural texts, particularly those that construct and legitimate certain subject positions, identities, values, and social relations that both celebrate pathologizing violence and render hyper-masculinity as a space in which to reinscribe the hierarchies of gender, race, sexuality, and politics.

[...]

At the very least, the emergence of films such as *Fight Club* suggests that progressives need a new civic language and vocabulary to address the contemporary relevance of culture, politics, and pedagogy. A new vocabulalry is necessary to understand not just how to read texts critically. It is crucial in order to comprehend how knowledge circulates through various circuits of power and promotes images, experiences, representations, and discourses that objectify others and create the ideological conditions for individuals to become indifferent to how violence in its diverse expressions promotes human suffering. This suggests developing forms of public pedagogy that critically engage how language, images, sounds, codes, and representations work to structure basic assumptions about freedom, citizenship, public memory, and history. It also means creating public pedagogies that are attentive to how the material relations of power that produce and circulate forms of common sense can be challenged and transformed on both a national and transnational level. In this instance, public pedagogy links knowledge to power in an effort to understand how to affect social change.

[...]

Any attempt to critically address *Fight Club* and the implications its presence suggests for the changing nature of representational politics must also acknowledge that power is never totalizing and that even within an increasingly corporatized social landscape there are always cracks, openings, and spaces for resistance. *Fight Club* reminds us of the need to reclaim the discourses of ethics, politics, and critical agency as important categories in the struggle against the rising tide of violence, human suffering, and the specter of fascism that threatens all vestiges of democratic public life. Precisely because of its ideological implications, *Fight Club* posits an important challenge to anyone concerned about the promise of democracy, and what it might mean for critical intellectuals and others to take a stand against the dominant media, while providing opportunities to develop, what Paul Gilroy calls in another context, 'minimal ethical principles'.[13] At the heart of such an engagement is the need to accentuate the tension between the growing threat to public life and the promise of a democracy that both remembers the history of human suffering and works to prevent its reoccurrence.

Notes

1. Zygmunt Bauman, *In Search of Politics* (Stanford: Stanford University Press, 1999), p. 65.
2. Zygmunt Bauman, *In Search of Politics* (Stanford: Stanford University Press, 1999), p. 63.
3. Cited in Robert W. McChesney, 'Introduction', in Noam Chomsky, *Profit Over People* (New York; Seven Stories Press, 1999), p. 9.
4. Pierre Bourdieu, *Acts of Resistance* (New York: Free Press, 1998), p. 32.
5. See, for example, Janet Maslin, 'Such a Very Long Way from Duvets to Danger,' *The New York Times*, (Friday, October 15, 1999), p. B14 and Amy Taubin, 'So Good It Hurts,' *Sight and Sound* (November 1999), p. 16.
6. Eleanor Byrne and Martin McQuillan, *Deconstructing Disney* (London: Pluto Press, 1999), pp. 3–4.
7. Homi Bhabha, 'Are You a Man or a Mouse?,' in Maurice Berger, Brian Wallis, and Simon Watson, eds. *Constructing Masculinity* (New York: Routledge, 1995), pp. 57–65.
8. For some excellent commentaries on the politics of masculinity, see R.W. Connell, *Masculinities* (Berkeley: University of California Press, 1995); Maurice Berger, Brian Wallis, and Simon Watson, eds. *Constructing Masculinities* (New York: Routledge, 1995); Paul Smith, ed., *Boys: Masculinities in Contemporary Culture* (Boulder, Colo. Westview Press, 1996).
9. Paul Gilroy, ' "After the Love Has Gone": Bio-Politics and Ethepoetics in the Black Public Sphere,' *Public Culture* 7:1 (1994), p. 58.
10. For a masterful analysis of the complexities of theorizing violence as well as a

critique of its romanticization, see John Keane, *Reflections on Violence* (New York: Verso, 1996).

11. Cited in Carol Becker, 'The Art of Testimony,' *Sculpture* (March 1997), p. 28.

12. Cited from the National Center Victims of Crime website. See: http://207.222.132.10/index%7E1.htm.

13. Paul Gilroy, *Against Race* (Cambridge: Harvard University Press, 2000), p. 5.

PRODUCING MEDIA VIOLENCE

One central question that has preoccupied violence researchers for many years is how media institutional structures, norms and values might contribute to the shaping of media content. For some, this has meant closely following the development of government policies addressing public concern over a range of issues around media violence (i.e. 'video nasties', child pornography on the internet, classification or censorship of violent films, etc.). The aim is to better understand how governments respond to public pressure to control, if not censor, content that they deem to be encouraging audiences to develop violent attitudes and behaviour. Others have focused their efforts on investigating the possible ways in which the economics of media production, that is to say, how specific forms of ownership (concentrated, conglomerate, and global) might persuade some producers in media corporations to increase the quantity, scope and intensity of violent content they produce in order to hold onto and increase their market share. Still other researchers have examined how the socialization of media professionals tends to construct certain norms and values around media violence, grounded in assumptions about gender, ethnicity, class, sexuality, and so forth. This section of the reader is organized to address many of these issues in the chapters that follow.

The section starts off with Christine L. Kellow and H. Leslie Steeves's examination of the role of the government-controlled Radio-Télévision Libre des Mille Collines (RTLM) in the 1994 Rwandan genocide, which involved mass killings both of and by civilians. After briefly considering the historical and political context of the genocide in order to situate their study, the authors then proceed to analyse excerpts from RTLM radio broadcasts and observational accounts interpreting the role played by radio in inciting the genocide. Kellow and Steeves conclude that extreme media dependency in Rwanda set the stage for campaigns to increase ethnic hatred and fear, leading to massacres. Under conditions of dependency, media campaigns appeared to serve as a catalyst for fear and collective reaction effects.

Staying with factual media but turning to examine a very different cultural context, Ann Jemphrey and Eileen Berrington's chapter explores UK press reporting in the immediate aftermath of the Hillsborough disaster in 1989 and the shootings at Dunblane Primary School in 1996. Some press reports of Hillsborough added to the burden of grief of the bereaved and survivors through their hostile portrayal of Liverpool football supporters and the clear suggestion of their culpability for events. By contrast, coverage of the Dunblane tragedy was markedly more compassionate in its tone to those most directly affected. The authors suggest that an explanation of the divergent tone and style of reporting of both these traumatic events involves an examination of the complex interplay between issues relating to the political economy of news production, the role of 'official discourse', hierarchies of media access and regulatory mechanisms governing the press.

From there, attention turns to the world of popular music, where Derek Iwamoto examines some of the ways in which hip hop and gangsta-rap have been publicly criticized for what some consider to be their promotion of personal violence. Taking this issue as the focus for his study, Iwamoto examines the life and work of the late gangsta-rap artist, Tupac Shakur, who was extensively reported in the media not only for his substantial record sales, but also because of his alleged notorious gangsta lifestyle. In Iwamoto's view, US culture defines and glorifies the violent masculinity which underpins gangsta-rap. Since there are only a limited number of masculine role models for men of colour, these men often take on hyper-masculinity as a way of coping with degrading effects of racism on their self-esteem. It has become too easy, in Iwamoto's view, to simply denounce hip hop and gangsta-rap for their violence and objectification of women. One only need look at the mainstream media to see that these same things are a recurrent feature of its output.

In the next chapter in this section, Medhi Semanti's essay explores tensions between the reality of recent political history in the Middle East, where he grew up, and the image of the Middle East in the popular imagination in the US. Focusing most of his analysis on Hollywood movies, Semanti suggests that among the most pronounced reactions to the September 11, 2001 attacks on the World Trade Center in New York was the degree to which press and public alike said that the events 'looked like a

movie'. The images of airplanes hitting the twin towers looked 'too fantastic to be real'. 'There are good reasons', claims Semanti, 'why Hollywood
images resonate with the horrors of September 11 in the public imagination. New York City has long been a favourite disaster site for Hollywood'
film makers. The author considers the possibility that the terrorists knew
and deployed these cinematic images with frightening efficacy. The 'symbolism' involved in their work shows how well they had mastered the power of
the image.

Attention then turns back to factual media, this time focusing on the role
of photography in representing the multiple realities of political violence
and human suffering. In his chapter addressing this topic, David Campbell
explores how the issue of death is imaged in contemporary media accounts
of atrocity. The author rejects the conventional view that sees the media as
replete with images of death and thereby contributing to a lessening in the
power of photography to provoke. Instead, he suggests that the intersection
of three economies (the economy of indifference to others, the economy of
'taste and decency' whereby the media itself regulates the representation of
death and atrocity, and the economy of display governing the details of an
image's production) means we have witnessed a disappearance of the dead
in contemporary coverage. As such, Campbell concludes, the possibility for
developing an ethical politics that exercises responsibility in the face of
crimes against humanity is severely restricted.

The final chapter in this section is based on the premise that the analysis
of some cyberethics problems would benefit from a feminist treatment.
Author Alison Adam argues that both cyberstalking and internet child
pornography are two such areas which have a 'gendered' aspect that has
rarely been explored. In Adam's view, what is needed are careful examinations of new behaviours which surround the creation and use of pornography on the internet in order to understand how far it encourages new
and more liberal modes of sexual expression, and on the darker side, how it
reinforces and even encourages abusive behaviour and relationships, particularly against women and children. The next step in producing a gendered
cyberethics, Adam suggests, will involve bringing the weight of arguments
from the considerable literature on feminist ethics to bear on more of such
problems to produce extended analyses of similar case studies against a
solid theoretical backdrop.

8 | THE ROLE OF RADIO IN THE RWANDAN GENOCIDE

Christine L. Kellow and H. Leslie Steeves

On April 6, 1994, the plane carrying President Juvenal Habyarimana of Rwanda and President Cyprien Ntaryamina of neighboring Burundi crashed under still undetermined circumstances. This event sparked a massive killing spree over the next 3 months that left up to 1 million Rwandans dead and 2 million refugees seeking safety in neighboring Zaire, Tanzania, and Burundi. Most of the killings were carried out by civilian Hutus against their Tutsi neighbors. Age, gender, and occupation were no criteria in the massacres. In hundreds of villages across Rwanda, where previously two ethnic groups had intermingled socially and coexisted peacefully, ordinary people were picking up machetes, sticks, or whatever was available, and killing their neighbors.

Rwandan media have been accused of inciting the hatred that led to violence by using an ethnic framework to report what was essentially a political struggle. They also have been accused of spreading fear, rumor, and panic by using a kill-or-be-killed frame, and of relaying directives about the necessity of killing the Tutsi people as well as instructions on how to do it. Accusers named several small publications, but principally the radio coverage of a single influential station, Radio-Télévision des Mille Collines (RTLM), which was owned and under the control of supporters of Hutu President Habyarimana. A Rwandan human rights activist lamented that, 'The political leaders, as well as all of us, have underestimated the force that RTLM represented . . . that was a lethal error' (Gatwa, 1995, p. 20). Two French journalists stated: 'If Rwandan crimes against humanity ever come to trial, the owners of Radio des Mille Collines will stand at the head of the accused' (Misser & Jaumain, 1994, p. 72).

For the first time since the Nazi war crimes tribunal at Nuremberg, journalists have testified in genocide trials. Western journalists have been among the witnesses. Rwandan journalists are among the accused. Alan Sigg, head of external relations at a United Nations tribunal investigating Rwanda's genocide, stated that international law dictates that journalists who incite killings are guilty. 'For these journalists, it won't be enough to say: "Sorry, I was just a small fish and I had orders." The standards of international law should be the same here in Rwanda' (quoted in Kaban, 1995).

Such accusations obviously pose concerns for politicians, journalists, and human rights organizations. They also pose questions for communication studies. Under what circumstances can and do media play an exceptionally powerful – and heinous – role? Can media incite genocide? Genocide is an extreme and infrequent occurrence. The circumstances and crimes vary enormously. In this essay, therefore, we report a preliminary investigation of the probable role of media, specifically radio, in the Rwandan genocide.

[. . .]

Interpreting the Role of Radio

In this study we interpret the probable role of radio in the Rwandan genocide. Our investigation is preliminary. A comprehensive study, including systematic interviews with Rwandans, remains to be carried out. There is much we cannot know without interviewing genocide survivors, including the extent of resistance to radio broadcasts and other messages inciting violence. Our study should be viewed as an early step in raising questions and suggesting interpretations about radio's role. The method may be described as a qualitative textual analysis, involving a close reading of available radio transcripts. Manning and Cullum-Swan (1994) divided the analysis of documentary data into three broad categories, with subdivisions under each: content and narrative analysis, structuralism, and semiotics. Our study falls into the category of macrotextual narrative analysis, which views texts as 'symbolic action,' and assumes the role of words in representing, dramatizing, and shaping society (p. 465). In this form of analysis, the researcher typically identifies and interprets the ways in which a dominant (hegemonic) societal position is supported in a text. Narrative techniques, including the use of cultural symbols and frames (Entman, 1993) may be interpreted as supportive, or possibly resistant, of dominant messages (e.g., Gitlin, 1980; Steeves, 1997). Research on context is crucial, as texts have little meaning apart from their cultural and political-economic origins.

[. . .]

[O]ur study draws heavily on historical and contextual information, including journalistic accounts and one eyewitness account (M. Bessey, personal communication, April 5, 1997). We acknowledge the assistance of prior writings implicating the role of radio in the genocide and reporting some firsthand observations, (i.e., African Rights, 1995; Berkeley, 1994; Chrétien et al., 1995; Gatwa, 1995; Misser & Jaumain, 1994).

We begin by describing the historical, political, and cultural context of the genocide, as the role of media cannot be assessed otherwise. We then draw on resources noted above, as well as communication theories and studies we reviewed, to narrate the sequence of events in Rwanda and interpret how the government used media, especially radio, as a tool in the genocide.

Historical and Political Context

Before the genocide, the Rwandan political situation was largely ignored by international media (Silverstein, 1994). Even after April 1994, Western reports neglected the politics at the root of the conflict and emphasized an ethnic frame (Wall, 1997). Yet socially, culturally, and linguistically, the Tutsis and Hutus of Rwanda have blended to the point that it is often difficult to identify one's ethnic origin observationally. In fact, it is questionable whether a distinction existed before colonial influence. Ethnicity in Rwanda, many argue, was overshadowed by an economic class system greatly distorted by the needs of various governments. A Hutu could become a Tutsi by the acquisition of wealth (e.g., Newbury, 1988).

[. . .]

The recent crisis in Rwanda began in late 1990, when the principally Tutsi Rwandan Patriotic Front (RPF) invaded Rwanda from Uganda to overthrow the predominantly Hutu regime of Major General Juvenal Habyarimana. They sought a return of the Tutsi refugees and recovery of political power.

[. . .]

By 1993, political dichotomization was extreme. There were only two poles from which everyone was forced to choose. At one end were those who wanted to maintain power at any cost. These included the president, his political entourage, and the army. At the other pole were those working for social and political change, including the RPF. It became impossible for any individual or organization to remain neutral. The media, the churches, the NGOs, and all the people were placed into one of the two camps (Gatwa, 1995, p. 20).

Role of the Media

Just as ethnicity was used as a tool of the government, so were the media. Many media and other forms of communication played a role in the genocide. Throughout 1992 and 1993, for instance, extremists toured the country inciting hate in public meetings (African Rights, 1995, p. 76). The press played a significant role. However, radio is a far more efficient means of reaching large numbers of people, and was much more significant as a catalyst.

[. . .]

To the extent that oral tradition remains strong and illiteracy is widespread, the radio may have great impact. According to Hachten (1974), 'Listeners tend to conceive it as literally the government itself speaking' (p. 396). African leaders, both insurgent and incumbent, have long recognized this impact (Bourgault, 1995; Hachten, 1974; and Mytton, 1983). Additionally, some African countries have strong traditions of hierarchy and authoritarianism, which increase the likelihood of blind obedience to the orders of officials on the radio. Norms of rote obedience were, and continue to be, exceptionally strong in Rwanda (African Rights, 1995, p. 1010; Chrétien et al., 1995, p. 57; Zarembo, 1997). A Tutsi businessman whose family disappeared in the attacks reflected that, 'The popular masses in Rwanda are poorly educated. Every time the powers that be say something, it's an order. They believe someone in political authority. Whatever this person demands, it's as if God is demanding it' (quoted in Berkeley, 1994, p. 19).

[. . .]

Preparation for genocide: 1990–1994

Media had been a pawn of the political and ethnic strife since the beginning of the war in 1990. When the RPF first struck from Uganda, the attack appeared to be 'a skillfully orchestrated media campaign' (Ntibantunganya, 1992, p. 34). Immediately upon the surrounding of Kagitumba in northern Rwanda, press agencies, leading radio stations, and many Western journalists reported the 'new national liberation war' (Ntibantunganya, 1992, p. 34). Although the attack took Habyarimana's government by surprise, the media were waiting at the border. In the early 1990s, media frequently issued appeals to racial hatred. These included official media – Radio Rwanda, the Rwandan Press Agency, and the periodicals, *Imvaho* and *La Relève* – as well as the privately owned paper, *Kangura* (Donnadieu, 1992, p. 28). Radio Muhabura was aligned with the opposite camp as an instrument of the RPF (Gatwa, 1995, p. 19). The accusations and counteraccusations of the media sometimes led to violence. For example, a March 1992 Radio Rwanda broadcast reported that an anonymous source in Nairobi knew about 20 planned assassinations of Hutu leaders by the Tutsis. Many blamed the broadcast when Hutus attacked Tutsis and burned their homes the following day (Dorsey, 1994, p. 145).

Tensions ran especially high after a November 1991 publication of a cartoon in an independent paper, *Kiberinka*, which denounced the government by depicting Habyarimana in priest's robes holding a bloody sacrament. The following day, Radio Nationale claimed that the biased reporting of the opposition press was aiding the RPF. The army pleaded for loyalty:

> They have set up a number of privately-owned papers in Rwanda which vilify our government. They have given financial support to existing papers for the same purpose. Every day their objectives are being realized through these papers, which no longer conceal their intentions, and which work openly for the enemy under the cover of freedom of expression. (quoted in Donnadieu, 1992, p. 29)
>
> [. . .]

Although revolving prison doors helped keep writers in check before April 1994, journalists were at the tops of lists of those who had to be killed during the genocide (African Rights, 1995, pp. 199–210). Deguine and Ménard (1994) declared that journalists have never been murdered in such numbers. Some were killed because of their ethnic backgrounds, but most because of their political involvement and professions (p. 55). One survivor of the massacres was André Sibomana, editor-in-chief of a Catholic weekly, *Kinyamateka*. Hunted as a Hutu, turned 'Tutsi accomplice' for 'thought crimes,' he managed to escape to the hills. 'We made a mistake: we underestimated the force of the propaganda. That was a mortal error' (quoted in Deguine & Ménard, 1994, p. 58). The propaganda relayed by the media was unrelenting and convincing during the years preceding the massacres. Thus psychological conditions for collective reaction effects were put in place.

Radio-Télévision Libre des Mille Collines

Although several Rwandan media have been accused of inciting the genocide that began in April, by far the most influential was Radio-Télévision Libre des Mille Collines (RTLM). Many survivors believe that the extent of the killing and later exodus would not have happened without RTLM. It became the government voice in demanding genocide.

RTLM was started in August 1993 to help ensure President Habyarimana's monopoly of power, and to counteract the RPF's Radio Muhabura (African Rights, 1995, p. 78; Gatwa, 1995, p. 19). Fifty shareholders invested 100 million Rwandan francs (US$1 million at that time). It was backed by the ruling inner circle, some with close links to the extreme Hutu nationalist party, the Coalition for the Defense of the Republic (CDR). Backers included Agatha Kanziga, Habyarimana's wife; Seraphin Rwabukumba, the father-in-law of one of Habyarimana's sons; and Joseph Nzirorera, political spokesman for Habyarimana's party. In Kigali, this group of RTLM backers was sometimes referred to discreetly as 'Habyarimana's wife's clan' (Misser & Jaumain, 1994, p. 73). The president of RTLM's board of directors was Felicien Kabuga, a businessman with close ties to the MRND and related by marriage to President Habyarimana (African Rights, 1995, p. 78). The station was located near the presidential palace and guarded by the government.

RTLM immediately attracted a large audience, especially among young people. Reggae and the music of Zairian, Congolese, and Camerounian artists were popular. However, the music that attracted much of the audience was played during times when fewer listened (i.e., 8–10 a.m. and 6–8 p.m.), so as not to compete with Radio Rwanda (Chrétien et al., 1995, p. 69). Following an attempted coup in Burundi and the execution of President Melchior Ndadaye in October 1993, RTLM started broadcasting openly ethnic commentaries and news. These were often inaccurate and inflammatory (African Rights, 1995, p. 78; Chrétien et al., 1995, p. 69). Announcers employed a popular variety of anecdotes, stories, insults, personal messages, and humorous remarks (Chrétien et al., 1995, p. 47; Deguine & Ménard, 1994; Gatwa, 1995). The station prided itself on *inkuruishushe* – 'hot news.' A political jingle was repeated all day long to keep the public keyed up: 'We have the latest hot news' (Chrétien et al., 1995, p. 69). Hot news included invented attacks and alleged misconduct in the lives of opposition party members (Gatwa, 1995, p. 19).

The station recruited excellent journalists and announcers from both the intellectual milieu and the working classes. Many of RTLM's journalists came from the press. This was part of a larger campaign to minimize the role of the press and increase Rwandans' dependence on government radio. Some publications folded as a result of RTLM's aggressive recruitment campaign (Chrétien et al., 1995, pp. 74–75). The increased role of RTLM, compared to the 'official' government station, Radio Rwanda, requires clarification. RTLM's broadcast range was limited to Kigali, whereas Radio Rwanda's reached the entire country. Radio Rwanda's power had been greatly increased by President Habyarimana, who provided small, inexpensive transistor radios to every region of the country. Radio Rwanda was located directly across from, and had a direct line to, the presidential palace, and was fed by a generator at the palace in case of power outage. RTLM had access to this direct line. Gradually, RTLM started using Radio Rwanda's airwaves more and more, so Radio Rwanda was broadcasting less and less. In this way, Radio Rwanda did not have to take responsibility for extremist hate messages. RTLM could be the main voice of extremist hate, and the official government station could wash its hands of it (Chrétien et al., 1995, p. 70).

Jean-Philippe Ceppi, a Western journalist present before and during the genocide, said he saw everybody listening to RTLM: 'military personnel or peasants, rebels or intellectuals in cafés, in cars, in the fields; the Rwandan people spend all their time with a receiver stuck to their ear' (quoted in Chrétien et al., 1995, p.74). Further, soldiers at every checkpoint had their own radio equipment and sometimes amplified the RTLM broadcasts so they could be heard throughout entire neighborhoods (Chrétien et al., 1995, p. 74). An interview with Media Bessey, a Rwandan who fled after the genocide began, confirmed these observations. Bessey also observed that RTLM's incitement of hatred of the Tutsis usually was in Kinyarwanda, the primary language of the station, whereas broadcasts in other languages – English, French, and Kiswahili – were more innocuous (personal communication, April 5, 1994).

RTLM genocide broadcasts

By April 6, 1994, the day the president's plane went down, RTLM was established as the propaganda arm of the Hutu government. It completely overshadowed Radio Rwanda. Excerpts from the broadcasts of the morning of April 6, gathered by Reporters Sans Frontières (1994), demonstrate that the station was well organized and in place to incite hatred and violence. The station immediately, and throughout the genocide, used a technique of reversal to encourage genocide. The station encouraged Hutu hatred and slaughter of the Tutsis by talking about Tutsi hate of the Hutus. The frequent use of popular culture, biblical references, and familiar historical context strengthened the power of the broadcasts. Additionally, although alternative voices had been largely silenced, RTLM repeatedly told listeners to ignore any oppositional information that might somehow reach them. The following excerpt, from the morning of April 6, 1994, was a dialogue, supposedly between two Tutsis. It was performed as a song, which includes lines of a popular poem titled *I Hate the Hutu*, by the poet and songwriter Simon Bikindi. The song containing phrases from the poem were regularly broadcast beyond April 6 and used to incite hatred (African Rights, 1995, p. 75; Chrétien et al., 1995, pp. 119, 202):

- The truth resists all ordeals, even the ordeal of fire. I talk to people who understand. Me, I hate Hutus. Me, I hate Hutus. Me, I hate Hutus who become Tutsis.
- What are you saying, Mutawa?
- Let me say it. I'm getting things off my chest. I'm going to tell you why I do hate them. Me, I hate the Hutu. I hate their 'Hutuness,' which makes them want to be our equals.
- Here, I agree with you.
- Me, I hate the Hutu. They're very arrogant with each other. The one who becomes important despises the other Hutus even though they are the same. Me I hate the Hutu. The greedy Hutus [take everything, give nothing], and they ignore me. They like to live as slaves, and practice slavery amongst themselves.
- Can we blame you for that [hating them]?
- How lucky we are that there are not many here who want to be our equals.

(Reporters Sans Frontières, 1994, parentheticals added by RSF)

Beginning on April 6, the RTLM broadcasts used the word *work* to mean killing. This terminology resonated with the culture by referring to the theme of communal work. For instance the word *interahamwe*, which means communal work parties, was used in many broadcasts to incite communal killing. The word work also resonated historically, because the same vocabulary was used in the revolution of 1959. Also, Interahamwe was the name of a youth party organization turned death squad during the genocide (e.g., African Rights, 1995, pp. 75–76; Chrétien et al., 1995, p. 305; Reporters Sans Frontières, 1994).

Throughout the weeks following April 6, RTLM relentlessly broadcast orders to exterminate all Tutsis, referring to them as *inkotanyi* (a common reference to the RPF) or as *inyenzi*, a derogatory term meaning cockroaches. According to African Rights (1995),

It told the Hutu population that 'the Tutsis need to be killed,' calling on the population to 'hunt out the Tutsi' and telling them that 'the RPF is coming to kill people; so defend yourselves.' It asked the population 'who will fill up the half-empty graves?' (p. 80)

Chrétien et al., (1995) referenced a June 4, 1994, excerpt: 'We must fight the inkotanyi. Finish them off . . . exterminate them . . . sweep them out of the country . . . because there is no refuge, no refuge then! There is none, there is none!' (p. 305).

Calls to genocide sometimes referred to the Bible, referring to Habyarimana as Christ (e.g., Chrétien et al., 1995, p. 326), and suggesting that the Virgin Mary sanctioned retaliation (p. 160). RTLM also often recalled historical events that would arouse emotion, especially the Revolution of 1959, when thousands of Tutsis were killed or fled, and the 1993 Arusha Accords, which RTLM framed as an abandonment of everything gained in 1959. For instance: 'I am convinced that we are in the middle of a revolution, a revolution similar to that of 1959, one that I think is an ultimate revolution' (Chrétien et al., 1995, p. 138).

Throughout the genocide the inkuruishushe (hot news) announcements emphasized a 'risk and danger,' 'kill or be killed' frame. Many of the directives to genocide employed the above-noted reversal technique, which described alleged, and unsubstantiated, Tutsi atrocities against the Hutus (Berkeley, 1994, p. 19). In fact, none of the Reporters Sans Frontières's excerpts that we translated explicitly instructed Hutus on how to kill Tutsis. Instructions always were framed as Tutsi acts. In this manner, RTLM suggested and legitimized the most extreme cruelties against the Tutsis. For instance, a May 20, 1994, broadcast described Tutsis as gathering guns, killing Hutu families and burning down their houses, then hiding in a church preparing for another attack. Thus, Hutus should destroy the church (Chrétien et al., 1995, p. 195). Sometimes, the broadcasts made up reasons why no Hutu bodies were visible. A broadcast of June 3, 1994, for instance, described how the inyenzi 'grabbed pregnant women, knocked them unconscious with a stick, and sliced open their stomach to extract the fetus, which, in turn, they tossed on the ground and killed after having sliced its stomach open too' (Chrétien et al., 1995, p. 338). Further, mothers and babies killed would be thrown into lakes and rivers like the Kangara, and the bodies would flow to Lake Victoria (Chrétien et al., 1995, p. 338). In another gruesome excerpt from June 14, 1994, the 'inyenzi-inkotanyi' were accused of killing Hutus by dissecting them alive, 'extracting certain organs,' for instance, the 'heart, liver, stomach.' The inyenzi-inkotanyi then ate the bodies. Therefore, no bodies could be found (Chrétien et al., 1995, p. 162).

As suggested in these excerpts, RTLM placed all Tutsis in one category. It blurred the distinction between rebel soldiers and Tutsi civilians (Berkeley, 1994, p. 19). The enemy also included moderate Hutus (e.g., Chrétien et al., 1995, p. 267). Belgians, who had historically aligned themselves with the Tutsis, also were targeted (Chrétien et al., 1995, p. 275; Misser & Jaumain, 1994, p. 74), and Belgian colonial policy privileging Tutsis was occasionally recalled in the broadcasts (e.g., Chrétien et al., 1995, p. 197).

Many broadcasts were directed to particular audiences (e.g., government staff maintaining roadblocks or distributing weapons), or directed attacks on specific buildings (e.g., churches, mosques, or schools) to which refugees had fled. African Rights (1995) reported that more than 300 were massacred in a mosque in the Nyamirambo district of Kigali after RTLM reported their location. RTLM constantly celebrated alleged retaliatory massacres as they occurred (pp. 80–81). According to African Rights (1995), many Rwandans heard RTLM broadcast the names of specific people targeted for killing, but no such broadcasts were recorded (p. 81). Nor do any Reporters Sans Frontières's excerpts we translated name individuals targeted, though a May 28 broadcast named a known Tutsi with a Hutu identity card who should have been killed, but was spared for paying a fine (Chrétien et al., 1995, pp. 192–193).

RTLM did not give clear or consistent instructions about how to distinguish Tutsis. An identity card alone was insufficient, as many with Hutu identity cards had known Tutsi ancestors. Personal appearance sometimes was emphasized as follows: '100,000 young men must be quickly recruited . . . we must kill the inkotanyi . . . the proof that we will exterminate them is that they are only a single ethnic group. Just look at one person, their physique and their physical appearance, look at their cute little nose and then break it' (Chrétien et al., 1995, p. 193). Other times, the radio cautioned that looks can be deceiving: 'Isn't there any Hutu with a long nose? What stops a Hutu from being noble? You understand that it is a shame to think that' (Chrétien et al., 1995, p. 202).

Some transcripts of RTLM broadcasts reportedly targeted people not named, but with metaphors and allusions that were perfectly understandable to the audience (Berkeley, 1994, p. 18). Broadcasts frequently attacked opposition party members, particularly Prime Minister Agathe Uwilingiyimana, who supported the 1993 Arusha agreement and had condemned RTLM. Many broadcasts also condemned leaders of surrounding countries perceived as Tutsi sympathizers, especially President Museveni of Uganda (African Rights, 1995; Chrétien et al., 1995).

RTLM managed to broadcast throughout the massacres. After being destroyed by RPF bombs around April 25, the station was on the air again in only 3 days from a mobile armored car. RTLM was evacuated from Kigali on July 3, and moved to Gisenyi in northwest Rwanda (African Rights, 1995, p. 83; 'Rwanda: Hutu,' 1994).

Although few other media were available during the genocide, RTLM was aware that some Rwandans (e.g., those with short-wave radios) would hear contesting versions of reality. RTLM frequently challenged these other reports. It told Rwandans to ignore them as biased and ill informed. The example below was broadcast May 14, 1994:

> This is nothing but propaganda from White people; we are used to it. However, we can still maintain that the inkotanyi, wherever they have gone, have massacred the Hutus ... after the 200,000 killed, the journalists say that the numbers today rise to 500,000 killed. Where do these other 300,000 come from? These other 300,000 are without a doubt Hutus. .... This war that we are fighting is a very important one ... it is, in fact, a war of extermination, a war started by the inkotanyi – because it is they who have started it with the purpose of exterminating the Hutus. (Chrétien et al., 1995, p. 202)

As the news of the mass killings spread globally, RTLM began to reassure Hutus that their safety was assured by a 'security zone' that would be set up by the French to 'welcome the Hutus fleeing the Tutsi terrorists who have gone crazy and want to decimate them' (Chrétien et al., 1995, p. 282). The Interahamwe would need to hide 'so that the inkotanyi would not pull their eyes out or eat their livers' (Chrétien et al., 1995, p. 337). Thus RTLM continued the fiction of genocidal Tutsi atrocities, while describing safe havens for Hutus. The station encouraged mass exodus at the same time it continued to incite genocide.

Discussion

Today, there are approximately 92,000 inmates in overcrowded prisons (Zarembo, 1997). Many were military personnel; many others were not. They await trial for genocide. Alfred Kiruhura, 29, an illiterate farmer from eastern Rwanda, is one of these. He states:

> I did not believe the Tutsis were coming to kill us, but when the government radio continued to broadcast that they were coming to take our land, were coming to kill the Hutus – when this was repeated over and over – I began to feel some kind of fear.

He admitted that he was a member of the Interahamwe, a youth party organization turned death squad. The stations 'were always telling people that if the RPF comes, it will return Rwanda to feudalism, that it would bring oppression. . . . We believed what the government told us' (quoted in Berkeley, 1994, p. 18). The same confusion is echoed over and over. Emmanuel Kamuhanda, 18, has admitted to killing 15 people in his home village:

> The government told us that the RPF is Tutsi and if it wins the war all the Hutus will be killed. As of now, I don't believe this is true. At the time, I believed that the government was telling the truth. (quoted in Berkeley, 1994, p. 19)

Rwandan theologian Tharcisse Gatwa (1995) believes that, before the 1990s, the genocide would have been inconceivable, and that it took 4 years of psychological preparation (p. 19). This psychological groundwork more typically takes place within the realm of the military, which works on captive audiences of young recruits. The process readjusts the notion of murder to a noble goal, duty, or obligation. Within tight structures and stratified hierarchies of power, soldiers are indoctrinated as to who the 'enemy' is. The deviation in the Rwandan genocide was that much of the killing involved civilians as perpetrators and victims. The radio and other media played a major part in their indoctrination. The radio, long established as the voice of government, defined the enemy as the Tutsis, and inspired an obligation by Hutus to protect themselves and their families. Further, Hutu extremists eliminated via assassination or recruitment almost all Rwandans who might have provided opposing views, including politicians, journalists, human rights activists, and lawyers. Strategies for eliminating or distorting outside information included cutting phone lines, imposing curfews, creating roadblocks, expelling foreign journalists, and encouraging ethnocentric reporting that massacres were hopelessly 'tribal' (African Rights, 1995).

The political dichotomization resulting from media campaigns was in place by the time of the April 6 plane crash and ensured that everyone was in one of the two camps. Mazrui (1990) stated that a 'dichotomous framework of world order perceptions amounts to an iron law of dualism, a persistent conceptualization of the world in terms of "us" and "them" ' (p. 13). One of the most persistent themes of humanity has been the notion of an 'us' and 'them' circumposed over a framework of 'good' and 'evil.' War has been fueled by the myth of an evil enemy: 'We first kill people with our minds, before we kill them with weapons. Whatever the conflict, the enemy is always the destroyer. We're on God's side; they're barbaric. We're good; they're evil' (Keen, 1991, p. 18). In 1994 Rwanda, politics, fueled by the media, had designed the framework for war. This war was framed in ethnicity – Hutu versus Tutsi.

[. . .]

Our study suggests consistency between RTLM radio's role in the genocide, and the dependency and collective reaction frameworks reviewed earlier. Rwandan media's micro-agenda-setting function accompanied Rwandans's increased dependence on media – especially radio – for political information. This function was firmly in place for many years before the ethnic wars that led to the genocide began in 1990. Then, at the macro-agenda-setting level, the media worked to instill a pronounced ethnic fear and hatred that previously had not been part of the everyday culture. The visible role of radio in the outcome of real events, as in attacks on Tutsis following broadcasts about planned assassinations in March 1992, obviously strengthened their power and potential to wage a full-fledged campaign and catalyze genocide. Many media contributed to the height-ened ethnic hatred and encouragement of violence during the ethnic wars between 1990 and 1994. However, when the genocide began in April 1990, nearly all media had been silenced, except RTLM radio.

During the genocide broadcasts, RTLM used several narrative techniques to incite killings. A relentless, 'risk and danger,' 'kill or be killed' frame, and related 'violence' and 'victims' frames, emphasizing gruesome consequences of violence for victims, were the most blatant. Hutus were told repeatedly that the Tutsis were killing Hutus in large numbers, and that Hutus, there-fore, must kill all Tutsis. Instructions on how to kill, perfectly understood, were described as Tutsi acts that demanded retaliation. The use of realistic contextual details and powerful cultural and religious symbols enhanced the credibility of the messages. Further, the absence of other information, group listening, and interpersonal communication contributed to the conditions necessary for the collective reaction effect of the genocide.

Cantril's (1940) study nearly 60 years ago of the impact of Orson Welles's radio drama offers some observations with parallels to the Rwandan situ-ation, although obviously there were vast differences in the timing, context, content, and outcomes of the *Invasion from Mars* broadcast in 1938 Amer-ica and the repeated RTLM broadcasts in 1994 Rwanda. These parallels support interpretations based on both dependency and collective reaction frameworks.

The first parallel is public confidence in the medium of radio. In the 1930s, radio in the U.S. had replaced newspapers as the primary source of news; most had great faith in the validity of radio (Cantril, 1940, pp. 68–69; Lowery & DeFleur, 1983, p. 55). In rural Rwanda, the radio's credibility and importance were even greater. Interpersonal networks were insufficient for political information, illiteracy was widespread, and the population had become increasingly dependent on radio. A second parallel is historical timing. The depression and the threat of another world war had produced political and economic instability by 1938 in the U.S. Rwanda, in 1994, faced much more extreme political and economic pressures. As noted earlier, unstable times may cause actual media effects to be greater. This has been suggested in many studies, including studies in the collective reaction, dependency, and **agenda-setting** traditions (McQuail, 1994). Cantril (1940) further credited the technical brilliance of the Welles drama for the large effect. The use of 'on-the-spot reporting,' the interviewing of 'experts,' and real place names inspired confidence in the validity of the Welles broadcast. RTLM broadcasts during the genocide were similarly well executed. The station employed expert journalists. Broadcasts referred to known historical context, drew on popular culture and religion, encouraged specific actions, targeted specific places, and celebrated specific massacres, adding realism. Cantril (1940) identified the listening situation as important to the interpretation and consequent reactions of the people. Social relationships were important. Many tuned in as a result of the contagion of fear and excitement of people who quickly called each other (pp. 83, 140, 144). In Africa, oral traditions, close ties with kin, and fewer radio receivers mean that group listening is common (Lewis & Booth, 1990, p. 170). People had each other to ignite fear and to corroborate their opinions, judgments, and reactions.

In sum, this study suggests that the strong establishment of media dependency for political information, alongside media's agenda-setting and framing roles, and an absence of alternative voices, can set the stage for unusually powerful propaganda campaigns. Such campaigns, in turn, may spark extreme fear and mass panic with catastrophic outcomes, even genocide. A favorable context for such collective reaction effects (of radio, in this instance) include public confidence in the medium, historic timing, the technical quality and realism of the production, and certain social factors such as group listening, that may support the spread of fear and violence.

[. . .]

[E]xtreme media dependency can set the stage for campaigns to increase ethnic hatred and fear, leading to massacres. Given a favorable historical and political context, fear is a powerful stimulus to panic and the irrational actions that accompany it. Under conditions of dependency, media campaigns may serve as a catalyst for fear and collective reaction effects. Yet, radio dependency and collective reaction effects alone cannot explain atrocities like the Rwandan genocide. They provide part of the interpretation in this instance. However, in-depth interviews are needed to understand further radio's role. Many Rwandans did resist the radio directives and peer pressure to participate in the genocide. Examining the degree of resistance, as well as compliance, should be a focus of further study.

References

African Rights. (1995). *Rwanda: Death, despair and defiance*. London: Author.

Berkeley, B. (1994). Sounds of violence: Rwanda's killer radio. *New Republic, 21*(8–9), 18–19.

Bourgault, L. M. (1995). *Mass media and Sub-Saharan Africa*. Bloomington: Indiana University Press.

Cantril, H. (1940). *The invasion from Mars: A study in the psychology of panic*. Princeton, NJ: Princeton University Press.

Chrétien, J., Dupaquier, J., Kabanda, M., Ngarambe, J., & Reporters Sans Frontières. (1995). *Rwanda: Les médias du génocide*. Paris: Karthala.

Deguine, H., & Ménard, R. (1994). Are there any journalists left in Rwanda? *Index on Censorship, 23*(6), 55–59.

Donnadieu, J. (1992). Rwanda takes its revenge on journalists. *Index on Censorship, 21*(4), 28–29.

Dorsey, L. (1994). *Historical dictionary of Rwanda*. Metuchen, NJ: Scarecrow.

Entman, R. M. (1993). Framing: Toward clarification of a fractured paradigm. *Journal of Communication, 43*(4), 51–58.

Gatwa, T. (1995). Ethnic conflict and the media: The case of Rwanda. *Media Development, 3*, 18–20.

Gitlin, T. (1980). *The whole world is watching: Mass media and the making and unmaking of the new left*. Berkeley: University of California Press.

Hachten, W. A. (1974). Broadcasting and political crisis. In S. W. Head (Ed.), *Broadcasting in Africa: A continental survey of radio and television* (pp. 395–398). Philadelphia: Temple University Press.

Kaban, E. (1995, Sept. 19). Rwanda: Rwanda genocide probers want journalist testimony. *Reuters News Service*, NEXIS.

Keen, S. (1991). Why peace isn't covered. *Media and Values, 56*, 18.

Lewis, P. M., & Booth, J. (1990). *The invisible medium: Public, commercial and community radio*. Washington, DC: Howard University Press.

Lowery, S., & DeFleur, M. L. (1983). *Milestones in mass communication research*. New York: Longman.

Manning, P. K., & Cullum-Swan, B. (1994). Narrative, content, and semiotic analysis. In N. K. Denzin & Y. S. Lincoln (Eds.), *Handbook of qualitative research* (pp. 463–477). Thousand Oaks, CA: Sage.

Mazrui, A. (1990). *Cultural forces in world politics*. London: James Currey.

McQuail, D. (1994). *Mass communication theory: An introduction*. London: Sage.

Misser, F., & Jaumain, Y. (1994). Death by radio. *Index on Censorship, 23*(4–5), 72–74.

Mytton, G. (1983). *Mass Communication in Africa*. London: Arnold.

Newbury, C. (1988). *The cohesion of oppression: Clientship and ethnicity in Rwanda, 1860–1960*. New York: Columbia University Press.

Ntibantunganya, S. (1992). Burundi and Rwanda: Nations at loggerheads. *Index on Censorship, 21*(7), 34–35.

Reporters Sans Frontières. (1994, April 6). *Morning radio broadcast and commentary from Radio Libre des Mille Collines, Kigali, Rwanda*. (Transcription by Herve Deguine and Ivan Duroy; Siegfried Praille, Trans.) [Online]. Available: http://www.intac.com/PubService/rwanda/RTLM/traduction.html.

Rwanda: Hutu extremist radio reportedly broadcasting from Gisenyi. (1994, July 13). *Reuters News Service*, NEXIS.

Silverstein, K. (1994). Guerrillas in the mist: Media misrepresentation of Rwanda. *Washington Monthly, 26*(9), 21–23.

Steeves, H. L. (1997). *Gender violence and the press: The St. Kizito story*. Athens: Ohio University, Center for International Studies.

Wall, M. (1997). The Rwanda crisis: An analysis of news magazine coverage. *Gazette, 59*(2), 121–134.

Wells, H. G. (1993). War of the worlds. In D. Y. Hughes & H. M. Geduld (Eds.), *A critical edition of the War of the Worlds: H. G. Wells's scientific romance* (pp. 41–193). Bloomington: Indiana University Press.

Zarembo, A. (1997, April). Judgment day. *Harpers, 294*(1763), 68–80.

9 | SURVIVING VIOLENCE
HILLSBOROUGH, DUNBLANE AND THE PRESS

Ann Jemphrey and Eileen Berrington

Disaster Reporting

The news media select, define and explain events that comprise 'the news'; they also influence public attitudes and opinion (Eldridge, 1995; Philo, 1995). Journalism combines social, cultural and political functions, by providing information about events beyond the immediate experience of readers and audiences, effectively constituting a 'window on the world'. In this way, news media construct rather than simply reflect events (Coleman *et al.*, 1990), interpreting and reconstructing incidents to create a distinctive 'media reality' (Scraton *et al.*, 1991). Much journalistic practice is routine, with stories sought and reported in accordance with pre-constructed news templates; only the names, dates or locations change. Disaster reporting, particularly in the immediate aftermath, seeks to establish the number of casualties, the apparent cause and the identity of those to whom blame can be apportioned. Additional reporting supplies supplementary information such as the ages and backgrounds of victims and survivors, expert comment, perhaps from the police and other emergency services, psychiatric profiling of perpetrators and statements from neighbours, relatives and friends of those involved. Editors may commission 'colour pieces', with the aim of depicting the community involved. This construction of community identity can be negative, as was the case for Hillsborough, or positive and, perhaps, even idealized, as in the coverage of Dunblane.

Previous studies suggest that the aftermath of disasters is frequently characterized by conflicting versions of what actually happened, and why (Gephart, 1984; Browning & Shetler, 1992; t'Hart, 1993). The aftermath of crises, then, are inherently political, with the ability of one group or interest to impose its account, over and above others, being a function of institutionalized power (Gephart, 1984). Organizations caught up in the crisis are aware of the importance of public relations and have become increasingly sophisticated in 'putting their message across' via the media. Issues of responsibility and liability may, moreover, create tensions between legal advisers and public relations staff 'as to what may be said and when' (Harrison, 1999, p. 171). Consequently, the media are crucially important in determining whether and how they reflect, amplify or minimize such conflict. Key elements in crisis management by the authorities will include efforts to 'frame' the crisis in a particular way. As t'Hart explains, 'Those who are able to define what the crisis is all about also hold the key to defining the appropriate strategies for resolution' (1993, p. 41).

Ericson *et al.* claim that, 'When sources do offer explanations, it is typically in pursuit of their own legitimacy and often through a process of blaming others' (1991, p. 268). It is important, therefore, that the media should remain sceptical of information from official sources when covering disasters (Elliot, 1989), but studies noted above suggest this is highly unlikely, given the routine construction of news (Schlesinger, 1978). Following disasters the media are more reliant than usual on official sources because of information management and other restrictions. The media may also favour official accounts when they dovetail with pre-existing news templates.

Reports of death and disaster inevitably focus on victims; but the media offer highly variable levels of sympathy for victims reflecting the specific context of their deaths. War reporting is one of the most obvious examples, where fatalities on 'our side' are presented differently from 'enemy casualties'. The former are typically depicted as tragic and heroic, or the result of acts of savagery by 'the enemy'. Clearly, the power to define and categorize determines 'who is victim and who is oppressor, the victims being regularly transmuted into savage tormentors of their innocent torturers' (Chomsky, 1994, p. 135). Many deaths in custody are reported with the minimum of publicity, with subsequent enquiry conducted within the parameters of official discourse (see Scraton and Chadwick, 1987). Assumed guilty, some victims are presented as undeserving of public sympathy.

[. . .]

Hillsborough

On 15 April 1989 Liverpool Football Club was scheduled to play Nottingham Forest in the semi-finals of the Football Association (FA) Cup at

Hillsborough, in Sheffield, England. The two clubs had met at the same stage of the competition, at the same ground, the previous year. Although the average attendance by Liverpool supporters was substantially higher than Nottingham Forest's, their ticket allocation on both occasions was for the Leppings Lane end of the stadium and the North Stand, giving them a smaller share of the tickets. This decision was made by the FA on advice from Sheffield Wednesday Football Club and the South Yorkshire Police, in the interests of traffic flow and segregation of rival supporters.

The match was timed to commence at 3 p.m. At 2.30 p.m. there was already a large build-up of supporters outside the turnstiles at the Leppings Lane end of the stadium. The police officer in charge of the area outside the ground became aware that the police were losing control of the situation (Scraton *et al.*, 1995, p. 102), and at 2.47 p.m. he requested that exit gates should be opened to reduce the pressure outside the turnstiles. The Match Commander gave the order to 'open the gates' and at 2.52 p.m. exit gate C was opened wide. During the 5 minutes it was open, some 2000 supporters were allowed to pass through; their tickets were unchecked. A large number of people headed for the tunnel in front of them (Taylor, 1989, p. 12). Although many supporters were unfamiliar with the ground layout, they received no direction and were allowed to enter the already crowded central pens. Just before 3 p.m. the match kicked off. Gate C, which had been closed at 2.57 p.m., was re-opened and supporters continued to enter the tunnel (*ibid.*, p. 13). In the ensuing crush, people could not escape to the emptier side pens because of the constraining radial fences; they could not reach the safety of the pitch because of the metal fencing erected to prevent pitch 'invasions' by 'football hooligans'. Ninety-six people lost their lives, hundreds were injured and thousands traumatized.

Pre-existing negative perceptions of Liverpool combined with journalistic selectivity were crucial in shaping press coverage. National newspapers produced a version of events which clearly implied that Liverpool supporters were responsible for much that happened. Less prominent was commentary which questioned serious issues such as police mismanagement and misinformation; ground safety; adequacy of facilities or the administration and financing of football, Britain's 'national game'.

Initial accounts focused on football hooliganism (an important political issue at the time) and alcohol as primary causal factors, thereby establishing those involved as less-than-innocent victims. With hindsight it has become clear that media coverage, specifically the focus on the behaviour of Liverpool supporters, had significant and debilitating consequences on the lives of the people directly involved. Although the Disaster occurred in Sheffield, much of the tone and style of reporting 'dovetailed into what had become habitual and institutionalised media coverage of Liverpool or Merseyside as the home of numerous "folk-devils" ' (Scraton *et al.*, 1995, p. 226).

Because of the chaos surrounding the Disaster, no police press conference was held until the evening (Coleman *et al.*, 1990). This led to a situation where journalists obtained first reports by taking statements from official spokespeople, most notably representatives from the FA and Sheffield Wednesday Football Club. Early reports, sourced to the Secretary of Sheffield Wednesday Football Club, who was reported as having spoken to 'the police officer in charge' (Coleman *et al.*, 1990, p. 55), stated unequivocally that Liverpool supporters had 'forced a gate', leading to the crush inside the ground (*ibid.*). In cross-examination during the Home Office Inquiry by Lord Justice Taylor (1989, p. 50, para 283), Chief Superintendent Duckenfield, the senior officer in charge, admitted that he had lied about supporters forcing the gates and 'apologised for blaming the Liverpool fans for causing the deaths' (*ibid.*, p. 50, para 285). Despite this denial Duckenfield's initial comment established an internationally reported myth which still persists.

It is clear that the faulty assumptions which usually underpin disaster are seldom overturned simply by the revelatory impact of a disaster's occurrence (Gephart, 1984). Rather, such beliefs may be vigorously defended, and indeed promoted, by those groups who have an interest in so doing. The identification of football supporters with 'hooliganism', which distorted South Yorkshire Police's planning and management of the Semi-Final and its aftermath (Coleman *et al.*, 1990; Taylor, 1989), was not restricted to a single police force. 'Hooliganism' was common political currency, deeply established as a 'way of seeing' within the media, and the population more generally. 'Hooliganism' was a received 'fact' in the law and order panics which so typically accompanied the ascendancy of 'Thatcherism'. The culpability of the police for the Hillsborough Disaster provided a motive for using their substantial public relations resources and consequent privileged influence on the media, to scapegoat others; the 'lens of hooliganism' provided them with the opportunity to do so. This underlay the way that the media was to victimize those who died and the survivors of Hillsborough.

Although early reports included some criticism of police failures, coverage was dominated by allegations of large numbers of fans without tickets attempting to force their way into the ground; themes repeated in national newspapers but expressed in stronger language in the following 48 hours (Coleman *et al.*, 1990). *Evening Standard* columnist, Peter McKay, was clear about where blame lay:

This catastrophe was caused, first and foremost by violent enthusiasm for soccer, in this case the tribal passions of Liverpool supporters.

They literally killed themselves and others to be at the game. (Coleman *et al.*, 1990, p. 61)

An editorial in *The Independent* fuelled these myths surrounding causation:

On Saturday, a mob of 1000's, many without tickets, thought it was alright to try to push into the ground and the police expected violence if they were not admitted. (*ibid.*, p. 61)

This demonization of supporters including, by inference at least, the dead and injured, was a feature of national reporting, although there were differences in emphasis. It was a dominant theme, which although couched in less sensational and offensive language than the tabloid press, none the less extended to the broadsheets. Accounts which identified accurately issues of causation were given comparatively limited space.

In the week following the disaster, allegations regarding supporters' behaviour became increasingly vitriolic, culminating in the infamous *Sun* headline 'The Truth' with its unsubstantiated allegation that: 'some fans picked pockets of victims; Some fans urinated on the brave cops; Some fans beat up PC giving kiss of life' (*Sun* 19 April 1989). These issues featured prominently in a range of national broadsheet and tabloid newspapers (Coleman *et al.*, 1990, pp. 69–70). Reports carried either unsupported allegations from anonymous police officers or quotes from the Police Federation. Although subsequently these reports were found to have been distorted or completely fabricated (*ibid.*), they continue to resurface.

[. . .]

Photographic coverage of the Hillsborough disaster was particularly distressing to the bereaved and survivors. While the operational procedures of live television coverage contributed to the problem, different circumstances applied when editorial decisions were taken which endorsed the publication of close-up photographs of squashed, distorted faces pressed against perimeter fencing, or pictures of those laid out on the pitch.

[. . .]

Public condemnation of the Hillsborough coverage was sufficiently widespread to warrant a Press Council Inquiry, with photographic coverage of the disaster as its primary focus. The Inquiry adjudicated against newspapers' use of close-up photographs of individuals or small groups crushed in the pens, the *Sun* article, 'The Truth' and newspapers' use of stylized logos to identify articles about the disaster (Coleman *et al.*, 1990, p. 106). The adjudication relating to photographic coverage was problematic in that 'broad pictures, taken from a distance, showing a large section of the crowd through a high steel fence, the front row crushed against it' were viewed as serving the 'public interest' and, therefore, publication was within the discretion of editors (*ibid.*, p. 103). The point at issue here seems to be the distance from which photographs were taken. However, for those who lost loved ones:

> there was no such distinction, given that individuals could be identified. For those who survived the crush and were injured, the sight of explicit photographs has been described as like 're-living it all over again'. (*ibid.*, p. 104)

[. . .]

Other major concerns emerging from the Hillsborough press coverage centred on media intrusion at hospitals and funerals, 'doorstepping' the bereaved and the use of deception, including posing as social workers, to gain information about those who died. These practices occurred despite the efforts of the Liverpool City Council Press and Publicity Unit to shield those involved from harassment and intrusion. The Unit's staff operated alongside Liverpool Social Services to liaise between the media and bereaved and injured people, holding daily press conferences and arranging contact with bereaved relatives who wished to speak to the media.

The publication of speculation, misconception and deliberate lies has undoubtedly influenced public perceptions, particularly of the cause of the disaster. In an opinion poll conducted in the immediate aftermath, football supporters, rather than the police, were considered 'mostly to blame' for the tragedy. Despite the persistent struggles of the Hillsborough Family Support Group and those who support their campaign for justice, there remains a strong belief that Liverpool supporters were primarily to blame for the Disaster. Such feelings are clearly evident in Sheffield. In a study conducted by the Liverpool University Football Research Unit, 1350 people in Liverpool and Sheffield were questioned about the tragedy. Over half of the Sheffield respondents 'still blame Liverpool fans'. There remained a perception of 'whingeing Scousers' and some hostility to the researchers' presence in Sheffield (*Daily Post* 15 April 1998). Sheffield newspapers continue to publish material sympathetic to the South Yorkshire Police version of events at Hillsborough and this provides one explanation for the strong levels of anti-Liverpool feeling within the Sheffield area. The research findings document the importance of the media, particularly early reports, in shaping public perceptions of events: 'Clearly views on the subject were formed very soon after the Disaster, and have barely changed in many cases' (Nash and Johnstone, 1998, p. 2).

In summary, the ideological cues resulting from coverage became influential in establishing the context within which the reporting of subsequent formal and legal proceedings took place, most notably the Inquiry conducted by Lord Justice Taylor and the Inquests. This further emphasizes the important and far-reaching consequences of journalism, and the heavy weight of responsibility on those constructing 'the news'.

Dunblane

On Wednesday 13 March 1996, shortly after 9 a.m., a class of 5 and 6 year-old children was in the gymnasium at Dunblane Primary School. Until that day relatively few people outside Scotland had heard of Dunblane, which is situated north of Stirling. Thomas Hamilton, who lived in Stirling, drove to the school that morning, walked into the gym and opened fire with four handguns, before fatally shooting himself. Sixteen children and their teacher were killed and a further 13 children and three adults were injured, many seriously (Cullen, 1996, p. 13, paras 3, 10–11). Only one child emerged from the gym unhurt. The news media picked up the story very quickly, and reporters hurried to the scene. Although initially these were mainly Scottish and English journalists, as the extent of the tragedy was revealed, reporters from the overseas media arrived.

The extent of public shock and grief in the immediate aftermath was overwhelming. It defied belief that so many young children in the safety of their school had been killed or injured in such harrowing circumstances. A Public Inquiry was conducted by Lord Cullen, whose remit was to establish 'the circumstances leading up to and surrounding the shootings' and to make recommendations for public protection from 'the misuse of firearms and other dangers' (Cullen, 1996, p. 1, para 1.1).

The involvement of so many young children, from one school and from one small, clearly defined neighbourhood, was an important influence leading to a more compassionate press response than is usual for an event of such magnitude. For many reporters it was 'a unique event in their memory' (interview) which necessitated different 'rules of engagement', although that is not to suggest that coverage was entirely unproblematic for bereaved families or the community. While there was general press agreement not to interview bereaved families immediately, by the second day most newspapers were seeking interviews. Other criticisms of the press concerned the behaviour of overseas journalists and the overwhelming presence of the world media, gathered in large numbers, within a small, contained location.

Interviews with journalists revealed that in their professional judgement the coverage of Dunblane was exceptional in terms of the level of restraint and sensitivity shown towards the bereaved, the survivors and the community. While this does not diminish the problems created by the sheer numbers of media personnel descending on Dunblane, it does raise questions about why coverage was less offensive or intrusive than the Hillsborough reporting.

The reporting process was described, unfortunately, given the circumstances, in militaristic terms:

> Of course *the rules of engagement* for Dunblane were a one-off . . . and it would be wrong to assume they will come into play the next time there's a Heysel or a Zeebrugge. But it will be a valuable lesson for all concerned: that we, the journalists, the community and the police, can find a way of dealing with it. (British Executive International Press Institute, 1996, p. 12, emphasis added)

When an important story breaks there is little time for reflection in the rush to 'get in there', get the story and transmit it to the newsdesk. Several journalists sent to cover Dunblane spoke of the 'adrenaline rush' accompanying this kind of story, and of operating on 'automatic pilot'. They were under immense pressure, not only to produce copy quickly, but to guarantee quality and accuracy. There was a heavy burden of responsibility, most keenly felt by local reporters:

> it was just nerve-racking, it was just terrifying. You had to make sure you got it right, because you did realize that it was a historic tragedy that you were reporting upon, and you wanted to make sure that the people looking back in years to come and reading your paper would realize that it was right first time and handled properly. It was just like really being thrown in at the deepest of the deep ends. (interview)

A senior journalist with many years of experience, including editorial, emphasized that reporting Dunblane was untypical because of the level of restraint exhibited by reporters, including those from the national tabloids. Journalists were 'influenced by the need not to offend the sensibilities of the people who had suffered. That's the last thing you want to do, to add further pain' (interview).

Editors and proprietors possess significant discretionary power over the tone and style of reporting. With Dunblane, most editors were immediately aware of the sensitive nature of the story and warned staff against causing offence or adding to the distress of those involved. Unusually, the police issued a strong warning to news editors against continued press invasion of victims' families' privacy (Harrison, 1999, p. 209). There was also a consensus among broadsheet editors that staff would not 'doorstep' bereaved people during the immediate aftermath. Reporters' reaction to this decision was one of overwhelming relief. Concern was expressed for those tabloid reporters:

> awaiting instructions from the paper which would tell them whether they should, against official advice, approach the parents and relatives of children who had died or been wounded. They looked washed out – and I offered up private thanks that I was no longer exposed to that kind of pressure. When the word came through from an unforgiving newsdesk, it was to the effect that they should begin knocking on doors. (Magnus Linklater in British Executive International Press Institute, 1996, p. 29)

[. . .]

Journalists had mixed views about the contribution of such interviews to understanding the tragedy. Some felt that parents needed to talk, that it was cathartic, a commemoration of their loved one. An interview with a bereaved mother (*Daily Record* 15 March 1996) focused on the one victim who did not appear in the class photograph, which featured prominently in news reporting. Several journalists said that they would not have felt comfortable with the assignment, but acknowledged that it had been handled with tact and sensitivity, and was a powerful and moving piece of journalism. There was, however, a general feeling that little or nothing could be added to people's knowledge of an event by stating the obvious. Early interviews with bereaved families would have led to 'the kind of stock grief-stricken clichéd responses you would expect' (interview) and, therefore, would not have been worth the anguish caused.

[. . .]

With Dunblane there was an immediate, unequivocal focus of blame – the gunman, the 'Monster' (*Daily Mail* 14 March 1997). Much of the coverage focused on him and his activities, to the point of demonization. Although later reports considered related issues such as gun control and, to a much lesser extent, school security, demonization of the gunman continued, including his alleged links with paedophile groups. There was little encouragement or incentive for journalists to explore issues such as militarism, machismo, male physique and athleticism or the bullying that is often a feature of boys' and young men's social relations. This focus on discipline and stamina was echoed in Hamilton's scouting and boys' clubs activities. His alleged obsession with guns and shooting linked in with these physical and militaristic themes. There was an attempt to raise these issues in an in-depth *Scotland on Sunday* investigation (17 March 1996) but, in general, as with the Hillsborough [. . .] example discussed earlier, it was easier for newspapers to frame the event in terms of individual pathology. In this case it was particularly easy to do. Hamilton was a 'nutter', a sexual deviant with a dysfunctional family background. He was from outside the community, literally (his home was in Stirling, not Dunblane) and meta-phorically (he was 'evil' and 'inhuman').

Scottish journalists voiced their frustration at the lack of informa-tion from senior police officers about the granting of firearms licences to Thomas Hamilton. The issue gathered momentum in the first few days after the disaster and continued beyond the publication of the **Cullen Report** in October 1996. One journalist felt information was withheld because 'there must have been a lot of police officers extremely worried about what was rebounding' (interview). Press interest mounted:

> The world's press were on the run with this and a lot of significant developments were starting to break – starting to name names – and all of a sudden, the Lord Advocate issued a statement which basically threatened that any paper that continued along this line would be in court for contempt. (interview)

In effect the Cullen Inquiry made many issues *sub judice*. The press interpreted the ruling as a ban on interviewing anyone who might be a witness at the Inquiry. This was described by one Deputy Editor as 'a classic Joseph Heller Catch 22 situation – you don't know if they'll be a witness until you have interviewed them!' (interview). The ruling was widely per-ceived as a 'gagging device' which allowed important lines of inquiry to 'run cold', maintaining official accounts of causation and inhibiting investigative journalism.

Conclusions

The complex relationships between media ownership, the market and the routines of journalistic practice exhibit many tensions. In disaster report-ing, journalists are under pressure to produce copy quickly and to drama-tize and sensationalize what are already dramatic stories. In complying with these editorial demands, the rights and expectations of bereaved people and survivors are endangered, and sensitivity is sacrificed to the business and managerial imperatives of publishing. Commercial issues relating to the press must be addressed, particularly the growing concentration in ownership and control. Further, in the battle for increased sales there is an important shared responsibility between proprietors, editors, journalists and the public. As long as there is a market for prurience, sensation and intrusion, newspapers will try to meet that public demand.

There is tension between journalists' need for information and the privacy of those affected by the event. Some people want to talk to the press, and may derive some comfort from a sensitively handled interview; others wish to be left alone. The 'therapeutic' nature of post-disaster interviews was commented on by several journalists. While this may be true, the press has a responsibility to those interviewed to present the published material in an appropriate tone and style of reporting, use of language and accompanying visuals. But it must be acknowledged that some people want to read intrusive material. Despite rhetorical protests against 'tabloid excesses', sensation and intrusion sell newspapers: 'There is a certain kind of hypocrisy out there among the punters' (interview).

With the exception of the local press, there was relatively little restraint exercised in Hillsborough reporting, particularly by the 'red-top' tabloids. Indeed, as one tabloid editor stated at the time, 'we cannot be expected to give over-riding consideration to the Hillsborough families in our coverage' (Coleman et al., 1990, p. 90). There were significant differences in the ages and backgrounds of Hillsborough victims, but Merseyside, with all its attendant negative imagery, was the perceived focal point. The deaths had occurred at a crowded football match, at a time when there was widespread concern over violence among spectators at games. The disaster was televised live, with sports commentators reporting what they thought they saw and what they were being told. Events were viewed through 'the lens of hooliganism' (Coleman et al., 1990) and reported as such. Although the victims' and survivors' class backgrounds differed, as football supporters they were perceived as traditionally working class.

The events surrounding Hillsborough required the police to protect themselves from blame and, therefore, to become active in scapegoating supporters. They had a ready set of prejudices, indeed a 'mindset' about football supporters which could be incorporated into their media-management strategies. These perceptions were mobilized to locate supporters' behaviour as the primary cause of the disaster, rather than to consider failures in crowd safety measures, emergency facilities, disaster planning and, particularly, the policing of the match.

The legacy for those directly affected by the disaster was one where grieving relatives, trying to deal with their loss, were faced with an additional burden of defending the innocence of loved ones. Survivors, many of whom had witnessed profoundly traumatizing events and suffered terrible injuries, were themselves subjected to having the 'finger of blame' pointed at them. This was fuelled by a style of press reporting which demonstrated an inability to distinguish between the hype surrounding recent football hooliganism debates and crucial issues of crowd safety. Instead, sections of the press were too eager to jump on the 'anti-Liverpool bandwagon', effectively 'rubbishing' the region and its inhabitants. This style and tone of reporting have meant that, despite many years of dogged campaigning by the bereaved people and survivors of the Hillsborough disaster to counteract the myths relating to blame and causation, misconceptions continue to influence debate.

By contrast, the deaths and injuries at Dunblane were the result of a criminal act whose perpetrator was dead. Undoubtedly this was a significant factor influencing the nature of reporting. Although there was criticism of Central Scotland Police Force over gun-licensing procedures, the police were not under the same pressure to justify their actions as had been the case after Hillsborough. Again, however, the police were in a position to shape reporting of the event through their control of journalists' access to information, shielding themselves from censure over Hamilton's guns and ammunition licences. The damage limitation process was aided by the prohibition of certain avenues of investigation by the Lord Advocate for the duration of the Cullen Inquiry. This prevented journalists from following up important lines of wider issues and concerns.

The 'demonizing' of Thomas Hamilton diverted press attention away from the police failure to question the number of weapons and amount of ammunition for which licences were issued. Newspapers made little attempt to digress from the simplified version of events by including analysis of threatening aspects of masculine behaviour. Hamilton's assumed deviation from the dominant, heterosexual masculine form and his alleged paedophile tendencies fitted a pre-existing template for reporting sexualized violence.

The press may have been conscious of the far-reaching and enduring effects of the campaigns by those offended by insensitive reporting such as Hillsborough. There was concern over the possible introduction of statutory measures to regulate and control the press if the industry's self-regulatory mechanisms were seen to be failing. However, 'Dunblane in itself was so horrific that sensationalism was unnecessary' (interview).

Overall there were few complaints about the Dunblane coverage, with most sections of the British media operating with sensitivity and restraint. The victims were mainly very young children, members of a small, defined locality and community. This facilitated the setting-up of measures to protect the privacy of those involved. Further, this was an event with which people could readily identify, as was demonstrated by the worldwide response. Class and status played a part, while local journalists' preconceptions were crucial to reporting. Many Scottish reporters lived in or had close personal links with the City, and their beliefs became part of the ideological context within which Dunblane's identity was constructed and disseminated to a worldwide audience. It was, in effect, a self-fulfilling prophecy: journalists observed and recorded what they expected to find – a safe, close-knit, middle-class community, quiet and 'respectable', 'the last place on earth' where an act of such violence would have taken place.

This positive and sympathetic portrayal of the community had an effect on the behaviour of journalists, particularly the British press. The agreement to leave before the funerals took place and not to cover them was described by journalists as 'unprecedented' (interviews). Such a decision by the national media is unusual, although the local press may be more sensitive to community feeling, as was evidenced in the decision by Merseyside newspapers not to intrude at the Hillsborough funerals.

Debates around privacy and intrusion continue to be driven by dramatic events and the complaints of high-profile figures, royalty and celebrities (see Scraton et al., 1998). There remains an urgent need for considering and putting into place effective safeguards against intrusion and the means of redress for ordinary members of the public who, often through no fault or desire of their own, become newsworthy: especially those caught up in personal tragedies. At present, the **Press Complaints Commission** (PCC) Code of Practice simply states that in relation to intrusion into grief or shock inquiries must be carried out and approaches made 'with sympathy and discretion', and publication must be handled 'sensitively at all times'. This is clearly inadequate, while the lack of effective sanctions further fails to protect the bereaved and survivors of disasters. Editors and proprietors possess considerable discretionary power over the tone and style of reporting. Ethical considerations and codes of conduct are easily sacrificed, with little fear of censure, in the harsh competitive climate of newspaper publishing. The reality for survivors and those bereaved by disasters is that they experience press intrusion at a time when they are least able to protect themselves or seek redress.

[. . .]

Unless the press demonstrates a collective will to honour the spirit of self-regulation in relation to the reporting of grief and sudden bereavement, it is unlikely that ordinary individuals will receive better protection from intrusion. Dunblane demonstrates that reporting can be conducted with relative restraint, and the needs of the bereaved and survivors acknowledged within that process. Instances of good practice must be built upon and incorporated into future reporting of disasters or sudden, dramatic deaths.

[. . .]

References

British Executive International Press Institute (1996) *Dunblane: reflecting tragedy.*

Browning, Larry and Shetler, Judy (1992) 'Communication in Crisis, Communication in Recovery: a postmodern commentary on the Exxon Valdez disaster', *International Journal of Mass Emergencies and Disasters* 10, pp. 477–98.

Chomsky, Noam (1994) *World Orders, Old and New*, London, Pluto.

Coleman, Sheila, Jemphrey, Ann, Scraton, Phil and Skidmore, Paula (1990) *Hillsborough and After: The Liverpool Experience*, Liverpool, Centre for Studies in Crime and Social Justice/Liverpool City Council.

Cullen, The Hon. Lord (1996) *The Public Inquiry into the Shootings at Dunblane Primary School on 13 March 1996*, Scottish Office, Cmnd 3386, October 1996.

Eldridge, John (Ed.) (1995) *Glasgow Media Group Reader*, Volume 1, London, Routledge.

Elliot, Deni (1989) 'Tales from the Darkside: Ethical Implications of Disaster Coverage', in Lynne Walters, Lee Wilkins and Tim Walters (Eds) *Bad Tidings. Communication and Catastrophe*, Hillsdale, New Jersey, Lawrence Erlbaum.

Ericson, Richard, Baranek, Patricia and Chan, Janet (1991) *Representing Order: Crime, Law and Justice in the News Media*, Milton Keynes, Open University Press.

Gephart, Robert (1984) 'Making Sense of Organisationally Based Environmental Disasters', *Journal of Management* 10, pp. 205–25.

Harrison, Shirley (Ed.) (1999) *Disasters and the Media: Managing Crisis Communications*, Houndmills, Macmillan.

Nash, Rex and Johnstone, Sam (1998) *Hillsborough Attitudes Survey Report*, Football Research Unit. University of Liverpool.

Philo, Greg (Ed.) (1995) *Glasgow Media Group Reader*, Volume 2, London, Routledge.

Schlesinger, Philip (1978) *Putting Reality Together: BBC News*, London, Constable.

Scraton, Phil, Berrington, Eileen and Jemphrey, Ann (1998) 'Intimate Intrusions? Press Freedom, Private Lives and Public Interest', *Communications Law: Journal of Media and Telecommunications Law* 3, pp. 174–82.

Scraton, Phil and Chadwick, Kathryn (1987) *In the Arms of the Law: Coroners' Inquests and Deaths in Custody*, London, Pluto.

Scraton, Phil and Chadwick, Kathryn (1991) 'The Theoretical and Political Imperatives of Critical Criminology', in Kevin Stenson and David Cowell (Eds), *The Politics of Crime Control*, London, Sage pp. 161–85.

Scraton, Phil, Jemphrey, Ann and Coleman, Sheila (1995) *No Last Rights: The Denial of Justice and the Promotion of Myth in the Aftermath of the Hillsborough Disaster*, Liverpool, Liverpool City Council.

Scraton, Phil, Sim, Joe and Skidmore, Paula (1991) *Prisons Under Protest*, Milton Keynes, Open University Press.

Taylor, Rt. Hon Lord Justice (1989) *The Hillsborough Stadium Disaster 15 April 1989: Interim Report*, Home Office, Cmnd 765, London, HMSO.

t'Hart, Paul (1993) 'Symbols, Rituals and Power: The Lost Dimensions of Crisis Management', *Journal of Contingencies and Crisis Management* 1, pp. 36–50.

TUPAC SHAKUR

UNDERSTANDING THE IDENTITY FORMATION OF HYPER-MASCULINITY OF A POPULAR HIP-HOP ARTIST

Derek Iwamoto

Hip hop and 'gangsta rap' have been widely criticized by the public as well as in numerous political (liberal and conservative) and religious arenas (Fried, 1999). Many critics declare that this type of music is not only extremely vulgar, but that it also perpetuates physical and sexual violence, and promotes sexism. One gangsta rapper in particular, the late Tupac Shakur (1971–1996), is said to encapsulate all of the above. In the mid-1990s he was one of the most popular rap stars. Even today he is considered a legend in the hip-hop world, and has sold over 22 million records, posthumously.

During his time, Tupac was constantly in the media limelight – for the revenue he generated selling millions of records and for the chaotic gangsta life he led. He was arrested a number of times for assault and was charged with sexual abuse, for which he was sentenced to four and a half years in prison (though he was bailed out shortly after). During the 1994 trial Tupac was shot five times and robbed of $40,000 worth in jewelry (Shakur, 1998). He was also one of the main instigators of the East Coast-West Coast rivalry in which the two sides often 'dissed' or put each other down. On September 7, 1996, he was again shot. This time it was fatal – seven days later Tupac passed away. His murder, along with that of fellow gangsta, Notorious B.I.G. (who was shot half a year later), received national attention, thus fueling concerns about 'this controversial music genre' (Farley, 1997, pg. 149).

These tragic examples heighten the concerns felt by religious and political groups which do not recognize:

any positive influence of rap music and have focused solely on the violent content of some rap and on the negative and harmful influences these lyrics may have . . . the press has focused primarily on rap music being harmful to society and being responsible for increased rates of murder and violent crime. (Fried, 1999, pg. 706)

But to others, his fans, under his rough and tough image and despite his gangsta lifestyle, Tupac is regarded as a sensitive and progressive person who was more knowledgeable than most people gave him credit for. It is my contention that Tupac was and still remains misunderstood by his critics. This paper will examine a number of his songs that represent specific aspects of his mentality and value system, including those that express his awareness of and empathy for women, as well as address issues such as racial oppression, and inner-city problems.

The Hyper-masculine Front

Fuck you and your fucking mama!
We going to kill all you motha fuckaz!

. . . All you mother fuckaz!
Fuck you, die slow, my 44 make sure all your kids don't grow!
You mother fuckaz can't be us or see us! ('Hit Em Up!')

These apparently extremely threatening lyrics in 'Hit Em Up' were directed toward arch-rival East Coast record company Bad Boy Records. Not only does this song indicate the immense tension of the bicoastal rivalry (between Bad Boy and Death Row Records – Tupac's label), but also it is symbolic of the hyper-masculine front that was characteristic of Tupac and other urban city and gang members. If viewed superficially, the song's message obviously will be seen as unacceptable and deviant by most people's standards. However, in its cultural context, the threatening vitriol of songs like 'Hit Em Up' is much more a matter of style than of substance. Our focus should not solely be on Tupac's violent expression, or even his violent actions, but also on social implications and the variables that shape violent behavior and feelings among gang members.

The most significant and often overlooked factor that perpetuates and reinforces extremely violent and competitive behavior is the way that the American culture defines and lionizes masculinity. The typical and idealized portrayal of a 'real man' in this society suggests that the male has to be anti-feminine – in the sense that he should be the opposite of what is traditionally considered feminine. In other words, he should not display openness, vulnerability or emotional expressiveness. A real man should be tough, aggressive, daring and have physical strength (Brannon, 1976). Men also are encouraged to have an 'emphasis on sexual prowess, sexual conquest, and sexual aggression' (Lindsey, 1997, p. 225). These characteristics often lead to behavior that is reflected in the disproportionably high number of males who commit crime.

Understandably, young men of color often enter into hyper-masculine behaviors to combat the degrading effects of racism on their self-esteem. Since 'there is little diversity of images in the media culture' (Katz, 1999), there is great pressure to conform to the limited masculine ideals provided by the cultural media. Moreover, due to poverty and neglect, black youth are often deprived of and under-exposed to cultural influences that differ from those of the mass media, which often negatively or one-dimensionally depict black men as villains, murderers, gang members, boxers (Latinos), and martial artists (Asians). These one-dimensional portrayals are indicative of the limiting stereotypical attitudes, beliefs, and values of the larger society.

One only needs to look at ethnic charicatures in recent movies to see how hyper-masculine characteristics are promoted in America today. In our society, men in general are socialized through movies (*Terminator 2, Casino, Die Hard*) to prove their manliness, as well as through sports and television shows (*Walker, Texas Ranger*). The superstar actors and sports figures have always been tough, aggressive, ultra-competitive, strong, and dominating. Given the fact that the media provide minorities only minimal and stereotypical representations of males, many minority youth exaggerate these hyper-masculine characteristics in their public personae, in order to prove themselves and be respected by their peers.

The 'Cool Pose'

Tupac, as well as many other young urban youth, adopted what Richard Majors and Janet Billson have termed the 'Cool Pose' (1992). The cool pose is a way for these young men to assert their manhood through a 'set of related physical postures, clothing style, social roles and social scripts, behaviors, styles of walk, and context and flow of speech, types of dances, hand shaking, and attitudes that are used to symbolically express masculinity' (Majors & Billson, 1992). The cool pose is a way to show others that a person has power and that 'everything is under control' (White and Cones, 1999, p. 92).

According to White and Cones (1999), the cool pose is also a coping mechanism to combat racial oppression, besides a way of validating one's manhood. There were times in Tupac's adolescence when he was teased by his peers due to his 'pretty-boy' and 'artsy' image (Dyson, 2001). This bothered him so much that he began to take on a more tough and manly attitude. Later, this pose was shown explicitly through many of his songs, in particular, 'Hit Em Up.' In the song he portrayed himself as a tough, hard, fearless and imposing figure. His brutally aggressive anger and threatening tone were intended to intimidate the members of Bad Boy and its affiliates:

We do our job, you think you the mob?!
We the motha fuckin mob!! ('Hit Em Up!')

The Thug Life

The gangster or mob image was one of the main cultural-media influences on the formation of Tupac's identity. Many rappers, including Tupac, took on the glamorized gangsta/mobster delineation of *The Godfather* series and other Mafia movies (Katz, 1999). The gangsta culture or 'thug' lifestyle reinforced Tupac's hyper-masculine values (gang values of toughness, fighting ability) and established his identity. Just as cultural-media forms such as mafia-type movies glamorize that particular lifestyle, Tupac too, made marked efforts with his media image to glamorize and legitimize the 'thug life,' in spite of the fact that the urban dwelling gang members are stigmatized by society. Through his music and videos, Tupac projected a sense of 'coolness' about living this lifestyle.

Moreover, Tupac himself wanted more than anything else, to be affiliated with the thug life: '*When I die/I wanna be a living legend/Say my name/Affiliated with this motha fucking game (No more pain).*' It is often noted that the collective hardships of witnessing death and the constant struggles poverty conditions tend to create a tight and unified bond among gang members (Mason, 2000). Likewise, Tupac's thug friends or 'crew' became a type of extended family to him, providing friendship, family, money, and security:

I hung around the thugs
And even though they sold drugs
They showed a young brotha love ('Dear Mama')

Tupac emulated the mob images of power, toughness, ruthlessness, elite, ruggedly classy, wealthy, and womanizing ways. Due to the lack of a positive and consistent male role model and father figure in his life, this was an idealized model – exaggerated toughness and physical strength that equated to respect and power – all characteristics of what he considered as defining a real man. What makes Tupac a special artist, cherished by the audience with whom he had much in common, is that while maintaining his cool pose and hypermasculinity, he was able in songs such as 'Dear Mama,' to express with truth and directness, as in an open letter, the effects of his father's abandonment on his emotional life:

> *Ain't no body tell us it was fair*
> *No love for my daddy because the coward wasn't there*
> *He passed away and I didn't cry*
> *Cause my anger wouldn't let me feel for a stranger*
> *They say I am wrong and I'm heartless*
> *But all along I was lookin for a father but he was gone.*
> ('Dear Mama')

Tupac the Ladies Man

Another outlet for Tupac to prove his manhood was through his hyper-sexual actions. Sex – how sexually active he could be, how many women he could sleep with – was a way for him to validate himself and to prove to others how manly he was. This is expressed in the song, 'How Do You Want It?':

> *Your body is banging baby*
> *I love it when you flaunt it*
> *Time to give it to daddy-anytime*
> *Tell me how you want it?*
> *. . . Tell me is it cool to fuck?*

His sexual prowess, displayed in song and in life, showed not only how manly he was, but also was a symbol of his social status. Tupac's ladies-man image and 'rider' (player of women) status ensured his cool pose and also was a sign of his immense success. The status of ' "livin" in the fast lane' signified his achievement – how a poor, inner-city black youth was able to overcome, against all odds, the economic and societal constraints placed on a person of that background.

But in conjunction to Tupac's hypermasculine attitudes and beliefs, were positive messages of communal change and mental liberation, passionately expressed through songs like 'Keep Your Head Up' and 'Dear Mama.'

These songs are narrations of the struggles and intense hardships people in poverty face on a daily basis. Through these songs, he elucidated inner-city conditions, such as the lack of accessibility to a decent education and low societal expectations for success. He elaborated upon the 'social and economic structures of society that systematically deigns [*sic*]' (Katz, 1999) these groups.

The song 'Keep Your Head Up,' demonstrates Tupac's awareness and concern, not only for the numerous problems of the inner city, but in particular for problems related to women's position and the treatment of women. 'Keep Your Head Up' provides hope and support for women, as well as constructively criticizing males in general:

> *I wonder why we take from our women*
> *Why we rape our women?*
> *Do we hate our women?*
> *I think it time to kill for our women*
> *Time to hear our women*
> *Be real to our women*

This passage, toward the end of the song, questions the societal violence against women and brings hope for solidifying relationships between partners. Even though he uses the phrase 'kill for our women,' which could be seen as antithetical to the holistic message of the song, 'kill,' again, is a hyper-masculine expression that may be interpreted as a reference to how men, or anybody, should do anything and everything in order to improve the conditions of and relationships with women.

Tupac realized that most men do not respect and listen to women – and he knew that men's actions and behaviors toward women are often times not right. He was aware of the cycle of sexism and the negative implications if it is not broken: '*If we don't we have a race of babies/That hate the ladies that make the babies.*'

Another prevalent theme in Tupac's lyrics is the salute to single mothers and those who are on welfare. This was very important to him, because he himself was raised by his mother, who was on welfare:

> *I give a holla to all my sisters on welfare*
> *Tupac cares . . . Don't nobody else care*
> *I know they like to beat you down a lot*
> *When you come around the block*
> *Brothers clown a lot*
> *Please don't cry; dry your eyes never let up . . .*
> *Girl keep your head up* ('Keep Your Head Up')

Though there have been many welfare reforms by the government over the past decade, the stereotype of the lazy, careless (black) 'welfare queen' has yet to be dispelled. Tupac knew that the stigmatization and pre-conceived notions about people on welfare are generally based on myth. Throughout his childhood his family was on welfare, even when his mother worked, so he was aware that government subsidy is much needed by families and that laziness has nothing to do with it. He realized that ultimately these people on welfare did not want to be dependent on the monthly government check. The theme of female empowerment is also evident in 'Keep Your Head Up.' Tupac knew there are a lot of dysfunctional and abusive (physical and mental) relationships:

> When he tells you ain't nothing
> Don't believe him
> And if you can't learn to love him
> You should leave him
> Sister you don't need him
> I ain't try to gash up
> I just swallow how I see it

In this passage, he stressed the fact that many men often degrade women by telling them '*you ain't nothing*,' which is a way for them to assert their dominance and bolster their own low self-esteem. The women may start believing in this false notion because they are financially and mentally dependent, and thereby continue to accept the conditions of abusive relationships. Tupac felt that these women needed to break out of being dependent on this type of relationship, and that they could find significant and positive people. He states 'I ain't trying to gash,' meaning, he was not generalizing (or dissing) about all the men out there, but only to those who knew what they were doing was wrong.

Continuing with the female empowerment theme, Tupac goes on to express his support for the right of women to choose whether or not they want a baby.

> . . . that will hate the ladies that make the babies . . .
> Since a man can't make one
> He has no right to tell a women where and when to create one
> So will the real men get up
> I know you fed up ladies
> Got to keep your head up ('Keep Your Head Up')

Here his pro-choice stance is clearly evident: women should have power over their own bodies. Oftentimes, based on the traditional male point-of-view, men believe they should get what they want (whether they want to be a father or their partner to have an abortion) even though it may conflict with the interests and desires of their partner. Again, Tupac was communicating a message to women to empower themselves with the right to choose, and encouraging males to respect women's choice.

Empowering his people as a whole and celebrating his blackness is also evident in this song. The first passage maintains:

> *Some say the blacker the berry the sweeter the juice*
> *I say the darker the flesh*
> *The deeper the roots* . . . ('Keep Your Head Up')

Embedded in this metaphor is the message that black is beautiful. Tupac believed that people with dark complexions are closer to their 'African' roots in a sense. The significance of skin color for Tupac is that blacks who are light skinned probably have some white in them (this could happen due to interracial marriages), but what he resented is that many of these people are lighter due to the rape of their ancestors by the white slave owner.

Tupac was obviously very concerned with race and often highlighted the tumultuous race relationships in America. Songs like 'White Man's World,' and 'Young Black Male' provide evidence of his concern. These songs probably make the white listener uncomfortable because they provoke a sense of guilt and discomfort – which was his desire – for he wanted America to 'come to grips with our attitudes towards race' (Mason, 2000, p. 123).

Tupac was definitely proud of being black and his idol, Marvin Gaye, facilitated his appreciation of being black:

> *I remember Marvin Gaye used to sing to me*
> *He had me feeling that black was the thing to be* . . .

Marvin Gaye seemed to be one of the few positive male role models in his life. Gaye is referenced positively in a number of his songs (e.g., 'Thug Mansion,' 'Keep Your Head Up'). Even though Gaye was not a direct acquaintance, it was apparent that Tupac felt a sense of pride, empathy, and appreciation for black culture through Gaye's songs. Tupac did not have many outlets where he could feel this and Gaye's music was one of the few. Gaye was definitely a source of empathy and inspiration for Tupac, but his main source that he looked up to and sought guidance from was his mother.

In both 'Keep Your Head Up' and 'Dear Mama,' he acknowledges her love, tenderness, affection, and commitment to raise him right. In fact, 'Dear Mama' was a sole dedication to his mother, which is uncommon in this genre of music. He wanted to show that he understood and appreciated all that she did for him. He realized that '*She nearly gave her life/ to raise me right.*' Even when she had a substance abuse problem, his admiration and love for her remained strong. '*Even as a crack fiend Mama/ You always a Black Queen Mama . . .*' Despite her problem, Tupac knew she was always there and that she provided as much as she could for him. Through his love and respect for his mother – the person he admired the most – he was able to gain a sympathetic awareness of the social conditions black females especially had to face.

In 'Dear Mama' and 'Keep Your Head Up' Tupac expressed his knowledge of what poor urban women have to go through. Another theme central to 'Keep Your Head Up' (as well as many of his other songs) was the effects of the racial oppression that many African Americans still have to face daily. This agony was voiced metaphorically: '*It seems like the rain will never let up/ I try to keep my head up and still keep from getting wetta.*' That was what Tupac felt and observed growing up in rough urban conditions. Little do the critics of Tupac mention the fact that he would sensitively address his community's lack of fundamental resources, such as adequate schools systems and health care, that middle-class people take for granted. He expressed his political agenda through his music, by criticizing major societal institutions and the government (Martinez, 1997) for being apathetic in regard to the urban communities' needs. '*They got money for wars/ But can't feed the poor.*' Tupac was angered by the political and economic system since it systematically hindered his community's progress. He wanted his people to recognize all of the injustices so they could break out of the negative cycles in the ghettos. Though he knew it would be a seemingly endless battle, he truly believed he and his community must fight through by keeping 'all of their heads up.'

Critics of hip-hop view music videos and self-righteously condemn the genre because of the violence and the blatant sexuality it contains. Yet everyday, women are objectified and sexualized on television, in movies and in the magazines at the checkout line of the local grocery store. It is time for America not to blame particular individuals or a particular music genre for these excesses, but to take a close examination of the fundamental structures of our society – a political economy that deprives people of basic necessities and opportunities – and a media culture that constantly reinforces negative values and promotes anti-social behavior. The hip-hop artist Tupac Shakur was a tragic example of a talented young black man, beautiful and damaged, who combined some of the worst excesses of the society that produced him with an acute awareness of the corrupt nature of that society.

References

Brannon, Robert (1976) *The Male Sex Role: Our Culture's Blueprint of Manhood and What It's Done For Us Lately*. In the 49% Majority. MA: Addison-Wesley.

Dyson, Michael Eric, *Holler If You Hear Me: Searching For Tupac Shakur* (New York: Basic Civitas Books, 2001).

Farley, Christopher J. (1997) 'Rhyme or Reason? (Murders of Rap Stars Tupac Shakur and Notorious B.I.G.),' *Time*, 149, 44–48.

Fried, C. B. (1999) 'Who's Afraid of Rap: Differential Reactions to Music Lyrics,' *Journal of Applied Social Psychology*, 29, (4), 705–721.

Katz, Jackson, dir., *Tough Guise* (1999). Video.

Lindsey, Linda L., *Gender Roles: A Sociological Perspective* (Upper Saddle River, NJ: Prentice Hall, 1997).

Majors, Richard & Billson, Janet, *Cool Pose: The Dilemma of Black Manhood in America* (New York: Lexington, 1992).

Martinez, T. (1997) 'Popular Culture as Oppositional Culture: Rap and Resistance,' *Sociological Perspectives* 40, (2), 265–286.

Mason, J. R. (2000) 'Pop Perspective: If Nietzsche Watched TV for Tragedy,' unpublished manuscript (Eugene: University of Oregon, 2000).

Parham, Thomas A., White, Joseph L., Adisa Ajamu, *The Psychology of Blacks: An African Centered Perspective* (Upper Saddle River, NJ: Prentice Hall, 1999).

Riggs, Marlon, dir., *Black is . . . Black Ain't* (1998) Video.

Shakur, Tupac, *Vibe* (New York: Three Rivers Press, 1998).

White, Joseph L. & Cones, James H., *Black Man Emerging* (New York: W. H. Freeman and Company, 1999).

Partial Discography

Tupac Shakur (1993). *Strictly 4 My N.I.G.G.A.Z.* Interscope records.

Death Row's Greatest Hits (1996). Death Row.

IMAGINE THE TERROR OF SEPTEMBER 11

Medhi Semanti

The monstrosities that took place on September 11 must be condemned unequivocally. There is no apology possible that would excuse the perpetrators, and we must hope those who still live will be brought to justice. But if we are to prevent such atrocities in the future, we cannot rest with condemnations and swift verdicts. We must seek a collective understanding of this atrocious act within its political, historical, and popular contexts. At the juncture of these contexts is a tension that I wish to explore here: the tension between the reality of recent political history in the Middle East, where I grew up, and the image of the Middle East in the popular imagination in America. Let me start with Hollywood.

Perhaps I seem untoward in advancing a connection between popular imagination and the political realities that contextualized the most egregious terrorist attack the United States has ever experienced. But consider: among the most pronounced reactions to the September 11 terrorist attacks in the United States was the degree to which press and public alike said that the events 'looked like a movie.' The images of those airplanes slicing the twin towers of the World Trade Center and their implosion looked too fantastic to be real. There are, of course, good reasons that Hollywood images resonate with the horrors of September 11 in the public imagination. New York City has been a favorite disaster site for Hollywood. In contemporary films such as *Godzilla*, *Armageddon*, and *Deep Impact*, Manhattan was the stage for disaster and mayhem. Quite recently in *The Siege*, major Manhattan landmarks were blown to pieces by a group of Arab terrorists. The image of New York City buildings imploding has enough fictional credibility to have framed the reality of September 11 for many of us.

I wish to consider the possibility that the terrorists knew and deployed these cinematic images with frightening efficacy. The 'symbolism' involved in their work shows how well they had mastered the power of the image. Is it possible that these terrorists appropriated Hollywood's disaster blockbuster? One critic suggested that the terrorists illustrated they could 'out-Hollywood Hollywood.' In this sense, geopolitical and cultural worlds came together on September 11 in a lethal and monstrous moment of blockbuster imagination.

What complicates the relationship between the cinematic and the real is the mediation of the televisual. In the eyewitness coverage of the horrors of the World Trade Center's destruction, the conscience of television, as Avital Ronell once put it, operated through the auspices of video. One film critic wondered whether the television networks aired the disaster scene in a wider view in order to avoid showing people waving for help in the windows of the massive buildings or jumping out of the windows. Was this all too real for network television obsessed with 'reality-based' television?

The relentless mediatization of the events of September 11 as an American phenomenon charts two directions for further discussion: the extent to which the American experience of the geopolitical is constructed through the cinematic and the mediation of the geopolitical by the televisual. On the one hand, there has been a proliferation of narratives of the Middle East in popular culture after the cold war. On the other hand, the American experience of recent conflicts has been highly mediatized (e.g., the Gulf War, Kosovo). The televisualization of international relations, the so-called CNN effect, is another element of this American phenomenon. And there is more: the shrinking public sphere, the erosion of formal politics, a notoriously ill-informed and internationally insulated population, and a journalism driven by ratings and fixated on the private (Monica Lewinsky and Gary Condit sagas as reality-based television). One begins to see why, in America, the geopolitical coordinates are lost in favor of the cinematic and the televisual.

A brief look at post-cold war Hollywood's Middle East reveals the contours of the interpretive framework provided by Hollywood for the geopolitical world and its synergistic relationship to the rhetoric of U.S. foreign policy. After a period of détente and 'peaceful coexistence' with the Soviets, America was perceived as a 'weakened superpower.' Signs of this weakness were seen in the presidency of Jimmy Carter ('soft' on communists), the 'loss' of Nicaragua and Iran, the invasion of Afghanistan by the Soviet Union, the hostage crisis in Iran, and Carter's preoccupation with human rights. Ronald Reagan's 'resurgent America' was the 1980s response. This was a call for the projection of American power around the globe. Aggressive militarism and a host of foreign interventions ensued. In that political-cultural context, 'terrorism' and its current cultural figurations emerged as potent ideological signifiers of the era. It was designated as 'Russia's secret weapon.' There was a call to fight the evil empire. Mujahedin in Afghanistan, including Osama bin Laden, were recruited and hailed as 'freedom fighters.'

Hollywood responded to Reagan's call by producing a series of films depicting resurgent America (e.g., *Top Gun*). Another series of films in the 1980s involved invasion and rescue scenarios set in the Middle East (*Iron Eagle, Delta Force*). During the 1990s, Hollywood remained preoccupied with terrorism. However, the end of the Reagan era and its aggressive foreign policy and the conclusion of the cold war ushered in a new 'kinder, gentler' sensibility in the cultural depiction of terrorism. In *True Lies* (1994), 'family values' rhetoric was incorporated in a sitcom caricature that turned the whole family into terrorist-killing heroes. *Executive Decision* (1996) reflected the 'kinder, gentler' sensibility by developing a self-reflexive stance in its depiction of the Middle Eastern terrorists. *The Siege* (1998) embodied the 1990s multicultural liberal and 'politically correct' sensibility in the way it at once deployed the conventions of depicting the Middle East and apologized for doing so.

The Siege deserves closer examination for the way it explicitly addressed Middle East politics, U.S. foreign policy, and the cultural anxieties about America's relationship with the Middle East. *The Siege* was released in 1998, a decade after the Reagan presidency and in the aftermath of the Oklahoma City bombing. Given this historical framework, it was in a position to tap into the political and cultural anxieties of the post-Reagan era and the political currents during the Clinton presidency. Although it is admittedly a run-of-the-mill thriller, *The Siege* may have unwittingly anticipated some of the political issues we now face with regard to the Middle East crisis. Its plot departs from other terrorist films of the decade in that its 'Arab' terrorists were actually trained by the CIA. Samir, the leader of the active terrorist cell in New York City, is a Palestinian character with whose help the CIA had been recruiting fighters to overthrow Saddam Hussein's government. Because of a 'policy shift,' reminiscent of George Bush's abandonment of anti-Saddam forces at the end of the Gulf War, the fighters were left on their own for Saddam to slaughter. Some of them survived and are now here in New York City 'doing what CIA taught them to do,' which is to make bombs and so on. The film also tries to give terrorists political grievances (e.g., Palestinians 'seduce you with their suffering'). The film's sympathetic portrayal of Samir's predicaments depicts terrorists as the victims of their own circumstances. Embodying the sensibility of the 1990s, the film portrays terrorists who play the role of the victim as 'good terrorists' and those who refuse to play the role as 'bad terrorists.'

The Siege as a piece of pop culture (even if it is caught up in **Orientalist** visions) is redeemed by the way it raises critical questions, in sharp contrast to much mindless militarized discussion of terrorism in the press in the aftermath of September 11. It taps into anxieties about our actions in the Middle East, expressing fears that, as Mohiaddin Mesbahi put it, we Americans can no longer pretend to live in a bubble – removed from our actions and policies overseas. The advantage of addressing the political context of terrorism is that it gives us a proper historical perspective, as opposed to the comfortable and feel-good talk about the 'clash of civilizations' (or what Edward Said has called 'the clash of ignorance'). Its good terrorist/bad terrorist dichotomy raises questions about our relationship with our 'allies' ('good Muslims') and our 'enemies' ('bad Muslims').

How are we to understand the notion of 'good terrorists' as victims? The contemporary universalization of the narratives of victimization, as Slavoj Žižek would say, achieves two objectives. On one hand, compassion with the local victims of the third world frames the liberal-democratic (mis)-conception of today's great divide between those who are with 'us' or those who are with 'them.' On the other hand, victimization of the liberal democratic subjects renders the Third World Other a threat.

It is here that the figure of 'the Muslim' becomes crucial in the cultural political discourse of the 'West.' Today, the Taliban cave dweller perfectly and conveniently embodies the image of the Muslim as premodern and backward. If there is anything haunting 'Western civilization,' it is the specter of 'Islamism.' The spectral nature of this phenomenon, as Bobby Sayyid argues, stems from the manner in which the Muslim presence in the eyes of the West has tended to be grounded in a 'hauntology' that easily conflates Muslims and ghosts (Jacques Derrida once said that the future belongs to ghosts and that modern image technology only increases the power of ghosts). Does this not explain the difficulty in finding and punishing the enemy in Afghanistan? You cannot kill a ghost, not with daisy cutter bombs (the largest conventional bombs ever made being dropped on Afghanistan), not with cluster bombs, and not even with peanut butter and jelly sandwiches.

More important, the figure of the Muslim is a symptom of the new world order. 'The international community' does not exist (the 'impossibility of society,' in Ernesto Laclau's language), and the Muslim is its symptom. The internal negativity, the immanent social antagonism in the midst of the 'community,' is projected onto the figure of the Muslim. In other words, the West is fighting its own demons in the Middle East. Incidentally, Žižek saw the war against Slobodan Miloševic in these same terms.

'Why do they hate us?' became the burning question after September 11. The mirror image of the innocence inherent in that question was the simple answer 'They hate us because we are the shining beacon of democracy.' And the mirror image is always bound up with blinding narcissism. Although I now live in America, I continue to visit the Middle East. I have yet to meet anyone who 'hates' America because of the freedom its citizens enjoy. Allow me to be autobiographical for a moment, not to express longing for narcissistic narratives of victimization, but to speak from the position of an embodied experience of American Middle Eastern policies. As a seventeen-year-old I lost many of my friends during the Iranian revolution that ousted the Shah's brutal regime. In America, the Shah was depicted as a 'moderate' monarch and an 'ally.' American had no 'clash of civilizations' with the Shah. When Saddam Hussein entered into a war with Iran after the revolution, the United States supported him. Millions of Iranians, including many families I know, experienced the war firsthand. The United States supported Saddam Hussein and had no 'clash of civilizations' with him. As someone who now lives in America, I am convinced that they do not hate us because we have freedom. They resent our policies that deprive them of their freedom when we support repressive regimes.

Recently, President George W. Bush pronounced that things would be better if the United States could explain itself to the people of the Middle East. Apparently, he thinks the crisis in the Middle East is a PR problem. This explains why recently Charlotte Beers, a former advertising guru known as 'the queen of branding,' was appointed as undersecretary of state for public diplomacy and public affairs. It was reported that her task is to create an 'ad campaign' with the aim of 'pitching' American views to 'young Muslims' in the Middle East. Contrary to the racist belief rampant in the media that people in the Middle East respond emotionally to images, they are savvy critics of image mongering. If the current U.S. propaganda of images fails to resonate with them, it is because they live the realities the images tend to obscure or dramatize. Palestinians, living under siege with quotidian terror as the ambience of their lives, need no camera crew to tell them which way the terror is coming. As Jean-Luc Godard used to say, 'This is not a just image. It is just an image.'

Only a just approach to the Middle East will bring about a safer future. We will never be able to convince fanatics about anything. But a just approach to the Middle East creates a context in which they wither away. Such an approach entails, among other things, promoting democratic values and norms in all parts of the Middle East, withdrawing our support of repressive regimes, and a just conclusion of the Palestinian question. Such an approach would deprive fanatics of their murderous cause and their legitimacy and legitimize our claims to the ideals we profess as a nation.

If the popular imagi*nation* is a reservoir of our hopes and fears, it may tell us via a discomfited pedagogy how the geopolitical reality is, in Meaghan Morris's words, 'media-shaped.' If the buoyant consumption of Hollywood terrorist blockbusters by Middle Easterners shows human capacity for conflicted subjectivities, and lessons in how to be a good sport, it gives me a unique vantage point. As I see on the screen the grotesque image of myself/body, and the place where I grew up, I can almost grasp the aesthetic power in violent conditions. Moreover, that image may just allow the American 'spectator' to see that I live a relation between that grotesque image and my self/body – one that is maintained in everyday life by the gaze of many others. This is a curiously ambivalent position: I may just be seen for my humanity or I may be subject to 'racial profiling.'

In the end, I am happy to be here, even if on September 11 I witnessed too closely the awesome violence I thought I left behind in a land and time far from here and now. September 11 may have seemed like a movie to some people, but to me it was a call to realism, one that Bertolt Brecht saw clearly must challenge us to realize a just and practical humanity: 'Realism is an issue not only for literature: it is a major political, philosophical, and practical issue and must be handled and explained as such – as a matter of general human interest.'

HORRIFIC BLINDNESS
PHOTOGRAPHIC IMAGES OF DEATH IN CONTEMPORARY MEDIA

David Campbell

Lynched Bodies
Southern trees bear strange fruit,
Blood on the leaves and blood at the root,
Black bodies swinging in the southern breeze,
Strange fruit hanging from the poplar trees.
Pastoral scene of the gallant south,
The bulging eyes and the twisted mouth,
Scent of magnolias, sweet and fresh,
Then the sudden smell of burning flesh.
Here is fruit for the crows to pluck,
For the rain to gather, for the wind to suck,
For the sun to rot, for the trees to drop,
Here is a strange and bitter cry.

(Margolis 2000, p. 15)

Strange Fruit evokes a practice and an era that seems long past in contemporary America. As one of that country's first protest songs, Billie Holiday's 1939 recording of Abel Meerpol's poem is a seminal statement of racial politics in American popular culture that has had many iterations. Numerous performers after Holiday have re-recorded the song or sampled its lyrics, academics draw upon it in college classes, judges cite it in legal cases, and politicians quote from it in speeches, though none have altered the original words. All seek to draw on its unvarnished portrayal of **lynching** in the South to make a statement about contemporary social issues (Margolis 2000).

Lynching has returned to America's consciousness in recent years, and this return recalls moments in the genealogy of *Strange Fruit*. Around 1930 Meerpol was exposed to a graphic photograph of a lynching that took place in Marion, Indiana. Haunted for days by the image he wrote a poem about it, first published in January 1937 with the title 'Bitter Fruit' before being set to music and performed by Holiday in 1939 (Margolis 2000, pp. 36–7). Photographs have again provoked an awareness of lynching, this time through an exhibition and publication entitled *Without Sanctuary* that records the death, mutilation and display of people lynched in the United States between 1883 and 1960 (Allen *et al.* 2000). The images compiled in *Without Sanctuary* record the deaths of only a small fraction of the total number of victims of extralegal violence. Between 1882 and 1968, there were 4,742 recorded lynchings of African Americans, with the likelihood of a larger number of unrecorded deaths. While the victims of lynchings were predominantly black, they also included Jews, white convicts, Hispanics, Native Americans, and Asian and European immigrants, the latter of whom were sometimes murdered because of their union involvement. And while the majority of lynchings took place in the South of the US, they were not unknown in the North, as evident by the lynching which inspired Meerpol to write his poem (Litwack 2000).

The photographs in *Without Sanctuary* are brutal. The victims' bodies have been broken, burnt, disfigured, dismembered and strung up. The experience of their death confronts the face of the viewer. No concession is offered to emotional sensitivity, and there is no use of abstraction or metaphor to signal what has taken place. Even more notable than this directness is the fact that many of the photographs show the white men who carried out the lynching standing around the corpse. Aware of the camera, they are sometimes accompanied by a crowd of on-lookers, including women and children, taking in the scene. The lynching photographs thus display the killers and their victims in the same manner as hunting pictures depict hunters showing off their prey.

The impunity with which lynching mobs recorded their deeds shocks us today, but are a product of the social circumstances surrounding the killings. Lynching, amazingly, was a social ritual attended by vast numbers of people who created a festive atmosphere. Often the killing would be advertised in advance. For example, *The Memphis Press* of 26 January 1921 carried on its front page a report in which it was said the crowd 'May Lynch 3 to 6 Negroes This Evening' (Smith 2000). As a public occasion, lynching required photographic recording to ensure its status as an historical event persisted long after the victim's death. The photographers who produced the lynching photos were not simply spectators to the killing but part of the lynching, integral to the public status and social meaning of the murder. The images they produced were printed in newspapers and made into postcards (often embossed with the photographer's name and business address) that circulated throughout the United States, sometimes as warnings to potential victims, but in many instances simply for use as personal notes (Allen *et al*. 2000). One journal recorded the various elements at work in an account of the 1915 lynching of Thomas Brooks in Fayette County, Tennessee:

> Hundreds of kodaks clicked all morning at the scene of the lynching. People in automobiles and carriages came from miles around to view the corpse dangling from the end of the rope . . . Picture card photographers installed a portable printing plant at the bridge and reaped a harvest in selling postcards showing a photograph of the lynched Negro. Women and children were there by the score. At a number of country schools the day's routine was delayed until boy and girl pupils could get back from viewing the lynched man. (Litwack 2000, p. 11)

The lynching photographs were popular because they functioned as 'icons of white supremacy' that dramatized the racial and gendered cleavages of a social order in which 'blacks were terrorized, white women were vulnerable, and white men were on top, invulnerable and free' (Rushdy 2000, p. 70). However, these photographs could also serve other purposes, especially when appropriated by the victim's family. When Emmet Till was lynched in 1955, his mother did not hide her son's body and insisted on an open-casket funeral so the congregation could witness for themselves the violence of Till's death. Photographs of Till's battered body were published, and readers of black-owned newspapers in which they appeared wrote in support of their appearance and the anger they generated. A photo essay of the Till lynching in *Jet* magazine mobilized many young African-Americans, some of whom went on to become student leaders in the civil rights movement (Rushdy 2000, pp. 72–3). This appropriation demonstrated that by the late 1950s shifting social attitudes manifested in the civil rights movement had altered the way lynching pictures were produced, used and read. As the public ritual of lynching attracted more widespread condemnation, photographs of the murders became increasingly rare. Moreover, those that did appear showed the once confident killers now hiding behind masks and avoiding public display of their quarry (Rushdy 2000, p. 73).

Not that the act of lynching itself disappeared. In June 1998, three white men killed James Byrd in Jasper, Texas. Reporting on the trial of one of these men, John William King, in February 1999, *The Guardian* described via the prosecutor's statement how Byrd died:

> The three men picked up Byrd, an unemployed, disabled vacuum cleaner salesman, at 2.30 am, as he was walking home along Martin Luther King Boulevard.

They stopped for cigarettes before heading out of town and down a secluded logging track. It was there that they beat him, sprayed his face with black paint, and chained him by his ankles to the back of Berry's pick-up.

Prosecutor Guy James Gray told prospective jurors that Byrd was 'not only alive, he was conscious at the time, and he was using his elbows and body in every way to keep his head and shoulders away from the pavement.'

He told them how Byrd was alive during the three-mile death ride until his head and shoulder hit a storm drain and he was beheaded. His torso was left in front of an African-American cemetery 'as some form of a message'. (*The Guardian* 1999)

Pictures of Byrd's body were shown by the prosecution to the jury during the trial of King. According to Ashraf Rushdy (2000, p. 74), those photos were unsparing in the suffering they conveyed: 'his knees, heels, buttocks, and elbows were ground to the bone; eight of his left ribs and nine of his right were broken; his ankles were cut to the bone by the chains that attached him to the truck. A pathologist testified that Byrd's "penis and testicles [were] shredded from his body" ', all prior to the moment he was decapitated and finally died. Jurors found the pictures horrendous, and had to force themselves to look (Rushdy 2000, p. 77). The images were central to the trial in East Texas, and helped a jury of eleven whites and one African American find King guilty and sentence him to death (Vulliamy 1999).

The function of the photograph in provoking different understandings of atrocity like lynching – from the original postcards collected in *Without Sanctuary*, to the image that led Meerpol to write the words for *Strange Fruit* and inspire other civil rights activists, and the police pictures that led to the conviction of James Byrd's killers – provides a platform from which to review some of the important issues surrounding the imaging of death in contemporary media. This article begins to address some of these issues by asking, how is death portrayed in accounts of contemporary atrocity, and what are the political effects of such representations? Are the pictures we witness able to engender a response sufficient to the crime portrayed?

Disappearing Bodies

To begin, let us return to the contemporary lynching of James Byrd in Texas. Despite the shocking story of Byrd's killing, and its evident newsworthiness, none of the photographs of Byrd's body have ever been published in the public domain. Indeed, few if any in the media have even seen the photographs of Byrd's body used by the prosecution in the trial of his killers. As a result, the accounts of Byrd's lynching have been illustrated with word pictures drawn from the trial testimony, or made graphic with photographs that represented indirectly the crime. The most direct American example of this was the *Boston Globe's* picture of dried blood on the road along which Byrd's torso had been dragged (Rushdy 2000, p. 75).

The disappearance (or non-appearance) of Byrd's body demonstrates that the media does not seize upon every opportunity for the display of death. It has become something like conventional wisdom to argue that media depictions of horror are commonplace, testimony to a commercially driven **voyeurism** by an immoral (if not amoral) industry. However, the fact that the public has been prevented from seeing the evidence of a contemporary lynching indicates otherwise. The failure to publish the available photographs of Byrd's body suggests the media, rather than always being voracious and voyeuristic, is at least sometimes cautious and discreet:

> Displays of the horror and hurt of bodies are a measure of the industry's mix of prurience and rectitude. The press errs on the side of caution in depicting death and destruction. It is careful to write more detail than it dares to show and often uses the metonymic power of photographs to remove harm from flesh to objects. When the press decides to picture bodies, the imagery tends (with notable exceptions) to be restrained. Newspapers do not revolt audiences for the sake of it. On the contrary, disgust forms a small part of the stock-in-trade and papers use it sparingly. (Taylor 1998, p. 193)

Indeed, as John Taylor makes clear in his analysis of how the British media handle horror, this apparent sensitivity when it comes to imaging death stems from industry standards governing the pictorial representation of death and violence. These standards reflect in part informal norms of decency and propriety. But they also involve formal codes devised and regulated by bodies in the UK such as the Press Complaints Commission and the Broadcasting Standards Commission. These formal codes are said to represent readers' and viewers' preferences, and readers and viewers generally want to be shielded from images of violence – 'I don't want to see these photos while I eat my breakfast', is a standard complaint in response to even the coded images of horror that newspapers use (Mayes 1999; Rushdy 2000, p. 74). These standards are aided and abetted by in-house regulations enforced by media producers themselves, such as the **BBC's Producer's Guidelines**, which prescribe the particular circumstances under which images of death could, if at all, be used (Taylor 1998, p. 5). All in all, these standards have effectively enshrined a system of censorship by and for the media with respect to the depiction of death and violence.

The disappearance of Byrd's body can be seen as part of a larger trend in the media coverage of violent death. The Vietnam War gave rise to numerous images of bodily violence, many of which were credited with changing public perceptions of the fighting and, eventually, undermining public support for American involvement. Notable in this respect were Eddie Adam's photograph of a Viet Cong suspect being executed on the streets of Saigon, and Huynh Cong Ut's 1972 photo of the Vietnamese girl fleeing a napalm attack. However, since the Vietnam War, governments have gone to considerable lengths to make such images, and the reactions they might provoke, difficult to come by.

[. . .]

This combination of official reporting structures and media sensibilities combined in the coverage of both the US-led invasions of Afghanistan (2001) and Iraq (2003) to further entrench sanitized reporting. From the mix of embedded journalists and cameramen, official briefings, violence against reporters in the field, government bans on filming particular events (such as the ceremonies at Dover air force base in Delaware to mark the return of American dead from Iraq) and media sensitivity about the portrayal of death has been constructed an image of these wars that is far from complete (Campbell 2003b, pp. 102–107, 2004, pp. 59–64; Lewis 2003; Wells 2003; Younge 2003).

Seeing Bodies

Why should we lament the disappearance of the dead? Why do we need to see the body? In the case of war reporting [. . .] one concern is that the disappearance obscures the fact that, 'War is real and war is terrible. War is a bad taste business' (Taylor 1998, p.75). But over and above this generalized sense of truth telling as an essential part of the portrayal of violence, we need to see the corpse and what was done to it, as Rushdy has argued with respect to James Byrd, because, 'It is possible that pictures of graphic violence still have to power to make an impression' (Rushdy 2000, p. 77). Just as the images of Emmet Till provoked an awareness of violence against African Americans, and an African American response to that violence, so too the photographs of James Byrd 'could also turn the tides of history once again.' How those photographs are used, and what context is chosen in which to deploy them, are vitally important. But their absence from the public domain has not diminished racism, prevented Byrd's killers becoming martyrs of the white supremacy movement, or stopped copycat crimes (Rushdy 2000, p. 76; Harden 1998). If their absence has not prevented such negative consequences, we can say that their presence through publication could not have been held responsible for furthering these problems. Publication could thus have had some positive benefits for the struggle against racism. Likewise, images of war dead could be the basis for mobilization against atrocity and violence. In this sense we can endorse Rushdy's view that 'images of terror – used responsibly – can foster a climate in which terror is no longer tolerated' (2000, p. 77).

This sense of the continuing power of photographs to provoke runs counter to the common view that proliferating pictures of atrocity creates compassion fatigue. This view holds that because the media is supposedly awash with images of death and horror, readers and viewers have been increasingly turned off by such pictures, and official policy has become increasingly resistant to calls for action. In Susan Moeller's (1999, p. 35) estimation, 'threatening and painful images cause people to turn away, and since the media prioritize bad-news images, this tendency may partially account for American's compassion fatigue.' Moeller's assurance is misplaced. Predicated on the questionable assumption that the media always pictures the worst, it focuses on governmental policy as the register of compassion. This overlooks the contrary evidence derived from the public response to charity appeals. The tens of millions of pounds donated to the Disasters Emergency Committee's consolidated national appeals in Britain shows that while state practice often appears lethargic in the face of disaster, public empathy, driven by powerful images, is anything but exhausted (Disasters Emergency Committee 2003).

The source of this belief about photographs and compassion fatigue can be traced back to Sontag's famous 1977 essay *On Photography* (Taylor 1998, p. 23). For Sontag, her discovery in 1945 of a book portraying the victims of the Holocaust was 'a negative epiphany' for the then 12-year-old (Sontag 1990, p. 19). Because they conveyed a horror at the limits of her comprehension, a horror not subsequently experienced by Sontag, she concludes that photographs themselves have increasingly anaesthetized the experience of atrocity: 'At the time of the first photographs of the Nazi camps, there was nothing banal about these images. After thirty years, a saturation point may have been reached. In these last decades, "concerned" photography had done at least as much to deaden conscience as to arouse it' (Sontag 1990, p. 21). While conceding that 'photographs can and do distress,' Sontag nonetheless maintains 'the aestheticizing tendency of photography is such that the medium which conveys distress ends by neutralizing it. Cameras miniaturize experience, transform history into spectacle. As much as they create sympathy, photographs cut sympathy, distance the emotions' (1990, pp. 109–110).

[. . .]

The compassion fatigue critique confuses a number of issues (state policy versus public empathy, for one). Moreover, insofar as it draws on Sontag's argument, it begins from a dubious premise. Because Sontag was never cut again so sharply as when she was 12 viewing the photos of Bergen-Belsen and Dachau while browsing a Santa Monica bookshop, she believes it is photographs *per se* which have lost their power. For Sontag, the repetition (whether as exact copies or generic icons) of such photographs means that all images of atrocity have become increasingly banalized. However, Sontag's personal appropriation of photographic epiphany denies this power to anyone else seeing those images for their own first time, or anyone else viewing any other images for the first time (Taylor 1998, p. 18).

That said, the often generic quality to certain atrocity photographs – such as the generic famine image of the starving African baby's face, staring pathetically into the camera lens, with flies buzzing around the child's nose and mouth – does run the risk of diminishing the sense of horror about the circumstances portrayed. However, to hold the pictures themselves solely responsible for this effect is to miss the important point that images never exist in isolation. Not only are they made available with an intertextual setting – where title, caption and text surround the particular content of the photograph – they are read within an historical, political and social context. Indeed, the lynching photographs of *Without Sanctuary* demonstrate above all else how the changing nature of this context radically refigures the meaning of the image. Whereas the postcards of lynchings were produced by and for white supremacists when the racial superiority of white over black was the societal norm in the US, they are being interpreted now within a context where such racism has lost its majoritarian support (if not its social significance). As a result, these photographs 'can be made public again only because now we ask them to carry an utterly different meaning than they once did – an outcry against racism rather than a reinforcement of it' (*New York Times* 2000). We are dealing here, therefore, with issues of cultural translation and transgression, whereby the same image does contrary work in different settings because of changes in the conditions of reception.

[. . .]

Foreign Bodies

When dead bodies do feature in the media, they are more often than not bodies of dead foreigners. And more often than not, images of dead foreigners are little more than a vehicle for the inscription of domestic spaces as superior, thereby furthering the 'cultural anaesthesia' produced through media representations of the other (Feldman 1994). But on occasion a photograph of a foreign body that differs from the norm is published. The film of the death of a 12-year-old Palestinian boy, Mohammed al-Durrah, contains one such image.

Mohammed al-Durrah was shot by Israeli troops at the Netzarin crossroads in Gaza on 30 September 2000. Huddling with his father against a wall in order to escape the live fire being exchanged by Palestinians and Israeli soldiers, al-Durrah's death was captured for television by a Palestinian cameraman working for a French network. Although Mohammed al-Durrah was pinned down during 40 minutes of gunfire, a handful of frames show his death. At first, the boy and his father squeeze themselves against a wall and behind a water barrel. Then Jamal al-Jurrah reaches back to shield his son, before turning to the cameraman to shout something. Mohammed al-Durrah is screaming in fear while his father gesticulates towards the Israeli guard post from where the fire is coming. At that point the film shows the worst – bullets hit father and son. The final frame – which has appeared subsequently as a single, haunting image – shows the father badly wounded, unconscious and slumped against the wall, a line of four bullet holes behind his head. His son lies dead, across his lap (Goldenberg 2000a). When screened as a television sequence, it disturbed millions of viewers, and brought a (contested) admission of responsibility from the Israeli army (Goldenberg 2000b, 2000c). In its subsequent publication as a still photograph, it has become a symbol of suffering circulating worldwide. As a frozen moment of horror, the photo of Mohammed al-Durrah says much about the violence in the Occupied Territories.

The directness of the photograph of Mohammed al-Durrah's death is rare. As such, it can be contrasted to another powerful image from the renewed violence in the Middle East. Two weeks after Mohammed al-Durrah was murdered, Vadim Norzich and a colleague – two reservists in the Israeli army – lost their way in Ramallah and were captured by an angry crowd of Palestinians. Their captors held aloft a poster of al-Durrah and his father, with images taken from the television coverage of their death. After Norzich and his fellow reservist were bundled into a Palestinian police station, a crowd stormed the building and attacked the men. In a frenzy of violence described by the Israeli prime minister as a 'cold-blooded lynching,'

Norzich was pummeled to death. From the television coverage of this incident came another single, horrific image, albeit one in which the body is absent. As a metonym for death, we see a young Palestinian man at the upstairs window of the police station. His arms are raised triumphantly, and he shows his blood-covered hands to the appreciative crowd below (Goldenberg 2000b). Eventually the burnt and mutilated bodies of Vadim Norzich and his colleague were returned to Israel, but no photographs of them were published. 'Use your apocalyptic imagination to figure out what they looked like,' said an army spokesman (Goldenberg 2000b).

The combined effect of the photographs of Mohammed al-Durrah and the killers of Vadim Norzich is likely to be the extinguishment of hope about the prospects of a resolution to the Israeli–Palestinian conflict. Moreover, the sense of balance that comes from linking the two underscores the limited opportunity for optimism (Corbin 2000). However, images of dead foreign bodies are not always produced or used in this way.

[. . .]

The filmed death of Mohammed al-Durrah [. . .] [was] able to create controversy because [it was] [. . .] shown. [. . .]. [R]egardless of who took the pictures, a wider public was able to view. .. [it] after. .. [it was] screened by broadcasters and printed in newspapers. That the potential power of an image depends in the first instance on its public circulation seems an obvious point. But what is not obvious is why some images and not others make it through the various layers of the media industry, across the desks of the many producers and editors involved in making a story possible, and finally onto the screen or the page.

[. . .]

Whatever the particular explanation might be [. . .], it will have to be an explanation that highlights the political economy of the news image as a pivotal context. Broadcasters in the UK have reduced their current affairs and documentary programs substantially; coverage of developing countries is down by more than 50% in the last ten years. Those program outlets that do remain have been shifted to the margins of the viewing schedule, further restricting audiences. Much of the remaining programming dealing with the South centers on the tourist industry and wildlife features, and ignores social and political concerns (Stone 2000; Vidal 2002). Standing in both a cause and effect relationship with this context are the cuts to broadcasters current affairs budgets. Not only have these financial restrictions meant less coverage, they have changed the way in which much of the coverage that exists is produced. Broadcasters often do not send their own personnel to cover conflicts, relying instead on the large news agencies such as Associated Press and Reuters to provide the pool images. However, those agencies are increasingly shunning the experienced and qualified freelance cameramen and photojournalists, who can investigate the stories as well as take the images. In their place, the agencies are subcontracting local sources to supply footage. Because they are often inexperienced, the locals hired to provide images can be at risk from this out-sourcing. For example, one small picture agency gave teenagers in Grozny $400 each if they provided pictures of the troops occupying the Chechen capital, something Maggie O'Kane (2000, p. 9) criticized as 'Russian roulette for television.'

Hidden Bodies

There are many situations that could serve as an example to highlight the horrific blindness that afflicts much current affairs coverage. There are, sadly, too many conflicts and crises that go uncovered, their crimes largely unknown to the wider world. But one stands out for the way in which its appearance on the world's visual radar occurs within a frame that masks a more disturbing story.

War in the Sudan, Africa's largest country, has been on going for more than four decades. Since the early 1980s, and especially after the overthrow of President Nimeri in 1985, the struggle between the authorities in Khartoum and the Sudanese People's Liberation Army in the south has produced devastating famines (African Rights 1997). Amongst the more than two million dead in the world's longest running 'civil war' are the hundreds of thousands of people who have perished because food resources have been part of the currency of power. The Bahr el Ghazal famine of 1998, which killed 250,000 in the south-western region of Sudan, was only one of the most recent consequences of this wider conflict (Human Rights Watch 1999).

The media coverage of the Bahr el Ghazal famine was short-lived in its intensity, lasting no more than a couple of months in June and July 1998. The media coverage required the clichés of famine photographs – 'the BBs,' or children with bloated bellies being held by the mothers, or fed by western aid workers – to present the story to a world audience ignorant of the context in which famine is produced (Moeller 1999, p. 35). The cruel irony is that such coverage of conditions in Bahr el Ghazal was possible only *after* the worst of the food shortages had eased. By the time vulnerable members of the community were dying, and thus made available for media stereotypes, the worst was over and relief (whether locally derived or internationally available) had arrived.

Such conventional media coverage of famine has the effect of reproducing an understanding of Sudan as being 'one of the hollow-bellied places of the world' (Salopek 2000). This meaning is well represented by a famous photograph the *New York Times* published in March 1993. Taken by Kevin Carter in Sudan, and awarded a Pulitzer Prize, it shows an emaciated child, alone and hunched over, with a vulture lurking in the background. The public response to the picture focused less on the child and her circumstances and more on the photographer and his actions, forcing the newspaper to issue an editorial statement making it clear that the child made it to a feeding centre and was unharmed by the vulture (Marinovich & Silva 2000). Nonetheless, the rancorous debate contributed to Carter's suicide, with his death memorialized in song (albeit one less poetic than Billie Holiday's ode to lynching).

Carter's photograph of the Sudanese girl was an example of what David Perlmutter calls an 'icon of outrage.' One of the paradoxes of such images is that the outrage they foster 'may stir controversy, accolades, and emotion, but *achieve* absolutely nothing . . . the little girl in Carter's picture was not plucked away by some special Western relief effort, nor did intervention stem the causes of her suffering . . . Far from a metonym, the photograph should be taken as an anomaly precisely because the human disaster of the Sudan, then as now, is largely ignored by the Western media' (Perlmutter 1998, p. 28).

Although not wrong about the specifics of the Carter photograph, Perlmutter's conclusion is too sweeping when we consider other attempts to document the famine in Sudan. Tom Stoddart's 1998 series from the Sudan bears comparison with Sebastiao Salgado's Sahel photographs (Stoddart *et al.* 1998; Campbell 2003a). They represent a committed form of photojournalism that persists, even with the limited opportunities for publication, and which prompts considerable financial support for aid agencies. Because of this, such photographs refute the notion that the public instinctively turns away from, and is immobilized by, such pictures.

However, what is lost in many photojournalistic accounts of Sudan which confer a passive and pathetic victim-hood on the suffering – even the better ones such as Stoddart's series – is any sense of the way famine is integral to the wider conflict. As a result, the larger story of the crimes against humanity (of which the diversion and withholding of food resources is but one) perpetrated in Sudan goes almost unnoticed. As in the majority of conflicts, no one side in Sudan can claim the mantle of virtue. But what has been missed by the generic famine imagery is the way the Government of Sudan's (GoS) campaign of aerial bombardment against civilians in the south –

notable for its random viciousness and its flagrant violation of the laws of war – creates the context for famine.

Using Russian-supplied Antanov cargo planes, GoS forces have indiscriminately bombed hospitals, markets, schools and villages (Médecins sans Frontières 2000a). In 2000, there were 152 bombing incidents recorded by fieldworkers, with 250 weapons dropped during 33 raids in July alone (US Committee for Refugees 2001; Sudan Working Group 2000). Because the Antanov is a cargo aircraft, which flies at a height (20,000 feet) sufficient to evade the few missiles possessed by the SPLA, it is a necessarily inaccurate platform from which to release weapons. Moreover, the devices dropped are crude: 25 gallon drums contain 20 pound bombs, packed into place with metal scraps that serve as shrapnel on detonation, function as crude cluster bombs. Significantly, there have also been substantiated reports of weapons containing chemicals being dropped from the Antanovs (Médecins sans Frontières 2000a: section 4.2). Not surprisingly, these attacks cause large-scale death and destruction. One attack on the southern town of Yei in November 2000 killed 18 people in a market place (*BBC News* 2000b).

The strategy behind these war crimes is the desire on the part of the GoS to generally terrorize the civilian population. Bringing about large-scale displacement serves the purpose of keeping the people in a state of chronic insecurity, fosters deprivation, and ensures the SPLA does not have a secure communal base from which to operate more effectively. The bombings also wreak havoc upon aid operations in southern Sudan. In August 2000, for example, the World Food Programme accused the GoS of deliberately attacking its operations after airstrips and United Nations and Red Cross aircraft (clearly marked with the ICRC flag) were bombed, causing relief work to be suspended (Médecins sans Frontières 2000b; *BBC News* 2000a). Notwithstanding progress in the negotiations for a comprehensive peace settlement in Sudan, the Khartoum Government's campaign against civilians is on-going (Human Rights Watch 2002; UN Office for the Coordination of Humanitarian Affairs 2002; International Crisis Group 2003).

Despite the potential newsworthiness of this story – which involves war crimes, military action, civilian deaths in a foreign land, and possibly chemical weapons – media coverage in the UK has been, to say the least, limited. An internet search of *The Guardian*'s archives for 2000, when there was widespread warfare against civilians, shows only two mentions of bombing in Sudan, both of them restricted to the 'In Brief' section where single paragraphs from news agencies are located at the margins of the page (*The Guardian* 2000a, 2000b). No photo essay recorded the campaign against civilians. No report that set the bombings in their overall context or drew the disturbing conclusions about their inhumanity and illegality was evident; although two articles in *The Observer* that year did highlight the role oil plays in the Sudan conflict (Flint 2000a, 2000b).

What explanation can there be for this relative silence? There is no shortage of information. As the citations to this section establish, agencies such as MSF and the US Committee for Refugees have documented the GoS bombing campaigns and their effects. Nor is there a complete absence of official responses. Governments have been reluctant to denounce clearly the GoS policy, but occasional statements have provided possible hooks upon which news stories could be built (UN Department for Public Information 2000; US Department of State 2000; European Union 2000). Nor are pictures totally unavailable (US Committee for Refugees 2001).

Conclusion

The media's blindness towards the war crimes committed in Sudan demonstrates again the significance of context. In relationship to images, context involves three dimensions: the economy of indifference to others (especially others who are culturally, racially and spatially foreign), the economy of 'taste and decency' whereby the media itself regulates the representation of death and atrocity, and the economy of display, wherein the meaning of images is produced by the intertextual relationship of captions, titles, surrounding arguments and sites for presentation.

Because of the interplay of these three contextual dimensions, Sudan does not regularly figure. When it does pierce the veil of ignorance, it does so in a way that confirms Sudan's status as one of the world's 'hollow bellied' places. The absence of a war crimes narrative to employ the relevant events and issues in Sudan prevents new meanings from developing. Pictures alone will not change the situation in Sudan. But the absence of photographs conveying something other than the pathetic victims of famine, as though the crisis were a natural disaster, can only help to perpetuate the current crisis.

Above all else, the significance of social context for the creation of pictorial meaning has been the theme of this article. The same pictures can mean different things at different times because of different concerns. The lynching photographs of *Without Sanctuary* were produced as celebratory icons of white supremacy, but are now read as powerful evidence of a deplorable racist history.

[. . .]

[The] dominant social understandings existing at the moment of production and reception are more important than the specific form or content of the image for the creation of meaning. When combined with issues of context that relate to the presentation of the image – the economy of display – the power of images cannot be said to result from qualities internal to the picture.

Nonetheless, images do bring a particular kind of power to the portrayal of death and violence. Seeing the body and what has been done to it are important. Images alone might not be responsible for a narrative's power, but narratives that are un-illustrated can struggle to convey the horror evident in many circumstances. Of course, there would be much to worry about if the media indulged in the simple proliferation of disturbing images. Making war pornography available for mass consumption would not address the concerns raised here. But the blindness produced by a combination of the social economy of taste and the media system of self-censorship constitutes a considerable injustice with regard to our collective understanding of the fate of the other.

[. . .]

References

African Rights (1997) *Food and Power in Sudan: A Critique of Humanitarianism*, African Rights, London.

Allen, J., Als, H., Lewis, J. & Litwack, L. F. (2000) *Without Sanctuary: Lynching Photography in America*, Twins Palms Publishers, Santa Fe, New Mexico.

BBC News (2000a) 'Sudan Government Accused of Aid Bombings', 9 Aug., [online] available at: http://news.bbc.co.uk/1/hi/world/africa/873328.stm.

BBC News (2000b) 'Sudan Market Bomb "Carnage" ' *BBC News On-Line*, 20 Nov. [online] available at: http://news.bbc.co.uk/1/hi/world/africa/1032791.stm.

Campbell, D. (2003a) 'Salgado and the Sahel: Documentary Photography and the Imaging of Famine', in *Rituals of Mediation: International Politics and Social Meaning*, ed. F. Debrix & C. Weber, University of Minnesota Press, Minneapolis, pp. 69–96.

Campbell, D. (2003b) 'Representing Contemporary War', *Ethics and International Affairs*, vol. 17, no. 2, pp. 99–108.

Campbell, D. (2004) 'Cultural Governance and Pictorial Resistance: Reflections on the Imaging of War', *Review of International Studies* 29, pp. 57–73.

Corbin, J. (2000) 'When Peace Died', *BBC Correspondent*, 17 Nov. [online] available at: http://news.bbc.co.uk/hi/english/audiovideo/programmes/correspondent/newsid_1026000/1026340.stm.

Disasters Emergency Committee (2003) 'Past Appeals' [online] available at: http://www.dec.org.uk/index.cfm/asset_id,132/index.html.

European Union (2000) 'Declaration by the Presidency on Behalf of the European Union on the Bombing of Civilian Targets in Sudan', 18 August [online] available at: http://wwww.reliefweb.int/w/rwb.nsf/f303799b16d2074285256830007 fb33f/ce2eafe0d09577c785256942006c9801?OpenDocument.

Feldman, A. (1994) 'On Cultural Anaesthesia: From Desert Storm to Rodney King', *American Ethnologist*, vol. 21, no. 2 May, pp. 404–18.

Flint, J. (2000a) 'Britain Backs Ugly War for Oil', *The Observer*, 16 April [online] available at: http://www.guardianunlimited.co.uk/Archive/Article/0,4273, 3986856,00.html.

Flint, J. (2000b) 'Nuba Face Destruction', *The Observer*, 7 May [online] available at: http://www.guardianunlimited.co.uk/Archive/Article/0,4273,4015547,00.html.

Goldenberg, S. (2000a) 'Making of a Martyr', *The Guardian (G2)*, 3 Oct. [online] available at: http://www.guardian.co.uk/israel/Story/0,2763,376639,00.html.

Goldenberg, S. (2000b) 'When They Blundered into the Baying Mob They Sealed Their Fate', *The Guardian*, 13 Oct., p. 3.

Goldenberg, S. (2000c) 'Arab Boy Haunts Army from the Grave', *The Guardian*, 9 Nov, p. 12.

The Guardian (1999) 'Texas Puts Racist on Trial for Murder', *The Guardian*, 16 Feb. [online] available at: http://www.guardianunlimited.co.uk/Archive/Article/ 0,4273,3822616,00.html.

The Guardian (2000a) 'In Brief: Sudan Civilian Targets Bombed', 23 Aug., p. 12.

The Guardian (2000b) 'In Brief: Sudan Jet Kills 10 in Market Attack', 21 Nov., p. 12.

Harden, B. (1998) 'Giuliani Suspends 2 N.Y. Firemen for "Display of Racism" At Parade; Participants Mocked Dragging Death of Black Man in Texas', *Washington Post*, 12 Sept., p. A06.

Human Rights Watch (1999) *Famine in Sudan, 1998: The Human Rights Causes*, Human Rights Watch, New York.

Human Rights Watch (2002) 'Sudan Bans All Relief to the South', 28 Sept. [online] available at: http://hrw.org/press/2002/09/sudan0928.htm.

International Crisis Group (2003) *Sudan's Oilfields Burn Again: Brinkmanship Endangers the Peace Process*, Nairobi/Brussels, 10 Feb. [online] available at: http://www.crisisweb.org/home/index.cfm?id=1807&l=1.

Lewis, J. (2003) 'Facts in the Line of Fire', *The Guardian*, 6 Nov. [online] available at: http://media.guardian.co.uk/broadcast/comment/0,7493,1078837,00.html.

Litwack, L. F. (2000) 'Hellhounds', in *Without Sanctuary: Lynching Photography in America*, eds J. Allen, H. Als, J. Lewis & L. F. Litwack, Twins Palms Publishers, Santa Fe, New Mexico, pp. 8–37.

Margolis, D. (2000) *Strange Fruit: Billie Holiday, Café Society and an Early Cry for Civil Rights*, Running Press, New York.

Marinovich, G. & Silva, J. (2000) *The Bang-Bang Club: Snapshots from a Hidden War*, William Heinemann, London.

Mayes, I. (1999) 'Close to Death', *The Guardian*, 8 May [online] available at: http:// www.guardianunlimited.co.uk/Archive/Article/0,4273,3862734,00.html.

Médecins sans Frontières (2000a) *Living Under Aerial Bombardments: Report of an Investigations in the Province of Equatoria, Southern Sudan*, Geneva, MSF Switzerland, February [online] available at: http://www.msf.ch/fr_asp/news/reports/ssudan/bombing.asp.

Médecins sans Frontières (2000b) 'MSF Suspends Operations Following Aerial Bombardments', Press release, 2 Aug. [online] available at: http://www.msf.org/projects/africa/sudan/reports/2000/08/pr-withdrawl/index.htm.

Moeller, S. D. (1999) *Compassion Fatigue: How the Media Sell Disease, Famine, War and Death*, Routledge, New York & London.

New York Times (2000) 'Death by Lynching', editorial, 16 Mar., New York Times [online] available at: http://query.nytimes.com/gst/abstract.html?res=F20615F7345F0C758DDDAA0894D8404482.

O'Kane, M. (2000) 'The Only Show in Town', *The Guardian (Media Supplement)*, 30 Oct., p. 9.

Perlmutter, D. D. (1998) *Photojournalism and Foreign Policy: Icons of Outrage in International Crises*, Praeger, Westport, Connecticut.

Rushdy, A. (2000) 'Exquisite Corpse', *Transition* 83, pp. 70–77.

Salopek, P. (2000) 'Famine in the Face of Plenty', *Chicago Tribune*, 11 June, p. 2.

Smith, R. (2000) 'An Ugly Legacy Lives On, Its Glare Unsoftened by Age', *New York Times*, 13 Jan. [online] available at: http://query.nytimes.com/gst/abstract.html?res=F30712FE3F5E0C708DDDA80894D8404482.

Sontag, S. (1990) *On Photography*, Anchor Books, New York.

Stoddart, T., Jacobsen, C. & Sweeney, J. (1998) 'Moving Pictures', *Reportage* 4, n.p.

Stone, J. (2000) *Losing Perspective: Global Affairs on British Terrestrial Television 1989–1999*, Third World and Environment Broadcasting Project, London.

Sudan Working Group (2000) 'Sudan: NGOs Condemn Bombing of Civilians', 9 Aug. [online] available at: http://wwww.reliefweb.int/w/rwb.nsf/s/C7114B3D604D9D17C1256938002EF1DC.

Taylor, J. (1998) *Body Horror: Photojournalism, Catastrophe and War*, Manchester University Press, Manchester.

UN Department of Public Information (2000) 'Concerned Over Bombings in Sudan, Security Council Requests Briefing', 10 Aug. [online] available at: http://www.reliefweb.int/w/rwb.nsf/s/C8547FF082D17A2DC12569380045D086.

UN Office for the Coordination of Humanitarian Affairs (2002) 'SUDAN: Two injured in government bombing', IRIN.org, 18 July [online] available at: http://www.irinnews.org/report.asp?ReportID/28876.

US Committee for Refugees (2001) 'Sudan Slide Show', January [online] available at: http://www.refugees.org/news/crisis/sudan/.

US Department of State (2000) 'State Department Comments on UN Relief Flights to Sudan', 17 Aug. [online] available at: http://wwww.reliefweb.int/w/rwb.nsf/f303799b16d2074285256830007fb33f/d3237181e06aaedc8525694200556aad?OpenDocument.

Vidal, J. (2002) 'Britons Sink into Ignorance as TV Turns to Trivia in Third World', *The Guardian*, 10 July, p. 7.

Vulliamy, E. (1999) 'American Graffiti: Deep South Turns its Back on the Klan's Region of Hate', *The Guardian*, 28 Feb. [online] available at: http://www.guardianunlimited.co.uk/Archive/Article/0,4273,3829087,00.html.

Wells, M. (2003) 'Embedded Reporters "Sanitised" Iraq War', *The Guardian*, 6 Nov. [online] available at: http://media.guardian.co.uk/broadcast/story/0,7493, 107864900.html.

Younge, G. (2003) 'Don't Mention the Dead', *The Guardian*, 7 Nov. [online] available at: http://www.guardian.co.uk/g2/story/0,3604,1079608,00.html.

CYBERSTALKING AND INTERNET PORNOGRAPHY
GENDERED VIOLENCE

Alison Adam

Introduction

This paper is based on the argument that a number of problems found within the domain of information or cyberethics would benefit from a more thorough gender analysis grounded in aspects of feminist theory. Such a position is particularly pertinent in relation to problems which involve the body, privacy violations physical or otherwise of bodies and bodily spaces, watching of and gazing at bodies. This is because of the long-standing tradition, prevalent in Western philosophy, of associating bodily matters primarily with women rather than men (Adam, 1998). Additionally, there is a tendency for advocates of cyberculture, from roboticists to cyberpunk science fiction writers, to ignore and even deny the primacy of the body. This reflects a turn to the virtual, which, at its extreme, sees the body as mere 'meat' (Adam, 1998).

If, as I suggest, philosophy has a tendency to equate women with the bodily realm, it may well be instructive to look afresh at gender relations to reclaim or reinvent the body, certainly within computer ethics. In arguing that it may be instructive to bring feminist theory to computer ethics problems, as much feminist thinking has centred on the body, this may also go some way to reclaiming the body in computer ethics. For instance, in regard to topics such as privacy, we may begin to think in terms of bodily invasions of privacy, where bodies are watched, looked at or subject to surveillance or indeed where bodies are actually violated and the violations are watched on-line. At the same time we must acknowledge that concepts of privacy may be different for men and women and may vary according to age, class, ethnicity and other cultural and social variables. Therefore my theoretical position involves weaving together a feminist approach to privacy and the concept of 'the gaze' and bringing this to bear on a number of empirical examples relating to cyberstalking and Internet pornography.

There is now considerable literature on gender and technology in general, as well as gender and information technology in particular. There is also no doubt that the subject of computer or information ethics has come of age, developing into a separate discipline in its own right with its own conferences and journal, a growing collection of textbooks and a semi-popular literature. Despite this, gender as an analytical variable is rarely given more than passing consideration in cyberethics literature.

[. . .]

The areas chosen for this paper are cyberstalking and Internet paedophile rings. The specific area of feminist theory which I wish to bring to the analysis is a feminist notion of 'the gaze.' This must be understood as an embodied gaze rather than as an anonymous 'view from nowhere' (Nagle, 1986). It has both a gazer and a gazed-upon subject. It is immediately clear that both cyberstalking and Internet paedophile rings have some gender dimension, e.g., most cyberstalkers are men, most victims women. Most individuals involved in Internet child pornography are men. However, while the predominance of men as perpetrators is well known and has been adduced in prominent policy documents, almost nothing seems to be made of this fact by the policy makers who write such documents (Reno, 1999). Additionally, policy documents fail to address the issue that, in finding the cause of the problem and ways to counter it, the question of gender might be highly relevant. However, if we are to get beyond a simple assertion that most criminal activity is perpetrated by men, we must begin to see how these specific activities can be analysed in terms of the ways in which men are constructed as perpetrators and women and children often construed as victims. The most effective tools in making such an analysis are feminist theory, particularly feminist ethics, theories of the body, legal theory and politics, but, although it is not possible to go into detail within the scope of the present paper, there is a very wide range of feminist literature which is potentially relevant in making a thorough gender analysis. This further underlines the point that cyberethics should not be understood in a narrow sense, philosophical or otherwise, but rather opens up into a broad spectrum of political, social and ethical discussion. However, to sharpen the present discussion I shall only focus on one area from feminist theory, namely that of the gaze, how it relates to privacy and violations of the body.

[. . .]

The paper proceeds by expanding these arguments with relation to cyber-stalking in detail, and Internet paedophile rings more briefly, both of which currently cause much concern in the media. As both cyberstalking and Internet paedophile rings involve violations of privacy, this gives a rationale for considering the ways in which different conceptions of privacy can be seen as gendered, and how the gaze can be better incorporated into our ideas of privacy. More especially, the ways in which virtual and non-virtual violations of the body enforce authority and reinforce the submission of the victim are an important element of a feminist analysis.

Recent feminist thinking argues against a 'victim' mentality, preferring to see ways in which, even if they cannot in many circumstances achieve empowerment, women can become active agents in resisting violations of their privacy. The Foucauldian notion of the 'gaze,' and its ambiguity in reinforcing or resisting submission are useful to explore here, and the ways in which the return gaze may be incorporated into an ethics of resistance of invasions of privacy, bodily or virtual. Clearly the gaze is used to terrible effect in Internet child pornography cases where the difficulty of finally removing all copies of the images from computer networks means that others may continue to gaze upon the images long after the original perpet-rator has been brought to justice. However, whilst the notion of the return gaze may be fruitful to explore with regard to women who have been cyber-stalked and women who are involved in Internet pornography, it would seem almost facile to offer the gaze as a means of resistance in cases of child abuse on the internet. In these cases, it is rather the gaze of the police and other authorities in the process of bringing offenders to book which reverses the power of the abuser's gaze.

Internet pornography, and especially child pornography is rarely the topic of academic discourse. Not surprisingly we are revolted by crimes against children. Nevertheless, it is important that a critical voice is added to the discussion, both to fight against the crime itself, and against knee-jerk reactions. Here the gaze can be turned back on the perpetrators in a way which whips up fears and prejudice and without necessarily making any difference to the quantity and type of crimes committed. In the summer of 2000, provoked by a tragic case where a young girl was abducted and mur-dered by a stranger, parts of the UK tabloid press began 'name and shame' campaigns, where names of child abusers were printed in newspapers result-ing in witch-hunts conducted on housing estates where locals claimed child abusers were living (Neustatter, 2000). Against the backcloth of police warnings that this would drive abusers underground and potentially out of sight of the authorities, it is hard to see how the tabloid campaign could make children safer. It is natural that anxious parents wish to gaze back and render visible potential abusers, but the dreadful irony is that this may serve to drive them out from our and the authorities' gaze altogether.

My discussion revolves around the events leading up to the sentencing of seven men in early 2001 for membership of the so-called 'Wonderland Club,' an international paedophile ring who traded three-quarters of a million images of child pornography on the Internet (Panorama, 2001). However, at the time of writing, the UK media report a series of arrests of Internet paedophiles after a lengthy police surveillance on a massive inter- national scale (*The Guardian*, 2001). This second example involves images on newsgroups which appear to be freely available, even to minors, rather than the apparently more underground activities of the 'Wonderland Club.'

The debate over Internet pornography can, in some senses, be seen as a contemporary reflection of much longer running debates over freedom of speech vs. censorship in relation to a more conventional adult sex industry. Internationally, laws vary as to the legality of adult pornography. On the Internet some authors regard adult Internet pornography as a business, a stimulus to e-commerce, whilst others regard it as but an extension of women's conventional exploitation in the sex industry (Lane, 2000). Authors such as MacKinnon and Dworkin, from the anti-pornography feminist movement, argue for a link between pornography and violence, yet others argue that it is not clear that the link has been proven definitively (Lane, 2000). However, child pornography is regarded as qualitatively dif- ferent from adult pornography. It is almost universally illegal and the link between paedophilia and child pornography seems incontrovertible (*The Guardian*, 2001). In addition, we now need to confront the possibility that the ease of use and relative anonymity afforded by the Internet leads some individuals to join with pathological Internet communities and acts as a further spur towards their committing terrible crimes. We have the possibil- ity of children being groomed for abuse and abuse taking place online and relayed to others as a video stream. This turns the spotlight onto the question of how far technology may act as a trigger for abusive and criminal activity.

Cyberstalking

Cyberstalking is the term which has been coined to describe the on-line variant of the much older crime of stalking (Meloy, 1998). Possibly because it has only received recognition as a specific phenomenon for around a decade or so, it has yet to be the subject of an extended empirical study. Whilst media reports abound (*USA Today*, 1999) academic discussion is somewhat thin on the ground (Adam, 2001). The upshot of this is, first of all, that, otherwise theoretically sophisticated authors working on the psychological aspects of stalking, fail to understand some of the important ramifications of the phenomenon, e.g., in terms of the possibilities for 'third party cyberstalking' and secondly, that the gendered nature of the problem has yet to be probed to any depth.

On the former point, Meloy (1998), an acknowledged expert on stalking, defines cyberstalking thus: 'The Internet as a means of stalking can be used for two criminal functions: (1) to gather private information on the target to further a pursuit; and (2) to communicate (in real time or not) with the target to implicitly or explicitly threaten or induce fear.' However he fails to understand the ready potential of the Internet for third-party stalking, i.e., the ability of the perpetrator to use features of the Internet, often to assume the identity of the victim on-line, to induce others to stalk or harass the victim in some way, a possibility which is much harder in the 'off-line' world.

Nevertheless, other authors have begun to describe the complexity of the cyberstalking phenomenon, particularly regarding efforts to design effective legislation. Packard (2000) explores current US state and federal stalking laws and how they relate to cyberstalking. A perennial problem with legislation concerning Internet crime in general is how to apply it across state and national boundaries. Current US federal stalking law is designed to apply only to stalkers who follow their victims across state lines. Clearly this makes little sense in an on-line environment; hence an amendment to the law prohibits certain forms of communication and protects victims from cyberstalkers who influence others to harass the victims.

Third-party cyberstalking

Three recent cases illustrate the complexities of what is involved in 'third-party' cyberstalking. In common with the Internet paedophile cases, it also becomes clear that the capabilities afforded by the technology act as a spur in the perpetrators' behaviour. In the first example, an author, Jayne Hitchcock, was cyberstalked when she, and other authors, exposed the dubious activities of a literary agency on the Internet (Mingo, 2000). The perpetrators posted counterfeit messages in various parts of the Internet, in her name, including explicit sexual invitations and details of her address and telephone number. Several men phoned her and called at her house. In a second case, a man angry that he had been spurned by a woman, posted personal information about her in Internet sex-chat rooms, again with explicit information, causing a number of men to try to break into her house (*The Guardian*, 1999). In a third case, Stephanie Brail found herself drawn into a 'flame war' in a news group discussing underground magazines (Brail, 1996). She rationalized this behaviour as resulting from her daring to speak up in the public space of the Internet. Although Brail does not attempt a conventionally feminist analysis, she clearly points to the root of her problem in terms of the results of a woman speaking out in public. As outcome of this, she began to be the victim of anonymous obscene postings, again with explicit invitations resulting in other people contacting her.

In all three cases the victim was a woman. In the Hitchcock case, the perpetrators appear to be a group of people, one of whom was a woman; in the other cases, the perpetrators were male. From the published accounts above, we know that the 'third-party' stalkers, those who were incited to contact the victims, were male. It is acknowledged that the majority of cyberstalking perpetrators are male and the majority of victims female yet, to date, commentators seemingly fail to make use of this aspect in their analyses, indeed missing the point that understanding the gendered nature of the phenomenon is crucial to achieving convincing explanations of why it occurs (Meloy, 1998).

Third-party stalking would seem to be a case in point. Given that, as discussed above, we are only just beginning to understand the range of third-party cyberstalking possibilities and given the gender breakdown of first and third party perpetrators and victims, I argue that it is vital to construct an analysis of this phenomenon which places gender centre stage.

A gender analysis of third-party cyberstalking

What is involved in making such a gender analysis? First of all, we should look to appropriate literatures in which to couch such an analysis. A prevailing view is that cyberstalking should be seen as a psychological phenomenon (Meloy, 1998). Appropriate psychological literature is clearly one relevant vector, but it needs to include the literature of feminist psychology, including studies on violence against women (Welsh, 2000). Immediately the question of a relevant theoretical locus opens up, and this extends from the purely psychological include social and cultural dimensions. In other words it is not just a question of individual psychology but also the wider culture in which individuals are situated.

An especially pertinent aspect of cyberstalking, and especially 'third-party' cyberstalking, relates to privacy. Although there has been considerable discussion of questions of on-line privacy (Moor, 2001), there has yet to be a similar level of interest in men's and women's differential views and expectations of their own privacy on-line. However, there is every reason to expect that the on-line world should mirror the 'real world' in this respect. MacKinnon (1979) has pointed out that the private sphere has traditionally been that of women, yet at the same time women have enjoyed few rights and the state is reluctant to interfere. For instance, witness the ways in which the eruption of domestic violence is often regarded as a lesser crime, than an act of violence directed towards a stranger. DeCew (1997) extends MacKinnon's argument to reason that as women have traditionally had few rights to privacy it is not easy for women, themselves, and others to see when these rights are being transgressed. Thomas and Kitzinger (1997) argue that one reason why **sexual harassment** took so long to be named (the phenomenon did not have a name until the mid-1970s) was that women were, and still are, reluctant to report it. The so-called 'backlash' writers, such as Roiphe (1993), reinforce this sense of 'having to put up with it' as a normal part of life's rich pattern, by attacking the concept of sexual harassment as part of a 'victim feminism' mentality. The trouble is that this can further reinforce women's diminished sense of personal privacy, and it would be unfortunate if this were to be translated into the on-line world.

Cyberstalking transgresses women's privacy in a direct way. Third-party cyberstalking transgresses women's privacy in the same way and also in a second way. This second notion of privacy transgression relates to the manner in which the original perpetrator becomes a voyeur, someone who invades and transgresses by watching and looking. This further reinforces the power that the perpetrator has over the victim.

[. . .]

Women's gaze in cyberstalking

In this description I have emphasized the gaze, in the context of cyberstalking, and especially third-party cyberstalking, as essentially a masculine phenomenon. However, there are two senses in which women can appropriate the gaze in cyberstalking. To illustrate the first sense, I analyse a relatively rare case of a woman who cyberstalked a man, in particular to describe what is different, in this case, with respect to the cases, described above, where men cyberstalked women. The second example involves interpreting what happens when women unmask or catch their male perpetrators, which can be cast as a feminine reinterpretation of the gaze.

Perhaps not surprisingly, as it is a predominantly masculine activity, detailed reports of female cyberstalking are rare. However, Burt (1997) reports a case which presents a distinct contrast to the cases described above and also which gives a further insight into notions of the 'gaze.' This involved a female college student who had been spending about eight hours a day monitoring a male relative's Internet usage using the 'finger' on-line tool. Given their cultural background a sexual relationship would not have been possible. She was able to discover that he frequently communicated with a woman from the university where he had just graduated and she phoned the woman and her parents in disguise, although we are not told whether or not these calls could be regarded as threatening in nature. Clearly we could interpret the activities of this woman as gazing at her male relative. But her case has different features to the predominantly masculine cases reported above. She experienced considerable shame and guilt over her feelings, that is, she knew that they were wrong in her culture. At the same time she knew that she was suffering from a psychological disorder as she eventually presented at a psychiatric outpatient clinic complaining of depression and severe, compulsive behaviour.

In this case the actor knew that she had a problem, that her behaviour was not normal and that she wished to have treatment to recover from it. At the same time, she seems to have held no intent to harm her relative, nor his woman friend, who probably never knew about her actions. There are, of course, cases where men cyberstalk women in this way, where the woman has no knowledge and may not be harmed. However, in the tragic Amy Boyer case, a man who was obsessed with the young woman in question emailed friends about his obsession and set up a web site (Burt, 1997). She, and her family, knew nothing of his obsession, until he murdered her outside her office.

A further aspect of the woman college student case is that, although she had held romantic longings for her male relative for a long time, she did not meet the criteria for obsessive compulsive disorder until she had access to the Internet. In this respect, as the quote below reinforces, she displayed similar attributes to men who use the Internet for stalking or pornography. For a susceptible person, the access to the technology seems enough to tip the balance and trigger this behaviour. A shy, secretive personality and a technical background are also salient factors, which are also often to be found in male perpetrators, although, of course, can be found in women too.

This opened an opportunity, a channel for behaviour that was congruent with the rest of her psychological makeup, and allowed her to express her obsessive thoughts through a unique, and previously unavailable mode of compulsive behaviour. Being shy and secretive but also mathematically oriented and technically skilful she had the appropriate background to use computers in order to manifest previously repressed thoughts and feelings

. . . she was able to make an intervention, a communication, that she had long longed for, without having to bear the anxiety-provoking aspects of a true interpersonal relationship (Burt, 1997).

Women reappropriate the gaze

Although I have characterized the three third-party cyberstalking cases above in terms of a masculine gaze, there are important ways in which we can interpret the women victims as reappropriating the gaze in order to bring some sort of satisfactory solution to their cases. In this case, we can see that these women, rather than being stereotypical passive recipients of the male gaze, were able to assert their authority as active moral agents in gazing back at their perpetrators in an ethics of resistance.

MacCannell and MacCannell (1993: 214) make it clear that the gaze is a two-way process.

> . . . the figure of authority turning its gaze on the victim and the victim looking back. But in the case of the instrumental gaze it is the 'looking' of authority that is crucial – snooping into the victim's affairs, maintaining an information base in order to maintain the effectiveness of threat and so on. In the case of identificatory gaze, the victims 'looking up' to authority is crucial – their desire to see themselves in the eyes of authority . . .

A feminist reading of the gaze underlines the juxtaposition of public 'state' surveillance and private individual watching in a patriarchal society, the two sides of the same coin. White (2001) has also noted that in the Internet games that she has surveyed, the female version of the gaze is often a submissive one, a 'looking up' to some sense of authority. But it is possible to develop a much stronger feminist reading of gazing where looking up can become instead, looking back or returning the gaze. In the three cases of cyberstalked women reported above, the return gaze is not just crucial in reversing the power balance of the original gaze, but it is also crucial in revealing the identity of the perpetrators of the gaze, who achieved much of their ability to stalk their victims, and thereby their power over their victims, through the anonymity afforded by the Internet. When their anonymity is stripped away through the power of the return gaze, they are either turned over to the authorities or they voluntarily stop their stalking behaviour.

In the Hitchcock case, Jayne Hitchcock and her fellow authors gazed back at the offending literary agency, exposed them for others to gaze upon, and ultimately to bring them to justice, although the case is complex and long running (Mingo, 2000). The perpetrator in the spurned lover case had assumed that he was protected by the anonymity of the Internet, yet he was lured into a trap, again on the Internet, by the victim's father, where his identity was revealed (*The Guardian*, 1999). The woman here, with the help of her family, was able to gaze back to identify her stalker. Finally in Brail's case, she was forced to increase her technical knowledge of UNIX, whereupon she was able to find the identity of her stalker (Brail, 1996). As soon as she turned the gaze upon him, by emailing him back to his original email address, rather than one of the aliases which he used, he stopped harassing her.

Internet Pornography

In this section, I briefly describe issues surrounding the question of Internet pornography, focusing on child pornography in particular. The first issue concerns the psychology of the, usually male, perpetrator and how it can be compared to the perpetrators of cyberstalking. Secondly, I discuss ways in which Internet pornography can be analysed in terms of the gaze.

Perpetrators of Internet child pornography

My discussion revolves around the events leading up to the sentencing of seven men in early 2001 for membership of the so-called 'Wonderland Club,' an international paedophile ring who traded three-quarters of a million images of child pornography on the Internet (Panorama, 2001). One of the perpetrators, David Hines, who received a criminal sentence, described how easy it was to obtain images of child pornography on the Internet – within 24 hours of first going on-line he had found material. He met other paedophiles. As with cyberstalking cases, this group of people thought they were protected by the anonymity of the Internet, so they traded sexually explicit images of children and talked about them. As a shy, introverted person, again similar to those who perpetrate cyberstalking crimes, he had found an instant set of friends. The problem was not just the trading of images, but also the way that paedophiles had an easy way to contact each other and to reinforce their beliefs that sex with children was not wrong, to promote the ghastly idea that somehow these children were 'in relationships' with adults. Paedophiles also shared information about how to 'groom' children for abuse.

 With cyberstalking, the availability of the technology has been the trigger for some perpetrators, as in the case of the woman college student fixated on a male relative. With Internet paedophile rings, the technology also seems to act as a trigger. Some members of the Wonderland Club abused children themselves so that the images would enhance their status amongst other members of the club. Reports of a more recent case reinforces further the notion of technology as trigger. More directly, a leading article in the UK newspaper, *The Guardian* (2001) points out that child pornography used to be rare and hard to find. However, in 'Operation Landmark' the police uncovered 60,000 images of children under 16 unloaded and traded on 33 newsgroups. The implication is, of course, that the quantity of child pornography has grown enormously and that there is a causal link between this and the widespread use of the Internet. However, we need to retain a degree of open-mindedness about this until there are further, more concrete data about the scale of activity afforded by new media.

Pornography and the gaze

In a very chilling sense, these people were turning an abusive, adult, authoritative, male gaze upon young children whose very age and innocence made it impossible to mount a defence for themselves in the way that the adult women were able to in the cyberstalking cases. Yet, here, the state authorities, the police, actually watched the paedophile ring live, and anonymously, on the Internet, over a period of two years, in order to gain enough evidence to charge and convict the perpetrators. However, the UK law under which they were charged (which has subsequently been amended), only allowed for maximum sentences of 18 months. This further underscores the need for Internet legislation to keep pace with criminal activity. Furthermore, the responsibility of the Internet Service Providers is called into question. Operation Landmark focused on open newsgroups where the ISP, Demon, allowed the police authorities unprecedented access to newsgroups to monitor them over a period of weeks. On the one hand, it could be argued that the ISP had not done enough to police its user groups itself. On the other hand, serious issues of freedom of speech are raised. This is especially problematic given that current rating and blocking systems on the Internet continue to excite controversy.

The gaze of the criminals on their victims and the gaze of the authorities on the criminal activity are two obvious senses of the gaze. Yet there is a further sense in which the gaze continues to fall upon these children whose lives have been wrecked by such abuse. Many of the children have never been identified and as their images have spread so far on the Internet they may be there for ever, gazed upon by others. A quote from a BBC documentary (Panorama, 2001) reinforces this:

> CORBIN (reporter): The policemen who patrol the Internet still see the faces of hundreds of Wonderland children. They are out there for ever.
> FOTTRELL (police): A lot of these are the equivalent of movie stars, they're famous, they're celebrities. All their pictures are well known.
> CORBIN: What is the effect on the children of their notoriety?
> FOTTRELL: They are going to be . . . their abuse is going to continue for the rest of their life. That documentation of their abuse is going to be part of their life forever.

In these chilling examples, it is hard to see how a gaze can be turned back on the abuser by the abused as the power relationship is so imbalanced. However, the official state surveillance of the police authorities, often covertly watching activities on-line for some time, is a gaze which can, in some senses, be turned against the abusers and bring them to justice. At the same time, as the above quote demonstrates, the nature of the technology is such that images of abused children can remain in corners of the Internet for ever, in a sense continuing their abuse indefinitely. There is also an unfortunate twist in the way that the Internet affords a negative sense of anonymity as many of the children whose images have been displayed are never identified.

Conclusion

My aim, in this paper, has been to highlight the way that some current cyberethics problems can be better analysed when they are the subject of feminist analyses which highlight the way that gender is a crucial variable in achieving an understanding of the problems in question. This argument is particularly pertinent for cyberstalking and Internet paedophile rings. As both involve severe violations of privacy and also voyeuristic and abusive aspects, I have found a feminist version of the concept of the 'gaze' and how it relates to bodies and privacy to be useful in analysis. However, I am conscious that the notion of gazing is but one aspect, and, indeed is probably not powerful enough on its own; rather, it must be combined with other aspects of feminist ethics to produce a sufficiently robust and far reaching analysis. Nevertheless, a number of issues have been raised for further discussion.

There is no doubt that the concept of the 'gaze' in the electronic world and the complexity of power relations that it raises are ripe for further analysis. Secondly, we must examine in more detail the suggestion made above that the technology may 'tip the balance' in susceptible individuals and act as a spur to antisocial, criminal or other undesirable behaviour. Technological determinism lies as a trap for the unwary along this path and dystopian views of the Internet as a haven for criminals somehow miss the point. Although technology as a trigger is a serious issue, it is impossible to say how individuals in reported cases would have behaved without it. Of course, we must take very seriously the suggestion that, as argued in the last section, serious cases of child abuse are taking place on the Internet, but it is very difficult to say if using the Internet causes an increase in the sum total of abuse in the world. This illustrates one of the most important messages from the scholarly community studying science and technology. No matter how much we inscribe a set of users and uses into the design of a technological artefact, we can never fully predict how it will be used (Wajcman, 1991). This is one of the strongest arguments to be made against technological determinism, or the view that the trajectories of technologies are predetermined and drive our behaviour rather than the other way around. This signals that we would do well to study the history of the creation and use of pornography through various technologies and to treat it as another topic for analysis in the arena of studies in science and technology.

[. . .]

An appropriate reaction to child pornography on the internet is surely reasonable. This suggests that we need to examine carefully the new behaviour which surrounds the creation and use of pornography on the Internet, to understand how far it encourages new and more liberal modes of sexual expression, and on the darker side, how it reinforces and even encourages abusive behaviour and relationships particularly against women and children. Authors correctly urge caution against the tide of moral panic (Edwards, 2000). Yet, at the same time, we need to analyse and better understand how technology is related to desire and the ways in which the technology has been the trigger for some perpetrators of antisocial and criminal behaviour. The next step in producing a gendered cyberethics will involve bringing the weight of arguments from the, by now, considerable literature on feminist ethics (Tong, 1999) to bear on more of such problems to produce extended analyses of similar case studies against a solid theoretical backdrop.

References

Adam, A. *Artificial Knowing: Gender and the Thinking Machine*. Routledge, London and New York, 1998.

Adam, A. Gender and Computer Ethics. *ACM Computers and Society*, 30(4): 17–24, 2000.

Adam, A. Computer Ethics in a Different Voice. *Information and Organization*, 11(4): 235–61, 2001.

Brail, S. The Price of Admission: Harassment and Free Speech in the Wild, Wild West. In L. Cherny, L. and E. Wise, editors, *Wired Women: Gender and New Realities in Cyberspace*, pages 141–157. Seal Press, Seattle, WA, 1996.

Burt, T. Stalking and Voyeurism over the Internet: Psychiatric and Forensic Issues. *Proc. Academy of Forensic Science*, 3: 172, 1997.

DeCew, J. *In Pursuit of Privacy: Law, Ethics, and the Rise of Technology*. Cornell University Press, Ithaca and London, 1997.

Edwards, L. Pornography and the Internet, In L. Edwards and C. Waelde, editors, *Law & the Internet: A Framework for Electronic Commerce*, pages 275–308. Oxford, Hart, 2000.

Lane, F. *Obscene Profits: The Entrepreneurs of Pornography in the Cyber Age*. Routledge, New York and London, 2000.

MacCannell, D., and MacCannell, J.F. Violence, Power and Pleasure: A Revisionist Reading of Foucault from the Victim Perspective. In C. Ramazanoglu, editor, *Up Against Foucault: Explorations of Some Tensions Between Foucault and Feminism*, pages 203–238. Routledge, London and New York, 1993.

MacKinnon, C. *The Sexual Harassment of Working Women*. Yale University Press, New Haven, CT, 1979.

Meloy, J. The Psychology of Stalking. In J. Meloy, editor, *The Psychology of Stalking: Clinical and Forensic Perspectives*, pages 1–23. Academic Press, New York, 1998.

Mingo, J. *Caught in the Net: An Online Posse Tracks Down an Internet Stalker*. Online. Available http://www.houstonpress. com/extra/cyberstalk.html (24 March 2000).

Moor, J. Towards a Theory of Privacy for the Information Age. In R.A. Spinello and H. T. Tavani, editors, *Readings in Cyberethics*, pages 349–359. Jones and Bartlett, Sudbury, MA, 2001.

Nagel, T. A View from Nowhere. Oxford University Press, Oxford, 1986.

Neustatter, A. Mind that Child. *Guardian Unlimited*, August, 15, 2000. Online. Available http://www.guardian.co.uk/ comment/story/0,3604,354423,00.html (21st February, 2002).

Packard, A. Does Proposed Federal Cyberstalking Legislation Meet Constitutional Requirements? *Communication Law and Policy*, 5: 505–538, 2000.

Panorama. Transcript of 'The Wonderland Club', Broadcast on 11th February, 2001. Online. Available http://www. bbc.co.uk/panorama (12th February, 2001).

Reno, J. *Cyberstalking: A New Challenge for Law Enforcement and Industry. A Report from the Attorney General to the Vice President.* Online. Available http://www.usdoj.gov/ ag/cyberstalkingreport.html (30 November 1999).

Roiphe, K. *The Morning After: Sex, Fear and Feminism.* Hamish Hamilton, London, 1993.

The Guardian. Cyber-Stalkers Make Computer New Tool of Terror. 29 November, broadsheet section, 13, 1999.

The Guardian. Nine Held in Net Child Porn Raids. 29 November, broadsheet section, 2, 2001.

Thomas, A. M., and Kitzinger, C. *Sexual Harassment: Contemporary Feminist Perspectives.* Open University Press, Buckingham, 1997.

Tong, R. Feminist Ethics. In E. Zalta, editor, *The Stanford Encyclopedia of Philosophy* (Fall 1999 Edition). Online. Available http://plato.stanford.edu/archives/fall1999/entries/feminism-ethics/ (24 November 1999).

USA Today. Gore Asks Reno to Study Cyberstalking. 26 February, 1999. Online. Available http://www.usatoday.com/life/cyber/tech/cte509.html (30 November, 1999).

Wajcman, J. *Feminism Confronts Technology.* Polity Press, Cambridge, UK, 1991.

Welsh, S. The Multidimensional Nature of Sexual Harassment: An Empirical Analysis of Women's Sexual Harassment Complaints. *Violence Against Women,* 6: 118–141, 2000.

White, M. Visual Pleasure in Textual Places: Gazing in Multi-User Object-Oriented Worlds. In E. Green and A. Adam, editors, *Virtual Gender: Technology, Consumption and Identity,* pages 124–149. Routledge, London and New York, 2001.

PART III

REPRESENTING MEDIA VIOLENCE

Within media and cultural studies research there is a long tradition of both quantitative and qualitative approaches to the analysis of media texts. This has equally been the case in studies that centre on representations of violence. Indeed, quantitative approaches have been enormously popular with government officials, media policy organizations and lobby groups who often commission investigators to count the frequency of media depictions of violence, especially in television programming. This has been done in an effort to quantify the range of violent actions and behaviour depicted, as well as the types of characters associated with that behaviour. From such analyses, based on the frequency with which audiences might encounter certain types of violent scenarios and characters, extrapolations are made about the likely negative cognitive and social effects of the depictions.

Critical researchers are often disparaging of quantitative content analyses, arguing that the mere counting of media representations of violence is woefully inadequate in identifying how representations are culturally encoded with meaning. These scholars have argued that any depiction of violence has to be considered in the context of its production and representation within the given medium in which it appears. This does not preclude the possibility of content analyses making useful contributions to media violence debates, but it does identify the need, as critical theorists argue, to consider how media violence draws on, and is embedded in, a whole range of social, cultural, and political discourses and power relations, not just those only about violence, but also about gender, sexuality, ethnicity, class, nationalism, etc.

Douglas R. Bruce's chapter, the first reading in this section, takes on the challenge posed by a growing number of researchers to broaden conceptual approaches to understanding media violence in children's television programming. To that end, Bruce uses the violence of *The Road Runner* cartoon series as a starting point for a mythical-rhetorical analysis of the cartoon's message system. He explores how the animated short cartoon re-enacts the Greek myth of Sisyphus. This tale of an absurd hero living a futile life, Bruce argues, is reproduced in *The Road Runner* in the context of the post-World War II technological boom in the US. The continual pursuit of technological progress, he suggests, is the source of most of the violence in the cartoon. The use of a 'children's' medium to critique reliance on technology offers substantial intellectual freedom to the animator, Bruce maintains, and, in turn, to the viewer and the critic. Examination of *The Road Runner* yields insights into the meanings of cartoon violence, how the media reproduce mythic structures, and into the potentially rich message systems of children's media.

From there, attention turns to an analysis of gendered violence found in many recent Hindi films. Srividya Ramasubramanian and Mary Beth Oliver's chapter presents an exploratory and critical content analysis which examines portrayals of **sexual violence** in these films. Nine were randomly selected from box office hits from the years 1997–1999. Employing conceptual insights drawn from script theory and social learning perspectives, the authors concluded that what they categorize as 'moderate sexual violence' is depicted as fun, enjoyable, and a normal expression of romantic love. Additionally, victims were more likely to be women rather than men, and sexual violence committed by heroes was a common portrayal, particularly moderate violence such as harassment or 'eve teasing' of women with whom the heroes ultimately became romantically involved. Finally, Ramasubramanian and Oliver suggest, that while severe sexual violence was portrayed as criminal and serious, 'moderate sexual violence' was treated as being fun and romantic.

Jennifer Paff Ogle, Molly Eckman and Catherine Amoroso Leslie's chapter moves the focus from fictional to factual violence in their study of newspaper representations of the 1999 shootings at Columbine High School in Colorado as an appearance-linked social problem. Using a '**social constructivist**' conceptual approach, the authors employed qualitative textual analysis to examine news reporting of this incident. The authors argue that news reports of the shootings seem to suggest that even wealthy US suburbs, where people tend to dress conservatively (in respectable, 'Republican' clothes), are not immune from the 'toxicity' wrought by 'antisocial' youth subcultures and their particular styles of dress such as the Trench Coat Mafia (to which the Columbine shooters, Eric Harris and Dylan Klebold belonged). Thus, any school campus, anywhere, could be at risk. Ogle, Eckman and Leslie conclude that the attempt to render the Columbine shootings as personal and as scary rather than as an indication of certain problems in the structures of US society reflect the news media's increasing orientation toward entertainment and away from political analysis.

We then turn back to an examination of fictional media violence in Magdala Peixoto Labre and Lisa Duke's study of the *Buffy the Vampire Slayer* video game based on the television series of the same name. Labre and Duke analyse the game's construction of Buffy as a hero who fights, in contradistinction to her rather different portrayal in the television show. The video game provides a one-dimensional construction of female heroism, based on the Warrior archetype and omitting the Caregiver/Martyr archetype often present in descriptions of female heroes. Like other fighting games, *Buffy the Vampire Slayer* exaggerates the sexual characteristics of its female characters. In so doing, it creates a certain ambiguity between feminine empowerment and subjugation. Labre and Duke argue that the construction of Buffy in the game provides support for the idea that female heroes can be powerful but must also conform to traditional constructions of femininity. In the end, the authors suggest, the game promotes anti-intellectualism and reinforces gender stereotypes about women.

The final chapter in this section is Debra Merskin's textual analysis of selected speeches to the nation given by George W. Bush in the weeks following the attacks on the US on September 11, 2001. Bush's rhetoric in these speeches, from his public statements on September 11, 2001 to January 29, 2002 built on stereotypical words and images already established in more than twenty years of US media and popular culture portrayals of Arabs as evil, bloodthirsty, animalistic terrorists. The author concludes that Bush's speeches reflected an identifiable model of enemy image construction that had, and continues to have, important human rights implications for Arab American citizens and non-citizens.

VIOLENCE IN CHILDREN'S CARTOONS

14

THE ROAD RUNNER AS MYTHICAL DISCOURSE

Douglas R. Bruce

Children spend a great deal of time watching animated cartoons, and scholars spend a great deal of time studying children watching cartoons. But for all the attention granted to children's cartoons, the range of studies is relatively limited. Outside of a few articles in popular culture and film studies journals, studies tend to be descriptive and normative: They count instances of violence, and they condemn them. Crawford (1991) notes that 'almost all discussion of TV cartoons for kids adheres to a single model and participates in a single discourse – the condemnation of cartoons on TV on the basis that they contribute to the corruption of children' (p. 113). When we begin from the assumption that children's programming is 'bad,' we limit our options for a full analysis of programs as a discourse with many possible messages for children.

I argue here for a broader discursive analysis of children's cartoons by focusing on 'The Road Runner' as one of the high points of the genre. Rather than finding violence so that it can be condemned, I undertake a criticism based on the messages transmitted by that violence; violent episodes will be seen as part of the complex and mythic discourse of the animation. In such a critical enterprise, the violence of the cartoon serves as a starting point for analysis rather than as a destination. I want to understand how the violence of 'The Road Runner' operates within a complex visual message system. The cartoon's violence can be taken to present a critique of the bases of America's historical-mythic creation of a cultural identity.

The Road Runner and the Children's Cartoon

Animation has a long history in the United States as a medium designed primarily – if not exclusively – for the entertainment of children. Animated films emerged along with the film industry, and major animation studios devoted themselves to producing mostly short subjects aimed at children, along with occasional feature-length films (Bendazzi, 1994, pp. 83–100). These cartoon shorts joined with original productions to become a staple of children's television, particularly on Saturday mornings (Crawford, 1991, p. 114).

Chuck Jones, one of the most talented animators at the Warner Brothers Studios, created 'The Road Runner' in 1948, at the juncture point between animated films and television cartoons. His animations have enjoyed a long run in both media. Many consider the series to be the finest work of both Jones and the Warner Brothers animation wing (Bendazzi, 1994, p. 134). The basic plot of 'The Road Runner' across all these years has been simple and repetitive: A hungry coyote, frustrated in his ability to capture a road runner, turns to human technologies and inventions, usually obtained via mail order from the Acme Corporation. His attempts to capture the road runner always fail, usually because the technology has let him down; more often than not, he 'dies' as a result, only to be reborn in the next futile sequence (see Maltin, 1980, p. 261). Bendazzi notes that Jones has recreated the myth of Sisyphus in this cartoon (p. 134). We can also easily derive from this cartoon a critique of the technological explosion of the postwar United States, as well as a sardonic commentary on the notion of a 'conquest of nature' via technology. Thus, the reproduction of the myth of Sisyphus here may be functional as well as structural – it serves a critical purpose as well as providing a basic narrative device. Moreover, the juxtaposition of the myth of Sisyphus with the historical conditions of the United States in the latter half of the twentieth century also bears a deeper examination.

Such an analysis will suggest that there is more at work in 'The Road Runner' than simple violence or 'mere' children's entertainment. I explore this surplus meaning through a discussion of the historical tendency to embed 'adult' messages in 'children's' media and through an analysis of the 'adult' messages recoverable through a mythic analysis of 'The Road Runner'. I will suggest that the children's animation may actually offer a more compelling and authentic critique of contemporary culture than is possible in more scholarly approaches.

Animated Cartoons as Social Documents

Animations are the rhetorical heirs of the nursery rhyme. Dismissed by the 'adult' world as a 'children's medium,' cartoons may say, do, and show all kinds of things that would be 'forbidden' in more serious cultural forms.

[. . .]

Animated children's cartoon [. . .] characters demonstrate all manner of anti-social, 'unacceptable' behaviors. They are rude, short-tempered, and willful. Mickey Mouse in 'Steamboat Willie' (1928) produces music by pulling on cats' tails. Bugs Bunny was 'cross dressing' more than a decade before Milton Berle and Billy Wilder brought this practice to human television and film behaviors (see Abel, 1995). Characters in the Warner Brothers' 'Looney Tunes' series were ridiculed for their speech impediments and other infirmities in ways that would be unthinkable in other media; and cartoons frequently display overt political, social, and economic messages without arousing much ire from the viewing public. Tex Avery, considered by many to be one of the greatest animators of the century, even managed to embed all sorts of erotic imagery in his cartoons (Bendazzi, 1994, p. 297), although the author of this essay has never been able to identify any in Avery's 'Droopy Dawg' series.

Over the past decade or so, film theorists have begun to explore the political messages of children's cartoons in more detail. Disney cartoons – especially the later Mickey Mouse cartoons, have been lambasted for their reproduction of bourgeois cultural values(see, e.g., George, 1990, p. 319); Donald Duck and other Disney standards have been taken as an icon of imperialism (Dorfman & Mattelart, 1975); Warner Brothers' cartoons have been studied for their parodic and 'deconstructive' elements (George, 1990, pp. 300–302); and the film *Who Framed Roger Rabbit* has been hailed as a masterpiece of deconstruction and postmodern textuality (Cholodenko, 1991b, see especially pp. 210–11). Ferrell (1991) argues that animations can call forth a Freudian sense of the 'uncanny,' calling to consciousness all sorts of repressed longings.

Cartoons can do forbidden and disruptive things because unlike 'adult' media they are not taken seriously. Consider the White House uproar against the film, *Contact*, for its relatively innocuous, but unauthorized use of film footage from a Clinton press conference. The president's press secretary portrayed this as an egregious attack on his privacy and his presidency (Shogren, 1997, p. A1), but when children's cartoons such as *Pinky and the Brain* and *The Simpsons* have caricatured Clinton as a brainless clod, the White House has not raised such public objections. These, after all, are 'only cartoons.' When we abandon such prejudices about animation, we may more fully appreciate the political and cultural import of its messages. As a first step in this abandonment, I turn to the most salient element of 'The Road Runner' for most students of children's programming: its violence.

'The Road Runner': Violence as Rhetoric

A viewer of 'The Road Runner' cartoons cannot escape their violence. They depict a violent situation: A predator seeks to capture prey, fails, and tries again. The means of capture usually are violent – explosives, catapults, bazookas, and other weapons of war; violent construction technologies such as jack-hammers and wrecking balls; and various medical technologies that do violence to the body (e.g. pills that instantly produce larger and stronger legs). And the outcome of each effort is violent: More often than not, Wile E. Coyote plunges off a cliff to smash into the ground in a canyon deep below, or he is 'blown up' (never to the point of permanent death) by the device intended to capture the Road Runner. He 'dies' at the end of most of the sequences in *The Bugs Bunny–Road Runner Movie*, as in most of the 27 animated shorts produced by Jones, only to live again at the beginning of the next sequence.

Even if we attune ourselves only to the violence in this cartoon, certain features of that violence stand out in the discourse. This is not a Disney style parable of the outdoors where the predator 'naturally' seeks and kills the prey. Although Wile E. Coyote, as a predator, has the *techne* to capture prey – speed, intelligence, experience – he specifically foreswears his natural *techne* in favor of human technology. Moreover, the violence of the cartoon is generated by this technology rather than by nature: The technologies themselves are, more often than not, military; even un-military technologies such as wings for flight are turned to violent ends; and the violent cataclysm with which Wile E. Coyote is defeated in each sequence results from a failure of the complex technology he has brought to bear on his simple task.

Here, then, we have multiple absurdities. A cartoon – an instrument of highly sophisticated technology – demonstrates to us that using technology results in continual failures. We have a depiction of what should be a 'naturally' violent behavior (predator captures prey) which never comes to pass; instead, we see an artificially generated violence of technologies gone bad. And we see disasters which should obliterate the protagonist instead simply renew the sequence of trial and failure. These absurdities suggest considerable manipulation of cartoon 'reality,' and thus rhetorical import.

'The Road Runner' may be read as a critique of 20th Century American culture on technological and social grounds.'

'The Road Runner' is, above all, an anti-technological use of technology. Where many technological cartoons celebrate the power of technology (*The Transformers* even accomplished their ends by changing from humans into technological beings, much like the movies' Robo-Cop), this one clearly abhors it. Technology here interferes with natural activity. The more sophisticated the machinery, the more spectacular the failure: Wile E. Coyote chases the Road Runner with a knife and fork (the simplest sort of human technology), and he merely fails to catch up with the speedy creature; he uses a bow to propel himself forward, and he simply falls; he adds an arrowhead to his own head, tries again with the bow, and this time is lodged within a telephone pole; when he uses a cannon, the cannon falls off a cliff (along with the hapless coyote), swivels in mid-air, and fires directly at him as they both fall to a canyon floor. In his effort to transcend his nature as a coyote, Wile E. finds that the very means of his liberation guarantee his failure. Technology makes things worse rather than better, adding injuries to insults, as it were.

[. . .]

As these technologies distance us from the natural world, they also may alienate us from each other and even from ourselves, as our lives revolve increasingly around using and maintaining technological gadgets: I have known people much more upset by a computer crash than by breakdowns in their personal relationships. In such a context, the social and cultural critique embodied in 'The Road Runner' acquires more meaning now than it had in the time it was created.

Here, then, we have violence clearly used in the service of a larger message system. Violence in 'The Road Runner' serves as an audio-visual punctuation mark; it locates the end of a sequence of actions at the failure of Wile E. Coyote. Indeed, it is the very emblem of failure and an announcement of futility. The notion that reliance on technology renders us inauthentic in our environments is suggested by the continual failure of Wile E. Coyote to accomplish his tasks using technology. This futility is the basis for the claim that the cartoon reproduces the myth of Sisyphus.

'The Road Runner' and the Myth of Sisyphus

Violence in 'The Road Runner' takes the form of a punishment. Wile E. Coyote suffers for his aspirations toward humanity. In this he shares the fate of Sisyphus, sentenced to his eternally futile task of rolling a boulder up a hill for his sin of aspiring to a god-like transcendence of death. (See Bendazzi, 1994, p. 134.)

[. . .]

Wile E. Coyote shares many of the characteristics of Sisyphus. Like Sisyphus, he aspires to partake of the life of beings different from himself: a creature of the wild who aims through economic and technological means to live the life of a human being; a cartoon character who seeks to be 'real.' His punishment also is to be given qualities of that alternative existence – here, access to technology rather than immortality – in a manner that renders them worse than useless to him. They are the instruments of his violent and spectacular failures.

Nonetheless, we should note that Wile E. Coyote is a peculiarly *American* version of Sisyphus. This Americanization of the myth can be seen in his boundless optimism. No failure is ever deemed permanent; he seems always to believe in the technologies he employs, and he never wavers in his confidence of success. This optimism blinds him to the other possibilities of his own nature. He does not seem to know that as a coyote he could catch prey without assistance. Nor does he know that as a cartoon character, he requires no sustenance. Nor does he seem aware of the violence he does to himself and to his natural surroundings by introducing unnecessary technologies. Whereas the absurd heroism of Sisyphus derives from his tragic knowledge of futility, Wile E. Coyote's inconceivable unawareness energizes the absurdity of 'The Road Runner.'

If Wile E. Coyote remains unaware of his fate, we cannot say the same for the viewer of the cartoon. The awareness of absurdity and the freedom purchased by this awareness reside not with the character but with the viewers. We assume for Wile E. Coyote the role of the absurd hero: We watch the action take place (perhaps even rooting for him to succeed) in full knowledge that his efforts are doomed to failure. The payoff for the viewers (our happiness) lies specifically in watching him fail. We want him to succeed, but we would be appalled if he did. Our mythic consciousness creates the absurdity we take from the cartoon.

[. . .]

Cartoons provide just such a dialogue between the life world and illusion. They present the illusion of life before the eyes of living audiences. They often re-create specific times and spaces, but they are not bound to do so. They can ignore the dictates of reason. Enjoyment of cartoons presupposes that we can both suspend our disbelief (accepting that the coyote can die again and again without ever 'actually' dying) and retain our awareness that this is 'just a cartoon' (whose characters can 'survive' catastrophes that we could not). Cartoons thus invoke our mythical consciousness, our willingness to accept things that are empirically or rationally 'untrue' (see Cassirer, 1955).

[. . .]

Mythical Qualities in 'The Road Runner'

'The Road Runner' takes place against a background of desert, mountains and plateaus. The scenery is that of the Western United States. Such a setting confers on the cartoon its particular mythic tone. History and popular culture have inscribed the American West as a the site of a dual conquest. The 'winning of the West' involved the 'taming' of the natural environment through construction, farming, and mining technologies; it also consisted in the use of military technologies to subdue the indigenous populations. While these two forms of conquest typified the entire process of colonization, the 'American myth' as recorded in histories and as enacted in Western movies, novels, and television programs identifies them most strongly with the West (see, e.g., Schulte, 1995).

'The Road Runner' re-enacts the participants in the battle for the West. Wile E. Coyote presents us with a stereotype of Western humanity – educated, urbane, and utterly reliant on technology to interpose between himself and the natural world. The Road Runner serves as a force of nature and as a reminder of the native populations – uneducated (by Western standards), but also possessed of a certain native intelligence (it occasionally contributes to the demise of the coyote's devices and sometimes returns to mock the coyote after a failure.); living in harmony with nature; and recognizing its own nature. Unlike Wile E. Coyote, the Road Runner does not aspire to be more than it is or to acquire the accoutrements of humanity. It never speaks (emitting only the double beep as the auditory marker of its presence), and only occasionally uses written language, in the form of a sign held up to explain something. Thus, Wile E. Coyote is a 'settler' of sorts, bringing Western cultural values to bear on the natural surroundings. The Road Runner is more typical of the native population, living as part of the land, having no need for Western technologies or practices. Moreover, the Road Runner as a creature of nature emerges in these cartoons as impervious and superior to the technologies of the coyote.

In such a scenario, the cartoon is not simply a re-enactment of the battle for the West – rather, it subverts that battle. The 'real' battle was a bloody and destructive conquest by a technological civilization over an indigenous one. In 'The Road Runner,' technology is insufficient to conquer either nature or the inhabitants of the natural world. Moreover, technology is the very instrument driving the failure of conquest. Wile E. Coyote is blown up by the bombs that were meant for the Road Runner; the machines meant to help him match speeds with the Road Runner carry him past his prey and over a cliff; his balloons and rockets fail him in mid-air, and he plunges into a canyon. The more complex the technology for conquering nature, the more pronounced the failure.

Within the space of 'The Road Runner' cartoon, the greatest sin seems to be a failure to live authentically or harmoniously. For Wile E. Coyote, the stark beauty and grandeur of the setting are wasted. They are simply the backdrop against which to carry out his machinations; in his aspiration to be human, they have no greater significance than as a tool. The Road Runner, by contrast, 'lives' within the boundaries of the scene. It is allowed to recognize its 'being' as a natural creature and as a cartoon character. Perhaps the best example of the contrast between these two modes of being resides in the famous scene in which the coyote attempts to capture the Road Runner by painting a false road on the side of a mountain, with the idea of stopping it dead when it collides with the mountain. The Road Runner, as an authentic cartoon character, recognizes the painted flat as its natural habitat, and continues down the 'road' as part of the natural ecology of its character. When the coyote tries to follow, he smashes into the wall. (This scene was redrawn many times. Its earliest appearance is probably in 'Fast and Furryous,' 1948.) By assuming the strictures of human 'reality,' Wile E. Coyote loses his ability to function within his 'natural' space.

[. . .]

[The] theme of 'The Road Runner' may well be that 'the conquest of the West' was at best an ironic feat. Both characters serve a role here. Wile E. Coyote symbolizes the futility of technology in the face of nature – a reminder that earthquakes, fires, mudslides and floods are more powerful and destructive than our technologies. The Road Runner can serve as a reminder of what we have destroyed in our zeal to conquer. We want it to succeed, to continue its quest to run freely through the Western scenery. (Indeed, we would be appalled and even outraged to see a cartoon in which it was killed and devoured.) But we know that the natural inhabitants of the West have not fared so well: They have been forced either to assimilate into the dominant culture or be confined to reservations, denied the ability to run freely through their ancestral homes. Only within the space of the cartoon do we glimpse their former freedom and harmony with nature.

[. . .]

'The Road Runner' shares with the myth of Sisyphus the quality of time-lessness in the form of endless repetition; the simple plot of 'Coyote employs technology to catch the Road Runner; Coyote fails' repeats both within the cartoon, from episode to episode, and in an endless cycle of Saturday mornings. Moreover, the necessity of death – our surest marker of the passage of time – is effaced in the cartoon; Wile E. Coyote is often 'killed' by his failures, but he never dies.

However, the cartoon also is strongly bound to time, both in the tech-nologies that bind it to the twentieth century and in the exactness of the six-minute duration of each episode. The episodes clearly reveal their location in the second half of the twentieth century through the military, construc-tion, and medical technologies used; while mail-order may pre-date this century, it also serves to temporalize 'The Road Runner,' as does the reli-ance on the specific mail-order entity, 'Acme,' as in the 'Acme Little Giant Do-It-Yourself Rocket-Sled Kit' which fails in a spectacular fashion at the end of *The Bugs Bunny–Road Runner Movie,* exploding into a fireworks display. More generally, the cartoon is bound to the modern and post-modern eras by the displayed (and ridiculed) theme of a technological con-quest of nature.

Jones reports that economic considerations dictated the six-minute length of the Warner Brothers' cartoon shorts. Distributors would not accept shorts of less than six minutes in duration, and the Warners refused to pay for cartoons longer than that (1991, p. 43). Perhaps, though, the confinement of this endless cycle of repetitions within a six-minute block of time may contribute to its mythic quality: we participate in a ritual within which traditional relationships of time and space are suspended, but one which has a precise and consistent duration in our own time. This ironic juxtaposition of timelessness and timeliness may create a space within which our world and the cartoon world co-exist, a balance in which we can lose ourselves in a cartoon whose regularity, rhythm, and repetition other-wise would seem simply boring.

The intrusion of 'normal' time into the idyllic time of the cartoon occurs as well in the matching of music to the animation. Brophy (1991, pp. 92–101) notes that Warner Brothers animators sought consciously to distinguish their musical scores from the Disney-style harmony with animations. Thus, Warner Brothers cartoons disrupt their classical accom-paniments with explosions, they introduce incongruous instruments such as banjos into symphonic performances, and they ridicule opera and sym-phony at every opportunity. Outside of the Road Runner's 'beep-beep,' music is the most salient auditory element for most of the cartoon, but the music suffers the same fate as the Coyote – doomed to endless, disruptive, and violent interruptions in its quest for harmony and completeness. The quotidian rhythm of the technological world cancels out the idealized rhythm of the symphonic world (see Brophy, 1991, pp. 103–104).

[. . .]

(Non)authorship and (Un)discipline in 'The Road Runner'

[. . .]

Chuck Jones worked in a 'children's medium,' a designation which, as noted earlier, gave him considerable freedom. The dismissal of his work from 'serious art and literature' opened up a space in which his credibility and his personal authority ceased to matter to viewers of his productions. Jones as an 'author' can be ignored in the cartoon in manners that we can never ignore the signification of 'authorship' in a more 'sophisticated' discursive form. One critic has suggested that Jones may be 'our greatest invisible actor' (Rose, 1984, p. 124).

[. . .]

Few people know that Ub Iwerks actually created Mickey Mouse, and few would identify a cartoon as a Chuck Jones or Tex Avery production. Rather, we know them by generic names (a cartoon short), by their series ('Looney Tunes'), or by their corporate identity (Warner Brothers, Hanna-Barbera, Disney). Thus, they are linked generically to other stories and folk tales for which authorship is irrelevant; the author of a nursery rhyme or a cartoon is not the source of its credibility or audience appeal (see Foucault, 1977, p. 125).

When Chuck Jones speaks through 'The Road Runner,' his voice is essentially silent. Moreover, the silence of his characters – Wile E. Coyote rarely spoke; the Road Runner only beeped – served to remove the authorial voice from the cartoon. The cartoonist's personality undoubtedly animated the animations. Wile E. Coyote and the Road Runner are manifestations of the comic and artistic genius of Chuck Jones, but this influence would be 'read' as the personality of his characters rather than as authorial presence. The means of production and dissemination of the animated cartoon short effectively conceal the 'return' of the viewer to the author: He drew still pictures, we perceive movement, his few words are mouthed by characters who clearly are not he, and the movie theater and television program give much less credence to authorship than is the case with the printed word.

[. . .]

Chuck Jones and the other Warner Brothers animators were largely *un*disciplined, in two senses of the word. First, they did not belong to any established discipline. They were engaged in a cultural practice – production of an economic good – rather than in disciplinary, intellectual activity. Moreover, their practice has tended to be overlooked or scorned by most disciplinary academics. Cholodenko has commented on the relative dearth of scholarly attention to animation for most of its history (1991a, pp. 9–12). More to the point, even as he introduces a volume designed to begin the remedying of that inattention, he draws a clear line between the animator and the scholar: 'With the exception of the talk by Chuck Jones which begins the book, it is *exclusively* of an academic nature, marked not only in the subjects addressed but in the approaches taken' (p. 12). While Cholodenko and his fellow writers accord Jones and his colleagues respect for what they do, they also clearly acknowledge that these animators are not members of the academic community.

This recognition accords Jones' cultural critique considerable freedom. Jones does not have to adhere to method or acknowledge his precursors. He could steal techniques from Disney with impunity; he could defy logic and scholarly convention to say what he wanted to say through his cartoon creations. While all discourses operate under constraints, the freedom from 'academic' constraints may well give Jones the license that Blair, Brown and Baxter (1994) would like to see for all writers.

Secondly, the animators at Warner Brothers were undisciplined in that they did largely what they wanted to do. While they did operate under strict time constraints, they otherwise were free to create. Jones noted this freedom in a 1988 keynote address: 'I've never overcome the wonder of that, that for over 57 or 58 years people have paid me for what I enjoy doing' (p. 37). The liberated creations consisted largely of destroying what others had done: parodying film genres and film stars; finding ways to duplicate what Disney had done so that they could destroy it; centering noise and confusion and destruction in their cartoons. Brophy (1991) describes their approach as anarchic and 'cacophonic' (pp. 86–87). Others have gone so far as to suggest that the Warner Brothers' cartoon shorts were a form of deconstruction (George, 1990, p. 300).

[. . .]

This lack of discipline seems to lie at the heart of 'The Road Runner.' It tells an historical story that never 'took place,' one in which the 'Conquest of Nature' is reversed. It turns the prevailing myths of American popular culture on their heads. It 'reconstructs' both the myth of Sisyphus and the myth of the conquest of the American West. Moreover, this deconstruction is accomplished without system, without scholarship, and without rigor. And it is all the better for the absence of these normalizing discursive demands.

The freedom from constraint enjoyed by the authors, along with their invisibility in the final product, also liberates the text for the audience. The cartoons as depicted here amount to elaborate 'inside jokes,' ones whose intended meanings would be accessible only to a handful of animators. With the 'intended' meanings subdued in the visual text, the reader is left to recover other meanings according to his or her conventions of interpretation. In the case of 'The Road Runner,' this liberation is extended by the relative absence of verbal cues to meaning; interpretation depends almost entirely on the processing of the visual field.

This is not to say, though, either that the animation is 'meaningless' or that it would support any interpretation (although there certainly can be valid interpretations other than the one offered here). Rather, the cartoon's meaning emerges from a combination of evoking mythic consciousness and subverting the specific mythic contents of Sisyphus and the 'conquest of the West.' The cartoon juxtaposes itself ironically with the viewer's normal senses of time, place, and number – offering a simple, familiar narrative sequence and setting, but interposing it with 'unreal' elements of animals undertaking human activities and with deaths that repeat endlessly.

[. . .]

These features of the animation allow a critic to construct a meaning system out of 'The Road Runner,' substituting cultural conventions of myth and mythic consciousness for the private visions of Jones and his fellow animators. Establishing a dialogue between the cartoon's violent images and American culture, in turn, allows the critic both to ground the reading in a close examination of the text and to use the text as cultural critique – turning the cartoon against certain cultural 'givens' rather than using those 'givens' to explain the cartoon. A text that results from an 'undisciplined' act of creation may serve the critic best in this regard: An act of authorial freedom sets the text free to 'speak' as it will, and that in turn frees the casual reader to appropriate the text as she or he will, and allows the critical reader to engage the text in ways that yield new meanings.

Conclusion

The potential of 'The Road Runner' to yield up such complex meanings suggests that the animated children's cartoon, like the nursery rhyme of earlier eras, is a sophisticated, if easily overlooked medium for message construction. If cartoons continue – and subvert – our mythic traditions, scholars have a reason to take them more seriously. They can serve as agents for cultural critique. Authentic cultural critique may be most possible when the reader contacts texts which were created with the greatest freedom from cultural constraints.

One of the strongest breaks from constraint in cartoons may be their violence. The vast majority of antisocial violence in children's programming occurs in cartoons (Wilson et al., 1998, p. 135). Studies of violence have, by and large, focused on the presence of violence as an empirical fact or on how violence sends a message *about* violence by the contexts in which it occurs. The analysis in this paper suggests that violence may be analyzed as an audio-visual cue to meanings about subjects other than itself – about technological failures, about persistence and optimism in the face of continued lack of success, about the ultimate failure of violent technologies to solve one's problems.

In 'The Road Runner,' violence is less about ends and means, justifications or lack thereof, and more of a punctuation mark. Moreover, its presence is less about serving good or evil purposes, and more about violence in the service of the absurd. When we view violence as a marker of other meanings, rather than a self-contained meaning system, we move the discussion of mediated violence away from the psychological questions of cause and effect, and toward rhetorical ones of meaning construction. Violence here has served as a catalyst to the interpretive process.

This claim is not meant to condone televisual violence; nor does it seek to undercut studies of cause and effect. Rather, I have aimed to show that the complex problem of mediated violence may provoke equally complex critical reactions. In the quest to understand violent programming, this approach may offer a small, missing piece of the puzzle, one that may help to clarify the outlines of the total picture.

[. . .]

References

Abel, S. (1995). The rabbit in drag: Camp and gender construction in the American animated cartoon. *Journal of Popular Culture, 29*, 183–202.

Bendazzi, G. (1994). *Cartoons: One hundred years of cinema animation* (A. Taraboletti-Segri, Trans.). Bloomington: Indiana University Press.

Blair, C., Brown, J. R., & Baxter, L. A. (1994). Disciplining the feminine. *Quarterly Journal of Speech, 80*, 383–404.

Brophy, P. (1991). The animation of sound. In A. Cholodenko (Ed.), *The illusion of life: Essays on animation* (pp. 67–112). Sydney: Power Publications.

Cassirer, E. (1955). *The philosophy of symbolic forms.* Volume 2: *Mythic thought* (pp. 88–92) (R. Mannheim, Trans.) New Haven: Yale University Press.

Cholodenko, A. (1991a). Introduction. In A. Cholodenko (Ed.), *The illusion of life: Essays on animation* (pp. 9–36). Sydney: Power Publications.

Cholodenko, A. (1991b). Who framed Roger Rabbit, or the framing of animation. In A. Cholodenko (Ed.), *The illusion of life: Essays on animation* (pp. 209–242). Sydney: Power Publications.

Crawford, B. (1991). Saturday morning fever In A. Cholodenko (Ed.), *The illusion of life: Essays on animation* (pp. 113–130). Sydney: Power Publications.

Dorfman, A., & Mattelart, A. (1975). *How to read Donald Duck: Imperialist ideology in the Disney comic* (D. Mingle, Trans.). New York: International General.

Ferrell, R. (1991). Life threatening life: Angela Carter and the uncanny. In A. Cholodenko (Ed.), *The illusion of life: essays on animation* (pp. 131–144). Sydney: Power Publications.

Foucault, M. (1977). What is an author? In D. F. Bouchard (Ed.), *Language, countermemory, practice: Essays and interviews by Michel Foucault* (D. Bouchard & S. Simon, Trans.). Ithica, NY: Cornell University Press.

George, R. (1990). Some spatial characteristics of the Hollywood cartoon. *Screen, 31*, 296–321.

Jones, C. (Producer). (1948). *Fast and furry-ous*. Animated Short.

Jones, C. (1991). What's up down under? Chuck Jones talks at the *Illusion of Life* conference. In A. Cholodenko (Ed.), *The illusion of life: Essays on animation* (pp. 37–66). Sydney: Power Publications.

Jones, C. (Producer). (1993). *The Bugs Bunny–Road Runner movie*.

Maltin, L. (1980). *Of mice and magic: A history of American animated cartoons.* New York: New American Library.

Rose, L. (1984, December). Our greatest invisible actor. *The Atlantic Monthly, 254*, 124–126.

Schulte, N. (1995). *The myth of the west: American as the last empire.* Grand Rapids, MI: William B. Eerdmans.

Shogren, E. (1997, July 15). White House protests film's use of Clinton. *The Los Angeles Times*. A1.

Wilson, B., Kunkel, D., Linz, D., Potter, J., Donnerstein, E., Smith, S., Blumenthal, E., & Berry, M. (1998). Part I: Violence in television programming overall: University of California, Santa Barbara study. In Center for Communication and Social Policy (Ed.), *National television violence study 2.* Thousand Oaks, CA: Sage.

PORTRAYALS OF SEXUAL VIOLENCE IN POPULAR HINDI FILMS

15

Srividya Ramasubramanian and Mary Beth Oliver

The incidence of sexual violence against women is greater in societies that have male-dominated ideologies and a history of violence, as is the case in India (Burt, 1980; Check & Malamuth, 1985; Linz & Malamuth, 1993). The number of registered cases of sexual crimes against women in India increased from 67,072 in 1989 to 84,000 in 1993 ('Crimes Against,' 1996). In 1995 alone, more than 25,000 cases of molestation and 12,000 cases of rape were reported in the capital city of New Delhi (West, 1996). It is estimated that well over 80% of sexual crimes go unreported ('Atrocities Against,' 2002). For example, only 7,643 of the estimated 50,000 instances of violence against women were reported to the police even in Kerala, a South Indian state with the highest women's literacy rate ('Atrocities Against,' 2002).

One specific form of sexual harassment called 'eve-teasing' is prevalent, especially in urban India. The term *eve-teasing* is used to refer to sexual harassment of women in public places such as the streets, public transportation, parks, beaches, and cinema halls. This type of public harassment by a lone man or gangs of men includes verbal assaults such as making passes or unwelcome sexual jokes; nonverbal assaults such as showing obscene gestures, winking, whistling, and staring; and physical assaults such as pinching, fondling, and rubbing against women in public places (Eve-teasing 1999; Stevens, 1984). In addition, in several instances eve-teasing has been followed by more violent assaults such as rape and murder. In trying to construct the profile of an eve-teaser, it is interesting to note that about 32% of eve-teasers are college students ('Films', 1998).

The severity of these incidents coupled with their high prevalence resulted in the legal declaration of eve-teasing as a punishable offense by the state government of Tamil Nadu in 1999, where it was announced that offenders would be penalized with up to 1 year of imprisonment or a fine of Rs. 10,000 or both ('Ordinance', 1999). Despite the seriousness of these incidents, research suggests that they are frighteningly commonplace. For example, a recent survey revealed that approximately 90% of college women in New Delhi have experienced sexual harassment in some shape or form ('Films', 1998). Yet, it is estimated that only about 1 in 10,000 eve-teasing occurrences are reported to the police ('Atrocities Against', 2002). The primary reasons why women abstain from reporting incidents of sexual violence are the unwieldy medico-legal process, concerns about continued violence, and fear of stigmatization (Prasad, 1999).

Mass Media and Sexuality in India

The variables that give rise to sexual violence in India are undoubtedly numerous and complex. However, for feminist media scholars, the idea that popular cinema plays a significant role in shaping notions about gender roles and gender identities within the Indian context is of special interest and concern (Bagchi, 1996; Ram, 2002). Cinema has been a dominant medium in India because of the sheer size and reach of its indigenous film industry. The Indian film industry produces about 800 feature films annually – the highest in the world (National Film Development Corporation, n.d.). Not only does India produce the largest numbers of films in the world, but also a sizeable amount of film consumption is common among almost all age groups, socioeconomic backgrounds, and geographical locations within India (Derne, 1995). It is estimated that every week approximately 90–100 million Indian viewers go to the cinema halls to watch films (Nair, Barman, & Chattopadhyay, 1999). Many cinema goers ritualistically make as many as 20–30 visits to the cinema hall in a month and repeatedly view a favorite film several dozens of times (Derne, 1999; Khare, 1985). Moreover, Indians films are popular not just in India but also amongst the Indian diaspora in countries such as the United States, United Kingdom, Canada, Fiji, Dubai, and Singapore (Bist, 2002). Indian-made films constitute the majority of the films watched by Indians; only about 5% of Indians watch non-Indian (mostly Hollywood) films (Anjum, 2002).

Apart from cinema halls, films also reach the Indian household through countdown shows on television that feature film-based song-and-dance hit numbers (Nair et al., 1999). In addition, access to cable television has also grown very rapidly in the last decade, with a penetration of over 50% of the urban Indian market as of 1997 (Nair et al., 1999). Futhermore, over 85%

of the cable television operators routinely screen two films a day through their own private local channels to attract their customers (Nair et al., 1999).

The importance of sexual portrayals in motion pictures is particularly relevant to Indian audiences, not only because these portrayals are viewed in abundance, but also because issues of sexuality are rarely discussed in other contexts (Derne, 1999). According to Derne (1999), Indian film portrayals form a 'privileged arena for construction of sexuality' for the common person, and serve as primary sources of information about how men and women are to behave in sexual relationships (p. 548). A recent study sponsored by UNICEF and Save the Children Fund in the Indian subcontinent showed that the film medium is influential, especially with teenaged boys, in teaching notions about masculinity, power, and violence in relationships with women (Poudyal, 2002). Similarly, researchers in the North American context have found that children and adolescents use media narratives (especially teen magazines and prime-time television programs) as sexual scripts for learning about dominant norms concerning gender, love, and sexuality (Carpenter, 1998; Pardun, 2002; Ward, 1995; Wood, 2001; Wood, Senn, Desmarais, Park, & Verberg, 2002).

Feminist scholars are particularly concerned that popular films in India too often portray women in stereotypical roles of subordination – accepting sexual violence as a normal part of relationships withmen (Dasgupta & Hegde, 1988; Gandhi & Shah, 1992). Further, they have pointed out that men's abuse of women is often glorified within Indian cinema (Derne, 1999). More specifically, critics have pointed out that the repeated glamorization of eve-teasing in films as a macho manifestation of a tough-acting, college student hero, who initially upsets the heroine but finally wins her attention, has fostered a climate supportive of such acts in real life (Birla, 2001; 'Films', 1998; Ravindran, 2001). Although many critics have voiced concerns, very few researchers have dealt with sexually violent portrayals in Indian films. In a rare study of its kind, Derne (1999) conducted a qualitative content analysis study of a selected few Hindi films in which violence and sexuality were often intertwined. Derne (1999) suggested that these films conveyed the notion that force and physical aggression were legitimate means of expressing romantic love. Therefore, sexual violence was not only 'normal' but also 'expected' in romantic relationships between heroes and heroines.

Links Between Media and Sexual Violence

Although little systematic research has explored the causal influences of Hindi films on sexual violence in India specifically, there is research in other cultures, particularly North America, that has explored the role of consumption of media portrayals of sexuality on viewers' behaviors. In this regard, some researchers have suggested that there is no causal relationship between access to sexually explicit material and the incidence of sexual crimes (Kutchinsky, 1991), that effects are observed only for individuals who are predisposed to be aggressive (Zillmann & Sapolsky, 1977), or that harmful effects are observed only for explicitly violent portrayals (Donnerstein, Linz, & Penrod, 1987). However, results of meta-analytic research suggest that there is a relationship between media consumption of sexually explicit materials (and particularly violent materials) and a number of variables related to sexual violence (Allen, D'Alessio, & Brezgel, 1995; Allen, Emmers, Gebhardt, & Giery, 1995). These analyses reported that exposure to sexually explicit media (both violent and nonviolent) was associated with increased rape-myth acceptance and with increased subsequent aggression, especially among angered participants (Allen, D'Alessio, et al., 1995; Allen, Emmers, et al., 1995). In addition, researchers have also reported that consumption of sexually explicit media (both violent and nonviolent) may lead to increased sexual callousness – the disregard or contempt for a woman's right to deny sexual access (Zillmann & Weaver, 1989). Similarly, other researchers have argued that consumption of media portrayals of sexual violence may lead to target desensitization – the belief that certain individuals are appropriate, natural, and safe targets of violence who are deserving of aggression (Check & Malamuth, 1985; Donnerstein & Berkowitz, 1981). Behavioral effects of exposure to sexually explicit material can take the form of imitation of new behaviors as well as lowered inhibitions to try out already learned behaviors (Russell, 1988). Finally, other researchers have examined the idea of sexual objectification, and have reported that the viewing of pornography can lead some male viewers to interpret subsequent interactions with women in inappropriate sexual or erotic terms (McKenzie-Mohr & Zanna, 1990).

[. . .]

The Present Research

Given the dearth of research on the effects of sexual violence with respect to popular Indian films and the need to investigate the effects of sexually explicit media amongst diverse populations, there is a need for research in the area of mediated sexual violence in India. The literature on effects of filmed sexual violence generally supports claims that Hindi films may be a contributory factor in sexual harassment. However, this would be true only if Hindi films actually depicted the types of images that are thought to play a role in influencing notions about sexuality in the Indian context. Hence, the first step in exploring this issue is to examine the types of portrayals that are commonly depicted in the films. At this point it is unclear if popular films meant for mass consumption would have any sexually violent material in the first place. In particular, because popular Hindi films are viewed by people of all age groups (rather than just by adults), one might expect that Hindi films would be unlikely to show sexual images. On the other hand, if Hindi films do provide an outlet for 'discussions' of sexual behaviors that serve to reinforce traditional views of women, then one might expect that Hindi films would be likely to show violence against women as normal and perhaps even enjoyable. Consequently, the purpose of this exploratory study was to examine the manner in which popular Hindi films portray sexual violence and the way in which violence might be associated with gender and romantic love. Specifically, we examined the following research questions:

RQ1: What proportion of sexual scenes contains violence?
RQ2: Is there a relationship between gender and likelihood of being the primary victim of sexual violence?
RQ3: Is there a relationship between character role and likelihood of being the primary perpetrator of sexual violence?
RQ4: Is there a relationship between severity of sexual violence and character role of the primary perpetrator of sexual violence?
RQ5: Against what type of character roles are heroes most likely to perpetrate sexual violence?
RQ6: Is there a relationship between scene type and severity of sexual violence?

Method

Sample
A sample of nine full-length feature films was randomly selected from a population of top-10 box office hits in the Hindi film industry released in the years 1997, 1998, and 1999. Within each of these 3 years, three films were randomly selected. Because we were interested in mass entertainment, especially films viewed by adolescents, films rated 'U' (universal audience) and

Table 1 List of films analysed in this study

Year	Film title
1997	*Pardes*
	Border
	Hero No. 1
1998	*Bandhan*
	Pyaar To Hona Hi Tha
	Kuch Kuch Hota Hai
1999	*Biwi No. 1*
	Hum Aapke Dil Mein Rehte Hain
	Sarfarosh

'UA' (public viewing with parental guidance for children under age 12) were included in the study but those rated 'A' (films restricted to adult audiences) were excluded (National Film Development Corporation, n.d.; see Table 1 for a list of the films analyzed).

Units of analysis
Two units of analysis were examined in this study: characters and sexual scenes. A scene was defined as a division of the film that presents continuous action in one place such as a single situation or unit of dialogue in the film (e.g., love scene or fight scene). Because we were interested in examining the nature of violence within the context of sexual interactions, only sexual scenes (both violent and nonviolent) were coded. The entire film was watched to locate the presence of sexual scenes. One hundred and eight such scenes were included in this study. A sexual scene was defined as one in which two or more characters were involved in activities such as having sex, kissing, petting, initiating or suggesting sexual contact, displaying nudity, engaging in sexual talk, bathing in an erotic way, wearing provocative or revealing clothes, or shown as a sexual object of gaze. This included actual depictions, suggestions of, and preparation for sexual activities. No instances of homosexual relationships were portrayed in any of the films selected. Therefore, only heterosexual relationships were considered within the scope of this study. Also, because we were interested in examining sexual interactions between individuals, two or more characters had to be present in a scene for it to be considered as a sexual scene. For example, a woman undressing for a bath was not considered for the study, but if a man undressed a woman, it was included within the study.

The second unit of analysis was the character. Seventy-seven characters were coded in this study. Only those characters who were shown speaking and were present in a sexual scene were included in the study. Characteristics of characters, such as gender and type of character role, were coded. Characters were observed for the entire film before coding their characteristics.

Coding scheme
A coding scheme was created for the variables of interest: presence of sexual violence, primary perpetrators/victims, gender, character role, severity of sexual violence, and fun/seriousness of scene.

Presence of sexual violence
Sexual scenes were of two types: mutually consenting scenes and sexually violent scenes. Mutually consenting scenes were those in which the characters involved showed interest in or expressed no objection to engaging in the sexual behavior, and there was no harm to any of the people involved. In contrast, a sexually violent scene was any sexual scene where there was actual depiction of, suggestion of, or preparation for sexual violence. Sexual violence was defined from the victim's perspective as any forced sexual act that was inappropriate, offensive, and/or harmful. Offensiveness to the victim was assessed using verbal and nonverbal expressions of disapproval, anger, or disgust (e.g., saying no, crying, pushing away, clenching fists). This included (but was not limited to) acts such as rape, verbal comments, kissing, disrobing, touching, staring, rubbing against, and obscene gestures. Rape was defined as the actual depiction of, suggestion of, or preparation for forced sexual intercourse.

Sexual violence was not just limited to rape but also included sexual harassment, eve-teasing, and domestic violence. Sexual harassment was defined as inappropriate, offensive, and/or harmful sexual behavior within the context of a workplace or academic environment wherein a power differential existed between the parties involved. For example, the sexual harassment of a student by a professor or of a subordinate by a boss was coded as sexual harassment. Eve-teasing was defined as sexual behavior displayed in public places (especially between strangers or acquaintances who are not committed to a relationship) that was inappropriate, harmful, and/or offensive to the victim. Domestic violence was defined as sexual aggression (e.g., forced kissing, disrobing, pinching) between couples that were in an intimate, committed sexual relationship (e.g., boyfriend/girlfriend, fiancé/fiancée, husband/wife) where the victim was hurt and/or offended by the sexual act.

Severity of sexual violence

Sexually violent scenes were further categorized as severe or moderate. Severe violence included actual depictions of, suggested, attempted, or preparation for rape or eroticized murder. Moderate sexual violence included all other forms of sexual violence, sexual harassment, eve-teasing, and domestic violence – that did not involve rape or murder.

Primary perpetrators/victims in a sexually violent scene

All sexually violent scenes had at least one perpetrator and one victim. The perpetrator was the one who initiated sexual aggression. A perpetrator was defined as someone who actually used, suggested the use of, attempted to use, or made preparations for using aggression in a sexual context. The victim was defined as the character who expressed lack of consent to the sexual act and/or was harmed by the act. It is important to note that sexual violence was defined more in terms of the harm caused to the victim rather than the intention of the perpetrator. This meant that even if the perpetrator did not intend to cause harm to the victim, it was considered as sexual violence if the victim was harmed.

Character role

Every character was coded as playing one of five character roles: hero, heroine, villain, comedian, or supporting character. A hero was defined as a character who played the role of the main, leading, male protagonist of the film. The heroine was defined as the main, leading, female protagonist in the film. The villain was anyone who was an antagonist (man or woman). A comedian is a character who is similar to a 'sidekick' in Hollywood films. A comedian was one whose role in the narrative was to provide comic relief (man or woman). Supporting characters included anybody who did not fall into the classification of hero, heroine, villain, or comedian. In a given film, more than one person could play these roles. For example, there were some films with two heroes.

Fun/seriousness of the scene

To understand fully the context within which sexuality was introduced into the plot of the films, it was crucial to code for the type of scenes that depicted sexuality. The sexual scenes were classified as either fun scenes or serious scenes. Serious scenes included drama, action, and mystery. Fun scenes included comedy, romance, and song–dance. Romance was defined as scenes that showed sexually attracted, dating, engaged, or married couples interacting with each other in a romantic fashion. Action was defined as scenes that showed fights, physical aggression, or violence.

Comedy was defined as scenes that depicted jokes and humor. Song–dance scenes were defined as musical episodes accompanied by dances by characters in the film. All other scenes were coded as drama scenes. Typically drama scenes showed conflict, were dialogue-oriented, and involved emotions such as anger or sadness.

[. . .]

Results

Presence of sexual violence

The first research question concerned the prevalence of sexual violence. An examination of the sexual scenes analyzed showed that slightly less than half of the sexual scenes (40.7%, $N = 44$) contained violence (see Table 2). The most common form of sexual violence depicted was eve-teasing (57% of sexually violent scenes, $N = 25$). Approximately 11% of the sexually violent scenes contained severe sexual violence such as rape or eroticized murder ($N = 5$). It should be noted here that one film (*Border*) showed that only mutually consenting sexual scenes whereas *Hero No. 1* depicted 72.2% of the sexual scenes as violent. However, most films depicted approximately 40% of the sexual scenes as sexually violent, suggesting that

Table 2 Summary of results

Sexual scenes	
With violence	40.7%
Without violence	59.3%
Gender of primary victims of sexual violence	
Women	77.0%
Men	23.0%
Character role of primary victims of sexual violence	
Heroines	95.0%
Other roles	5.0%
Primary perpetrators of sexual violence	
Heroes	67.8%
Villains	32.2%
Primary perpetrators of moderate sexual violence	
Heroes	78.2%
Villains	21.7%
Portrayal of moderate sexual violence	
Fun	69.2%
Serious	30.7%

although there is clearly variation in the percentage of sexually violent scenes portrayed, the majority of these films contained a substantial proportion of sexual scenes containing violence.

Gender and primary victim of a sexually violent scene
The second research question asked if there was any relationship between gender and the primary victim in sexually violent scenes. A chi-square test of the primary victims in sexual scenes revealed that women were more likely than men to be victims. Namely, of all victims coded in sexually violent scenes, 77% were women and 23% were men, χ^2 (1, N = 43) = 12.30, p <.001, V^* = 0.29 (see Table 3). For example, in *Kuch Kuch Hota Hai*, a typical college-based eve-teasing is used as a means to enhance the sexual appeal of the heroine Tina (played by Rani Mukherjee). When Tina enters the college campus wearing a very short mini-skirt and tight top, she is accosted by a gang of men in her college who stare at her legs, whistle, hoot, and make lewd remarks at her even though she expresses her disgust at their behavior. However, it appears that the intention of the scene is more to invite the audience to view the heroine as a sex object rather than to empathize with her experience.

Character role and primary perpetrator
The third research question focused on the relationship between the character role (hero vs. villain) and the primary perpetrator in sexually violent scenes. A chi-square analysis of heroes and villains showed that heroes (67.8%) were more likely than villains (32.2%) to be the primary perpetrator in sexually violent scenes. However, these differences only approached statistical significance, χ^2 (1, N = 28) = 3.57, p = .06, V^* = 0.13 (see Table 2). For example, films such as *Biwi No. 1* and *Hum Aapke Dil Mein Rehte Hain* show the hero eve-teasing women by singing lewd songs, making sexual remarks, and touching the heroine in sexual ways despite knowing that the heroine does not like these acts. On the other hand, in *Pardes*, the evil, villainous boyfriend tries to force his fiancée to have sex with him and rips off parts of her clothes after taking her to a hotel room. However, such depictions are much fewer than instances where the hero is the perpetrator.

Character roles and severity of sexual violence
The fourth research question examined the relationship between character of the primary perpetrator and the severity of sexual violence portrayed. A chi-square analysis of character role and severity of sexual violence revealed that villains were more likely to be featured as perpetrators of severe sexual

violence whereas heroes were more likely to be featured as perpetrators of moderate sexual violence. Specifically, primary perpetrators in severe scenes were more often villains (80.0%) than heroes (20.0%), whereas primary perpetrators in moderate scenes were more often heroes (78.2%) than villains (21.7%), χ^2 (1, N = 28) = 6.39, $p < .05$, $V^* = 0.48$ (see Table 2). In films such as *Kuch Kuch Hota Hai* and *Hero No. 1* there are several instances in which the hero eve-teases attractive young women to win their attention. These acts are treated in a very casual and trivial manner. However, later in the same film (*Hero No. 1*), the hero is shown enraged when the villains try to rape another young girl in the streets. The sexual violence in the latter scene is dramatized as something evil and wrong.

Character role and primary victim

The fifth research question focused on the types of character roles against whom heroes were most likely to perpetrate sexual violence. All sexually violent scenes where the hero was the primary perpetrator were selected for this analysis. A chi-square analysis of the primary victims in these scenes revealed that heroines (95%) were much more likely to be the victim than were other characters (5%), χ^2 (1, N = 19) = 15.21, $p < 0.001$, $V^* = 0.85$ (see Table 2). For example, a typical scene showing a boy–girl romantic confrontation using eve-teasing can be seen in *Hero No. 1*. The hero waylays the unsuspecting heroine (both are strangers to each other until this point in the story) at the airport, follows her around to the train station, makes obscene passes at her, rubs against her body, and even sits on her lap in the train, even though all through the sequence, the heroine constantly expresses her disapproval of these actions by the stranger (hero). As the entire encounter is against the background of a catchy song-and-dance sequence, the sexual harassment is presented to the audience as light-hearted fun.

Severity of sexual violence and fun/seriousness of scene

The sixth research question asked if there was a relationship between severity of sexual violence and the type of scene. The findings suggest that severe sexual violence is more likely to be portrayed as serious whereas moderate sexual violence is more likely to be portrayed as fun. Specifically, a chi-square analysis revealed that severe crimes were more often portrayed as serious (80.0%) than as fun (20.0%) whereas moderate crimes were more often portrayed as fun (69.2%) than as serious (30.7%), χ^2 (1, N = 44) = 4.64, $p < .05$, $V^* = .33$ (see Table 2). For instance, in *Bandhan*, the hero (played by Salman Khan) constantly eve-teases the heroine (played by Rambha), but the entire situation is couched in slapstick comedy, which distracts

the viewer from the sexual harassment per se. On the other hand, la.
the same film when the villains stop the heroine in an isolated field and eve-
tease her, the scene takes on more serious proportions with dialogue and
drama rather than song and dance.

Discussion

conclusion

The results of this study lend support to the idea that a substantial proportion of sexual scenes in popular Hindi films depict sexual violence, even in
those films meant for viewing by audiences of all age groups or with parental guidance if under 12 years. However, it is not just the amount of
sexual violence in the films that is cause of concern but also the nature of
these portrayals.

First, these films indicate a gender divide when it comes to perpetrators
and victims of sexual violence. Almost all films show female characters as
victims of sexual violence, whereas male characters are shown as perpetrators of these incidents. This seems to be consistent with traditional gendered beliefs in India that women should be submissive and men should be
aggressive in social relationships. This repeated pairing of women with
violence is problematic because it might reinforce existing beliefs that it is
acceptable to aggress against women and that women should tolerate
violence from men. *representations*

Another aspect of these portrayals that is a cause for concern is that
the perpetrators of sexual violence were not just villains, but also heroes.
Heroes were somewhat more likely than villains to be the primary perpetrators in sexually violent scenes. It is a cause for concern that heroes, who
often represented the essence of 'ideal manhood' and male sexuality, were
often perpetrators of sexual violence. This lends some support to the idea
that being aggressive is depicted as 'being manly.'

The idea that heroes would be shown engaging in sexual violence is
cause for concern, as social learning perspectives suggest that when likable,
attractive characters such as heroes perpetrate sexual violence on screen,
they are more likely to be imitated by viewers. That is, research on social
learning from media portrayals suggests that viewers are more likely to
emulate behaviors that they see in the media when the modeled behavior is
portrayed as rewarded (or at least not punished; see Bandura, 1994). This
line of reasoning suggests that film portrayals of women as victims of
sexual aggression are particularly problematic because such behavior
might be learned and imitated by the viewers. In addition, the viewer's
modeling of a media character's behaviors is particularly likely to occur
when the character is portrayed as attractive, likable, and heroic. In terms

of the present research, this suggests that Indian male viewers may be especially likely to emulate sexually violent behavior perpetrated by heroes.

Heroes and villains differed in the types of sexual violence that they perpetrated. Heroes were more likely to perpetrate moderate crimes such as eve-teasing, sexual harassment, and domestic violence, whereas villains were more likely to perpetrate severe crimes including rape and eroticized murder. Thus, moderate sexual violence seems not to be condemned and might even be rewarded. As we saw above, heroes, by definition, seem to protect moral good and to fight evil. Therefore, the association of heroes with moderate sexual violence may run the risk of sending a message to viewers that only severe crimes are bad and that moderate sexual violence is not bad (and may be even perceived as good). Therefore, these findings suggest that only rape and eroticized murder might be considered crimes by the audiences, but that eve-teasing, sexual harassment, and domestic violence may be socially acceptable sexual behaviors. Furthermore, moderate sexual violence is often depicted in the context of fun and happiness, whereas severe sexual crimes are depicted as serious and dramatic. This pairing of fun with moderate sexual violence implies that such crimes are not bad but enjoyable for all involved.

Moreover, the finding that heroes more often aggressed against heroines than against any other characters is consistent with the argument that aggression is portrayed as a desirable attribute in Hindi films. It should be noted that in all the films in this study, the hero and heroine were romantically involved. This suggests that it was appropriate, normal, and perhaps even romantic for men to aggress against the women with whom they were romantically involved. From the perspective of sexual script theory, these portrayals may suggest to viewers (especially young adults, adolescents, and children) that these recurring themes of violence among romantically involved couples in the media represent acceptable ways of behaving in sexual relationships. The films analyzed in the current study were not adult films but those rated U and UA. Thus, it is highly likely that these films' audiences include younger age groups who are also likely to be learning social norms related to gender and sexuality. Moreover, as mentioned previously, eve-teasing statistics report that about one-third of the perpetrators in real life are college-age youth ('Films', 1998). This situation suggests that social learning and sexual script theories might be at work although clearly, experimental research needs to be conducted to determine the specific nature of the effects that these films may be having on their viewing audiences.

[. . .]

The results of this exploratory study seem to suggest that Indian films tend to present moderate forms of sexual violence to its audience as normal, fun, and heroic. The effect that such sexually violent portrayals have on viewers is an area of study that is deserving of research attention. Overall, our data support the criticism that eve-teasing in Indian films is not generally portrayed as a crime that ought to be punished, but rather as an act of romantic love aesthetically woven into the narrative as fun and enjoyable.

[. . .]

References

Allen, M., D'Alessio, D., & Brezgel, K. (1995). A meta-analysis summarizing the effects of pornography: II. Aggression after exposure. *Human Communication Research, 22,* 258–283.

Allen, M., Emmers, T., Gebhardt, L., & Giery, M. A. (1995). Exposure to pornography and acceptance of rape myths. *Journal of Communication, 45*(1), 5–26.

Anjum, Z. (2002, February/March). Hollywood calling, Bollywood falling. *Aaj Magazine.* Retrieved August 13, 2002, from http://www.aajmag.com/hollybollywood.html

Atrocities against women on the rise in state. (2002, April 11). *The Hindu.* Retrieved August 12, 2002, from the Lexis-Nexis Academic Universe database, http://web.lexis-nexis.com/universe

Bagchi, A. (1996, December 18). *Women in Indian cinema.* Retrieved August 12, 2002, from http://www.cs.jhu.edu/»bagchi/women.html

Bandura, A. (1994). Social cognitive theory of mass communication. In J. Bryant & D. Zillmann (Eds.), *Media effects: Advances in theory and research* (pp. 61–90). Hillsdale, NJ: Erlbaum.

Birla, P. (2001, March 31). *Helping kids get street-smart on sex education.* Retrieved August 18, 2002, from the Health Education Library for People Web site: http://www.healthlibrary.com/news/25 31 march/31 sex.htm

Bist, R. (2002, October 12). *Bollywood takes on the world.* Retrieved December 6, 2002, from *Asia Times* (Online) Web site: http://www.atimes.com/atimes/South Asia/DJ12Df01.html

Burt, M. R. (1980). Cultural myths and supports for rape. *Journal of Personality and Social Psychology, 38,* 217–230.

Carpenter, L. (1998). From girls into women: Scripts for sexuality and romance in *Seventeen* magazine, 1974–1994. *Journal of Sex Research, 35,* 158–168.

Check, J.V. P., & Malamuth, N. M. (1985). An empirical assessment of some feminist hypotheses about rape. *International Journal of Women's Studies, 8,* 414–423.

Crimes against women rise in India. (1996, August 27). *Xinhua News Agency.*

Retrieved February 11, 2002, from the Lexis-Nexis Academic Universe database, http://web.lexis-nexis.com/universe

Dasgupta, S. D., & Hegde, R. S. (1988). The eternal receptacle: A study of mistreatment of women in Hindi films. In R. Ghadially (Ed.), *Women in Indian society: A reader* (pp. 209–216). New Delhi, India Sage.

Derne, S. (1995). *Culture in action: Family life, emotion and male dominance in Banaras, India*. Albany: State University of New York Press.

Derne, S. (1999). Making sex violent: Love as force in recent Hindi films. *Violence Against Women, 5,* 548–575.

Donnerstein, E., & Berkowitz, L. (1981). Victims' reactions in aggressive erotic films as a factor in violence against women. *Journal of Personality and Social Psychology, 41,* 710–724.

Donnerstein, E., Linz, D., & Penrod, S. (1987). *The question of pornography: Research findings and policy implications*. New York: Free Press.

Eve-teasing – The menace refuses to die. (1999, June 12). *The Hindu*. Retrieved August 12, 2002, from the Lexis-Nexis Academic Universe database, http://web.lexis-nexis.com/universe

Films, TV serials have contributed to increasing acts of eve-teasing. (1998, September 22). *The Hindu*. Retrieved February 11, 2002, from the Lexis-Nexis Academic Universe database, http://web.lexis-nexis.com/universe

Gandhi, N., & Shah, N. (1992). *The issues at stake: Theory and practice in the contemporary women's movement in India*. New Delhi, India: Kali for Women.

Khare, V. (1985). The Dinman Hindi film inquiry: A summary. In B. Pfleiderer & L. Lutze (Eds.), *The Hindi film: Agent and re-agent of cultural change* (pp. 139–148). New Delhi, India: Manohar.

Kutchinsky, B. (1991). Pornography and rape: Theory and practice? Evidence from crime data in four countries where pornography is easily available. *International Journal of Law and Psychiatry, 14,* 47–64.

Linz, D., & Malamuth, N. M. (1993). *Pornography*. Newbury Park, CA: Sage.

McKenzie-Mohr, D., & Zanna, M. P. (1990). Treating women as sexual objects: Look to the (gender-schematic) male who has viewed pornography. *Personality and Social Psychology Bulletin, 16,* 296–308.

Nair, N. K., Barman, A. K., & Chattopadhyay, U. (1999, December 15). *Study on copyright piracy in India*. Retrieved August 11, 2002, from the Government of India Department of Education Web site: http://www.education.nic.in/html web/cr piracy study

National Film Development Corporation. (n.d.). *Cinema history*. Retrieved February 11, 2002, from http://www.nfdcindia.com/history.htm

Ordinance against eve-teasing issued. (1999, July 30). *The Hindu*. Retrieved February 11, 2002, from the Lexis-Nexis Academic Universe database, http://web.lexis-nexis.com/universe

Pardun, C. J. (2002). Romancing the script: Identifying the romantic agenda in top-grossing movies. In J. D. Brown, J. R. Steele, & K. Walsh-Childers (Eds.),

Sexual teens, sexual media: Investigating media's influence on adolescent sexuality (pp. 211–225). Mahwah, NJ: Erlbaum.

Poudyal, R. (2002, June 12). *Boys on film: Challenging masculinities in South Asia.* Retrieved August 11, 2002, from http://www.id21.org/society/6arp1.html

Prasad, S. (1999). Medicolegal response to violence against women in India. *Violence Against Women, 5,* 478–506.

Ram, A. (2002). Framing the feminine: Diasporic readings of gender in popular Indian cinema. *Women's Studies in Communication, 25*(1), 25–52.

Ravindran, V. (2001, September 10). Victims of whims. *The Hindu.* Retrieved August 12, 2002, from the Lexis-Nexis Academic Universe database, http://web.lexis-nexis.com/universe

Russell, D. E. (1988). Pornography and rape: A causal model. *Political Psychology, 19,* 41–73.

Stevens, W. K. (1984, March 17). For women of India, a rite of spring is sour. *The New York Times,* p. 24. Retrieved February 11, 2002, from the Lexis-Nexis Academic Universe database, http://web.lexis-nexis.com/universe

Ward, M. (1995). Talking about sex: Common themes about sexuality in the prime-time television programs children and adolescents view most. *Journal of Youth and Adolescence, 24,* 595–615.

West, J. (1996, August 11). Police 'tease' is slapped in jail: India applies the law to curb gropers. *Sunday Telegraph,* p. 25. Retrieved February 11, 2002, from the Lexis-Nexis Academic Universe database, http://web.lexis-nexis.com/universe

Wood, E., Senn, C.Y., Desmarais, S., Park, L., & Verberg, N. (2002). Sources of information about dating and their perceived influence on adolescents. *Journal of Adolescent Research, 17,* 401–417.

Wood, J. (2001). The normalization of violence in heterosexual romantic relationships: Women's narratives of love and violence. *Journal of Social and Personal Relationships, 18,* 239–261.

Zillmann, D., & Sapolsky, B. S. (1977). What mediates the effects of mild erotica on annoyance and hostile behavior in males? *Journal of Personality and Social Psychology, 35,* 587–596.

Zillmann, D., & Weaver, J. (1989). Pornography and men's sexual callousness toward women. In D. Zillmann & J. Bryant (Eds.), *Pornography: Research advances and policy considerations* (pp. 95–126). Hillsdale, NJ: Erlbaum.

PERSONAL APPEARANCE AS A SOCIAL PROBLEM

16

NEWSPAPER COVERAGE OF THE COLUMBINE HIGH SCHOOL SHOOTINGS

Jennifer Paff Ogle, Molly Eckman and Catherine Amoroso Leslie

On April 20, 1999, at Columbine High School in Littleton, Colorado, Eric Harris and Dylan Klebold took their own lives and those of 12 students and one teacher in the worst school shooting in terms of fatalities on U.S. soil to date. In addition, several other students and staff members were injured from the gunfire or from bombs that Harris and Klebold had planted in the school before the shootings.

In the days, weeks, and months that followed the Columbine shootings, the local and national media provided considerable coverage of this act of school violence. By the first anniversary of the shootings, the two major newspapers in the Denver metropolitan area had published over 1,000 articles about it. From the outset, the media made linkages between the Columbine shootings and appearance cues, with numerous references to the appearances of the gunmen and their alleged associates, the appearances of their victims, and the appearances of the many others who were somehow implicated in the incident at Columbine High. Very quickly, appearance had become a factor in the Columbine investigation, or more precisely, a factor in the media's interpretation of the incident, the ensuing investigation, and the public's reaction to the incident and investigation.

With the present work, we used an interpretive approach to explore print media (newspaper) representations of the relationship between appearance and the tragedy at Columbine High School. Our work was guided by the **social constructionist** definition of a social problem. Of particular interest to us was the process by which the print media transformed the Columbine incident into an appearance issue, or a social problem linking school violence to appearance. Further, we were interested in examining the role of the popular press as a public forum for negotiating meanings about various appearances.

Theoretical Framework

Scholars have invoked the basic tenet of constructionism – and in particular, the notion that knowledge is subject to and the product of social forces – to develop a sociological theory of social problems. Constructionists are interested in exploring how individuals conceptualize an issue as a social problem and how they go about constructing an issue as a social problem in the eyes of others. To this end, constructionists explore the *claims-making activities* that allow for the 'discursive reproduction of social problems' (Ibarra and Kitsuse 1993, p. 22).

Claims-making refers to the activities of individuals and groups who make assertions about an issue (Spector and Kitsuse 1977). Typically, claims are assumed to reflect the interests of the social actors or constituents who make them (Best 1987). Thus, claims are not held as 'objective truths,' but rather, are viewed as rhetoric, or 'claims-makers' attempts to persuade others of the validity of their claims (Best 1987, 1989). Presumably, it is through these persuasion tactics that the 'trick' of social construction is carried out, in that at least some messages are eventually taken for granted as 'real' or 'true.'

Best distinguishes between two types of claims-makers: primary and secondary (1989). Claims-making begins when primary claims-makers, or individuals with special knowledge (e.g., experts, victims, witnesses), draw attention to an issue in an attempt to incite awareness or change. Media coverage of primary claims-making activities (especially those launched by nonexperts) may facilitate efforts to highlight an issue. However, the media do not merely restate claims, transmitting them to a larger audience (Best 1989). The conventions of the mass media 'transform' claims (Best 1989); claims presented in the media play a key role in ordering and maintaining audience perceptions of social reality. As such, according to Best (1989), the mass media are secondary claims-makers.

Research Questions

Our work was guided by the following research questions:

1. How and why did the media craft the Columbine shootings as an

appearance-related social problem? What role did primary and secondary claims-makers play in constructing the shootings in this manner?

2. How, according to claims presented in the media, did this construction of the shootings affect those who were implicated as either key or tangential players in the crime or in broader appearance-related social problems? Did those affected by the media's claims launch counterclaims in their defense? If so, how was this dialogue played out in the media?

These questions are important to address. Media reach a broad audience, offer coverage of primary claims-making, and have the potential to shape the ways in which viewers define reality or, as here, a specific social problem (i.e., the 'why' behind the Columbine shooting). The role of claims presented in the media may have been especially pivotal in constructing the 'reality' of the Columbine shootings, as those with the most primary or 'expert' knowledge of the incident (i.e., Harris and Klebold) did not survive and thus played a very minor role in constructing an explanation for their actions. Further, media coverage may shape public policy developed in response to a perceived social problem (Altheide and Michalowski 1999).

Method

An interpretive approach was used to explore print media interpretations of the role of dress in the Columbine incident. Newspaper articles and editorials addressing the Columbine incident were collected from the two major newspapers in the Denver area, the *Denver Post (DP)* and the *Rocky Mountain News (RMN)*.

Data were collected in several waves that reflected the flow and ebb of events related to the Columbine investigation and the corresponding media coverage. A total of 1,051 articles and 211 editorials related to the Columbine incident and published between April 20, 1999 (the day of the shooting) and May 16, 2000 (the day *The Columbine Report* was released) were identified.

In keeping with the constructionist tradition, analyses focused not only upon the content of claims presented, but also upon the process by which these claims were made, including who made them and for what possible reason. For the purposes of this research, primary claims included quoted information attributed to a specific individual or group. Examples of primary claims-makers included students (witnesses, victims), parents of victims or Columbine students, law enforcement officials, members of subcultural groups linked to the shootings, and citizens who wrote letters to the editor. Secondary claims were defined as those made by journalists, including professional media writers such as reporters and editorialists.

Results

Bringing appearance into the discussion

Reconstructing the crime

Within hours of the Columbine shootings, the media's construction of the crime as an appearance-related social problem had begun. The initial media reports related to this incident were rife with content addressing the appearances of the gunmen and their victims. By April 22, 1999, the *DP* and the *RMN* had published 31 and 22 references to the appearances of the gunmen and their victims, respectively.

Most of the initial references to the appearances of the gunmen were made by primary claims-makers, particularly Columbine students, who provided first-hand accounts of the shooting. At the time, little was known about the incident, and the gunmen had yet to be identified. Media writers apparently invoked these accounts to assist in reconstructing for their readers the details of this mysterious and horrific event. For the most part, these earliest accounts were descriptive in nature, yielding little explanation for the gunmen's dress:

> Sophomore Amanda Stair, 15, was in the library when the shooting started. She also heard what sounded like grenades going off. 'We hid under different tables,' Stair said. 'Two guys in black trench coats walked in. They said "Get up," or they would shoot us.' (*RMN* 4/20/99)
>
> [. . .]

Early news reports concerning the victims' appearances also featured claims made by witnesses to the crime, once again in an apparent attempt to describe for readers the events of April 20, 1999. Several students, most of whom were in the Columbine library during the shooting, were quoted as saying that Harris and Klebold had targeted athletes or 'jocks' in their shooting spree. According to these primary accounts, the gunmen had ascribed 'jock status' to students who were wearing white baseball hats:

> Meanwhile, Brittany Bollerud, 16, hid under a library table and saw only the gunmen's shoes and long trench coats. 'They yelled, "This is

revenge," ' she said. They asked people if they were jocks. If they were wearing a sports hat, they would shoot them. (*DP*4/21/99)

'They said, "All jocks are dead. All jocks stand up. Any jock wearing white baseball caps stand up!"' said sophomore Joshua Lapp, who was in the library [during the shooting]. (*RMN*4/27/99)

In one article, a student was quoted as suggesting that ethnicity had also played a role in the gunmen's selection of victims:

They shot a black kid. They called him a nigger. They said they didn't like niggers, so they shot him in the face. (*DP*4/21/99)

Quotes from three other students supported the claim that the shooters had made racial slurs during the shooting, but these students did not intimate that the killers used ethnicity as a mechanism with which to select their victims.

Intermingled with student accounts of the gunmen's actions were the interpretations of media writers. In the days following the shooting, comments made by several media writers reiterated the notion that Harris and Klebold had targeted both athletes and ethnic minorities in their act of violence, despite the fact that only one witness had indicated that ethnicity played such a role:

The masked shooters first targeted specific victims, especially ethnic minorities and athletes and then randomly sprayed the school hallways about 11:30 a.m. with bullets and shotgun blasts witnesses said. The bloody rampage spanned four hours. (*DP*4/21/99)

That at least some readers embraced the claim that appearance cues, such as white hats and skin color, were used by the killers to target victims is clear from the following quotes, published nearly a year apart. The first remark was made by the father of a Columbine student and was published two days after the shooting. The second comment was made on the anniversary of the shooting by a grade-school child.

'I'm just glad that Valerie didn't have her cheerleading uniform on,' he said. . . . 'I know they would have targeted the cheerleaders.' (*RMN*4/22/99)

'Does anybody know what happened last year?' [said a teacher to her class]. 'I know what happened, two boys shot some kids. . . . They shot Isaiah because he was black.'(*DP*4/21/00)

Moving beyond reconstruction: building a foundation for further hypotheses
Soon after the media had established 'what' the gunmen had looked like on the day of the shooting, they began to focus more attention upon the meanings of these appearances as well as the 'everyday appearances' of the two boys. At this stage, which was still within days of the shooting, media writers played an active role in establishing or validating the black trench coat as a symbol of violence and the profane. In some cases, trench coats were imbued with negative meanings merely by linking them with Harris and Klebold, who in turn, had been characterized by media writers as somehow antisocial or deviant:

> Trouble at Columbine. Gunshots. Suddenly, existence boiled down to what mattered most. And strange kids in trench coats were threatening to yank it away. (*DP*4/21/99)

> The story is tragic and it's heartbreaking and it's got kids wearing trench coats who spout German and who are called Goths and who kill their classmates. (*RMN*5/2/99)

In other instances, claims were used to project assumed negative characteristics of Harris and Klebold onto the garments cloaking their bodies during the rampage. For example, on both April 21, 1999, and April 22, 1999, *DP* writers invoked a quotation from Columbine senior Wade Frank, whose reference to one of the killers as 'the trench coat' personified trench coats, imparting a sense of malice and evil to these inanimate objects:

> The trench coat walked up and shot the boy point blank in the back. (*DP*4/21/99, 4/22/99)

In discussing the dress of Harris and Klebold, media writers also drew upon pre-existing meanings that had been linked to trench coats in other cultural contexts. Several reporters suggested that Harris and Klebold might have chosen to wear trench coats on the day of the shootings because characters in films such as *The Matrix* or *The Basketball Diaries* had donned similar garments to commit acts of gun-related violence:

> The Columbine shooting suspects, Eric Harris and Dylan Klebold, favored trench coats like the one DiCaprio wears [in *The Basketball Diaries*]. (*RMN* 4/23/99)

> In the enormously popular new movie *Matrix*, Keanu Reeves wears a black duster and battles the forces of evil with two-fisted bursts of gunfire. He stages an attack on the conspiracy that has turned his life into a living hell. The movie already is being mentioned as a possible

> source of influence on the Trench Coat Mafia, two of whose members entered Columbine High School Tuesday carrying weapons and wearing long black coats. (*RMN* 4/22/99)

Similarly, another media writer suggested that Harris and Klebold had modeled their April 20 appearances after Kip Kinkel, an Oregon boy who had worn a black trench coat while killing one classmate and injuring 23 others on his school campus in 1998. Here, then, media writers presented trench coats as 'props' already suffused with dark meanings and selected by the gunmen to help them 'take on' their roles as adolescent killers. The following text imparts this notion of the trench coat as a 'role dress' for violence:

> As [Brooks Brown, a Columbine student] stood outside a door that leads to the cafeteria, Eric Harris came up the walk. Gone was the flannel shirt [that Harris had been wearing earlier that day], replaced by a long, black trench coat. (*RMN* 4/25/99)

In addition, references to the everyday dress of Harris and Klebold began to appear in the news within a week of the shooting. Media writers infused their reports with claims that Harris and Klebold had regularly sported not only trench coats, but berets and T-shirts emblazoned with swastikas and German slogans as well. Although media writers often cited 'students' as the source of this information ('students said'), these claims were secondary in that they were not the direct words of a primary claims-maker (i.e., a student). Some students, however, were quoted as saying that they had been 'frightened' of Harris and Klebold, in part because of their dress. Further, media writers referenced student comments that demonstrated a pattern in the dress of the gunmen and a linkage of this dress to the act of violence they committed:

> Junior Chris Reilly said when he heard that the two gunmen wore black trench coats, he had five students in mind. 'Eric and Dylan were two of them,' he said. (*RMN* 4/22/99)

Taken together, then, these media reports created an image of two young men who routinely adorned themselves in symbols of violence, both before and during the shootings at Columbine. These (largely secondary) claims seemingly established a pattern of potential for violence that led up to the shootings. And it was this association between the gunmen's dress and violence that provided the platform from which media writers began to construct more speculative claims in which appearance was presented as a cause of the shootings.

Locating cause: how can appearance explain why this happened?

Within the first week after the shooting, entire articles were devoted to the appearances of the gunmen and related others. References to appearance were no longer provided simply as details germane to the Columbine incident; appearance had become a media story in its own right. The apparent thesis of many of these appearance-focused reports was the location of cause for the shootings: media attention had switched from 'what' the gunmen and their victims were wearing to 'why' they were wearing it and 'how' it might have contributed to their act of violence. In seeking to understand and/or explain the shootings at Columbine, three claims were invoked with respect to appearance: the subcultural-group claim, the social-tensions/ revenge claim, and the dress as-facilitator claim.

The subcultural group claim

Soon after the shooting, claims made by media writers linked Harris and Klebold to a variety of adolescent subcultures whose membership was symbolized in part by appearance cues. Most often, these secondary claims identified the gunmen as members of the Trench Coat Mafia, a group of Columbine outcasts who were said to wear black trench coats, embrace violence and hatred, and worship death. In several instances, secondary claims also drew linkages between the Trench Coat Mafia and other subcultures, primarily the Goths, Marilyn Manson fans, satanic cults, and neo-Nazi groups. Frequently, media writers augmented their claims with loose references to information sources (e.g., 'fellow students,' 'experts'), perhaps in an attempt to add credibility:

> Fellow students describe the shooting suspects as part of a clique of generally quiet, brooding outcasts with penchants for dark trench coats, shaved heads, and militant armbands. By several accounts, the group also is interested in the occult, mutilation shock-rocker Marilyn Manson and Adolf Hitler, whose birthday was Tuesday [the day of the shooting].(*DP* 4/21/99)

> Masked gunmen Eric Harris, 18, and Dylan Klebold, 17, are said to have hung out with the so-called mafia, a small, self-styled group drawing on the satanic 'Goth' scene and neo-Nazi paramiltarism. Underlying both those subcultures, experts say, are preoccupation with death, feelings of being misunderstood and isolated, and often unspeakable anger. Classmates say Klebold and Harris—who apparently killed themselves—wore swastikas and worshipped Adolf Hitler. Some say their clique drove hearses, tested friendships by cutting each

other with knives, engaged in endless hours of macabre Internet chat-
ter and relished a bloody fantasy game called 'Doom' on their computers. Several Columbine students say the group idolized Marilyn
Manson, who claims to be a satanic priest. (*DP* 4/22/99)

By drawing these sorts of linkages between the gunmen and subcultures
associated with interests and appearances outside of the mainstream, media
writers offered one explanation as to the 'why' behind this shooting. The
association of the gunmen with these groups cast them as *not normal* or as
deviant. Implicit here was the notion that normal kids—that is, those who
did not associate with these underground cultures and who did not embrace
antisocial values such as hatred—would not or could not commit the acts of
violence undertaken by Harris and Klebold. Perhaps, however, kids drawn
into the violent underworld of the Trench Coat Mafia or the Goths *could* do
such a thing.

[. . .]

The supposed usefulness of appearance in recognizing potential danger
or violence was further highlighted when the media published 'checklists' to
admonish readers to be on the alert for the 'warning signs' of violence such
as the wearing of trench coats, the adoption of no mainstream appearances,
or general changes in children's appearances. Indeed, the notion that potentially violent youth could be recognized or identified by something as readily apparent as appearance may have provided some sense of control for a
community anxious to understand and remedy a very disconcerting situation. That the public policy proposed in response to the shootings was
rooted in this claim (i.e., the assumption of an appearance violence linkage)
supports this notion of a desire for a clear and controlled answer to the
Columbine problem.

The social-tensions/revenge claim
The claim that the gunmen's involvement in the Trench Coat Mafia contributed to their act of violence spawned a second, related explanation for the
Columbine shootings. This line of reasoning, the product of both primary
and secondary claims, suggested that the shootings were the gunmen's
response to social tensions between the Trench Coat Mafia and Columbine's athletes. In effect, this claim identified the shootings as an act of
revenge undertaken by the gunmen to 'pay back' Columbine's athletes for
past trespasses against them. The roots of the revenge hypothesis were
planted when the *DP* and the *RMN* published the previously discussed
claim that Harris and Klebold had targeted jocks during the shootings.
Comments made by students and media writers also established that

Columbine's athletes had teased the gunmen and members of the Trench Coat Mafia, often about appearance:

'Everywhere they went, they were taunted and teased about how they dress . . .' says Typher, the girl Harris went out with briefly after his freshman year. (*DP* 5/2/99)

That this taunting contributed to the gunmen's dislike for the jocks is reflected in claims staged by both students and media writers about comments made by the gunmen during their shootings:

'[During the shootings, Harris and Klebold] kept saying jocks made them feel like outcasts. Then they said they were going to the cafeteria to get more people,' said Todd. (*RMN* 4/22/99)

'This is for all of the people who made fun of us all these years,' the two boys in trench coats said, laughing as they opened fire. (*DP* 4/23/ 99)

[. . .]

Finally, a primary claim made by Harris himself in the Columbine tapes and published posthumously in the *DP* verified the proposition that feelings of insecurity and hatred induced by peer teasing may have incited Harris' acts of violence against his Columbine peers. A media writer describing the content of the tapes wrote:

Harris talks of always being the new, 'white scrawny' kid. 'I had to go through that s— so many times,' Harris says. (*DP* 12/14/99)

The dress-as-facilitator claim

The final claim offering an explanation for the role of dress in the Columbine shootings concerned the instrumental role that the boys' trench coats had played in facilitating this crime. These claims were advanced by media writers, who charged that the boys had used their outer garments to hide their contraband—including guns and bombs—on the day of the shootings:

The two came to school Tuesday in fatigues, pipe bombs strapped to their chests and shotguns and high-powered pistols under long black coats. (*RMN* 4/21/99)

Several months later, the release of the Columbine tapes renewed the discussion concerning the use of clothing to hide weapons. According to media writers' reports, the tapes included two separate segments in which Klebold experiments with the use of his trench coat to hide his gun. One of these 'experiments,' dubbed a 'dress rehearsal' by the media, occurred three days prior to the shootings:

> During Klebold's dress rehearsal on April 17, in the only piece of the tapes made at the Klebold residence, he worries that his gun is making his black trench coat look bulky. (*DP*12/14/99)

Staging a backlash: the media as a forum for counterclaims

As mentioned, shortly after the shootings, adolescents whose appearances resembled those of Harris and Klebold were targeted as additional suspects in the Columbine investigation. Although each of these students was eventually cleared of wrongdoing by the police, the claims published within the media had cast them and others who looked like them or who associated with the same adolescent peer groups as scapegoats for the crime. According to primary claims published in media reports, some individuals associated with the Trench Coat Mafia or the Goths (or believed to be associated with these groups) had become the targets of harassment by others:

> 'There are a lot of us [people who dress in Goth-style clothing] who are starting to get afraid of the people who think we were part of [the Columbine shootings],' he said. 'The jocks and yuppies are constantly driving by, calling us "faggots" or yelling, "I'm going to kick your asses." It's happening a lot more now after Columbine. We can't let our girlfriends or our sisters walk out alone anymore. We're scared of drive-bys.' He said his group is 'not about violence or killing.' (*DP* 4/24/99)

Further, claims made by members of the Goth and Trench Coat Mafia communities and other primary claims-makers (e.g., school employees, businesspeople serving the Goth community, representatives of the American Civil Liberties Union [ACLU]) suggested that individuals in these groups were alarmed and angry that others would implicate them as involved in the shootings. To defend the honor of and to protect individuals who had been implicated as somehow involved in the Columbine shootings, a variety of counterclaims were submitted by varied claims-makers to challenge previous accusations of 'guilt by association.' For instance, counterclaims were made to distance subcultural group members from Harris and Klebold and their act of violence. To this end, members of the Trench Coat Mafia denied the claim that Harris and Klebold were actively involved in this clique.

[. . .]

Other claims-makers disputed the allegation that members of the Trench Coat Mafia and/or the Goths embraced violence or the hatred of others. These claims often were submitted by members of these groups or by those who associated with them. However, as in the second quote below, secondary claims-makers also offered their version of this claim:

'They're [the Goths] not violent. They're not racist. They're not into the whole hate mentality,' said Sweet [a researcher who had studied Goth culture]. (DP 4/22/99)

The two Columbine gunmen embraced some Goth trappings but also embraced racism and violence that most in the Goth world reject. (DP 5/10/99)

[. . .]

Further, some claims-makers suggested that the inordinate amount of attention focused upon the appearances of the gunmen (and others linked to them) represented a misguided investigative effort that should be focused upon variables other than appearance. This sentiment is reflected in the following comments excerpted from a letter to the editor of the DP:

Harris and Klebold didn't try to blow up Columbine High School and slaughter its students because they wore black clothes and listened to German music. They did it because at some point their minds curled in the heat of high school social pressure and because they could get guns and because their parents apparently didn't notice that anything was amiss. To make this an issue of deviant dress is a counterproductive effort on the part of the mainstream . . . (DP 4/24/99)

Proposing solutions to the Columbine problem

The Columbine problem was constructed as appearance-related. Thus, the solutions advocated by claims-makers as remedies to the problem often focused upon appearance as well. Two solutions in particular involved modifications in appearance management: (a) the adoption of school dress codes or uniforms and (b) the adoption of RESPECT patches.

The adoption of school dress codes or uniforms

Within two days of the shooting, claims-makers proposed the implementation of dress codes or school uniforms as a solution to the Columbine problem. Proposed dress codes entailed the banning of certain types of apparel, particularly trench coats and—to a lesser extent—baseball hats and dress associated with the Goth movement (e.g., leather collars). In turn, the suggestion of dress regulation as a solution to Columbine sparked a dialogue in which claims-makers divided themselves along two lines: those for and those against school dress codes and uniforms.

Claims made to support school dress codes or uniforms were made by primary claims-makers, including parents and school officials. In addition, media writers frequently highlighted the pro-uniform view by describing policies adopted by area school districts. These claims-makers offered a variety of justifications in support of dress codes and uniforms. Implicit in each of their justifications were the assumptions (a) that dress can shape the behavior and thoughts of wearers and/or perceivers (i.e., those who view wearers) (see Lennon, Johnson, and Schulz 1999) and (b) that dress codes or school uniforms were an appropriate response to prior claims locating cause of the incident. Specifically, dress-code/ uniform advocates presented claims that the regulation of student appearances had the potential to (a) decrease gang activity and school violence, (b) increase student achievement, (c) create an environment that facilitated learning, (d) assist in identification of school trespassers, (e) deter students from hiding weapons in their clothing, and (f) deter students from expressing class divisions or hatred against others. Further, school and law enforcement officials suggested that banning trench coats would (a) protect students who might find trench coats frightening given the events at Columbine and (b) safeguard students who might wear such coats from others who might (mis)interpret the garments as indicative of violence:

'We have excluded the long black coat because it makes it hard for us to guarantee the safety of our students,' said Susan Carlson, spokeswoman for the Adams 12 schools. Wearing such a coat, she said, can also be 'alarming enough to others that it disrupts the educational environment.' (*RMN* 4/22/99)

I would also like to suggest we revisit the idea of school uniforms that take away the opportunities to hide weapons and express rage and class divisions within our schools. (Excerpted from a letter to the editor, *RMN* 4/22/99)

Claims-makers opposing the adoption of school dress codes or uniforms as a solution to the Columbine problem were afforded less media coverage than were those who embraced this solution and included students, parents, civil liberties experts (e.g., ACLU officials), and media writers. Typically, the claims of this contingent concerned three issues. First, these claims-makers argued that the regulation of dress or appearance represented harassment of one's person and the violation of one's freedom of speech and right to self-expression. Often, these claims were advanced by students (or their parents) whose dress had been regulated after the Columbine shooting:

> Neil [an Englewood student who was ticketed for the wearing of Gothic-style accessories], for his part, said, 'I should be able to express myself however I want, to wear whatever I want, as long as it's not hurting anybody.' (*DP* 4/23/99)

Second, anti-dress-code/uniform claims-makers challenged the logic that dress can be used to infer that a wearer may behave in a certain way (e.g., violently) or hold certain attitudes (e.g., hatred toward others), an argument that was also drawn upon to counter the claim that individuals with specified appearances were somehow involved in or responsible for the Columbine shootings:

> One [student] statement read: 'I wonder how long it'll be before we're allowed to wear our trench coats anymore. You know those screwed-up kids in Colorado were wearing them, so that means I will also kill someone and so will all my friends.' (*DP* 5/10/99)

Finally, those opposing dress codes intimated that such a 'solution' was a superficial and unrealistic way to address the acts of violence executed by Harris and Klebold. These claimants perceived that a 'real' solution to the Columbine problem would need to address more 'serious' issues than appearance (this sentiment also was used as a counterclaim in the backlash against the construction of Columbine as an appearance problem):

> If Eric Harris and Dylan Klebold had been wearing Denver Broncos jerseys with No. 7 on the back, would school systems be so quick to ban those? This banning of trench coats is a ridiculous response promoted by people who refuse to deal with the real underlying causes of violence. (*DP* 4/24/99)

The adoption of Columbine RESPECT patches

Media coverage also focused upon a second appearance-related solution to the Columbine problem: the adoption of RESPECT patches. According to media writers and individuals affiliated with the Colorado High School Activities Association, the association created the patches to be worn by student members of athletic, music, speech, and student-government groups. Claims such as those below suggested that the patches were developed as a response to the claim that the shootings were a product of disrespect and tension between adolescent cliques at Columbine High School:

[. . .]

…es are meant to spotlight a critical concept that emerged
…mbine siege and to promote it universally, in a way that
students and all adults, officials said. (*DP* 8/4/99)

[. . .]

Revisiting and clarifying the issues: The Columbine Report

In May 2000, an official summary of the crime investigation, *The
Columbine Report*, was released. Newspaper articles concerning *The
Report* clarified and/or revisited several key claims broadly disseminated
within previous coverage of the shootings. First, despite prior claims by
students that they had observed three gunmen—two in trench coats and one
in a white-tee shirt—newspaper articles about *The Report* cited ballistics
evidence to confirm that only two gunmen had been involved. In *The
Report*, the confusion concerning the gunmen's dress was attributed to the
fact that Harris had shed his coat before entering the school. Second,
media coverage of *The Report* also indicated that Harris and Klebold did
not use appearance as a cue with which to select their victims, suggesting
instead that the gunmen 'hated everybody' and thus, were indiscriminate
in their shooting (DP, 3/12/00). Finally, media content about *The Report*
questioned the gunmen's involvement in the Trench Coat Mafia and the
suggestion that the group's members behaved violently or advocated
the hatred of others. According to newspaper articles about *The Report*, the
gunmen did not regularly wear symbols of violence or the Goth culture, but
rather, 'appeared outwardly normal, [sharing] their dark side only with
each other' (DP, 3/12/00). This claim seemingly undermines earlier claims
suggesting that an adolescent's appearance is a reliable indication of violent
tendencies.

Discussion and Conclusions

Constructionism was an effective framework for analyzing media representations of the Columbine shootings as an appearance-linked social problem.[. . .] Claims made by both primary and secondary claims-makers drew
linkages between this incident of youth violence and appearance. Primary
claims-makers provided eye-witness accounts of the Columbine incident
and previous experiences with the Columbine gunmen, launched claims
and/or counter-claims to dispute or revise allegations advanced in prior
claims, and proposed appearance-linked solutions to prior claims.

[. . .]

[S]econdary claims-makers covered, validated, and transformed the content of primary claims. Although media writers highlighted the claims of primary claims-makers by offering them coverage within the media, media writers' decisions about which primary claims to cover and how to cover them simultaneously and necessarily transformed these primary claims. Thus, even primary claims presented in the manufacture of this social problem were media constructions or rhetoric, shaped and tailored by media writers as they staged secondary claims. For instance, media writers played a key role in promulgating the claim that the gunmen used ethnicity to identify their victims, despite the 'fact' (as presented by the media) that only one primary claims-maker had made such a claim. Similarly, both primary and secondary claims-makers addressed the everyday appearances of the gunmen and the meanings of these appearances. Often, secondary claims-makers even invoked student comments in support of their claims. However, media writers' claims were considerably more speculative than those of students. Students' claims asserted that the gunmen wore trench coats on a regular basis and that they (i.e., the students) were afraid of the gunmen, but media writers' claims went one step further, suggesting that the gunmen regularly wore symbols of violence and the profane. [. . .] As such, our findings support the notion that although the content of primary and secondary claims may 'overlap' (O'Neal 1997, p. 348), the claims made by these different claims-makers are not synonymous.

[. . .]

Media coverage concerning the Columbine shootings was rife with themes of fear and intimidation. In this vein, several secondary claims intimated that the lives of readers could be touched by youth violence like that exhibited by the Columbine gunmen, a strategy that Best (1989, p. 264) has referred to as 'personalizing the issues.' For instance, media claims suggested that parents observe their own children for appearance-linked 'warning signs' that might allude to violent tendencies—any child with an affinity for black clothes could be the next Harris or Klebold. Further, appearance-related media claims pointed to the Columbine shootings as an example that even unlikely places—such as affluent and suburban Littleton (where people typically wear 'respectable, Republican' clothes)—were not immune from the 'toxicity' wrought by youth affiliated with 'antisocial' subcultures such as the Trench Coat Mafia; any school campus, anywhere, could be at risk. This seeming attempt to render the Columbine shootings as personal and as scary may reflect the news media's alleged entertainment orientation.

[. . .]

Although media writers constructed Columbine as a personally threatening issue, they also presented it as a social risk that could be 'kept at bay' through proper policing, control, and/or prevention (Ericson and Haggerty 1997; Staples 1997). To this end, appearance was presented as both a scapegoat for and a solution to the Columbine problem. The notion that a readily identifiable and malleable characteristic such as appearance could be at the heart of the Columbine problem may reflect an attempt on the part of the media to reassure readers by offering them a ready and tidy solution to a problem that had been presented as scary and threatening. Further, presenting simple explanations for and easily implemented solutions to complex issues is consistent with an entertainment orientation of the news media; entertainment has been said to 'abhor ambiguity,' relying instead upon neat and unequivocal claims (Altheide and Michalowski 1999, p. 499).

Finally, it is important to consider the possible implications of claims made within the media and related to the role of appearance in the Columbine shootings. Granted, primary and secondary claims-makers eventually recanted or minimized the scope of claims casting appearance as cause of and solution to the acts of violence perpetrated by Harris and Klebold. However, these 'corrective' claims were published more than a year after the original claims were made. In the months between the media coverage of the initial claims and the revised claims, the reality of Columbine as an appearance problem was produced in the eyes of the public; meanings about the appearances of the gunmen, their victims, and their alleged associates were negotiated in the forum of the print media. As an apparent result of this dialogue, innocent individuals perceived themselves as unjustly implicated in the crime on the basis of their appearance and were moved to stage counterclaims defending their innocence. Further, by constructing Columbine as an appearance-related problem and formulating appearance-based solutions accordingly, the media may have shortchanged the discussion of an opportunity for 'real' social change as away to prevent future school shootings. In their analyses of media coverage related to threats to children and killing for clothes, Best (1989) and O'Neal (1997) discovered similar patterns in which the location of cause for a problem shaped the resultant public policy and precluded discussions necessary for true social change. Taken together, then, these implications certainly constitute a call for continued research related to the media's role in the construction and explanation of issues as 'social problems.'

[. . .]

References

Altheide, David L., and R. Sam Michalowski. 1999. 'Fear in the News: A Discourse in Control.' *The Sociological Quarterly* 40: 475–503.

Best, Joel. 1987. 'Rhetoric in Claims-Making: Constructing the Missing Children Problem. *Social Problems* 34: 101–21.

Best, Joel. 1989. 'Secondary Claims-Making: Claims about Threats to Children on the Network News.' *Perspectives on Social Problems* 1: 259–82.

Ericson, Richard V., and Kevin D. Haggerty. 1997. *Policing the Risk Society.* Toronto: University of Toronto Press.

Ibarra, P. R., and John I. Kitsuse. 1993. 'Vernacular Constituents of Moral Discourse: An Interactionist Proposal for the Study of Social Problems.' pp. 21–54 in *Constructionist Controversies*, edited by Gale Miller and James A. Holstein. New York: Aldine De Gruyter Press.

Lennon, Sharron J., Kim K. P. Johnson, and Theresa L. Schulz. 1999. 'Forging Linkages between Dress and the Law in the U.S. Part 2: Dress Codes.' *Clothing and Textiles Research Journal* 17: 157–67.

O'Neal, Gwendolyn. 1997. 'Clothes to Kill For: An Analysis of Primary and Secondary Claims-Making in Print Media.' *Sociological Inquiry* 67: 336–49.

Spector, Malcolm, and John I. Kitsuse. 1977. *Constructing Social Problems.* Menlo Park, CA: Cummings Publishing Company.

Staples, William G. 1997. *The Culture of Surveillance: Discipline and Social Control in the United States.* New York: St. Martin's Press.

BETWEEN FEMININE EMPOWERMENT AND SUBJUGATION

SEXUALIZING THE VIOLENT FEMALE HERO IN THE *BUFFY THE VAMPIRE SLAYER* VIDEO GAME

17

Magdala Peixoto Labre and Lisa Duke

Introduction

Throughout time, heroism has described deeds of men who must overcome adversity through a showing of physical prowess, valor, and bravery – usually on the battlefield. Historically, heroism has been ascribed to women with relative infrequency and in muted form. Feminine heroism traditionally has had less to do with physical strength and daring than emotional fortitude and selflessness (Polster 1992). However, recent media research indicates that typical, gender-oriented portrayals of heroism are changing. Television shows such as *Xena: Warrior Princess* developed a following among fans who enjoyed seeing a woman regularly best male opponents both physically and intellectually. Another more recent example is *Buffy the Vampire Slayer* (BVS), a television cult series about a California 'valley girl' who slays vampires and other demons. The show, which completed its seventh and final season in 2003, has attracted substantial scholarly attention from feminist, postmodernist, and other academics who point to Buffy as exemplary of a new breed of mediated female hero. She is powerful and in control, a woman who does the rescuing. The success of the program inspired Fox Interactive to develop a *BVS* videogame, released in August 2002.

The Buffy video game is unusual because it builds on a show primarily watched by women, portrays a female as the hero, and yet is also a fighting game – a genre traditionally preferred by males between the ages of eighteen and thirty-four, who make up the majority of video game players. This article provides a critical analysis of the Buffy video game, describing the construction of Buffy as a female hero, comparing it with her portrayal in the television series, and discussing the reasons for and possible repercussions of this type of representation.

The hero

[. . .]

In the past, portrayals of female heroes in the media featured characters (e.g., Wonder Woman, Super Girl, Charlie's Angels, The Bionic Woman) that exemplified the feminine heroism described by Pearson (1986). They were attractive, emotional, and caring and often used their intellects and relationships rather than sheer strength to solve problems. Although they engaged in fights when needed, combat scenes were mild and killings were seen as a last resort. These female heroes were caregivers and problem solvers first, warriors second.

In the past decade, however, a new breed of female heroes has emerged. Exemplified by the lead characters in the television shows *Xena: Warrior Princess, La Femme Nikita, BVS*, and *Alias*, the new female heroes are warriors. Although caring and compassionate, they are fighters willing to engage in hand-to-hand combat and use a variety of weapons and techniques to conquer their foes. Like their male counterparts, they can be ruthless and destructive. In the new imagery that has surfaced in the media, the male shadow of excessive aggression manifests itself in both male and female heroes (Calvert et al. 2001).

Two of these new female heroes, Xena and Buffy, have attracted substantial scholarly attention. *Xena: Warrior Princess*, an action-adventure show that attracted a diverse audience of devout followers, was one the first television shows to place a woman in the role of the archetypal hero on a quest (Morreale 1998). Xena, who first appeared as an evil character in the *Hercules: The Legendary Journeys* fantasy-action series, had to overcome her dark side, or male shadow, to avenge the innocent. However, the shadow never completely receded, and throughout her journey, she had to fight the evil forces outside and inside herself (Calvert et al. 2001).

[. . .]

Gender and video games

The *BVS* video game was released in August 2002 for the X-Box game system. It was labeled as 'action/adventure,' with a rating of *T*, for teen, with content deemed suitable for persons ages thirteen and older. The game joined a rapidly growing market of titles, played on computers or on consoles such as Microsoft's X-Box and Sony's Play Station 2, that have become extremely popular, with more than 215 million games sold in 1999 alone – an average of more than two per household (Jenkins 2000).

Video games have always been considered a male-dominated form of entertainment. Males make up the majority of players, video game characters, and game developers or producers (Cassell and Jenkins 1998). Boys have been found to play video games more than girls at every age group (Wright et al. 2001), and at least 90 percent of video game magazine readers are male (Kinder 1996). Until recently, girls made up less than 25 percent of the videogame market (Cassell and Jenkins 1998). And while the past decade has witnessed the emergence of a movement toward the creation of video game companies and products targeting girls, the majority of games in the market continue to be developed for male tastes, featuring a high level of violence and stereotypical portrayals of women as victims or sexual objects.

Studies suggest that violence or aggression is present in more than 70 percent of video games (Braun and Giroux 1989; Dietz 1998). Although evidence regarding the games' promotion of antisocial or 'aggressive' values or behavior is mixed (Dominick 1984; Gibb et al. 1983; Graybill, Kirsh, and Esselman 1985; Kestenbaum and Weinstein 1985; Silvern and Williamson, 1987), several recent studies suggest that video game use is associated with short- and long-term increases in aggression (Anderson and Dill 2000; Ballard and Lineberger 1999; Ballard and Wiest 1996; Bartholow and Anderson 2002; Dill and Dill 1998).

Although Buffy is not the first female hero to be featured in a video game, very few games have portrayed women as heroes (Dietz 1998). Studies have found that women are generally absent or underrepresented in these games (Beasley and Standley 2002; Dietz 1998; Provenzo 1991). When women characters are included, they often are stereotyped as subordinate, as victims of male aggression (e.g., damsels in distress), or as sexual objects (Beasely and Standley 2002; Dietz 1998). A recent study of forty-seven video games found that female characters were more likely to show skin than male characters and that many of the female characters were 'unrealistically large breasted' (Beasely and Standley 2002). In another study, the few female characters who were presented as heroes (15 percent of characters) were often dressed in stereotypical female colors and or clothing (Dietz 1998). As noted by Subrahmanyam and Greenfield (1998), female hero-character Lara Croft of the *Tomb Raider* game has a tiny waist, extremely large breasts, and a mainly male audience.

Research on the effects of the under-representation of women in video-games and of the stereotypical portrayals of female characters in these games is lacking. However, critics suggest that these games may contribute to negative attitudes toward women by helping children internalize the idea that 'women are to be viewed as weak, as victims, and as sex objects' (Dietz 1998, 438).

Although video games have traditionally targeted males, games specifically aimed at girls began to be developed when marketers realized that the most readily available games, which primarily featured violent combat and good versus evil themes, were not appealing to this audience. While studies suggest that boys prefer games with violent action, sports, and realistic human violence, girls routinely indicate a preference for games with components of spatial relations, education, or cartoon fantasy violence (Gailey 1996; Buchman and Funk 1996; Funk, Germann, and Buchanan 1997). The violent nature of many video games has been shown to alienate girls (Greenfield 1996; Malone 1981), who are said to be more interested in non fantasy themes related to exploration, negotiation, cooperation, the building of social relationships, and nurturance (Cassell and Jenkins 1998; Subrahmanyam and Greenfield 1998). However, as noted by organizations of female gamers, to maintain that girls prefer only one type of game and that boys prefer another is an oversimplification that helps support gender stereotypes: 'Underlying the position that there are fundamental differences between what boys and girls want from computer games is a discourse that posits essential differences in girls' and boys' cultural tastes, interests, and competencies' (Cassell and Jenkins 1998, 25). Some girls and women may, in fact, enjoy violent combat games and view them as empowering avenues for developing a sense of control and mastery over the environment. As noted by a woman who enjoys playing these games,

I keep reading about articles and studies where experts say girls don't like shooting and blasting games but instead prefer quiet, contemplative games with well rounded characters and storylines that stimulate their imagination. I'd venture to say, however, that these studies are a reflection of how we condition girls to be passive. The image of woman with gun is too shocking, too disruptive and threatening to the male dominant order of things. (Cybergrrl Aliza Sherman quoted in Jenkins 1998, 335)

The development of violent video games for boys and relationship-building games for girls can therefore be seen as perpetuating the tradition of gendered toys, thereby supporting the social construction of girls as passive and nurturing and of boys as aggressive and dominating.

Research Focus and Method

To analyse the construction of Buffy as a female hero in the video game [. . .] the authors conducted a textual analysis of the Buffy game. We also consulted with representatives from the video game makers to gain a better understanding of the target audience for the game, how well it was selling, and their future plans regarding the game. The code sheet from a previous qualitative content analysis of archetypal depictions of male and female heroism as portrayed in advertising (Goodman, Duke, and Sutherland 2002) was examined for categories relevant to the current study. This code sheet lists an adaptation of primary Jungian heroic archetypes, such as the Warrior, Magician, Martyr/Caregiver, or Innocent, and enumerates the goals, fears, problem response, task, and gifts of each. For example, the Warrior's goal is to succeed against adversity; her fear is weakness; her response to a problem is to use force to overcome an opponent; her task is to fight for right; and her gifts are courage, discipline, and skill. This archetype contrasts starkly with the stereotypical female hero, who is a Martyr/Caregiver. Her goal is goodness – her fear, selfishness. She rectifies and protects without harming wrongdoers and achieves her objectives with compassion and generosity (see Pearson 1986). A graduate student and an undergraduate student, both males, were recruited to play the BVS game while the two researchers took detailed notes on pertinent, preexisting codes, as well as numerous elements unique to the Buffy character, story, and video game format.

With the exception of the first level, a training level that was included to provide players with an opportunity to learn how to play the game (e.g., how to open doors), the other levels were remarkably similar to each other. In each, Buffy walks through a particular locale, such as a cemetery, fighting the enemies that appear. After the students had completed five levels of the game, the researchers determined that saturation had been reached regarding Buffy's portrayal and that the playing of subsequent levels of the game would contribute little to the analysis.

After each level of play was completed, the researchers compared observations and created preliminary categorizations of data. The two students played all five levels of the game on separate days, allowing the research team to capture the essential visual and verbal elements of the scene and narrative. In addition, the graduate student game player, who is very familiar with the genre, served as an expert consultant on the play of the game, for example, to provide feedback about the level of difficulty, conventions of battle, understanding of narrative and clues to advancement, and his level of engagement in characters and tasks. This feedback was of interest since our player assistant falls into the primary target for the game: males aged eighteen to thirty-four. After all levels of play were completed the researchers were debriefed on their observations and established agreement on interpretations of the game's signs, gaming conventions, use and development of characters and narrative, and departures or adherences to the signature elements of the television show.

The Buffy Video Game: an Analysis

Unlike video games targeted to girls, *BVS* is a fighting game, containing high levels of violence against nonhuman (but human-appearing) opponents. The game was written as a lost episode and fits in as an early episode in season three, when Buffy was still in high school and Cordelia and Angel had not moved on to the spin-off series, *Angel*. Other characters in the game include Giles, Willow, Xander, and the dangerous British vampire Spike. [. . .] The text is narrated by the actor who plays Giles in the series, as are all other regular characters included in the video game, with the exception of Buffy, whose voice double does a good imitation of Gellar. The score features creepy sounds and fast-paced instrumental music that serve as the background for some of the fighting scenes. Much of the action takes place in dark, foreboding locations such as a cemetery or mausoleum.

The game begins by introducing Buffy as a cheerleader, interrupted at practice by a sudden influx of demons. The *S* on Buffy's cheerleading uniform could stand for the name of her school, Sunnydale, but it also reminds the viewer of her slayer status. While male high school athletes wear jerseys with numbers to identify them as individuals on a team, girls on high school cheerleading squads wear a common letter, marking them as undifferentiated parts of a team.

This ambiguity between feminine empowerment and subjugation is extended through the name of the main character: Buffy. 'Buff,' her nickname – meaning in shape, toned, able to do battle, in admirable physical condition – contrasts sharply with 'Buffy,' the ultimate girly-girl name. In the video game, Buffy says that she finds the cheerleading experience 'very empowering,' signaling that she is equally at ease using extreme, stereotypically feminine and masculine tools to succeed and does not privilege one over the other. She is the cheerleader with a valley-girl cadence who demolishes opponents with flip comments, a cavalier attitude, and kickboxing prowess.

The construction of Buffy in the video game provides support for the idea that female heroes can be powerful but must conversely conform to traditional constructions of femininity, so as not to be perceived as too masculine or elicit suspicions of lesbianism (Inness 1999). Buffy is portrayed as physically powerful despite the fact she is slim, petite, unusual, and stereotypically female in her physical presentation. But she is not like any other female. As one character in the game notes, 'Ever seen a girl kick ass like that before?' She is atypical. She is not one of us. She did not build a high level of strength, agility, and skill through effort alone – she was born this way.

[. . .]

[T]he game promotes anti-intellectualism and reinforces gender stereotypes about women. For example, when Giles gives Buffy a list of new techniques to study, she responds, 'Wait, you didn't say there was reading involved.' At another point, Willow uses the word *inured* and then says, 'Isn't it exciting? I never used that word in conversation before.' This is particularly interesting given that Willow is the self-proclaimed nerd in the group. This type of exchange supports the construction of women as frivolous and anti-intellectual. Self-deprecation also minimizes Buffy's success as a warrior; she undercuts her victories with flip comments to those whom she has beaten and consistently understates or makes light of the import of her achievements, for example, 'Oh, look, another pointy thing to add to my collection of pointy things.'

[. . .]

While in the television series, much of the action revolves around relationship building and collective problem solving, these more positive, traditionally feminine characteristics are stripped from the video game, which focuses almost exclusively on combat. Most of the time is spent kicking, punching, and staking vampires and demons, using a variety of weapons including stakes, a crossbow, a double-edged blade, a super soaker that can shoot flames or holy water, and improvised weapons such as mops, rakes, and bats.

Although Buffy must at times look for keys or place stones in particular positions to open doors or achieve other goals, puzzles do not take up much game time. Nor do relationships. There are times during play, usually at the beginning of a new level, when the main characters assemble at the library and Buffy speaks briefly to each of them. For example, Xander tells her about a new weapon he has made for her, Giles gives her new fighting techniques, and Willow asks her to bring back crystals that she can use to make Buffy more powerful. In reply, Buffy usually makes quick, glib retort and moves quickly into combat mode.

In the game, Buffy is a killing machine with a 'whatever!' attitude. Fearless to the point of foolhardiness, she taunts her opponents: 'You want a piece of me? I'll give you the whole damn pie!' or 'This is my town!' She ends each killing with a remark such as the following: 'I feel like a new slayer'; 'Nothing like a brisk walk and a spot of demon slaughter to make a girl's night'; 'Guess who wishes he'd stayed home tonight'; 'Oops, I did it again'; or 'Let that be a lesson to you or, you know, those who pass by your mangled corpse.' Although in the television series, Buffy also uses cutting remarks such as 'I'm Buffy, and you're . . . history' (quoted in Pender 2002), in the game, these are repeated incessantly, serving to construct a character that is more arrogant than witty.

In the television show, Buffy often works closely with her friends to brainstorm responses to demon threats and other problems, and she often brings them along in her most difficult battles. In the video game, she is the lone warrior who goes on the hunt. For example, when Xander offers to go with her on her mission, she responds, 'Sorry, Xander, this is a solo slayer mission.' This one-dimensional construction of Buffy in the video game is not surprising given that it fits within the normal parameters for a fighting game. Although there is some dialogue, the focus is on the battles.

In game-play scenarios, Buffy is driven by an ethic of justice – snuffing out the lives of the bad guys who have hurt others in the game. Her ethic of care, a significant characteristic in the television show, is not evident in the game. The game does not allow for 'unexciting' plot and character development – it is an action-oriented format. There is no room for slow-moving scenes of empathy or compassion. One does not win anything for expression of care. Although Buffy saves her friends by killing vampires and other evil creatures in the game, she is bereft of the caring qualities she exhibits on the series. She often passes victims as if stepping around road kill, never asking if they are alright or offering solace. Most of the time, she does not speak to victims and cannot touch them (the game literally does not allow the player to physically interact with victims). The injured and frightened are left behind as Buffy chases after an endless array of evildoers. She must kill to advance. The death of opponents empowers her. She is unfeeling, uncaring, a cyborg with a blond ponytail.

The video game almost completely eliminates Buffy's care-giving side as a hero, even as it amps up the portrayal of her sexual characteristics. Although not as sexually exaggerated as Lara Croft, Buffy has round breasts that are always in view. Buffy's sexualization is intensified by the color of her outfit through several levels of the game: red and black, colors associated with sex and passion (Sharpe 1974). The lighting used on her black, low-cut top and tight red pants often draws attention to her cleavage and butt. In fact, all female characters have medium to large breasts, including Willow, who has small breasts in the series. Female vampires generally wear tight, low-cut jeans, with midriff-baring tops. A particularly strong female vampire wears a black leather, dominatrix-style outfit that leaves most of her breasts exposed. Cleavage shots objectify Buffy and other women in the game, making them into objects of desire, which suggests that game makers desired to make the game appealing specifically to male players. Because of the darkness of the game, Buffy's breasts and rear are a constant 'highlight,' beacons in the shadows, leading the player through the game.

Not only are sexual characteristics emphasized in the game, but much of the dialogue is also sexually charged. More than once, a male vampire will taunt Buffy saying, 'I want you, babe, but not in a good way.' At another point in the game, Buffy's friend Xander says her cheerleader outfit (tight red pants and a yellow, sleeveless crop top) is hot. When she mentions that she is starting to think that the outfit is a vampire magnet, he responds that it will also attract lecherous middle-aged men.

When fighting female demons, Buffy often comments on their appearance, saying things like 'Your outfit is killing me' or 'Just between us girls, you're a little worn around the eyes.' Fights with female opponents are often introduced by a voice saying 'chick fight.' Although these types of comments have appeared in the television show, in the game, they occur with much greater frequency. In addition, Buffy and others in the game often use sexist put-downs not common in the television series. For example, when Willow is captured by the female vampire in the dominatrix outfit, she says, 'Maybe you didn't hear me, you skanky bloodsucking ho.' Later, when fighting this vampire, Buffy says, 'That outfit just screams biker slut,' and 'I know you guys take the whole fetish scene way too seriously, but there's a fine line between femme fatale and tacky tramp.' At another point in the game, Cordelia says something about Buffy's saving their football team's tight end from a 'skank slut' who was hitting on him at the local nightclub frequented by characters on the show. The game also differs from the television show in its presentation of violence.

Although violence occurs more frequently in the video game than in the television show, the type of violence seems less graphic. First, the characters in the game are obviously cartoons, not real people. Vampires turn to dust when killed; there are no gory scenes of bloody evisceration that are common in other fighting video games. At the same time, however, because the game is interactive, its violence may have a different type of impact. When playing the game as Buffy, at some level, the player feels that he or she is the character and is focused on avoiding annihilation. The goal of the game is morbidly personal: not only do you want to move the next level, but you also do not want to die!

The point of production

Our analysis raised questions that could not be ignored in a thoughtful consideration of the game. For example, although the majority of video game players are male, it was difficult to see how *BVS* could attract and sustain a substantial male playing audience. The audience for the television show, after all, skews heavily female and the game allowed the player to become only one character – Buffy. To address this and other related questions, we consulted with an executive who was in charge of developing the *BVS* game at Fox Interactive, one of the game's two publishers. (The other is Electronic Arts.) Although neither of the respondents in this section requested anonymity, we have chosen not to use their names in this study.

The Fox Interactive executive noted that because the game was introduced as an X-Box exclusive, the target audience for the game was, by caveat, current owners of the X-Box – or males ages eighteen to thirty-four. Although the game 'could be played by anyone' and enjoyed a burst of success in the first two weeks of its release, sales in the subsequent months had been 'disappointing.' The executive noted that improvements had been made to the upcoming second version of the game, including allowing players to choose to become a variety of characters (phone interview, October 2002).

We also interviewed one of the head creative people at The Collective, which designed and developed the game. The creative professional noted that there are special problems in developing a game based on a popular television show. First, in this case, the program and gaming audiences are of different sexes. The game was developed in a way that would maximize sales, that is, 'ultimately, it's an action game. A relationship-oriented or adventure game wouldn't sell. . . . How often do you hear a woman say "Let's bust out the PlayStation and get some games going?" ' The creative professional also noted that there is a difference between games that can be played on a personal computer without special equipment and those that require a console. The latter make up the bulk of game sales and are more likely to be purchased by boys. The Collective specializes in action console games and, according to this respondent, the company has never created a game especially for girls. Second, the creative professional said that television producers can 'get away' with more than can video game producers. For example, there are restrictions on how blood can be portrayed in games with human or humanlike characters. Again, to make the game as marketable to as large an audience as possible, it was decided that the game needed to pull a *T* rating, meaning it was suitable for teens over the age of thirteen, rather than a mature audience rating, which would allow more gore but 'limit its sales potential.' Also, restrictions on secondary use of intellectual property limited the ways Buffy could make her typical references to popular culture. For example, her group of friends is called the Scooby gang on the television show, but the game developers were prohibited from using this reference.

Finally, the creative professional noted two important factors in deciding how Buffy's body was to be portrayed in the game. 'If you try to use strictly human proportions,' the respondent said, 'the figure doesn't read very well onscreen. You want to bulk up slim characters, round them out a bit.' However, the Buffy character was never going to take on the unlikely proportions of a Lara Croft – the developers had to secure 'likeness approvals' from Sarah Michelle Gellar's representatives before the game was released (all from phone interview, October 2002).

Market considerations can account for the game's relentless focus on Warrior modes of combat – boys dominate the market and therefore dictate the forms that games will take – even, apparently, games based on media vehicles originally intended to appeal to and empower girls. The types of games that focus more on narrative and relationships – hallmarks of the *BVS* television show – are seen as less profitable by video game producers. The decreased violence and sexualization of the main female character were dictated by different market considerations. More (male) players of younger ages can buy the game if it features less graphic violence, while Gellar's control over the marketing of her likeness prevents (or, conceivably, could also enable) hypersexualization of her character. The fact that she is an extremely slender woman may have helped keep the focus of the game on the fighting rather than her figure. Too much deviation would have destroyed the resemblance to the decidedly uncurvy Gellar.

Conclusion

As discussed above, the type of female heroism portrayed in the Buffy video game is characterized by the Warrior archetype, the male shadow, and an ethic of justice rather than an ethic of care.

[. . .]

The video game's construction of Buffy as a warrior hero can be viewed as providing an alternative, nontraditional representation of females, allowing young women to view themselves not as victims but as heroes in charge of their own destinies. These images may be empowering to women by allowing them to consider roles and activities that might otherwise be perceived as inappropriate and unavailable to them.

Although women can be assertive in American society, aggression is a character trait that is still largely viewed as inappropriate (Rubin, Bukowski, and Parker 1998). Portrayals of female warriors such as Buffy allow female viewers to envision themselves and others as strong, capable, and fearless heroes rather than helpless victims awaiting rescue.

[. . .]

At the same time, however, this one-dimensional construction promotes the martial and masculine values of domination and destruction, where powerlessness is replaced by seeking power over others. It is significant to note that when Buffy kills an opponent, she gains his or her energy. Killing is not something done as a last resort; it is a way to gain strength.

Like other video games, the *BVS* game promotes the objectification of women's bodies, by exaggerating the sexual characteristics of female characters and contributing to the idea that powerful women must also be sex objects. In addition, the game features sexist language that denigrates women and associates them with anti-intellectualism. Lines spoken by Buffy such as 'Oops, I did it again,' serve to associate this strong hero with the highly sexualized, anti-intellectual pop star Britney Spears.

Despite these shortcomings, within the genre of fighting video games, Buffy's representation seems less problematic than that of other female heroes such as Lara Croft. As noted earlier, because the video game characters had to resemble the actors in the television show, the sexual characteristics of female characters could not be as exaggerated as in other video games. Moreover, to secure a *T* rating, the game had to feature a lower level of violence than other fighting games. This type of game could therefore be viewed as representing a 'female version' of the fighting game, providing an alternative for some of the girls and women who enjoy playing this genre (others may prefer the more traditional fighting games).

Video games are unique cultural texts characterized by greater interactivity, more narrow demographics, and quasi-subcultural status (relative to television). Further research on girls' interaction with the game is needed to gain an understanding of the possible repercussions of this new type of entertainment (e.g., the game's sequel, *Chaos Bleeds*, released in August 2003, features a multiplayer mode, a feature worthy of study on many levels). Given that the most recent literature indicates that playing violent video games can increase aggressiveness in children, it is plausible that such negative behaviors would show an overall increase should fighting games become more popular with girls. To date, however, females have only just begun to be perceived by marketers of such games as a potentially profitable audience segment. Observations of and interviews with female players might help shed some light on the uses and potential effects of this new genre of video game as well as identify other possible portrayals that girls may find more useful and appealing.

References

Anderson, Craig A., and Karen E. Dill. 2000. Video games and aggressive thoughts, feelings, and behavior in the laboratory and in life. *Journal of Personality and Social Psychology* 78: 772–90.

Ballard, Mary E., and Robert Lineberger. 1999. Video game violence and confederate gender: Effects on reward and punishment given by college males. *Sex Roles* 41 (7/8): 541–58.

Ballard, Mary E., and J. R. Wiest. 1996. Mortal Kombat™: The effects of violent video gameplay on males' hostility and cardiovascular responding. *Journal of Applied Social Psychology* 26: 717–30.

Bartholow, Bruce D., and Craig A. Anderson 2002. Effects of violent video games on aggressive behavior: Potential sex differences. *Journal of Experimental Social Psychology* 38: 283–90.

Beasley, Berrin, and Tracy Collins Standley. 2002. Shirts vs. skins: Clothing as an indicator of gender role stereotyping in video games. *Mass Communication and Society* 5 (3): 279–93.

Braun, Claude M. J., and Josette Giroux. 1989. Arcade video games: Proxemic, cognitive and content analyses. *Journal of Leisure Research* 21 (2): 92–105.

Buchman, Debra D., and Jeanne B. Funk. 1996. Video and computer games in the '90s: Children's time commitment and game preference. *Children Today* 24 (1): 12–15.

Calvert, Sandra L., Tracy A. Kondla, Karen A. Ertel, and Douglas S. Meisel. 2001. Young adults' perceptions and memories of a televised woman hero. *Sex Roles* 45 (1/2): 31–52.

Cassell, Justine, and Henry Jenkins. 1998. Chess for girls? In *From Barbie to Mortal Kombat: Gender and computer games*, edited by Justine Cassell and Henry Jenkins, 2–45. Cambridge, MA: MIT Press.

Dietz, Tracy L. 1998. An examination of violence and gender role portrayals in video games: Implications for gender socialization and aggressive behavior. *Sex Roles* 38 (5/6): 425–42.

Dill, Karen E., and Jody C. Dill. 1998. Video game violence: A review of the empirical literature. *Aggression and Violent Behavior: A Review Journal* 3 (4): 407–28.

Dominick, Joseph R. 1984. Video games, television violence, and aggression in teenagers. *Journal of Communication* 34: 136–47.

Funk, Jeanne B., Julie N. Germann, and Debra D. Buchanan. 1997. Children and electronic games in the United States. *Trends in Communications* 2: 111–26.

Gailey, Christine Ward. 1996. Mediated messages: Gender, class, and cosmos in home videogames. In *Interacting with video*, edited by Patricia M. Greenfield and Rodney R. Cocking, 9–23. Norwood, NJ: Ablex.

Gibb, Gerald D., James R. Bailey, Thomas T. Lambirth, and William P. Wilson. 1983. Personality differences between high and low electronic video game users. *Journal of Psychology* 114: 159–65.

Goodman, Robyn, Lisa Duke, and John Sutherland. 2002. Olympic athletes and heroism in advertising: Gendered concepts of valor? *Journalism and Mass Communication Quarterly* 79 (2): 374–93.

Graybill, Daniel, Janice R. Kirsch, and Edward D. Esselman. 1985. Effects of playing violent versus non-violent video games on the aggressive ideation of aggressive and non-aggressive children. *Child Study Journal* 15 (3): 199–205.

Greenfield, P. M. 1996. Video games as cultural artifacts. In *Interacting with video*, edited by Patricia M. Greenfield and Rodney R. Cocking, 85–94. Norwood, NJ: Ablex.

Inness, Sherrie A. 1999. *Tough girls: Women warriors and wonder women in popular culture*. Philadelphia: University of Pennsylvania Press.

Jenkins, Henry. 1998. Voices from the combat zone: Game grrlz talk back. In *From Barbie to Mortal Kombat: Gender and computer games*, edited by Justine Cassell and Henry Jenkins, 328–41. Cambridge, MA: MIT Press.

Jenkins, Henry. 2000. A patron for video games. *Technology Review* 103 (5): 117–20.

Kestenbaum, Gerald I., and Lisa Weinstein. 1985. Personality, psychopathology, and development issues in male adolescent video game use. *Journal of the American Academy of Child Psychiatry* 24 (3): 329–33.

Kinder, Marsha. 1996. Contextualizing video game violence: From Teenage Mutant Ninja Turtles 1 to Mortal Kombat 2. In *Interacting with video*, edited by Patricia M. Greenfield and Rodney R. Cocking, 25–38. Norwood, NJ: Ablex.

Malone, Thomas W. 1981. Toward a theory of intrinsically motivating instruction. *Cognitive Science* 5: 333–70.

Morreale, Joanne. 1998. *Xena: Warrior Princess* as a feminist camp. *Journal of Popular Culture* 32 (2): 79–86.

Pearson, Carol. 1986. *The hero within: Six archetypes to live by*. San Francisco: Harper and Row.

Pender, Patricia. 2002. 'I'm Buffy, and you're . . . history' The postmodern politics of *Buffy*. In *Fighting the forces: What's at stake in* Buffy the Vampire Slayer, edited by Rhonda V. Wilcox and David Lavery, 35–44. Lanham, MD: Rowman and Littlefield.

Polster, Miriam. 1992. *Eve's daughters: The forbidden heroism of women*. San Francisco: Jossey-Bass.

Provenzo, Eugene F. 1991. *Video kids: Making sense of Nintendo*. Cambridge, MA: Harvard University Press.

Rubin, Kenneth H., William M. Bukowski, and Jeffrey G. Parker. 1998. Peer interactions, relationships, and groups. In *Handbook of child psychology: Vol. 3. Social, emotional, and personality development*, edited by William Damon

(Series Ed.) and Nancy Eisenberg (Vol. Ed.), 5th ed., 619–700. New York: Wiley.

Sharpe, Deborah T. 1974. *The psychology of color and design.* Chicago: Nelson-Hall.

Silvern, Steven B., and Peter A. Williamson. 1987. The effects of video game play on young children's aggressive, fantasy, and prosocial behavior. *Journal of Applied Developmental Psychology* 8 (4): 453–62.

Subrahmanyam, Kaveri, and Patricia M. Greenfield. 1998. Computer games for girls: What makes them play? In *From Barbie to Mortal Kombat: Gender and computer games*, edited by Justine Cassell and Henry Jenkins, 46–71. Cambridge, MA: MIT Press.

Wright, John C., Aletha C. Huston, Elizabeth A. Vandewater, David S. Bickham, Ronda M. Scantlin, Jennifer A. Kotler, Allison Gilman Caplovitz, June H. Lee, Sandra Hofferth, and Jonathan Finkelstein. 2001. American children's use of electronic media in 1997: A national survey. *Applied Developmental Psychology* 22: 31–47.

18

CONSTRUCTING ARABS AS ENEMIES AFTER SEPTEMBER 11

AN ANALYSIS OF SELECTED SPEECHES BY GEORGE W. BUSH

Debra Merskin

Make no mistake, we will find the enemy and we will kill the enemy. (*The Siege*, 1998)

Make no mistake, the U.S. government will hunt down and punish those responsible for these cowardly acts. (George W. Bush, 2001)

Just as the media have anthropomorphized courage and bravery in the post-September 11 world, a face has also been put on terror and it is Arab. The political rhetoric of George W. Bush following the September 11, 2001, attacks on the World Trade Center and Pentagon employed words and expressions – 'us,' 'them,' 'they,' 'evil,' 'those people,' 'demons,' 'wanted: dead or alive' – to characterize people of Arab/Middle Eastern descent. Although these descriptions have largely been applied to non-U.S. citizens, they cannot help but include the approximately three million Arab individuals living in the United States, many of whom were born in the United States as well as others who have adopted America as home – Iraqis, Iranians, Palestinians, Egyptians, Arabs, Yemenis, and others.

Popular culture and mass media in the United States have generated and sustained stereotypes of a monolithic evil Arab; these stereotypes constructed all Muslims as Arab and all Arabs as terrorists. Using representations and language in news, movies, cartoons, and magazine stories, the media and popular culture have participated in the construction of an evil Arab stereotype that encompasses a wide variety of people, ideas, beliefs, religions, and assumptions (Ghareeb, 1983; Hamada, 2001; Jackson, 1996; Shaheen, 1998, 2001; Suleiman, 1988, 1999; Terry, 1985). For example, movies such as those listed earlier and several newsmagazines present dark images of Middle Eastern men, or what Shaheen (1995, p. 191) calls 'America's bogeyman.' In recent films, 'Barbarism and cruelty are the most common traits associated with Arabs' (Jackson, 1996, p. 65). These stereotypes, 'which tend to lump Arabs, Muslim, Middle East into one highly negative image of violence and danger,' are composed largely from collective memory, rather than from actual experience (Jackson, 1996, p. 65).

Historically, a combination of (mis)information has worked to construct an enemy image in the popular imagination that has an important function in the maintenance of political power, or **hegemony**, through ideology. Consequently, the 'Face of Terror' is not only that of Osama bin Laden and Saddam Hussein but also all persons of Arab descent, evoking the simulacrum of all Middle Eastern-looking men as the face of terrorism (Ghareeb, 1983; Hamada, 2001; Suleiman, 1999).

This article links stereotypes of Arabs, enemy image construction, and ideology to the rhetoric of President George W. Bush as delivered during five speeches and a memorial service subsequent to the September 11, 2001, attacks. Spillman and Spillman's (1997, pp. 50–51) model of enemy image construction is used as a framework for an interpretive textual analysis (Chandler, 2002; Hall, 1975) that chronologically traces the development of the Arab enemy image in this rhetoric. This model posits that feelings and reactions to enmity can be described as a syndrome, one that draws on a historically constructed foundation from which stereotypes are built and enemy images emerge. The resultant extraction of an enemy image reinforces ancient ideological dichotomies of good versus evil and us versus them, rigidifying an agreed upon stereotype with referential function. Over time, an *enemy image*, defined as a 'culturally influenced, very negative and stereotyped evaluation of the "other" ' (Fiebig-von Hase, 1997, p. 2), is reinforced and reinvigorated via the words of political opinion leaders and mass media representations.

This study reveals that the accumulation of historically, politically, and culturally cultivated negative images of Arabs resembles the word choices and allusions used in the carefully constructed, post-September 11 speeches of President George W. Bush. A necessary part of this analysis is to 'bracket the historical question of guilt and innocence, and focus on the recurring images that have been used . . . to characterize the enemy' (Keen, 1986, p. 13). The analysis demonstrates how presidential verbal rhetoric was built on and informed by cultural artifacts (movies, television, newspaper stories, and comics) and is consistent with Spillman and Spillman's (1997) model of enemy image construction. There is a standard repertoire of propagandistic words and images that serves to dehumanize the 'other' as part of the construction of an enemy image in the popular imagination and thus makes a retaliatory backlash against human beings seem logical and natural. The results of this study are important for scholars, governmental decision makers, media creators, and citizens. They add to the limited literature on the construction of enemy images and Arab stereotyping in the media and extend and exemplify the Spillman and Spillman (1997) model.

[. . .]

Making Enemies

Nations 'need' enemies. Governments use the idea of a common enemy as a method of social control, of reinforcing values of the dominant system, and of garnering participation in the maintenance of those beliefs (Keen, 1986; Spillman & Spillman, 1997). As a hegemonic device, a common enemy can serve to distract attention and divert aggression and energy toward a common threat. In addition, a common enemy is important in organizing evolutionary-based survival strategies that rely on perceptual and behavioral patterns that are a fundamental part of human nature.

Differences in age, race, religion, culture, age, or appearance can be the characteristic(s) that stimulate resentment toward other groups. The unfamiliar and strange evoke strong emotions and reactions such as aggression, fear, hate, aversion, and expulsion. Xenophobic and racist reactions create 'an artificial binary opposition that is resolved through the physical annihilation of one side by the other' (Kibbey, 2003, paragraph 2). The resultant 'we-they' dichotomy produces a kind of 'group think' that supports separation of particular racial, religious, ethnic, or cultural groups, positioning them as hostile and alien. As Said (1997) pointed out, 'Sensationalism, crude xenophobia, and insensitive belligerence are the order of the day, with results on both sides of the imaginary line between "us" and "them" that are extremely unedifying' (p. xlviii).

Cultural factors also play an important role in forming and regulating human behavior as part of the 'phenomenology of the hostile imagination' (Keen, 1986, p. 13). Despite changing times and circumstances, the 'hostile imagination has a certain standard repertoire of images it uses to dehumanize the enemy' (Keen, 1986, p. 13). This process includes what Jung refers to as the shadow archetype, which, in this case, becomes the 'archetype of the enemy' (Hyde & McGuinness, 1994, p. 86). In the collective sense, according to this theory, shadowy qualities and unsavory characteristics are often projected onto other people resulting in 'paranoia, suspiciousness, and lack of intimacy, all of which afflict individuals, groups, and even entire nations' (Hopcke, 1989, p. 82). Spillmann and Spillmann (1997) explained the development of the collective unconscious that comes to support viewing others as enemies. They describe enemy image construction as a syndrome of deeply rooted perceptual evaluations that take on the following characteristics:

- *Negative anticipation.* All acts of the enemy, in the past, present, and future become attributed to destructive intentions toward one's own group. Whatever the enemy undertakes is meant to harm us.
- *Putting blame on the enemy.* The enemy is thought to be the source of any stress on a group. They are guilty of causing the existing strain and current negative conditions.
- *Identification with evil.* The values of the enemy represent the negation of one's own value system and the enemy is intent on destroying the dominant value system as well. The enemy embodies the opposite of that which we are and strive for; the enemy wishes to destroy our highest values and must therefore be destroyed.
- *Zero-sum thinking.* What is good for the enemy is bad for us and vice versa.
- *Stereotyping and de-individualization.* Anyone who belongs to the enemy group is ipso facto our enemy.
- *Refusal to show empathy.* Consideration for anyone in the enemy group is repressed due to perceived threat and feelings of opposition. There is nothing in common and no way to alter that perception (pp. 50–51).

Stereotypes and Propaganda

First the image, then the enemy. (Keen, 1986, p. 10)

Thought of as over-generalized, reductionist beliefs, *stereotypes* are collections of traits or characteristics that present members of a group as being all the same. This signifying mental practice provides convenient shorthand in the identification of a particular group of people.

[. . .]

In the absence of direct personal experience, stereotypes serve as a way of filling in the blanks in terms of expectations (or lack thereof) of those different from the individual imagining them. Construction of an enemy image becomes the 'mental background for aggression, distrust, guilt, projection, identification with all evil, and stereotyping' (Fiebeg-von Hase, 1997, p. 2).

The people and government of the United States, for example, have a long history of selectively demonizing and dehumanizing others, including their own citizenry, in the interest of acquisition and preservation of resources and power (Said, 1997; Takaki, 1993; Zinn, 1995).

[. . .]

Further, a joining of politics and religion is useful in propagating hegemonic beliefs. To accomplish this, both theologians and political rhetoricians frequently invoke images of Satan (Pagels, 1996). [. . .] For purposes of this article, however, there are ample examples in the recent past that can best be explained under the rubric of two structural factors tied to enmity: (a) 'some concrete facts that permit the enemy image to appear as plausible and real' and (b) 'the political system itself' (Fiebig-von Hase, 1997, p. 24).

[. . .]

During the Persian Gulf War, the September 1990 *Atlantic Monthly* cover [. . .] titled 'The Roots of Muslim Rage,' featured the image of a large, turbaned, slanty-eyed man whose angry eyes had irises in the shape of the American flag. There is nothing to suggest that the man has any humanity; rather, what is important is that he is 'unlike us. We need have no sympathy, no guilt, when we destroy him' (Keen, 1986, p. 16).

Through the use of symbols or symbolic words that are not only popular but also resonate with pre-existing points of view, propagandist representations must spontaneously induce acceptance and elicit necessary changes to bring about permanent adaptation. Stereotypes, 'especially negative ones of Arabs, have been used as a weapon that has proved to be as effective as some of the military, economic, or political weapons' (Suleiman, 1988, p. ix).

The Arab Stereotype in American Popular Culture

Al tikrar biallem il hmar. [By repetition, even the donkey learns]. (Arab proverb)

All the information a child or young adult learns becomes assimilated into a particular worldview and is compressed into categories of understanding (stereotypes) that are consistent with widespread social norms (Gandy, 1998; Hall, 1997; Merskin, 2001; Spyrou, 2002). From early childhood on, media and popular culture teach both Arabs and non-Arabs about 'Arabness' by bombarding them 'with rigid, repetitive and repulsive depictions that demonize and delegitimize the Arab' (Shaheen, 1990, paragraph 7) and appear to represent consensus. These distorted representations can be found in music (remember 'Ahab the Arab'?) cartoons, advertisements, comic strips, editorials, political rhetoric, and even children's textbooks (Ghareeb, 1983; Hamada, 2001; Shaheen, 1988, 2001; Terry, 1985). The movie quotations at the beginning of this article suggest Hollywood has been a particularly powerful and consistent outlet for vilification of others. According to Basinger (Lyman, 2001, p. E1), 'we've had the IRA as villains, we've had international drug dealers, we've had Arabs, we've had vague Asians who weren't quite sure what country they were from.' In other words 'the media are not simply institutions that reflect consensus but also institutions that produce consensus and "manufacture consent" ' (Hall, as quoted in Gavrilos, 2002, p. 428). The system of representation thereby 'becomes a stable cultural convention that is taught and learned by members of a society' (Kates & Shaw-Garlock, 1999, p. 34). Markers of the nation state, these signifiers serve as key components of ideology in a hegemonic system that requires a great number of people to 'buy in' to the dominant belief system, the one held to be 'right.' Stories and beliefs about what is 'true' thereby becomes fertile fodder for the construction and maintenance of Arab stereotypes.

In an exhaustive study of more than 900 films over the last 20 years that portray Arab men, women, and children, Shaheen (2001) found that, in all but a few, Arabs were presented as 'Public Enemy #1 – brutal, heartless, uncivilized religious fanatics, and money-mad cultural "others" bent on terrorizing civilized Westerners, especially Christians and Jews.' Other examples include stereotypical representations such as 'brute murderers, sleazy rapists, religious fanatics, oil-rich dimwits, and abusers of women' (Shaheen, 2001, pp. 1–2), as well as 'A-rabs, camel jockeys, towel-heads, sand-niggers, genie, sheik, greasy merchant, ruthless, violent, treacherous, barbaric, all Arabs as Muslims–All Muslims as Arabs' (http://www.adc.org, 2002).

After the dismemberment of the Soviet Union and the end of the Cold War, America needed a new enemy, a global bad guy, 'a new foreign devil' (Said, 1997, p. xxviii). Cultural, political, educational, and media environments were well in place to make the threat Arab. The 1991 Gulf war provoked 'an ugly wave of anti-Arab racism in the United States with Arab-Americans insulted or beaten or threatened with death. Bumper stickers said, "I don't brake for Iraqis" ' (Zinn, 1995, p. 587). By then, the construction of an enemy 'of Middle Eastern descent' was well established, as evidenced by the rush to judgment when an Arab American man (Abraham Ahmad) was arrested only a few hours after the April 19, 1995, Oklahoma City bombing. Ahmad said that he was singled out, 'because of his Middle Eastern appearance and name and because he was flying to Jordan' ('Suspect sues,' 1995, 3A).

[. . .]

Method

An interpretive textual analysis was used to examine six speeches, remarks, and a memorial address given by President George W. Bush shortly after September 11, 2001. Specifically, the September 11 presidential address to the nation, remarks in a photo opportunity with the National Security Team on September 12, a September 14 prayer service at Washington National Cathedral for the September 11 victims, remarks Bush made upon arrival at the White House from the South Lawn on September 16, a speech before a joint meeting of Congress on September 20, and the State of the Union address on January 29, 2002. These speeches were selected because the discourse provides insight into the enemy-building process that Spillman and Spillman (1997) described.

The first step of the analysis involved 'a long preliminary soak' (Hall, 1975, p. 15) in the text by studying complete speeches. This step was followed by a 'close reading' to identify the rhetorical characteristics of enemy image construction and an interpretation of the findings within the Spillman and Spillman (1997) model (Feldstein & Acosta-Alzuru, 2003, p. 159). Representative quotes of each characteristic (negative anticipation, putting blame on the enemy, identification with evil, zero-sum thinking, stereotyping and de-individualization, and refusal to show empathy) are presented in this analysis. Transcripts were collected from http://www.whitehouse.gov. Because the Spillman and Spillman (1997) categories are not mutually exclusive, the results are presented and discussed chronologically.

Analysis

September 11, 2001: Statement by the President in His Address to the Nation

In this brief (593-word) address to the nation, President Bush laid the foundation on which his future rhetoric would build, solidifying the evil enemy image. The term 'evil' was mentioned four times in this first address, God once, and Psalm 23, 'Even though I walk through the valley of the shadow of death, I fear no evil, for You are with me' was recited. The Spillman and Spillman (1997) characteristics of enemy construction, negative anticipation, blaming the enemy, identification with evil, stereotyping and de-individualization, are pulled together in this rhetoric. For example, in the first few sentences, Bush invoked the concepts of good versus evil and us versus them when he provided an initial reason for the attack: 'Our very freedom came under attack. . . . America was targeted for attack because we're the brightest beacon for freedom and opportunity in the world . . . thousands of lives were suddenly ended by evil, despicable acts of terror.' This is the first of many uses of the word 'evil' that transmogrified into 'evil folks' and 'evildoers' in later addresses. He noted that 'today, our nation saw evil' and that 'the search is underway for those who are behind these evil acts.' Zero-sum thinking, stereotyping, and de-individualization are evident in the statement 'we will make no distinction between the terrorists who committed these acts and those who harbor them.'

September 12, 2001: Remarks by the President in photo opportunity with the National Security Team

Animalistic stereotypical Jungian shadow imagery was evoked in these remarks by Bush in references to an enemy who 'hides in the shadows and has no regard for human life' and is different from those of previous conflicts because 'this is an enemy who preys on innocent and unsuspecting people, then runs for cover. This is an enemy who tries to hide.'

Bush reminded Americans that 'Freedom and democracy are under attack' not only in America but also among 'all freedom-loving people everywhere in the world.' He said that U.S. retaliation 'will be a monumental struggle of good versus evil . . . but good will prevail.' Drawing from the movie *The Siege* (1998), in which the villains were Islamic terrorists, he declared 'Make no mistake about it: We will win.' This expression was repeated in the State of the Union Address on January 29, 2002.

September 14, 2001: Washington prayer service

On September 14, Bush delivered a prayer service, which on its face is not unusual. However, such an intensely religious, Christian event suggests an administration more zealous than that of Carter. Critics have called the Bush presidency the 'most resolutely "faith based" in modern times' (Fineman, 2003, p. 22) and noted President George W. Bush's high level of public, Evangelical Christian religiosity (Balmer, 2003; Carver, 2003; Fineman, 2003; McNamara & George, 2001). Although Carter is also an Evangelical Christian, 'Bush's God is the "eye for an eye" God, the God of vengeance and retribution' (Balmer, 2003, p. 7). During the December 13, 2000, Republican debate, for example, Bush was asked who his favorite philosopher was, to which he replied 'Jesus' (Balmer, 2003, p. 7). Although on at least two occasions Bush 'made a point of praising Islam as "a religion of peace" ' (Fineman, 2003, p. 22), this effort was adumbrated by persistent mentions of evil, God's power, and fire and brimstone imagery: 'we have seen the images of fire and ashes and bent steel.'

In this address, Bush referred to God or the Lord no less than seven times and made references to evil as well. Bush reassured the nation that

> God's signs are not always the ones we look for. We learn in tragedy that his purposes are not always our own. The world he created is of moral design. And the Lord of life hold all who die and all who mourn.

The power of prayer was declared when Bush proselytized,

> Yet the prayers and private suffering . . . are prayers that help us last through the day or endure the night. There are prayers of friends and strangers. . . . There are prayers that yield our will to a will greater than our own.

He concluded this speech with the words 'Neither death nor life, nor angels, nor principalities, nor powers, nor things to come, nor height, nor depth, can separate us from God's love. May He bless the souls of the departed, may he comfort our own.' According to Balmer (2003), rather than drawing on '20th century liberal nostrums about human goodness' (p. 7), Bush applied Protestant theologian Reinhold Niebuhr's 'theology of crisis,' which demands 'that people of faith abandon their quaint naïveté about human progress and unite to resist evil – by force if necessary' (as quoted in Balmer, 2003, p. 7).

Shadow imagery and the word *evil* have historically and contemporarily been used to summon the image of a dark, ominous, stereotypical threat – and they were used, too, in Bush's rhetoric. By referring to the enemy as a dark, faceless, soul-less source of evil, and referencing the forthcoming war as a 'crusade,' Bush positioned the retaliation as a battle between the forces of good and evil. Although this kind of discourse is thought to bring a nation (tribe) closer together, it instead tends to have a polarizing effect. For example, Bush pointed out that the 'civilized world' (which implies that 'we' are civilized and the monolithic 'they' are not) 'was rallying to America's side.' Spillman and Spillman's (1997) negative anticipation and stereotyping are evident in Bush's rallying cry to Americans that it is the United States's responsibility to 'rid the world of evil' as 'war has been waged against us by stealth and deceit and murder.' Bush positioned America as the world's leader of obvious virtues when he declared, 'we are freedom's defender' and 'whether we bring our enemies to justice or bring justice to our enemies, justice will be done.'

September 16, 2001: Remarks by the President upon arrival at the White House

George W. Bush's remarks to the nation from the South Lawn of the White House offered less scripted, more spontaneous rhetoric. At this point, terms such as 'evildoers,' 'evil folks,' and 'barbarism' had entered the vernacular. Arab enemy image construction is evident in the President's persistent references to evil in his speeches and the accompanying pervasive images of Arab suspects in the news media. In his remarks from the South Lawn, Bush said,

> We're a nation that can't be cowed by evildoers. . . . We will rid the world of evildoers. . . . There are evil people in this world. . . . Evil folks still lurk out there, never did anybody's thought process [sic] about how to protect America did we think that the evildoers would fly not one, but four commercial aircraft into precious U.S. targets. That's why I say to the American people we've never seen this kind of evil before. But the evildoers have never seen the American people in action, before, either – and they're about to find out.

The idea of evil in Bush's remarks was accompanied by the idea of goodness, frequently expressed in Christian terms and expressions. In this speech, the word 'faith' was used six times, either in references to Sunday, September 16, being 'the Lord's day,' 'this day of faith,' or of the American people having 'great faith.' Bush said he had 'faith in our military,' 'faith in America,' and 'great faith in the resiliency of the economy.'

The animalistic nature of stereotyping and de-individualization are evident as well in his assurance that 'my administration is determined to find, to get 'em running, and to haunt [sic] 'em down, those who did this to America.'

September 20, 2001: President Bush's address before a joint meeting of Congress

In this speech, Bush identified four questions he felt Americans were asking: (a) Who attacked our country?, (b) Why do they hate us?, (c) How will we fight this war?, and (d) What is expected of us? In response to the first question, Bush engaged negative anticipation by pointing out previous attacks and bombings by Arabic affiliated groups. At this time, he not only used terms such as 'evildoers' but also began referring to a more precise group identified as Taliban. Bush described how the Taliban would pay a price for not meeting his demands. He drew on the stereotypical, de-individualized characteristics of enemy image construction when he described the people as animalistic and brutal in act and ideology: 'The terrorists may burrow deeper into caves and other entrenched hiding places. Our military action is also designed to clear the way for . . . relentless operations to drive them out and bring them to justice' because 'they hide in your land.' Zero-sum thinking is illustrated by the statement to the Taliban that they must act immediately and 'hand over the terrorists or they will share in their fate.'

In commenting that the Muslim faith is respected and freely practiced by individuals in America and around the world, Bush's ecumenical effort to be inclusive was subsumed by the statement that followed, one that was loaded with the return to identification with evil: 'Those who commit evil in the name of Allah blaspheme the name of Allah.' Many Americans are not well-schooled in the details of Islamic faith and thus cannot make the fine distinctions necessary to understand the significance of this statement. According to Hathout (1999, paragraph 1), 'Islam is probably the most misunderstood American reality' and 'studies have shown that American's knowledge of the Islamic faith is "tragically laughable." ' As a result, 'Most of the time we're mentioned, it's sensationalized, ugly, or weird. And when a group is generalized, it becomes an object of fear' (Hathout, 1999, paragraph 1).

'Why do they hate us?' was the second question Bush posed. His response: They hate us because 'Americans show a deep commitment to one another and an abiding love for country.' The implication was that 'they' do not share a similar sense of national pride. Bush compared an unknown image to a known stereotype by stating, 'Al Qaeda is to terror what the Mafia is to crime.' The act of blaming the enemy – and the representation of the enemy as greedy, insatiable, and possessing no limits or boundaries – provides justification for doing whatever is necessary to preserve the American way of life. In this speech, Bush used the abstract concept of freedom as being under attack, not individuals. For example, he said that, 'enemies of freedom committed an act of war against our country.' He pointed out that the 'terrorists' directive commands them to kill Christians and Jews.' Negative anticipation is illustrated in this speech when Bush stated that America and Americans are hated because of

> what they [the terrorists] see right here in this chamber, a demo-
> cratically elected government. Their leaders are self-appointed.
> They hate our freedoms, our freedom of religion, our freedom of
> speech, our freedom to vote and assemble and disagree with each
> other.

A clear example of zero-sum thinking is found in Bush's ultimatum:

> Every nation in every region now has a decision to make. Either you are with us or you are with the terrorists. From this day forward, any nation that continues to harbor or support terrorism will be regarded by the United States as a hostile regime.

Refusal to show empathy is illustrated when Bush made this declaration about sympathizing nations: 'they will hand over the terrorists or they will share in their fate.' The American military would either 'bring our enemies to justice or bring justice to our enemies.' It was alongside this statement that Bush announced the creation of a cabinet level position that would report directly to him – the Office of Homeland Security.

[. . .]

When he presented the third question, 'How will we fight this war?,' Bush's response returned to the characterization of the enemy as evil, barbaric, and animalistic when he said the U.S. military would 'starve terrorists of funding, turn them one against another, drive them from place to place until there is no refuge or no rest.'

Finally, negative anticipation, identification with evil, blaming the enemy for domestic tensions, zero-sum thinking, and stereotyping came together in Bush's response to the fourth question, 'What is expected of us?' In describing the meaning of patriotism, Bush assimilated the U.S. economy into the symbolic meaning of the World Trade Center: 'terrorists attacked a symbol of American prosperity.' Religiosity also came into play when Bush implored Americans 'to continue to pray,' as 'prayer has comforted us in sorrow and will help strengthen the journey ahead.' Dark and light imagery again were used as points of opposition when Bush stated, 'Our nation, this generation, will lift the dark threat of violence from our people and our future.' He concluded with his own request: 'God grant us wisdom and may he watch over the United States of America.'

January 29, 2002: State of the Union Address

By the time of this important address, the enemy was fully constructed, infused by more than 20 years of media and popular culture images equating Muslims and Arabs as terrorists. The United States was firmly positioned, at least in the minds of the Bush Administration, as global caretaker supported by faith in God. The enemy was a dirty, dehumanized animal that scurried to 'caves' and dark places. Anyone or any country that empathized or harbored the enemy became the enemy. 'They' clearly were no longer individuals but rather demonized as evildoers 'who send other people's children on missions of suicide and murder. They embrace tyranny and death as a cause and a creed,' and it is 'equaled by the madness of the destruction they design.'

In this speech, Spillman and Spillman's (1997) identification with evil was evident when Bush identified the nations of North Korea, Iran, and Iraq as the 'axis of evil,' a collection of countries that were 'arming to threaten the peace of the world' with their 'weapons of mass destruction.' While going into detail about what these countries have done to their own and other countries' people, he pointed out, 'This is a regime that has something to hide from the civilized world. States like these, and their terrorist allies, constitute an axis of evil, arming to threaten the peace of the world.' Movie-speak entered presidential discourse as Bush again declared 'Make no mistake about it: If they do not act [governments "timid in the face of terror"] America will.'

[. . .]

Discussion

The purpose of this study was to examine post-September 11, 2001, presidential rhetoric to see if the use of particular words, phrases, and allusions fit Spillman and Spillman's (1997, pp. 50–51) enemy image construction model. In this case, although some of the characteristics played a stronger role than others did (stereotyping and de-individualization, identification with evil, and zero-sum thinking), it is clear that the carefully chosen, mostly scripted words in President Bush's speech were grounded in powerful connections to universal notions of enmity. In particular, historical as well as current popular culture portrayals of people of Arab/ Middle Eastern descent were coupled with a rhetoric that was able to draw upon collective consciousness to revivify, reinforce, and ratify the Arab as terrorist stereotype. Pre-existing stereotypical media portrayals and presidential verbiage consistent with dominant ideology about Arabs provided the context for rigidifying the constructed Arab terrorist stereotype in a way that made such associations seem normal and logical. Combined with verbal and visual portrayals that consistently construct Arabs as terrorists, the tragic events of September 11 gave a real face and, for many Americans, a real reason to retaliate. Presidential propaganda thereby became a powerful hegemonic tool in the organization of public support and energy in the 'Hunt for bin Laden' and investment in homeland security.

The construction of all Arabs as terrorists and all Muslims as Arab terrorists – through political rhetoric reducing vast populations into a single dark image – has significant consequences not only for the civil rights of individuals living in the United States but also for many other citizens of the world. Ultimately, such patterns have not only consequences for organizing citizen support for government operations, but also a serious impact on the quality of life for Arab Americans. Families have suffered violence and there have been numerous hate crimes, illegal detentions, and even murders (May & Modood, 2001). Children have experienced humiliation and fear among their schoolmates and the climate of prejudice and hate only deepens the wound of discrimination. The constitutionality of the Patriot Act, in conjunction with concerns over the legality of actions by the Department of Homeland Security, will also be topics of conversation, scholarship, debate, and media attention for years to come.

Are we likely to see an end to the construction of enemy images? Probably not. Television programming largely omits Arabs from stories and movies continue to rely on a monolithic Arab stereotype 'complete with glinty eyes and a passionate desire to kill Americans' (Said, 1997, p. xxvii). In the absence of a continuum of roles, characters, and occupations, there are very few alternative media sources for non-Arabs to draw on in their understanding of Arab cultures. Considering how all but European Americans are identified by some level of hyphenation, differences serve as constant reminders of 'otherness' to some imaginary *real* American. If the United States truly is a democratic nation and Arabs and Muslims are truly 'our friends,' then it is important to reflect this not only in media content, but also in the hiring of writers and producers who can work in cooperation with television, news, and movie executives. Delivery of a more balanced, informed, and fairer image of Arabs (and all other minorities for that matter) to viewers is a pedagogically crucial, long overdue move toward professional respect and responsibility to all persons in the United States and elsewhere in the world. Perhaps then, in an odd twist of fate, the experiences of Arab Americans after September 11 will ironically serve as a crucible of our times.

[. . .]

References

Balmer, R. (2003, March 27). Bush and God. *The Nation*, pp. 7–8.

Carver, T. (2003, April 6). Bush puts God on his side. *BBC News*. Retrieved April 28, 2003, from http://www.news.bbc.co.uk

Chandler, D. (2002). *Semiotics: The basics*. London: Routledge.

Feldstein, F. P., & Acosta-Alzuru, C. (2003). Argentinean Jews as scapegoat:

A textual analysis of the bombing of AMIA. *Journal of Communication Inquiry, 27*, 152–170.

Fiebig-von Hase, R. (1997). Introduction. In R. Fiebig-von Has & U. Lehmkuhl (Eds.), *Enemy images in American history* (pp. 1–42). Providence, RI: Berghahn.

Fineman, R. (2003, March 10). Bush and God [Electronic version]. *Newsweek*, p. 22.

Gandy, O. H., Jr. (1998). *Communication and race: A structural perspective.* London: Arnold.

Gavrilos, D. (2002). Arab Americans in a nation's imagined community: How news constructed Arab American reactions to the Gulf War. *Journal of Communication Inquiry, 26*, 426–445.

Ghareeb, E. (Ed.). (1983). *Split vision: The portrayal of Arabs in the American media.* Washington, DC: American-Arab Affairs Council.

Hall, S. (1975). Introduction. In A. C. H. Smith (Ed.), *Paper voices: The popular press and social change, 1935–1965* (pp. 11–24). London: Chatto & Windus.

Hall, S. (1997). The spectacle of the 'other.' In S. Hall (Ed.), *Representation: Cultural representations and signifying practices* (pp. 223–279). London: Sage.

Hamada, B. I. (2001). The Arab image in the minds of western image-makers. *The Journal of International Communication, 7*(1), 7–35.

Hathout, M. (1999, March 29). Group looks to bridge gap. In. C. Jones (Ed.), *View*. Retrieved April 20, 2003, from http://www.viewnews.com

Hopcke, R. H. (1989). *A guided tour of the collected works of C. G. Jung.* Boston: Shambala.

Hyde, M., & McGuinness, M. (1994). *Introducing Jung.* New York: Totem Books.

Jackson, N. B. (1996). Arab Americans: Middle East conflicts hit home. In P. M. Lester (Ed.), *Images that injure: Pictorial stereotypes in the media* (pp. 63–66). Westport, CT: Praeger.

Kates, S. M., & Shaw-Garlock, G. (1999). The ever-entangling web: A study of ideologies and discourses in advertising to women. *Journal of Advertising, 28*(2), 33–49.

Keen, S. (1986). *Faces of the enemy: Reflections of the hostile imagination.* San Francisco: Harper & Row.

Kibbey, A. (2003). Editorial: Gender and the American ideology of war. *Genders Online Journal, 37*. Retrieved March 6, 2003, from http://www.genders.org

Lyman, R. (2001, October 3). Bad guys for bad times: Hollywood struggles to create villains for a new climate [Electronic version]. *The New York Times*, p. E1.

May, S., & Modood, T. (2001). Editorial. *Ethnicities, 1*(3), 291–294.

McNamara, M., & George, L. (2001, September 19). After the attack: When evil itself becomes the primary foe. *Los Angeles Times*, p. A3.

Merskin, D. (2001). Winnebagos, Cherokees, Apaches, and Dakotas: The persistence of stereotyping of American Indians in American advertising brands. *The Howard Journal of Communication, 12*, 159–169.

Pagels, E. (1996). *The origin of Satan*. New York: Vintage.

Said, E. S. (1997). *Covering Islam: How the media and the experts determine how we see the rest of the world*. New York: Vintage.

Shaheen, J. G. (1988). Perspectives on the television Arab. In L. Gross, J. Katz, and J. Ruby (Eds.), *Image ethics: The moral rights of subjects in photographs, film, and television* (pp. 203–219). New York: Oxford.

Shaheen, J. G. (1990, August 19). Our cultural demon – The 'ugly Arab': Ignorance, economics create an unshakeable stereotype. *Des Moines Register*, p. A7.

Shaheen, J. G. (1995). TV Arabs. In P. Rothenberg (Ed.), *Race, class, and gender in the United States* (pp. 197–199). New York: St. Martin's.

Shaheen, J. G. (1998). We've seen this plot too many times. *The Washington Post*, p. C3.

Shaheen, J. G. (2001). *Reel bad Arabs: How Hollywood vilifies a people*. Northampton, MA: Olive Branch Press.

Spillman, K. R., & Spillman, K. (1997). Some sociobiological and psychological aspects of 'Images of the Enemy.' In R. Fiebig-von Has & U. Lehmkuhl (Eds.), *Enemy images in American history* (pp. 43–64). Providence, RI: Berghahn.

Spyrou, S. (2002). Images of the 'other': 'The Turk' in Greek Cypriot children's imaginations. *Race, Ethnicity, & Education, 5*, 255–272.

Suleiman, M. W. (1988). *The Arabs in the mind of America*. Battleboro, VT: Amana.

Suleiman, M. W. (1999). Islam, Muslims, and Arabs in America: The other of the other of the other. . . . *Journal of Muslim Minority Affairs, 19*, 33–48.

Suspect sues for false arrest. (1995, November 10). *Eugene Register-Guard*, p. A3.

Takaki, R. T. (1993). *A different mirror: A history of multicultural America*. Boston: Little, Brown.

Terry, J. J. (1985). *Mistaken identity: Arab stereotypes in popular writing*. Washington, DC: American–Arab Affairs Council.

White House history: A non-partisan evaluation of the past. (2004). Retrieved January 11, 2004, from http://whitehouse.org/history

Zinn, H. (1995). *A people's history of the United States 1492 – present*. New York: Harper Perennial.

MEDIA VIOLENCE AUDIENCES

Understanding whether and how media content has the power to shape social perceptions and attitudes toward violence has long been a central focus of media violence scholarship. Early researchers focused on investigating how watching depictions of violence might lead to imitation – especially amongst 'vulnerable' groups in society, such as children. This 'effects' tradition of media scholarship held considerable sway in media violence debates for over seventy years, and its arguments have permeated popular social thinking about the 'effects' of the media in a way that critical approaches have not.

Over the past few decades, critical media violence scholarship has shifted conceptual emphasis away from statistically quantifying the behavioural effects of violent media content on audiences, to understanding how audiences negotiate that content. Analyses from this perspective have sought to investigate how different audiences engage with and make sense of depictions of violence, and how their **subjective identities** contribute to the interpretative process. Additionally, critical researchers argue that media violence must be understood in the contexts of both the production and variable consumption of violent media content, and in relation to the wider cultural circulation of hegemonic discourses in society. In these terms, they are also interested in examining how violent media content and its interpretation by audiences contribute to those discourses.

The primary focus of most media violence 'effects' research has been on how violent media content might adversely affect children. For this reason, we begin this section with David Buckingham's reading on how children, and concept of 'childhood', have featured in concerns about media violence.

Buckingham argues that research needs to be more precise in how media 'effects' are defined, differentiating between behavioural, emotional, and ideological or attitudinal effects. He also questions whether the commonly identified negative effects of engaging with mediated violence (worry, fear, sadness) are in fact always 'harmful' effects – at times, they might be entirely appropriate responses to particular events. Buckingham's overview of his own research with children identifies the need to understand the considerable complexity involved in their relationship with, and interpretations of, both fictional and factual violent media content, as well as their motivations for engaging with this content.

The second reading in this section offers a rare insight into how the internet can be used to advocate racial violence. Authors Jack Glasner, Jay Dixit and Donald Green's research exploited the anonymous potential of computer-mediated communication to infiltrate white racist chat rooms. They posted comments in such chat rooms suggesting that there are certain economic (job competition), geographic (blacks moving into a white neighbourhood) and genetic (interracial marriage) threats posed against white people by blacks. The comments were designed to test the conditions under which chat room participants 'would be willing to advocate violence in response to a racial threat'. This study is particularly valuable in investigating how media channels can operate as sites for the expression of users' own violent attitudes and ideologies. The investigation also raises interesting ethical dilemmas in terms of researchers' undisclosed infiltration of chat rooms for the purposes of data collection.

With Valerie Palmer-Mehta and Kellie Hay's chapter the emphasis moves to reader responses to an anti-gay hate crime story in the *Green Lantern* comic. Such crimes often go unreported due to victims' feelings of shame about their sexuality and fears of public exposure and attack. Palmer-Mehta and Kellie Hay used *Green Lantern*'s anti-gay hate crime story as an opportunity to analyse how readers responded to the violence contained within it. The research was conducted through both an on-line survey and an analysis of letters sent to the comic's editor and the writer of the storyline. The findings demonstrate how the comic succeeded in highlighting the social discrimination and violence that gays can experience, and that many readers were sympathetic to the plight of individual gay characters. However, not all readers saw the *Green Lantern*'s inclusion of content promoting understanding and tolerance of homosexuality as acceptable. Some considered the comic as tending to be too liberal in its portrayal of gays and unsuitable content for children.

A post-modern analysis of audience engagement with violent media content is provided in Charles Piot's reading. Here the focus of attention is on the violent content of video games such as *Duke Nukem, Quake, Doom,* and *Mortal Kombat,* played by teenagers in shopping arcades and on home television and computer gaming consoles. Originally stimulated by his young daughter's avid game playing, Piot set out to identify, through ethnographic analysis, what elements of video games make them such compelling entertainment for teenagers, and how the extravagant spectacle of violence in them can be understood. Why have video arcades, often situated in suburban malls, become popular spaces for dystopic, end-of-the-world scenarios that are played out on video screens and in the imaginations of these teens? The commodity form, Piot suggests, depends on and inscribes alienation, violence and exclusion. The commodity is embodied violence, and the shopping mall is a product of that violence. Piot thus concludes that popularity of such games might lie in their ability to allow young people to re-imagine their identities and bodies outside consumerism in ways that are exciting and empowering.

Jenny Kitzinger's reading shifts our focus to an advertising campaign designed to change social attitudes toward domestic violence against women. The author explores how audiences responded to the feminist-informed 'Zero Tolerance' campaign communicated to the public via large poster hoardings hung along the main street of Scotland's capital city, Edinburgh, in the mid-1990s. Kitzinger's study is unusual in its examination of the extent to which provocative messages about violence are successful, or not, in changing public attitudes. Most people understood and agreed with the central message of the ZT campaign, which was to challenge the mainstream media's misleading focus on stranger-danger in order to prioritise the issue of sexual abuse by men known to, and trusted by, their victims. Many, however, were resistant to the campaign's attempt to re-frame sexual violence debates in feminist terms, highlighting questions around gender and power. Even so, the degree of positive support for the campaign and the extent to which it encouraged people to think about the issues were testimony to its success.

The final reading in this section is Birgitta Höijer's analysis of how audiences emotionally engage with media reporting about victims of war, political conflicts, and other violent events. Whether motivated by humanitarian and/or commercial reasons, the depiction of human suffering has become of central focus of contemporary journalism. Yet, discourses of humanitarian compassion have also been utilized by governments in the United States, the UK, Australia and by the United Nations, for example, to justify military intervention in countries such as Iraq, Afghanistan and Kosovo. It is also through humanitarian discourses that aid agencies and human rights organizations appeal for public support and donations. It is in this context that Höijer positions her research looking into how the media, and especially television news reporting, might contribute to 'fostering of a collective global compassion'. The findings reveal different emotional forms of compassion among the viewers, and how age and gender contributes toward differences in audience response.

19

CHILDREN VIEWING VIOLENCE

David Buckingham

Over the past two decades, media violence has become implicated in a series of much broader 'moral panics'[1] about childhood. In the process, questions about the impact of the media have frequently been caught up with debates about the impact of real-life events. Indeed, media violence is often seen as itself a form of violence *against* children, committed by adults whose only motivation is that of financial greed. According to many campaigners, it represents a form of electronic child abuse, which is all but indistinguishable from physical abuse and cruelty.[2]

At the same time, of course, media violence is routinely identified as the primary cause of what is seen as a rising tide of youth crime. It is rare to read reports of violent crime that do not at some point attempt to attribute responsibility to the media. Coverage of the murder of London headteacher Philip Lawrence, for example, and the spate of random killings in US high schools – not to mention the mass murders at Dunblane and **Port Arthur** – dwelt at length on the question of media influence, despite its complete irrelevance to the circumstances of all these crimes.

The furore around the impact of violent videos which followed the murder of two-year-old James Bulger by two ten-year-old boys in 1993 is probably the most spectacular recent example of this kind of 'media panic' in Britain, and certainly the most widely discussed.[3] In this instance, as in many others, the media were clearly used as a convenient scapegoat for events which were too complicated, or simply too horrible, to explain. Yet there was no evidence that the killers of James Bulger had even seen the film that had apparently provoked them, let alone that the murder was in any sense a 'copycat' crime.[4]

Nevertheless, this kind of connection between 'bad' media and violent crime has become part of a commonsense demonology, which can easily be invoked by politicians and others seeking to demonstrate their moral authority and responsibility – and in the process, to distract attention from more deep-seated causes of violence in society. Proposals to regulate media violence are less likely to encounter opposition than attempts to address what are by any estimation more significant contributory causes of violent crime, such as poverty and family breakdown – or, in the United States, the ready availability of lethal weapons. What is perhaps most strik-ing here is how, in many apparently secular societies, forms of evangelical Christianity have been so successful in defining the terms of public debate on this issue.[5]

These anxieties typically lead to calls for stricter control – for increasing censorship and other forms of centralised regulation. Here, the addition of children to the equation provides a crucial element of rhetorical strength that might otherwise be lacking. While censorship directed at adults could be rejected as authoritarian or as an infringement of individual liberty, the call to protect children is much harder to resist. Particularly in the United States, the notion of childhood has increasingly come to replace the notion of 'national security' as a justification for censorship, not least because of its ability to command political assent. Children, apparently depraved by a 'diet' of media sex and violence, have implicitly come to be seen as an *internal* threat to the continuation of the social order.

[. . .]

Reading 'Effects'

If we are to generate a more informed debate about these matters we need to be much more precise about the *kinds* of effects which are at stake here. Violence on television, for example, may have *behavioural* effects – for example, in leading to aggression, or in encouraging people to take steps to protect themselves. It may have *emotional* effects – for example, producing shock, disgust or excitement. And it may have *ideological* or *attitudinal* effects – for example, by encouraging viewers to believe that they are more likely to be victimised by particular kinds of people, or in particular kinds of situations, and hence that specific forms of legislation or social policy are necessary to prevent this. These different levels of 'effect' might be related – emotional responses might lead to certain kinds of behaviour, for example – but the connections between them are likely to be complex and diverse. And the question of whether any of these effects might ultimately be seen as harmful or beneficial is equally complex, depending upon the criteria one uses in making the judgement.

In my research in this field, I have concentrated specifically on the emotional 'effects' of television and video on children. In this area at least, it is clear that television frequently has very powerful effects – and indeed that children often choose to watch it precisely in order to experience such effects. Television can provoke 'negative' responses such as worry, fear and sadness, just as it can generate 'positive' responses such as amusement, excitement and pleasure – and indeed, it often generates 'positive' and 'negative' responses at one and the same time.

Nevertheless, the question of whether these responses are to be seen as harmful or as beneficial is far from straightforward. Emotional responses which are perceived as 'negative' may have 'positive' consequences, for example in terms of children's learning or their future behaviour. Thus, children (and adults) may be extremely distressed by images of violent crime or social conflict shown on the news; but many people would argue that such experiences are a necessary part of becoming an informed citizen – and indeed, this is an argument that children frequently make on their own behalf. A fear of crime, for example, of the kind that is sometimes seen to be induced by television reporting, can lead to an illogical desire to retreat from the outside world; but it may also be a necessary prerequisite for crime prevention. Likewise, children's fiction has always played on 'negative' responses such as fear and sadness, on the grounds that experiencing such emotions in a fictional context can enable children to conquer the fears they experience in real life. Experiences that are perceived as negative in the short term may have positive benefits over the longer term. In this respect, therefore, the *consequences* of such emotional responses cannot easily be categorised as either 'positive' or 'negative'.

One fundamental distinction that needs to be made here – and it is one that is often ignored in public debates on the issue – is that between fact and fiction. Many children are certainly frightened by horror movies, and by some explicit representations of crime, particularly where they involve threats to the person. But they can also be very upset and even frightened by what they watch on the news or in documentary programmes.

My research suggested that children develop a range of strategies for coping with the unwelcome feelings induced by fictional material. These range from straightforward avoidance (simply refusing to watch, or – more ambivalently – hiding behind the sofa) to forms of psychological monitoring (self-consciously preparing oneself, or attempting to 'think happy thoughts'). While these strategies are clearly carried over from responses to stressful situations in real life, children also develop forms of generic knowledge – or 'media literacy' – which enable them to cope specifically with media experiences. For example, they will attempt to predict the outcome of a narrative on the basis of their previous experience of the genre; they will use information from beyond the text, both from conversations with others and from publicity material of various kinds; and they will use their understanding of how the illusion of realism is created, for example through editing and special effects. In all these ways, they seek reassurance from the knowledge that what they are watching is, precisely, fictional. Of course, this is not to suggest that any of these strategies is necessarily always effective, or that 'mistakes' of various kinds cannot be made: indeed, it would be impossible to learn such strategies without at some point having such negative experiences.

These strategies are simultaneously 'cognitive' and 'social': they involve forms of internal self-awareness and self-control, but they are also manifested in social performances of various kinds, both in the immediate context of viewing and subsequently in talk. To a large extent, they depend upon prior knowledge or experience; and there is some evidence that they can be explicitly taught, for example by parents or older siblings.[6] Nevertheless, there will clearly be differences in this respect between experienced and less experienced viewers – a point that applies to both adults and children. 'Fans', who commit themselves to a particular genre, are likely to be much better at predicting what will happen – and hence at monitoring or controlling their responses – than casual or infrequent viewers. Indeed, a crucial aspect of the appeal of genres such as horror and 'action' movies is the way in which they play to and feed upon the knowledgeability of their fans – their familiarity with the established conventions of narrative, characterisation and dialogue.[7] A great deal of the irony and sardonic humour that infuses the use of 'violence' in such genres will simply be lost on the less experienced viewer, who will be inclined to take it literally – except perhaps where the humour is at its most overt, for example in movies such as *Demolition Man* or *Scream*.

By contrast, children often find it much harder to cope with the negative feelings induced by *non-fictional* material. They may learn to control their fear of Freddy Kruger by reassuring themselves that he is merely fictional; yet such reassurances are simply not available when one is confronted with news reports about grisly serial killings or images of suffering and war in Bosnia or Rwanda. As they gain experience of watching fictional violence, children may indeed become 'desensitised' to fictional violence, or at least develop strategies for coping with it; although the notion that they are thereby 'desensitised' to *real-life* violence has yet to be substantiated.[8] By contrast, however, there may be very little that children can *do* in order to come to terms with their 'negative' responses to non-fictional material, precisely because they are so powerless to intervene in issues that concern them. In my research, for example, children frequently described the disturbing effects of news reports about violent crime; and they reported experiencing much greater anxiety about the media reporting of the Bulger case than they did about the film that had allegedly provoked it.

Nevertheless, this distinction between fact and fiction is not always clear cut. Within these different forms, children are also learning to make fine distinctions between what they perceive to be more or less realistic or plausible.[9] As I have implied, these distinctions depend upon the nature and context of the violence; and upon children's existing expectations and knowledge of the genre and the medium. *Child's Play 3*, for example, was described by many of the children in my research as a comedy (in my view quite accurately); yet other horror movies, such as *Pet Sematary* and even *The Omen* appeared to be seen as more plausible, and hence more likely to prove upsetting. Fictional programmes that were judged to be more realistic (such as the hospital drama *Casualty*) were granted considerable credibility and power to disturb; while factual programmes that used 'fictional' devices, such as crime reconstructions, were sometimes treated in a more irreverent way.

Significantly, however, the programme that was often described as the most frightening was one that deliberately set out to violate these distinctions: it was not a 'video nasty' but a television play called *Ghostwatch*, transmitted by the BBC at Halloween in 1992. This programme apparently featured a real-life ghost hunt being conducted at a house on the outskirts of London; and by using all the conventions of a 'live' outside broadcast report, including well-known presenters playing themselves, it appears to have succeeded in fooling many viewers. Yet while several children found the programme very disturbing, a number of the older ones expressed considerable interest in seeing it again; and video copies are still in circulation, testifying to its continuing cult status. As this implies, the distinction between fact and fiction is not a fixed or straightforward one; yet playing on the boundaries between them provides a distinctly risky kind of pleasure.

So Why Do Children Watch?

Rather than simply condemning screen violence, therefore, it makes sense to begin by asking *why* people – and children in particular – actively choose to watch it. Research on such issues typically seeks to answer this question by recourse to a pathological conception of the viewer. A taste for violence is seen to be a symptom of sexual immaturity, lack of intelligence, or more fundamental personality defects. Ultimately, it would seem that people only watch this stuff because there is something fundamentally *wrong* with them.

The potential appeal of screen violence is, on one level, fairly easy to understand. For many viewers, there is a visceral thrill in watching graphic representations of violence – a thrill that has of course been recognised since the tragedies of the Ancient Greeks. Critics will occasionally enthuse about the 'poetry' or 'beauty' of set piece instances of screen violence; while others acknowledge its vaguely 'counter-cultural', subversive appeal.[10] As I have implied, many films encourage a self-conscious irony, a 'sick' humour, in responses to screen violence which suggest that it is not to be taken literally. The publicity come-ons for violent movies – 'can you take it?' – also attest to the pleasure that can be gained from self-consciously 'testing' one's own psychological responses.[11] Extreme instances of graphic violence can raise challenging moral and philosophical questions about our own complicity in it, not just in 'art movies' such as *Man Bites Dog* or *Broken Mirrors* but also in more mainstream entertainment such as *Reservoir Dogs* or *Natural Born Killers*.[12]

All these are potentially significant aspects of the experience and the pleasure of screen violence *per se* – and few of them have been acknowledged, let alone systematically investigated, by mainstream research. Yet the presence or absence of 'violence' may not in itself be a sufficient – or even a particularly meaningful – explanation of why people choose to expose themselves to such material. Here again, we need to look *beyond* 'violence' to the generic and dramatic contexts in which it occurs.

Let us consider the example of horror. Insofar as they do generate negative emotions, apparently violent genres such as horror may be popular because they enable us to understand and deal with real life anxieties and concerns in the comparatively 'safe' arena of fiction. Indeed, many horror films would seem to be implicitly addressed to children, or at least to 'the child in us all'. It is no surprise that so many of the apparently horrific books, films and television programmes children prefer are those which play on their fear of the large and incomprehensible 'monsters' that surround them. Alternatively, they are about child-like figures, or repressed dimensions of childhood, taking revenge on the adult world. This may well be why the figure of Chucky from *Child's Play 3* proved to be so offensive to many adults: he represents a direct and highly self-conscious affront to cherished notions of childhood innocence.

In my research on children's responses to horror, I found a considerable degree of ambivalence. On the one hand, the children's accounts of horror films were frequently accompanied by a good deal of disclaiming. Many vehemently denied that they were scared by horror films, and occasionally mocked those who said they were. Many were keen to assert that they were no longer scared by such material, even if they had been when they were younger. Some of the children re-told extremely gory scenes of torture and dismembering, yet in a studied deadpan tone, as if to guarantee their fearlessness.

Many of the children attempted to use their limited knowledge of the genre, and their understandings about the production process, to distance themselves from the fears such films had evidently invoked – although for the younger or less experienced viewers, this knowledge was uncertain, and its effects could not always be guaranteed. Films like *Child's Play* and *Nightmare on Elm Street* were often described as 'unrealistic' and even as laughable, particularly by the older children. Many were keen to draw attention to the liberal use of 'tomato ketchup' and make-up; although they also expressed a kind of aesthetic appreciation of special effects that were done well.

On the other hand, there was plenty of evidence that horror films do frighten children, and that such responses are occasionally quite lasting. Such experiences often seemed to crystallise around a single decontextualised image or scene which the children would 're-wind' in their heads. In many instances, the children described how the experience of fear intensified after viewing. Some spoke of the fear of going into a dark bedroom or out to the kitchen to get a drink after they had seen a horror film. Others described how clothes hanging on a door or a shadow on the curtain could temporarily appear like a shape from *Alien* – although of course such fears are commonplace, and do not solely result from viewing. [. . .] What is perhaps most crucial to emphasise here, however, is that in almost all the children's accounts, they took on the position of the victim rather than the 'monster'.

[. . .]

While many of the children described how they had been scared and given nightmares as a result of watching horror, their prime motivation for doing so was clearly to do with pleasure. Even where it was acknowledged that films were scary, this was often seen to be synonymous with the enjoyment they offered. Many of the children expressed the wish to watch 'scary' things again, even where their first experiences of them appeared to have been quite traumatic. The wish to 'see it again' – and the practice of repeat viewing – is on one level, simply about re-living the pleasure. Many children claimed to have seen favourite horror films 'over and over again'; while others described how they would use the video to fast-forward to the 'best bits' – that is, the scariest or most 'violent' moments – or to watch those parts again.[13] At the same time, repeat viewing of this kind also helps children to cope with negative feelings: rewinding the tape enables you to 'see how it's done' and hence to conquer your fear.

This suggests a rather different view of the impact of technology than is often promoted in public debate. As I have noted, the 'problem' of video in this context is that it is seen to undermine centralised regulation; and it is also sometimes seen to encourage an obsessive and unhealthy preoccupation with decontextualised moments of violence. Yet, as I have implied, it may also afford much more positive control for viewers themselves, and play a part in developing their competencies as viewers.

Even for the more enthusiastic horror viewers, therefore, pleasure was seen to be inextricably tied up with the possibility of pain – although the balance between the two was sometimes difficult to achieve. This ambivalence is perhaps most clearly manifested in the characteristic pose of the horror viewer, described by several children: peering over the top of the cushion, or peeking through half-closed fingers, this pose allows you to feel 'safe' and yet also to fulfil the desire to know the outcome of the narrative.

Nevertheless, transgression and disruption were the major focus of the children's pleasure in the genre. They did not, by and large, choose to focus on the restoration of order or the demise of the monster, but on the films' violation of social, sexual and physical taboos. It is an enormous leap to suggest, as some critics have done, that these transgressions are somehow politically 'progressive', or indeed psychically therapeutic – that the monster somehow stands in for all the underprivileged social groups, or for the repressed sexual energies, whose inherent threat must be contained by bourgeois society.[14] Nevertheless, much of the appeal of horror must surely lie, not only in the pleasure of watching evil destroyed or controlled, but also in watching it triumph, however temporarily. This is not to suggest that viewers simply 'identify' with the monster – if anything, the opposite is the case. Nevertheless, it is to imply that the 'pain' of viewing should not be seen simply as the polar opposite of the pleasure, as though the presence of one implied the absence or removal of the other.

The ambivalence and complexity of children's experiences of horror should lead us to question many of the assumptions that are frequently made about it – assumptions that are often based on ignorance, not merely of children, but also of the genre itself. To be sure, children do often get frightened or disgusted by horror films, but then so do adults. The notion that the experience is therefore necessarily negative and traumatic – or indeed that it inevitably 'depraves and corrupts' – is no more valid than the idea that it is somehow automatically therapeutic. It may be the case that, as adults, it is our responsibility to help children learn to cope with such experiences; but it is important that we do so in a way that respects the complexity of the process, and empowers children to make decisions on their own behalf.

Notes

1. This term derives from the work of Stan Cohen (1972). For a later reconsideration, see Cohen (1985).
2. This analogy is pursued in the notorious report by Elizabeth Newson (1994) which fuelled the controversy surrounding the James Bulger case: see Barker (1997).
3. See Buckingham (1996), Chapter 2; and Franklin and Petley (1996).
4. This was acknowledged by a Parliamentary Select Committee in July 1994.
5. The so-called Campaign for Christian Democracy played a vital behind-the-scenes role in the debates that followed the Bulger case, for example.
6. See Messaris (1986).
7. For a discussion in relation to action movies, see Andrews (1996); on horror, see Kermode (1997).
8. Of all the popular hypotheses about the effects of television violence, this is the one that is least effectively supported by the available evidence: see Buckingham and Allerton (1996).
9. This issue of children's perceptions of reality in television has been widely researched. My own research in this area can be found in Buckingham (1993), Chapter Nine, and Buckingham (1996), Chapter Seven.
10. See the contributions to French (1996), particularly those by Martin Amis, Poppy Z. Brite and John Waters. For some empirical work on this issue, see Barker and Brooks (1998).
11. For an empirical investigation of this process, see Hill (1997).
12. On the latter, see Self (1996).
13. See Wood (1993).
14. See, for example, Wood (1985). An obvious alternative here would be to see the genre as a kind of psychological 'safety valve' (Docherty, Morrison and Tracey, 1987).

References

Andrews, N. (1996) Muscle Wars, in K. French (ed.), *Screen Violence*. London: Bloomsbury.
Barker, M. (1997) The Newson Report: A cast study in 'common sense', in M.

Barker and J. Petley (eds), *Ill Effects: The Media Violence Debate*. London: Routledge.

Barker, M. and Brooks, K. (1998) *Knowing Audiences: Judge Dredd, Its Friends, Fans and Foes*. Luton: University of Luton Press.

Buckingham, D. (ed.) (1993) *Reading Audiences: Young People and the Media*, Manchester: Manchester University Press, Ch. 9.

Buckingham, D. (1996) *Moving Images: Understanding Children's Emotional Responses to Television* Manchester: Manchester University Press, Chs 2 and 7.

Buckingham, D. and Allerton, M. (1996) *Fear, Fright and Distress: A Review of Research on Children's 'Negative' Emotional Responses to Television*. London: Broadcasting Standards Council.

Cohen, S. (1972) *Folk Devils and Moral Panics*. London: Paladin.

Cohen, S. (1985) *Visions of Social Control: Crime, Punishment and Classification*. Cambridge: Polity.

Docherty, D., Morrison, D. and Tracey, M. (1987) *The Last Picture Show? Britain's Changing Film Audience*. London: BFI.

French, K. (ed) (1996) *Screen Violence*. London: Bloomsbury.

Hill, A. (1997) *Shocking Entertainment: Responses to Violent Movies*. London: University of Luton Press.

Kermode, M. (1997) I was a teenage horror fan: or 'How I learned to stop worrying and love Linda Blair', in M. Barker and J. Petley (eds), *Ill Effects: The Media Violence Debate*. London: Routledge.

Messaris, P. (1986) Parents, children and television, in G. Gumpert and R. Cathcart (eds), *Inter Media: Interpersonal Communication in a Media World*. New York: Oxford University Press.

Newson, E. (1994) Video violence and the protection of children, *Journal of Mental Health* 3: 221-226.

Petley, J. and Franklin, B. (1996) Killing the age of innocence: Newspaper reporting of the death of James Bulger, in J. Pilger and S. Wagg (eds), *Thatcher's Children: Politics, Childhood and Society in the 1980s and 1990s*. London: Falmer.

Self, W. (1996) The American vice, in K. French (ed.), *Screen Violence*. London: Bloomsbury.

Wood, J. (1993). Repeatable pleasures: notes on young people's use of video, in Buckingham, D. (ed.), *Reading Audiences: Young People and the Media*, Manchester: Manchester University Press.

Wood, R. (1985). An introduction to the American horror film, in B. Nichols (ed.), *Movies and Methods*, vol.2. Berkeley: University of California Press.

20

INTERNET RESEARCH ON HATE CRIME
WHAT MAKES RACISTS ADVOCATE VIOLENCE?

Jack Glaser, Jay Dixit and Donald P. Green

[. . .]

Under what conditions do people advocate racial violence? In particular, are people who openly embrace ideologies of racial hierarchy in a constant state of readiness to respond to racial threats, or are certain types of threats particularly evocative? Since Myrdal (1944), scholars have observed that threats of miscegenation tend to evoke the strongest emotional reactions from avowed racists, yet at the same time, there exists an extensive literature that explains racial animus by reference to economic competition and other 'realistic' sources of conflict (e.g., Olzak, 1990; Tolnay & Beck, 1995).

This topic, like so many in the domain of intergroup conflict, presents the researcher with a wide array of measurement problems. In addition to problems of dissembling and self-presentation (Crosby, Bromley, & Saxe, 1980), special ideological populations, such as those belonging to **White separatist** movements, are often deeply suspicious of authorities and outsiders. Although interviews with avowed racists have been conducted in past research (Ezekiel, 1995), it remains unclear whether the views expressed have been tailored to the interview setting.

In order to observe this population as unobtrusively as possible, we used the Internet, applying a randomized survey procedure to examine the conditions under which individuals who participate in White racist chat rooms would be willing to advocate violence in response to a racial threat. This approach benefits from a combination of features unique to the Internet: the guarantees of anonymity in communication, and the abundance of hate group communication forums there. It should be noted at the outset, however, that our study does not measure actual illegal conduct. Rather, our approach is to study the advocacy of racially motivated crime, under the assumption that the causes of advocacy are related to the causes of illegal conduct itself.

Motifs of Ethnic Violence

[. . .]

The [. . .] analysis focuses on hate crime against African Americans and will compare the factors that have most prominently been thought to precipitate such acts: economic competition, turf violation, and interracial dating, marriage, and/or sex. We focus on anti-Black hate crime for several reasons. First, because the nature of hate crime appears to vary as a function of the target group, it is prudent to focus on one group in order to isolate predictor variables. Given that, we chose to focus on anti-Black hate crime in part because Blacks are by far the most frequently victimized group according to federal statistics (e.g., U.S. Department of Justice, 1997). [. . .]

Societal factors and motivation

What kinds of threats trigger the most vigorous racist reaction? Historical analyses have attributed Hitler's rise to poor macroeconomic conditions (e.g., Eberhard, 1998; Turner, 1996). Similarly, dominant social science approaches to understanding hate crime assume instrumental antecedents like competition for material resources (e.g., Bobo, 1988; Olzak, 1990) [. . .] However, recent analyses of historical and contemporary data indicate that economic variables are not reliable predictors of hate crime (Green, Abelson, & Garnett, 1999; Green, Glaser, & Rich, 1998; Green, Strolovitch, & Wong, 1998). [. . .]

What little is known about the motives of those who belong to racist groups or engage in racially motivated crime also suggests the importance of noneconomic factors. [. . .] Green et al. (1999) conducted a telephone survey [. . .] [and] found that, in comparison to a general-public control sample, supremacists and hate crime perpetrators were not more economically frustrated or pessimistic about future finances. However, they were considerably more opposed to interracial marriage and migration of minorities into traditionally White communities. Supremacists in particular also appeared more concerned with threats to cultural identity (e.g., banning of the Confederate flag).

[. . .]

Thus, we theorize that hate crime against African Americans typically results not so much from economic concerns or frustrations, or competition for material resources, but more often from the perceived threat to the integrity, separateness, and hegemony of the ingroup. We set out to test this thesis by examining the differential effects of economic, geographic, and genetic threat on White racists' advocacy of hate crime. All three threats are interrelated, but our hypothesis is that the threat of genetic incursion is the most evocative.

[. . .]

The purpose of the [. . .] research is to employ and test an Internet-based, unobtrusive survey method to determine the social factors that are most likely to incite bias-motivated violence. The question is, what form of threat by minorities, in this case African Americans, is most likely to yield an inclination by racists to commit violence against them? Accordingly, we posed scenarios that might be perceived as threatening, regarding interracial marriage, minority in-migration (i.e., Blacks moving into one's neighborhood), and job competition (i.e., competing with a Black person for a job). These were selected to reflect genetic, geographic, and economic threats, respectively, each representing fundamental and prototypical examples of these types of threats in the interracial realm. In addition to investigating the effects of different types of threats, we assess the impact of threat proximity, that is, whether the threat occurs at the personal, local, or national level. This factor is potentially important because White separatist rhetoric often dovetails with nationalistic concerns (i.e., many separatists advocate deporting racial and ethnic minorities to other countries or continents), but for practical reasons it seems likely that action (e.g., violence) will be taken or advocated when threat is immediate or proximal.

Method

The utility of the Internet

[. . .]

Over 100 million Americans used the Internet in 1999 (Cole et al., 2000). White pride Web sites appear to be particularly active on the Internet (Anti-Defamation League, 1999; Whine, 1999). Organized racist presence on the Internet began no later than 1985 (Anti-Defamation League, 1999) and has increased to include hundreds of Web sites, file archives, chat rooms, mailing lists, newsgroups, etc. (Franklin, 2000; Klanwatch, 1998).

Racists on the Internet tend to express their views rather freely, at least when they are interacting with those they perceive to be like-minded. For this reason, and because of their prevalence there, we decided to use the Internet Relay Chat (IRC) 'rooms' affiliated with racist organizations as our venue, and the participants therein as our sample. In this manner we can assess attitudes and behavioral inclinations that racists might otherwise be reluctant to reveal.

Our goal was to compare factors that are likely to inspire hate crime, specifically those discussed above: economic threat (i.e., job competition), territorial threat (i.e., minority in-migration to neighborhoods), and genetic threat (interracial marriage). In order to accomplish this, we visited various IRC chat rooms sponsored by White supremacist groups and conducted randomized interviews. Posing as a new visitor to the chat rooms, our interviewer presented scenarios of different kinds of threats and recorded the responses. These responses were then coded for their advocacy of violence so that we could compare the extent to which different types of threat differentially inspire advocacy of hate crime.

Design

We employed a 3 (threat type: interracial marriage, minority in-migration, job competition) by 3 (threat level: personal, local, national) design. One important feature of the design is that it was neither fully within- or between-participants, nor was it a mixed-factorial design in the typical, orthogonal sense. We adopted an unusual, pseudo-Latin square design to maximize the number of respondents in each condition of the experiment. Although there are a large number of racist Web sites, the number of chat rooms is more limited, and our preliminary monitoring of these rooms indicated that many of the participants were the same people, jumping around from room to room. Consequently, there appeared to be a universe of only several hundred at the most. Because we anticipated that only a subset of this population would be willing to converse one-on-one with a chat room neophyte (the interviewer) with whom they were not familiar, we attempted to increase the number of respondents in each condition of the experiment by utilizing a partial within-participants design. It most likely would be awkward and suspicious for the respondents if all nine scenarios were posed to each of them, or if they were posed a series of similar questions with only one parameter changed. It was decided that we could pose three scenarios each, if only one was drawn from each level of each variable. Specifically, one group of respondents got all the scenarios in the diagonal of Table 1 (personal interracial marriage, local in-migration,

Table 1 Scenarios comprising 3 × 3 design of the quasi-experimental survey

	Marriage	In-migration	Job competition
Personal	My sister is talking about getting married to this Black man.	I found out this Black couple is moving in next door to me.	I found out I'm competing with a Black man for my promotion at work.
Local	Lots of White women in my neighborhood are getting married to Black men.	Lots of Blacks are moving into my neighborhood.	At my work, White people have to compete with Blacks for promotions.
National	All over the country, Black men are getting married to White women.	All over the country, Blacks are moving into White neighborhoods.	All over the country, Blacks are taking White people's jobs.

and national job competition). Similarly, another group heard about personal in-migration, local job competition, and national interracial marriage. Finally, another group was asked about personal job competition, local interracial marriage, and national in-migration. In this manner, all nine conditions were filled with a limited sized sample without raising suspicion.

Ethics

In order for us to gather candid responses without raising suspicion, we could not obtain informed consent. The Yale human participants committee agreed that respondents would have been very unlikely to participate, that those who did would not have been representative, and that responses would have been significantly biased. We believe, and the Yale committee concurred, that the lack of informed consent was acceptable because respondents participated without coercion, in a public forum, discussing topics that were common subjects of conversation there. Finally, respondents' identities were protected, through the use of their own pseudonyms and our careful separation in the data set of these pseudonyms from the responses they provided.

Procedure

The interviewer entered various chat rooms, posing as a curious neophyte. In an IRC chat room one can engage in real-time conversations with any or all of the visitors there. Chat rooms are ideal for this study because their participants are especially likely to express otherwise socially taboo sentiments and proclivities (McKenna & Bargh, 1998, 2000). In each visit, the interviewer made small talk until he was able to engage an individual in a dialogue. At this point the interviewer randomly selected a sequence of experimental conditions (e.g., personal-marriage, local-in-migration, and then national-job competition). There were 18 possible orderings to ensure that scenario order would be a random variable and that the interviewer would not be able to anticipate the next scenario he was to give. The interviewer posed each scenario after the respondent appeared to have played out his or her response to the previous scenario. The interviewer typically carried out the discussion 'in view of' the chat room but did not engage other participants in the same room on the same day.

We employed a semistructured interview approach (Smith, Harré & Von Langenhove, 1995) where in the interviewers engages in a relatively free flowing discussion, making sure to cover all topics. This approach allowed for a realistic discussion with survey questions embedded naturalistically, thereby increasing the likelihood of candid and representative responses. The danger that the interviewer's own hypotheses might bias his interactions with respondents was mitigated by the random selection of the conditions just prior to posing each scenario.

As described above, three of the nine scenarios were posed to each respondent. A few respondents left the chat room after responding to only one or two of the three scenarios, thus reducing the total number of responses from the expected 114 to 107. Responses were recorded by logging the text of the discussions and downloading it for later coding. The responses were coded for the extent to which the respondent advocated violence in some form during the course of his or her response. Blind to the condition of the experiment, the interviewer and another author rated each response on a 6-point scale from 0 (no advocacy of violence) to 5 (advocacy of extreme violence). It is plausible that the interviewer could have recognized the responses and recalled the condition, but this was impossible for the other author, who had not seen the data prior to coding. Nevertheless, the interrater correlation was reasonably high ($r = .82$).

[. . .]

Results

Narrative analysis

Perhaps the greatest power of this study lies in the qualitative analysis of the types of responses the different scenarios evoked. The specific statements made by our respondents were often very strongly worded, revealing clear opinions that differed substantially as a function of threat type. They offer a rich source for analysis of racists' attitudes toward minorities and committing violence against them. It should be noted that the style of communication in chat rooms is very informal and, even more so than with e-mail, typing is often sloppy. We have not corrected errors in the following quotes.

Interracial marriage

The data clearly reveal that responses with regard to interracial marriage, especially at the personal level, were the most volatile. For example, one respondent stated, 'better kill her. kill him and her. pull a oj . . . im not kidding. i would do it if it was my sister. i would gladly go to prison then live a free life knowing some mud babies were calling me uncle whitey.' Another respondent advised, in a manner reminiscent of the days of lynchings, 'Hang his black ass.' One person cautiously suggested the following: 'Im not saying how I would stop it, nor am I encouraging you to do this, but, there are many murders in America today, some for the better of our race, and it is fairly easy to get away with one. Not that I am telling you to go out and murder someone though!' It is not certain, but this respondent appears to be advocating violence while being careful not to do so directly.

[. . .]

A few people responded to the personal-interracial marriage scenario without advocating violence (e.g., 'well I wouldn't have anything to do with her if I were you.'), but the clear majority (9 out of 13) expressed some advocacy of violence, mostly extreme violence. Further evidence for the evocative nature of interracial marriage is available in spontaneous responses to other threats. For example, one respondent stated with regard to in-migration, 'I don't let it get to me, they stay with their space and I stay in mine. . . . The thing that upsets me most is seeing so many white girls dating black guys.'

Responses to interracial marriage at the local level were, in contrast, notably brief and bland. Respondents expressed some concern (e.g., 'Thats sad. Yuck that makes me sick,' 'man that to bad,' 'then move'), but were generally more passive and helpless (e.g., 'sorry man, I don't know what to say'). Only 1 respondent out of 14 in this condition indicated a disposition toward violence, recounting his own assault of a Black man who married his cousin, for which he claimed to have been prosecuted.

At the national level, the responses to interracial marriage were somewhere between the personal and local in terms of advocacy of violence, with most being tepid, but a few exhibiting support for extreme violence (e.g., 'They should all be shot.').

Minority in-migration

At least at the personal level, in-migration evoked a range of responses. Many were mild and even restrained, such as, 'I don't like it but we can['t] do anything.' Others were more extreme: 'I would run the niggers and all non-whites oit of my city . . . kill some nigger ass.' Others recommended specific action that would qualify as hate crime but was not necessarily violent (e.g., 'Spraypaint "niggers beware" on the door before they even move in. If they catch wind of it, I doubt they will even finalize the buy'). At the local and national levels, in-migration moved only a few respondents to advocate some form of action (e.g., 'make his ass move out of there') but for the most part responses were passive and even resigned (e.g., 'move,' 'Yep. . . . It's happening everywhere').

Job competition

The threat of job competition elicited a more consistently mild reaction. Although one respondent did advocate extreme violence ('kill him') with regard to a personal-level scenario, most responses were tepid and reasoned, such as, 'all you can do is try your best.' In response to the personal-level threat, several inquired about the qualifications of the Black competitor, one suggesting filing suit for reverse discrimination. At the local level, responses were similar, with the exception of one person who advocated framing the Black competitor: 'I say set em up for a bust get em fired and away from our women.' Notably, in this case, spontaneous reference is again made to interracial dating/marriage, suggesting that it is a chronically salient threat. At the national level as well, responses tended to be political, focusing on issues of affirmative action, rather than violent. One person volunteered, 'asian are taking white jobs too!' suggesting that whereas job competition from Blacks may not be much of a threat, competition from other groups may be.

The clear differences in the types of reactions to different scenarios reveals to some extent that the threat to the integrity of the group, be it cultural or genetic, is a relatively potent predictor of violent tendencies toward outgroup members. The genetic aspect of this is evidenced by the specific references to the outcome of interracial marriage: 'mud babies.'

This conclusion is bolstered by data from additional inquiries we made. On one occasion, after completing the relatively structured part of the interview, the experimenter asked, more comparatively, 'Of blacks marrying white women, blacks moving into white neighborhoods, and blacks taking white jobs, which of these do you think is the most threatening?' The response was 'integration of races, obviously!' When the interviewer pressed further the respondent indicated that he meant integration through intermarriage, restating, 'obviously'.

Quantitative analysis

Although the analytic strength of this research appears to lie in the compelling narrative of the responses, the data can also be analysed quantitatively. Accordingly, Table 2 reports the mean degree of advocacy of violence in each condition of the experiment, based on the 6-point (0–5) scale ratings. These results reinforce our qualitative assessment. The average level of advocated violence was greatest when respondents were presented with the issue of interracial marriage as compared to job competition or in-migration. Averages were also higher when these threats were framed in personal terms. Local threats elicited low levels of advocated violence, with national threats falling in between.[1]

[. . .]

Table 2 Advocacy of violence as a function of threat type and level

| Threat type | Threat level | | | |
	Personal	Local	National	Row mean
Interracial	2.46	0.18	1.43	1.34
Marriage	(2.21)	(0.67)	(2.44)	(2.04)
	n = 14	n = 14	n = 7	n = 35
In-migration	1.5	0.0	0.0	0.46
	(2.23)	(0.0)	(0.0)	(1.38)
	n = 11	n = 16	n = 9	n = 36
Job competition	0.54	0.0	0.29	0.32
	(1.47)	(0.0)	(1.21)	(1.18)
	n = 12	n = 7	n = 17	n = 36
Column mean	1.54	0.07	0.46	
	(2.11)	(0.41)	(1.46)	
	n = 37	n = 37	n = 33	

Note. Scores represent mean responses from ratings on a 6-point scale from 0 (no advocacy of violence) to 5 (advocacy of extreme violence). Standard deviations are in parentheses.

Discussion

> The greatest existing cause of lynching is the perpetration, especially
> by black men, of the heinous crime of rape . . .
> – Theodore Roosevelt (cf. Wright, 1990, p. 77)

The thousands of lynchings of Southern Blacks, often on trumped up
charges, during the post-Reconstruction period represent an early form of
what we now might call 'hate crime.' President Roosevelt's take on the cause
of lynching about a century ago must be considered within the historical
context of the time. Accounts of lynchings often involved the accusation of
the rape of a White woman by a Black man. Although Roosevelt's conclusion, influenced by the propaganda of the time, was almost certainly misguided, it nevertheless may offer a valuable insight into the mind of the hate
crime perpetrator: that violence against members of other races may be
particularly linked to concerns over interracial mixing.

Indeed, it is clear from the present study that interracial marriage is the
idea that most upsets racists on the Internet and is likely to drive them to
advocate anti-Black hate crime. Consistent with Green, Strolovitch, and
Wong (1998) and Green et al. (1999), there is also some response to territorial incursion, but only at the personal level. In keeping with the findings
of Green, Glaser, and Rich (1998) as well as Green et al. (1999), but incon-
sistent with Hovland and Sears (1940) and studies that followed, job competition, an economic variable, inspired very little advocacy of violence
against Blacks at any level. The propensity for interracial marriage and
minority in-migration to evoke extreme responses among White racists on
the Internet is perhaps exemplified in the frequent, spontaneous invocations
of the expression '14 words.' This is White separatist code for, 'We must
secure the existence of our people and a future for White children' and it
serves as a rallying cry of sorts, but clearly reflects concerns about race
mixing.

The effect of threat level, although of less theoretical interest than threat
type, was fairly clear. Scenarios posed at the personal level were by far the
most evocative. This may be the case because scenarios of this sort are the
most concrete and conducive to giving advice. Specifically, it seems more
likely that one would advocate some form of action to someone who faces a
'problem' personally and so, in this respect, this variable is not very
informative or interesting. However, this was not equally true across types
of threat. Job competition had the same small effect at the national and
personal levels, where responses often indicated that such threats either
were beyond one's control or would work themselves out, this based on the

belief that Blacks are inferior and will not be able to retain such jobs. We must also consider why the national level evoked some advocacy of violence but the local level had no effect whatsoever. The most plausible explanation for this is probably that threats posed at the national level triggered thoughts tied to the rhetoric of hate groups who tend to speak nationalistically and lament the declining state of the country, which they often attribute to 'lazy' and criminal minorities and immigrants. The local threat level, on the other hand, may have been too abstract, tapping neither the empathic response of the personal level nor nationalist dogma. It is nevertheless surprising that this level evoked virtually no advocacy of violence, especially with regard to minority in-migration, which is often a community concern, or at least perceived to be.

Impact of the Internet on race relations

The utility of the Internet as a venue for studying racist extremists is a derivative of a potentially troubling reality: that such groups are prevalent in cyberspace. Although their prevalence is undisputed, there is some debate over whether or not the Internet has been a boon for racist groups. In fact, a web site called Hatewatch that had functioned to list and monitor web-based hate groups since 1995 recently shut itself down, offering the explanation that it had completed its mission and concluding that the Internet has had a negative impact on hate (Dixit, 2001). Although white racist groups have proliferated on the Internet in recent years, there appears to have been no corresponding increase in membership in these groups or in hate crime rates. In fact, one might argue that the prevalence of racist groups on the Internet works to reduce hate crime, perhaps by providing less physical, more rhetorical outlets for hate. Furthermore, the presence of hate groups on the Internet has in many ways made them more transparent to the public, which in turn facilitates monitoring by watchdog groups, government and private alike, not to mention social scientists. Nevertheless, perhaps in part because of the inherently underground nature of white separatist groups, extending back to the days of the hooded Ku Klux Klan, there is no direct evidence available that the Internet has not helped to proliferate hate groups. Furthermore, the potential of the Internet as a tool for communication, organization, and information dissemination among extremist groups is undeniable, and although it may have its incidental benefits (e.g., transparency), it clearly warrants scrutiny.

Methodological considerations

In addition to providing insight into the mentality of white separatists and perhaps the antecedents of hate crime, the present study offers a methodological innovation that should generalize to other research questions and prove useful in the future. Specifically, by unobtrusively surveying people on the highly anonymous, yet public, forum of the Internet, and specifically in chat rooms, we are able to open up avenues of research not previously available to most researchers. There are numerous groups that are difficult to gain access to, either because of their marginality or because of illicit aspects of their behaviors that make self-disclosure potentially costly.

In order to carry out such research, however, we must consider the thorny issues of deceit and informed consent. As noted above, deceit with regard to the identity of the interviewer (and, in fact, that he was an interviewer at all) was essential for the success of the study. Otherwise, respondents would have been very unlikely to participate, or to respond candidly if they did. For the same reasons, obtaining informed consent was impossible. Fortunately, the use of the Internet had the added advantage of ensuring the anonymity of our respondents, all of whom use pseudonyms in the chat rooms. We further promoted their anonymity and confidentiality by separating even their pseudonyms from their data, assigning random numerical codes. Additionally, the public forum nature of the chat rooms mitigates the need for informed consent. Nevertheless, such research should always be carried out with the utmost regard for the confidentiality and safety of the sample.

Limitations

Despite the seeming clarity of the results, there are several limitations of the study that should be acknowledged. First, this study was conducted at one moment in time, and only through replication can one ascertain whether, for example, the motive power of economic threat was undermined by the generally favorable economic conditions that prevailed at the time of our study. This investigation is also limited by the relatively small size of the sample.

[...]

We are somewhat more sanguine about other aspects of the study, in particular the sincerity with which respondents expressed their views. One respondent went so far as to reveal the types of code words that are used over ham radios to form posses and plan hate crimes. Of greater concern than the sincerity of the responses is the possibility that, because of the anonymity of the Internet and the culture of the chat rooms, responses reflected a greater level of endorsement of violence than respondents actually felt. Nevertheless, as far as we can tell, there is little cause for concern that respondents were not genuine.

[. . .]

Perhaps more complex is the issue of how advocacy of violence relates to actual illegal conduct. It is telling that several respondents, but by no means a majority, indicated that they had, indeed, themselves committed violent hate crimes in the past and provided some detail of them. Needless to say, we cannot be sure that such statements are true. They could simply reflect a certain form of false bravado, even under conditions of anonymity. The possibility remains, however, that some overlap exists between racist ideology and racist action (Green et al., 1999).

[. . .]

Conclusion

In sum, because of the nature of Internet-based communication, particularly chat rooms, we were able to observe a group and form of behavior that would otherwise be difficult for scientists to study. By assessing their responses to various types of threat, we develop a better understanding of the motives and beliefs that animate those who advocate and perhaps commit hate crimes. These results are consistent with our past findings that economic threat, whether in the form of declining cotton prices, increases in unemployment, or heightened job competition, does not in itself trigger violent ideation. Rather, perceived threats to white hegemony and separateness, via in-migration and especially interracial sex and marriage, generate a visceral reaction against outgroups. These findings are important insofar as they shed light on the parlance used to incite fear by racist ideologues, both past and present.

Note

1. Differences were also tested for statistical significance. Interracial marriage evoked significantly more violent responses relative to in-migration and job competition. Personal level threats evoked significantly more violence than did national, which evoked significantly more violence than did local level threats. See Glaser, Dixit, & Green (2002) for a full inferential statistical analysis of the quantitative data.

References

Anti-Defamation League. (1999). *Poisoning the Web: Hatred online.* Washington, DC: Author.

Bobo, L. (1988). Group conflict, prejudice, and the paradox of contemporary racial attitudes. In P. A. Katz & D. A. Taylor (Eds.), *Eliminating racism* (pp. 85–114). New York: Plenum.

Cole, J. I., Suman, M., Schramm, P., van Bel, D., Lunn, B., Maguire, P., Hanson, K., Singh, R., Aquino, J., & Lebo, H. (2000). *The UCLA Internet report: Surveying the digital future.* Los Angeles: University of California at Los Angeles, Center for Communication Policy.

Crosby, F., Bromley, S., & Saxe, L. (1980). Recent unobtrusive studies of Black and White discrimination and prejudice: A literature review. *Psychological Bulletin,* 87, 546–563.

Dixit, J. (2001, May 9). A banner day for neo-Nazis [On-line]. Available: www.salon.com/tech/ feature/2001/05/09/hatewatch/index.html

Eberhard, K. (1988). *The Weimar Republic.* Boston, MA: Unwin Hyman.

Ezekiel, R. S. (1995). *The racist mind: Portraits of American neo-Nazis and Klansmen.* New York: Viking.

Franklin, R. A. (2000). The hate directory [Internet Website]. Available: www.hatedirectory.com

Glaser, J., Dixit, J. and Green, D.P. (2002). 'Studying Hate Crime with the Internet: What Makes Racists Advocate Racial Violence?', *Journal of Social Issues,* 58(1), 177–93

Green, D. P., Abelson, R. P., & Garnett, M. (1999). The distinctive political views of hate-crime perpetrators and White supremacists. In D. A. Prentice & D. T. Miller (Eds.), *Cultural divides: Understanding and overcoming group conflict* (pp. 429–464). New York: Russell Sage Foundation.

Green, D. P., Glaser, J., & Rich, A. O. (1998). From lynching to gay-bashing: The elusive connection between economic conditions and hate crime. *Journal of Personality and Social Psychology,* 75, 82–92.

Green, D. P., Strolovitch, D., & Wong, J. (1998). Defended neighborhoods, integration, and racially motivated crime. *American Journal of Sociology,* 104, 372–403.

Hovland, C. I., & Sears, R. R. (1940). Minor studies of aggression: VI. Correlation of lynchings with economic indices. *Journal of Psychology,* 9, 301–310.

Klanwatch. (1998). 474 hate groups blanket America: God, rock 'n' roll and the Net fuel the rage. *Intelligence Report Special Issue: 1997, the Year in Hate,* Winter, 1998, 89.

McKenna, K. Y. A., & Bargh, J. A. (1998). Coming out in the age of the Internet: Identity 'demarginalization' through virtual group participation. *Journal of Personality and Social Psychology,* 75, 681–694.

McKenna, K. Y. A., & Bargh, J. A. (2000). Plan 9 from cyberspace: The implications of the Internet for personality and social psychology. *Personality and Social Psychology Review*, 4, 57–75.

Myrdal, G. (1944). *An American dilemma: The Negro problem and modern democracy*. New York: Harper.

Olzak, S. (1990). The political context of competition: Lynching and urban racial violence, 1882–1914. *Social Forces*, 69, 395–421.

Smith, J. A., Harré, R., & Von Langenhove, L. (1995). *Rethinking methods in psychology*. New York: Sage.

Tolnay, S. E., & Beck, E. M. (1995). *A festival of violence: An analysis of Southern lynchings, 1882–1930*. Urbana, IL: University of Illinois Press.

Turner, H. A. (1996). *Hitler's thirty days to power: January 1933*. Reading, MA: Addison-Wesley.

U.S. Department of Justice. (1997). *Hate crime statistics 1997*. Washington, D.C.: U.S. Department of Justice, FBI Criminal Justice Information Services Division.

Whine, M. (1999). The use of the Internet by far right extremists [On-line]. Available: http://www.ict.org.il/articles/right-wing-net.htm

Wright, G. C. (1990). *Racial violence in Kentucky, 1865–1940: Lynchings, mob rule, and 'legal lynchings.'* Baton Rouge, LA: Louisiana State University Press.

READER RESPONSES TO THE ANTI-GAY HATE CRIME STORY LINE IN DC COMICS' GREEN LANTERN

Valerie Palmer-Mehta and Kellie Hay

[. . .]

Crimes of hate create a terrifying space where violence and incivility crash against our most taken for granted assumptions about citizenship and social justice. While the widespread media coverage of the Matthew Shepard case in 1998 and the Brandon Teena case in 1993 compelled U.S. society to reflect more carefully on the material effects of homophobia, there are many more nameless and faceless victims who endure hate in a personal way every day. According to the Federal Bureau of Investigations (2000), 2,151 hate crime incidents against 2,475 gay, lesbian, bisexual and transgender (GLBT) individuals were reported in 2000. While the number of anti-gay violence incidents reported in 2000 represents a 1% decline from 1999, police refused complaints in 49% more instances (Moore, 2001). Of course, many more anti-gay hate crimes are never even reported to police for a variety of reasons, including shame and fear of exposure. While organizations are able to suggest a figure, however tentative, for the actual number of people who have endured anti-gay violence, there is no similar method to quantify the broader impact such violence has on the emotional well being of the GLBT community and their family and friends. Hate crimes are epidemic in U.S. culture and they warrant our careful consideration and reflection, whether in real life or in the realm of representation.

Recently, the representation of anti-gay hate crimes has emerged in an unlikely place: comic books. In the U.S. alone, the comic book industry is a $425 million enterprise, with 4,000 comic book stores scattered throughout the nation (McAllister, 2001, p. 17). There are hundreds of comic book Web-sites on the Internet, and many online chat rooms where comic book fans converge to discuss the latest events transpiring in the stories and in the industry. Although there is a common belief that adolescents are the main audience of comic books, Morris Franklin III (2001) reports that the actual age of most readers is between 25 and 40 and male readers typically outnumber females twenty to one (p. 248).

The comic book industry has addressed a number of pressing social issues in its narratives through the years, including alcoholism, gun control, and urban poverty. More recently, both DC and Marvel Comics have added the complexities of gay identity and anti-gay hate crimes to the list. While there are many comic book companies, DC Comics and Marvel Comics are the nation's top two comic book producers, controlling approximately 60% of the market (McAllister, 2001, p. 19). These two leaders in the field have introduced various gay and lesbian characters in their mainstream comic books since 1988, most of them in minor roles (Franklin, 2001, p. 224). In 2001 the longstanding comic book *Green Lantern*, reaching approximately 65,000 readers every month, introduced a well adjusted, proudly out central character, Terry Berg, in its issue #137. The issue won an award from the Gay and Lesbian Alliance Against Defamation (GLAAD) for being the year's best comic book. DC Comics pushed the envelope even further in the September and October 2002 issues of *Green Lantern* by becoming the first mainstream comic book to focus a major story line on a central character, the aforementioned Terry Berg, whose experience of anti-gay violence leaves him on the verge of death.

The *Green Lantern* hate crime story line has received considerable attention in a range of media outlets. News stories have appeared in many mainstream outlets such as the *New York Times, CNN* and the *Associated Press*. Additionally, the *Green Lantern*'s writer, Judd Winnick, was featured on an episode of MSNBC's *Donahue* discussing the influence of the story. *Out Magazine's* December 2002 issue features Judd Winnick drawn in drag comic art being hailed as a new 'straight alliance.' Further, *Out Magazine* exclaims, *Green Lantern*'s writer is a 'superhero for gays.' Bob Schreck, editor of the *Green Lantern*, explains that, 'It's a story that needs to be told . . . We've tried to reasonably, intelligently educate people that we're not all on one note' (Gustines, 2002). As if to underscore the urgency of the topic, as the first installment of the two-part story line hit the stands in September 2002, three men in West Hollywood were victims of antigay violence (*Associated Press*, September 24, 2002).

[. . .]

The hate crime story line in the *Green Lantern* provides a compelling opportunity to examine a groundbreaking event in the history of the comic book industry as well as a chance to probe cultural and ideological perceptions regarding the GLBT community and anti-gay hate crimes. Seizing this opportunity, we analyzed readers' response to the story line in two ways, through an online survey and through an analysis of unsolicited letters to the editor and writer. But before presenting the results of these analyses, we will give a synopsis of the hate crime story line in issues 154 & 155 of the *Green Lantern*.

The *Green Lantern* Hate Crime Story Line

At the end of issue 153, Kyle Rayner, who is the human form of the Green Lantern (the names are used interchangeably to refer to the same person), receives a phone call from his friend John Stewart indicating that something bad has happened to 17 year old Terry Berg. Terry is Kyle's assistant at work and one of his close friends. In the last panel of the issue, Kyle bows his head and says, 'Oh, God' as a tear rolls down his face.

The cover of issue 154 shows two large, muscle bound white males baring their teeth, with blood spattered on their arms. One of the men is pulling Terry's head up by his hair and both men are holding him, presumably under his arms. [. . .] Blood is dripping profusely from around Terry's nose and mouth and it looks like one of his teeth is missing. The area around his left eye is swollen, and his clothes are torn and spattered with blood.

The first panel on the first page of issue 154 shows Terry's boyfriend, David, with tears streaming down his face. Distraught, he explains that he and Terry were walking home after visiting a dance club. David was charged up from the fun they were having, and this prompts David to lean over and kiss Terry, while they are out in the street. David laments having engaged in this public display of affection because, although at the moment it appeared that they were alone, three men have witnessed the kiss and begin whistling at them. This by itself concerns Terry and David, but then they hear the men shout the word 'faggot' and start running towards them. [. . .] In a panic, Terry and David decide to split up in order to distract their pursuers. The men follow after Terry, chase him down, and beat him ruthlessly. Moments later, David musters the courage to go back and look for Terry. When he finally finds him, David is able to recognize Terry only by his shoes because he is so badly beaten. Once Terry is in the hospital, we learn that he suffers from a skull fracture, a broken arm, two broken legs, four broken ribs, and a collapsed lung, and he is also in danger of losing his left eye. He is on a respirator, in a coma, and struggling for life. Visually and textually, the comic book creates a very compelling and heart-wrenching scene.

Everyone, especially David, is deeply shaken by what has happened. The situation is made worse for David because Terry's father refuses to let him into Terry's hospital room to see him. In issue 155, [. . .], Jen, Kyle's girlfriend, confronts Terry's father in order to gain entry for David. Terry's father exclaims, 'I do not want him in the room with Terry! You hear me?! [. . .] Jen protests, saying, '[. . .] Please. David has the right to see Terry. He's his boyfriend.' Mr. Berg replies:

> You shut the hell up with that kind of talk! All this business is what got Terry attacked in the first place! Because of people like him [Mr. Berg points to David]! If Terry hadn't met him then he'd be home right now. None of this would ever have happened. No one would have laid a finger on him! He'd be safe. He wouldn't . . . be here in this god-forsaken hospital . . . he'd be home (p. 2–3).

In this angry statement, Mr. Berg blames David, rather than the three perpetrators, even suggesting that David is the reason that Terry is gay.

Shortly after the incident, a police officer questions Kyle, asking him if Terry uses drugs and suggesting that Terry might have tried to 'pick up' the perpetrators, thereby prompting the attack [. . .]. Kyle is enraged by this line of questioning which, similar to Mr. Berg's statements, attempts to blame the victims. During the interview the officer is called away by another officer. Kyle eavesdrops on their conversation and finds out that one of the three perpetrators has been caught and is being held at Riker's Island House of Detention. He also hears that if the perpetrator who is caught does not inform on his buddies soon, the other two may never be caught.

Using his super powers, Kyle Rayner as the Green Lantern enters the prisoner's cell and demands to know where the other two perpetrators are. When the prisoner refuses, the Green Lantern lifts him out of his bed, turns him upside down and threatens to break his wrists. After both of his wrists have been broken the perpetrator finally tells the Green Lantern the location of his accomplices. The Green Lantern hunts them down and beats them both brutally in retaliation. [. . .] Afterwards, the Green Lantern, now back to his Kyle Rayner persona, returns to Terry's bedside and says, 'I did my part, now you've gotta do yours' [. . .]. Terry still has not emerged from his coma.

In issue 155, [. . .] the Green Lantern goes to the Justice League of America Watchtower to ask the superhero Flash if he will turn back time, so that the Green Lantern can intervene in the attack and save Terry. [. . .] The Flash acknowledges the brutality of the crime, but [says] he cannot turn back time every single moment someone is the victim of injustice. Flash's unwillingness to fulfill his request angers the Green Lantern greatly [. . .]. In the midst of his grief driven anger, Hal Jordan, the Green Lantern's predecessor, appears and gives him advice and consolation before auspiciously sending him back to the hospital. At the hospital, the Green Lantern, now back in his Kyle persona, finds out that Terry has emerged from his coma, and he is overjoyed. However, Kyle/Green Lantern is still distraught by the evil that prompted Terry's injuries and, consequently, he has lost his will to protect the people of the earth. [. . .]

On-line Survey Method and Results

The anonymous, on-line survey of *Green Lantern* readers was conducted between November 13, 2002 and December 9, 2002. [. . .]

165 responses were received. 55% (n = 91) of the responses provided demographic information and 45% (n = 74) did not have demographic information. Of those responses that provided demographic information, almost all were male (95%, n = 86, versus 5% female, n = 5). The majority indicated a heterosexual preference (64%, n = 58), although a substantial minority indicated a homosexual preference (32%, n = 29), while four (4%, n = 4) listed a bisexual preference. As for ethnicity, the vast majority identified as white (84%, n = 76) with only 7% (n = 6) Hispanic, 5% (n = 5) Asian/Pacific Islander, 1% (n = 1) African American, and 3% (n = 3) indicating 'other.' The readers' ages ranged from 12 to 55, with most falling into the 20–29 group (44%, n = 39) and the 30–39 group (38%, n = 33). The remainder were: 9% (n = 8) people aged 12–19; 8% (n = 7) people aged 40–49; and 1% (n = 1) person aged 50–59. (Percentages for age are based on the 88 respondents who gave this information.) These data on age and sex are consistent with Franklin's demographics on comic book readers as noted above. In what follows, we provide the survey questions, summations of responses, and a brief discussion of survey answers.

Public displays of affection

Questions one and two assessed respondents' perceptions regarding heterosexual and same sex displays of affection in public, such as holding hands or kissing. The third question probes respondents' perceptions regarding whether violence is justified if same sex affection is displayed in public. By probing respondents' comfort level with same sex public affection as well as whether public affection warrants violence, we hoped to gain some sense of respondents' general dispositions towards the gay community.

[. . .]

The majority (56%) of respondents indicated that heterosexual displays of public affection are appropriate. Almost half (48%) also indicated that homosexual public displays of affection are appropriate. These findings suggest that the majority of the respondents are not averse to same sex public displays of affection. 97% (n = 160) of respondents indicated that violence is not justified in the event that same sex affection is displayed in public. Moreover, no one responded affirmatively to this question.

Although no respondents gave an unqualified 'yes' to question three [whether violence is justified if same sex affection is displayed in public], it is noteworthy that 3% (n = 5) responded with 'sometimes.' Four of the five respondents provided demographic data, which is extremely mixed. Two were heterosexual white males aged 12 and 18, one was a bisexual female between the ages of 20–29, and one was a gay Asian / Pacific Islander male between the ages of 20–29. That gay and bisexual readers thought violence is sometimes warranted concerns us because this might suggest internalized oppression and self-blame. Internalized oppression occurs when individuals who are socialized within the dominant community take on the opinions or ideologies of that community, even when such opinions work to oppress, marginalize, and diminish the individual. When members of the GLBT community reinforce dominant ideologies that oppress the self, such as 'sometimes' supporting violence imposed on the GLBT community in response to mild public affection, 'we collude in our own demise' and 'become our own oppressors from within' (Harro, 2000, p. 19).

Motivation and blame

In questions four through seven, we probe specific points in the story line of the Green Lantern. In question four, we zero in on issues of motivation and blame regarding the hate crime, referring to Terry's father's position.

[. . .]

The overwhelming majority of readers, 92% (n = 152), did not think David was to blame. This is significant because public discourse surrounding anti-gay hate crimes often has located blame within the sexual orientation of the victim rather than with some fault related to the perpetrator of the crime. Perhaps the reason respondents do not blame David is the result of the way in which the story was represented in the comic book. [. . .] The decision to have David's complicity questioned by Terry's father and even David himself and to have Jen explain that the situation was not his fault, was a conscious decision made by writer Judd Winnick. Winnick (personal communication, October 3, 2002) explains that he made this decision because blaming the victims was 'the most realistic thing to occur,' but he also wanted to underscore how harmful that point of view is to the victim.

[. . .]

Winnick's thoughtful consideration of the complexities of GLBT family life results in a story line that explores the tensions felt by family members and concerns felt by victims while also pointing out that the hate crime was not caused by the victims.

Even so, a fair number of respondents, 8% (n = 13), blamed David [. . .] Like the majority of the survey respondents, the majority of those who blamed David were male, white, and heterosexual. However, [. . .] one Pacific Islander gay male and one white bisexual female were among those who did blame David for the hate crime, continuing the theme of internalized oppression and self-blame.

Response to the crime

In addition to assessing reader perception of 'who is to blame' for the incident, reader perception regarding the appropriateness of the Green Lantern's response to the crime was gauged. In the story line, the Green Lantern pursues the perpetrators of the crime and he beats them all brutally. [. . .] That the Green Lantern chooses to use his super powers to beat up people who are not his equal is a controversial matter in the realm of super heroes and comic books. Question five assesse[d] reader reaction to this unusual decision [in asking] [. . .] Was the Green Lantern's response justified?

The readers were split on this question [with 50.3% answering 'Yes' (n=83), and 49.7% (n=82) answering 'No'], and some written responses reflected a dialectical tension many of them felt between understanding why the Green Lantern would want to respond with violence, and why he should not have done so.

[. . .]

Those who thought Green Lantern's response was justified indicated that, given the circumstances, they understood why the Green Lantern would feel enraged, but some stated that they had hoped that he would have chosen a less violent, vengeful way to handle the situation. As one reader put it, 'it is his ultimate action of not following through and killing the attackers that helps to set him apart as a heroic character, but still with the human fragility.' Because super heroes are supposed to represent a 'higher ideal,' many respondents were troubled by the fact that the Green Lantern fought violence with violence, especially against non-super powered adversaries, putting him at a distinct advantage. One respondent wrote, 'violence in response to violence is not justifiable, under any circumstance,' and another wrote, 'I feel that a hero – a superhero even – should not let his own rage direct his power. Green Lantern should have been better than that.'

Inclusion of the anti-gay hate crime

Question six assessed whether or not the reader thinks the anti-gay hate crime story line was appropriate for inclusion in the comic book.

[. . .]

Most survey respondents (78%) indicated that the story line was appropriate because [. . .] it reflects a 'real world issue,' which is a common trend in comic books, and 'comics shouldn't be afraid to reflect the world we live in.' For example, one reader said that:

Why not? Hate crimes exist. They occur far more often than a mad-man trying to take over the world. And that subject occurs frequently in comics. There's no reason why comic books cannot reflect real life.

Another reader thought it was important to include the issue in order to challenge readers' beliefs:

I think that the topic of hate crimes has not been well covered in comics and since comic readers tend to be mostly young men, it could serve as a valuable opportunity to challenge some of their beliefs and educate them about the issue . . .

[. . .]

Even a respondent who disapproved of same-sex relationships wrote, 'I don't agree with the homosexual lifestyle and dislike seeing it glorified, but I have extremely more negative feelings toward violence and prejudice.'

However, even though 128 readers found the story line appropriate, 37 [22%] found that it was not appropriate for a comic book. 26 of these 37 people provided demographic information. 21 were heterosexual white males, one was a heterosexual Hispanic male, one was a heterosexual Asian Pacific Islander male, one was a heterosexual 'other' male, one was a gay Asian Pacific Islander male, and one was a bisexual white female. Some of them objected to the theme as inappropriate for children; as one survey respondent put it, 'I thought this was a mainstream comic marketed to kids.' Another reader elaborated on this point:

[. . .] Most comics are kids stuff, and shouldn't be indoctrinating kids for the pro-gay agenda. I as a parent won't even allow my kids to read the *Green Lantern* now.

This person then added another criticism of the story line, objecting that, 'I don't like the fact that this [story line] perpetrates that a "hate crime" is worse than a regular beating. [. . .]' [W]e feel that it is important for readers to note that the purpose of designating certain crimes as 'hate crimes' was not to diminish other acts of violence. Rather, hate crime laws have functioned to serve as a deterrent for those who would single out victims simply based on marked dimensions of difference, as often has been the case in U.S. society.

[. . .]

Letters to the Writer and Editor

The second group of data is derived from unsolicited letters to the editor and to the writer of *Green Lantern*, Bob Schreck and Judd Winnick, respectively. [. . .] There were 31 letters sent in response to the hate crime story line. 26 (84%) of the letters came from males, two (6%) came from females and three (10%) letters were from individuals whose gender could not be identified. In what follows, the letters are grouped according to their content and tone. 6.45% (n = 2) of the letters were not categorized because they did not fit into a clear category. [. . .] The rest of the letters are categorized as follows: resistance to gay issues being probed in a mainstream outlet, concern about Green Lantern's vigilante violence, concern about the representation of GLBT characters, and, the largest category, appreciative letters. In what follows, an examination of each of the categories is provided.

Resistance to gay issues being probed in a mainstream outlet

16% (n = 5) of the letters express dissatisfaction with the story line because it focuses on an issue of concern to the GLBT community, and these authors are not sympathetic to the community. Three of the five letters provide emphatic statements about the immorality of homosexuality and the influence such a topic might have on young readers. In the first letter, a *Green Lantern* reader writes:

> [. . .] This is a book that kids read and you're telling them that it's o.k. to be gay. In issue #137 you had GL himself say that being gay is not a sin. [. . .] Leviticus 18:22 clearly states that being gay is an abomination unto the Lord. If you are a Christian you need to take another look at the Bible . . . I will not support a company that let's [sic] you write garbage like that.

The second letter also evokes images of immorality and concern for children: '. . . Isn't the real world immoral enough without bringing this into the imaginary. [. . .] I do wish to thank you for saving me money by not having to purchase anymore DC Comics so my kids won't have to be exposed to this trash . . .'

The third letter expresses concern with the story line because 'adolescents should not have to deal with gay bashing . . . The notion that a gay comic is cute and appropriate for any child is outrageous.' All of these letters echo the same sentiments, those of moral outrage and concern for the pollution of children. Implicit is the assumption that comics are for kids, that children are primary readers of comic books. As mentioned above, our data and other studies show that this is not the case; the average comic book reader is between the ages of 25 and 40. Underneath this child protection rhetoric is a sad reality – the GBLT community and representations of it are not perceived as socially legitimate, or ethical. What is more, Christianity is hailed as the moral backdrop that justifies the omission of not only gay social issues surfacing in the realm of representation, but also gayness itself.

[. . .]

Rather than educating young people about the diversity of life that surrounds us, some parents are more comfortable subverting meaningful issues that adolescents are already facing in school and in the media. Such silencing may explain why young gay adolescents often experience isolation and confusion, and why their heterosexual counterparts are so willing to harass them in school when their sexuality is evident. [. . .]

Regardless of how the story had been written, the previous *Green Lantern* readers would not have been happy with it. In the following letter, however, the reader suggests that he would have been more tolerant of the issue had it been written differently:

Oh boy, here comes the obligatory homophobic violence issue! 'One shocking moment' indeed. I seriously doubt that any of your readers haven't seen this one coming since the last time you preached the joys and wonders of homosexuals to us. I suppose we could always hope that the issue will be dealt with in a manner that includes good writing, accurate human portrayals, and a touching lesson in comparative morality. Unfortunately, it has already been proven that the only thing we can expect is a good message turned into a hammer with which you will bludgeon your readers to death. You've successfully turned Terry into my least favorite character in all comics. Rather than feel anxiety for his fate, I find myself hoping he's beaten severe enough that I'll never have to read about him again.

This writer suggests that had the story line been dealt with more skillfully he might have been drawn in. Yet the hostility that permeates his letter makes this assertion questionable. [. . .] His opening remarks suggest that he is sick of GLBT issues before opening this issue of the *Green Lantern*. Without giving any concrete examples of poor writing or inaccurate portrayals, he simply alleges that GL readers have been 'bludgeoned with a hammer' (note the metaphor), then even expresses a wish that Terry would receive the bludgeoning – but with a mortal outcome. Rhetorically, this reader's 'lesson in comparative morality' is curiously undercut by images of imagined violence and murder and by a tone of sarcastic superiority and contempt.

[. . .]

Concern about Green Lantern's vigilante violence

19% (n = 6) of the letter writers express concern with the vigilante violence that the Green Lantern engages in to avenge Terry's attack. While most of these letter writers indicate that they understand why the Green Lantern was pushed to act as he did, they all suggest that his behavior was inappropriate for a super hero, an extraordinary being who is supposed to be beyond such base human responses. For example, one letter writer laments that the 'Green Lantern used to be so much more than a petty thug.' Another letter writer suggests that the Green Lantern has taken a 'fall from grace' and yet another writer begs, 'Please don't make him a bad guy.' A fourth writer argues:

> Just because he is a super hero doesn't mean that he can take the law into his own hands, even though he does it everyday fighting super villains. This was a different situation. The bad guys weren't super villains, they were just some stupid kids who did something they never should have done. So what I guess I'm really saying is that unlike most people I wasn't bothered by the gay factor in issue 154, but I was bothered by Kyle's response.

A fifth letter writer is disturbed by the premeditation that the Green Lantern engages in before torturing the thugs who beat up Terry:

> Face it, the character [Green Lantern] [. . .] hooked the bad guy up like a slab of meat and slowly broke his wrists. How do these actions make him any better than the thugs he was going against? [. . .]

[. . .]

The investment [that these letter writers] have in the integrity of the

Green Lantern as a superhuman hero is striking. They are not hostile, only deeply concerned about issues of character and ethics.

[. . .]

Concern with representation of GLBT characters

6.45% (n = 2) of the letter writers express concern with the ways in which the GLBT community is portrayed in the media and, in particular, in comics. The first letter writer exhibits anxiety regarding what will happen to Terry in the forthcoming issue. He has read the teaser in issue 153 that suggests that something terribly wrong has happened:

> . . . I trust you to do the right thing with our characters, like Terry in the upcoming issue 154 . . . [. . .] We do need Terry to keep on showing us something, every month, but crises make the universe interesting, so I trust.

The comment that 'we do need Terry' suggests that the reader is concerned that Terry will die in the forthcoming issue. The reader perhaps recognizes that historically, in the media, the bodies of women, minorities and the gay community have borne the burden of society's ills and they have died disproportionately in comparison to straight, white male characters. Writer Judd Winnick recognized this pattern in the media and, early on, decided that would not happen to the character of Terry. 'That's the cliché in all mediums. Who dies in movies? Gay people, people of color. Killing him seemed like too much. We wanted a little bit of hope' (Gustines, 2002).

The second letter writer also has read issue 153 and is anxious and somewhat pessimistic regarding what is going to happen to Terry:

> NO. No, you are NOT going there. I just finished reading GL #153 . . . and I think it's very obvious . . . that Kyle's young gay assistant Terry has either been injured or even killed as a result of a hate crime act . . . I applaud the fact that you at DC have even attempted to present the topic of homosexuality in your various titles. But let me also tell you that you have not always been kind and certainly not helpful in doing so. . . .

The fan refers to various gay characters who have emerged in comics through the years and laments the fact that many of them have been portrayed in a very stereotypical fashion. He worries that the same will hold true for Terry:

> And now we have Terry, a regular non-meta gay character who is

probably about to fall victim to yet another gay stereotype. All gays are not disease ridden, all gays are not fem or butch, all gays are not borderline psychotic, and all gays are not potential victims of a violent demise (any more than anyone else is!) Yes, I know that this is just comic book fiction, but there are people who believe everything they read. The stories in your books are capable of spreading very dangerous and false information ... Please be careful where this story is leading.

For some people, their only exposure to the gay community is through the media. Hence, their perceptions of the community are based largely on what they read or view. It is not surprising, then, that this reader would show concern regarding the way in which Terry's situation will be handled, especially since Terry is one of few characters in the mainstream media that has been portrayed in such a positive manner.

Appreciative letters

52% (n = 16) of the letters, more than half of all letters received, express appreciation that DC Comics was bold enough to provide a story line that deals with an anti-gay hate crime. Comments ranged from 'thank you for having the courage to release such a controversial comic' and 'this is so progressive' to 'it's too important to hide events like this in the closet.' Some readers even recounted their own experience of harassment or violence:

> I'm also a 25-year-old gay man. I came out at 16 and was subjected to some of the brutality young queers face in America. [. . .] During that time, I longed for positive queer characters to help me justify myself and my feelings. I found a handful, but also discovered that queer characters who survived to the end of the novel were exceedingly few. [. . .] My hope is that a closeted teenager will read that comic book and think 'someone will fight for me. Someone who is respected and powerful will stand up for me and my rights. . .' My hope is that a homophobe will pick up that comic and think.

Self-disclosure is a powerful communication practice for this reader, one which both accomplishes catharsis and holds up hope for gay youth, providing a nice twist to the earlier readers' tales about the pollution of children through gay texts. Such disclosure opens a space for dialogue and potentially fuels GL's writers and editors with a wide range of story lines to learn from.

Another reader was moved to recount his experience of anti-gay violence in a New Jersey City street twelve years ago:

> Nobody saved me that night. Clothing was ripped. Bones were broken. I had two black eyes, and a scar on my forehead that reminds me of the incident twelve years later. I grew up on comic books, and I never remembered Superman or Batman or the Flash fighting one fag-basher. But I did remember they fought for justice, and so the next morning, I went down to the police station to report the crime. I was still wearing the ripped and bloody t-shirt [that had the name of a gay political organization on it]. The police officer asked, 'Don't you think you were asking for it, wearing a t-shirt like that?' When I asked if I could file a report, he told me that it was useless.

The candor and emotion in this letter demonstrate the power of the *Green Lantern* story line. It is rare that people feel safe enough to recount such a horrific experience, let alone to an audience that they have never met. The story line seems to have had a greater effect than one could anticipate: it has created a forum where individuals can discuss anti-gay hate crimes and a space where individuals who have been the victim of harassment and violence may share their experiences.

[. . .]

Concluding remarks

Throughout this paper, we have sought to assess reader reaction to the anti-gay hate crime story line in the *Green Lantern* comic book. The range of responses has been broad and varied, but overall they suggest that these respondents were positive regarding this GLBT issue being raised in their mainstream comic book. ~Truth about rape,

[. . .]

It is refreshing to note that, in the year 2002, even mainstream corporations such as DC and Marvel Comics are taking risks and engaging politically volatile social issues. As writer Judd Winnick (personal communication, October 3, 2002) remarked, 'I think it is important to create dialogue, to make people think twice, to check their mindsets.' As mainstream corporations take on the challenge of creating dialogue regarding controversial issues, they risk reduction in their market share, losing advertisers, or negative publicity. Our study, on the other hand, paints what may seem an overly bright picture of a readership that largely approves of these efforts and is mainly troubled by their super hero's descending to exact revenge on the perpetrators of the hate crime. This rosy assessment must be tempered by the self-selected nature of our respondents; they are the readers who cared enough to go to a Web-site, fill out a survey, or write a letter. But perhaps these are the readers who, in the long run, count the most.

Acknowledgement

We thank the Center for the Study of Media and Society for funding to conduct this project, and Van Cagle for his assistance on the project.

References

Associated Press. (2002, September 24). Gay man beaten in West Hollywood. *New York Times*. Retrieved September 24, 2002 from: http://www.nytimes.com/aponline/national/AP-LA-Hate-Crimes.html?ex=1033919667&ei=1&en=8d24a6f4b05c7432

Federal Bureau of Investigations. (2000). *Crime in the United States, 2000*. Washington, D.C.: Federal Bureau of Investigations, United States Department of Justice.

Franklin, M. E. (2001). Coming out in comic books: Letter columns, readers, and gay and lesbian characters. In M. P. McAllister, E.H. Sewel & I. Gordon (Eds.), *Comics and Ideology* (pp. 221–250). New York: Peter Lang.

Gustines, G. G. (2002, August 13). A comic book gets serious on gay issues. *New York Times*. Early edition.

Harro, B. (2000). The cycle of socialization. In M. Adams, W. J. Blumenfeld, R. Castaneda, H. Hackman and X. Zuniga (Eds.), *Readings for diversity and social justice: An anthology on racism, sexism, classism, anti-Semitism, heterosexism, and ableism* (pp. 15–21). New York: Routledge.

McAllister, M. P. (2001). Ownership concentration in the U.S. comic book industry. In M. P. McAllister, E. H. Sewell, & I. Gordon (Eds.), *Comics and ideology* (pp. 15–28). New York: Peter Lang.

Moore, K. (2001). *Anti-lesbian, gay, transgender and bisexual violence in 2000*. New York: New York City Gay and Lesbian Anti-Violence Project.

22

REVELLING IN THE GORE IN THE ROOM NEXT DOOR

VIDEO GAME VIOLENCE AND US TEEN CULTURE

Charles Piot

The facts alone are arresting. Over 50 per cent of homes in the United States own a video game system, and another 10–20 per cent rent them. Eighty per cent of American boys play video games regularly – at home or in the arcades. The video game industry nets more money annually ($10–13 billion) than the entire movie industry. In December of 2002 alone, video game companies realized a profit of 2 billion dollars. And profits continue to grow. Moreover, within the different genres of video games – sports games, racing games, adventure games, non-violent action games, and violent games – it is the last, violent, and often extremely violent, games that dominate. These, for instance, are the games of choice in the video arcades in suburban malls and movie theater lobbies where our teens congregate (or, as one put it to me recently, 'where we hang and chill'), as well as on the 32- and 64-bit games that protrude, like life-support systems, from television sets in middle- and upper-middle-class households across the United States, and throughout the post-industrial world. Violent videos alone gross three-quarters of the money spent on video games annually.

Picture yourself, then, in the arcade at your nearby shopping mall. Clusters of teenagers (mostly boys) huddle in front of a giant video screen, taking turns punching, kicking, shooting, torching, flaming, maiming, dismembering, and decapitating various enemies. In doing so, they deploy a vast arsenal of weaponry – flame throwers, crossbows, bazookas, gatling guns, hand grenades, buffalo rifles, napalm cannons, plasma guns, laser guns, chain-saws, to name only a few – and operate an equally diverse fleet of attack craft – tanks, turbo vehicles, helicopters, fighter planes, nuclear missiles. The arms and legs of enemies are blown off or burned, and blood spurts from bullet wounds, dripping onto the screen, forming huge red pools. In one of the more startling scenes from recent gaming history the protagonist (that is, you the player) rips the heart out of a dying victim's chest and gloatingly holds it aloft. The undisputed rule of thumb in videoland is the more gore the better. Games like *Mortal Kombat* made their mark, and sucked millions of dollars in quarters from teens in the arcades, precisely because of the supposed 'realism' (and the transgressive displaying) that the special effects of on-screen blood-letting achieved.[1]

It is on such violence, its excess and (marketing) success that I focus in this essay. Why is violence – especially bodily violence – and the display and spectacularization ('special effecting') of blood so compelling for this (largely middle-class, largely male) teen population? And why have video arcades – nestled as they are in suburban malls, those meccas of bourgeois consumption, filled with circulating, sated and (presumably) happy shoppers – become popular staging grounds for the dystopic, end-of-the-world scenarios that are played out on the video screens and in the imaginations of these teens? There seems something oddly out-of-whack here.

'Participant' Observation: Research In and Out of the Personal

[. . .]

The research on which this article is based was conducted through a mix of scattered, multi sited, often-improvised ethnographic techniques – auto-ethnography, family ethnography, living room and classroom ethnography, arcade viewing, and textual analysis. While I conducted many interviews with individual teens and pre-teens, and on occasion with groups of teens, my research generally did not follow conventional research norms. However, I came to see this set of unorthodox strategies as a strength, for it offered an approach that mirrored the disjunctions and fleeting contacts that characterize the late-twentieth- and early twenty-first-century world we live in. Caught up in the dual role of parent and researcher, I also found myself privileging my own family (my daughter and her friends, and my partner's sons and theirs), and indeed myself, as a site of ethnography – and came to see such privileging of the personal as a gain.

[. . .]

Textual Terrain

Consider some video game scripts – all the while keeping in mind the social and cultural space of the shopping mall arcade, with its teens huddled around a video screen, challengers lining up their quarters on the console next to the control sticks. Not surprisingly, perhaps, the story-lines for these games are incredibly thin and remarkably similar from game to game. Take, for instance, the one that appears in the instruction booklet for a recent, enormously popular game called *Quake*, a game that plays in all three major video game venues – on home television systems, on personal computers, and in the arcades:

> You receive an early-morning call from your commanding officer, who assigns you to lead a covert mission called operation Counterstrike. It seems that Quake, an enemy from a distant dimension, is preparing to launch an offensive assault upon Earth, using devices called Slipgates to instantly transport his armies into position. But a secret government installation researching the top-secret Slipgate technology has made an important breakthrough that will allow you and your team to strike first. Upon arriving at the complex, you find that things have gone horribly wrong. Quake's minions have struck first, overrunning the Slipgate Complex. In one swift blow, Operation Counterstrike has been wiped out. As the only survivor, your mission is clear: You must take the Slipgate in the center of the complex to Quake's dimension and defeat his minions before it's too late for Earth. Maybe you can even get to Quake personally. Pump a round into your shotgun and get moving.[2]

Or, this, from the instruction booklet for another popular and inordinately violent game called *Duke Nukem*:

> As Duke Nukem, your mission is simple: save the earth (especially the babes) from the hideous alien menace. Each level presents you with new enemies and new challenges, which you will need to overcome before you can progress. The alien plot is master-minded by loathsome creatures of awesome power, and your ultimate aim is to find these monsters and scatter their body parts over a great area.[3]
>
> [. . .]

And, again, from an ad for [. . .] *Brute Force*:

> The year is 2340 and more than fifty star systems are populated with colonies. But when an alien invasion threatens to put every living organism on the endangered species list, the Confederation of worlds must dispatch its elite special forces unit, code-named Brute Force. That's you. As Brute Force, you command four separate intergalactic

mercenaries. The trigger-happy assault trooper, cyborg sniper, stealthy assassin and feral alien are all played by you. As you guide these shooters through 20 missions and 6 exotic worlds, your knowledge of squad based combat will be severely tested. . . . Good luck to all four of you.

Other current and recently-popular games, such as *Turok, Tomb Raider, Street Fighter, Resident Evil, Mortal Kombat, Flesh Feast, LAPD 2100, Doom, Half-Life, Metal Gear Solid, Counter-Strike, Killer Instinct,* and *Maximum Carnage,* all have plots that are strikingly similar to these.

The common element, then, to many of these plots is that the earth is under attack by enemies (often commandos or monsters from an alien planet or 'dimension') and it is your mission (as player) to save it by seeking and destroying the enemy. (So what our twisted teens in the malls are really doing is saving the world from attacking aliens!) Notice, too, however, the lack of specificity or reference to actual places/countries and real people in these texts. Occasionally, there is a real-city referent – Los Angeles, New York, Tokyo – but, more often than not, both enemies and protagonists are totally fictional characters like 'Duke Nukem'. Such lack of real-world referents stands in striking contrast to another genre of video games – sports games like *NBA Jam, Tournament Edition* and *Quarterback Club* – in which the teams are peopled with the real teams' stars – the Los Angeles Lakers with Shaquille O'Neal and Kobe Bryant; the Green Bay Packers with Brett Favre and Reggie White – and the scenarios provided are those of real playoff series from past years. I will return to the nameless, placeless, non-locatable feature of the violent video genre later.

The game action in these mythic video encounters involves the main character (that is, you) moving from room to room, or building to building, and then from level to level. (Each game has multiple 'levels' that the action moves through, and you win and defeat the game when you have moved through all the levels.) Your goal is to shoot and kill enemies – commandos, monsters (who are often half-animal, half-human) – that appear suddenly around corners or jump at you from above. You have many weapons at your command, as do they – guns, swords, missiles, mines, and occasionally cleverly inventive devices such as the hologram double that Duke Nukem plants which enemies fire at, thinking it is Duke himself. When played in the arcades or on networked computers – or a recent wrinkle: networked arcades, where a player in an arcade in St Louis can play against someone in an arcade in Los Angeles – you play not against the machine but against another player – who you try to annihilate.

While the levels you move through may only involve moving from room to room in the same building, or from building to building in the same city (as in the ironic, reflexive backdrop to *Duke Nukem* which finds you chasing enemies through a shopping mall, a video arcade, and a movie theater – a backdrop which moved one of my teen informants, an academic's 15-year-old son, to comment when playing this game, 'Check this out man. It's really postmodern'), they often also involve moving from landscape to landscape around the world, and often incredibly disjunctive ones at that. Thus, as with the landscapes in Nintendo's famous line of *Mario* games, you find yourself moving from a snowy alpine forest, to a desert, to a bayou swamp, to an ice cave, to a lava pool. These natural (and often prehistoric) landscapes are also juxtaposed with industrial, post-industrial and futuristic urban scapes – scapes that are often oozing with toxic slime and nuclear waste. There is here a weird mix of fantasy scapes – El Dorados and Shangri-Las, snowy forests and steamy jungles – with apocalyptic, dystopic Blade-Runner-like urban wastelands – wastelands that are eerily empty of people. (The *Quake* manual, recall, tells you that 'you are almost certainly the only survivor'.)

In all of these settings, natural/prehistoric and urban/futuristic alike, it is the surfaces and colors that leap out, that grab the attention. And it is this that many of the players I spoke to talk about. The advances in video games' graphic technology in the last five years have been extraordinary. The intensity of color, the recently-added three-dimensional nature of the characters and settings, the speed and variety of movement (kicks, punches, aerial attacks, moves described as 'circle strafes' and 'rocket jumps'), as well as the explosions, the smoke trails, the blood pools, and, of course, the multitudinous forms of bodily mutilation (the ad for a recent Play Station game, *Bloody Roar*, for example, boasted that you can 'maim, crush, and devour your enemies in over 200 different ways'!) – it is this extraordinary graphic technology, the gaming action it permits, and the intensities it elicits, that wrap and enhance and overwhelm virtually all else. Another wrinkle that all the latest games have incorporated is the ability to change camera angle and perspective – you can choose to engage the action from behind the eyes of the character you're playing, or you can step back and watch the action from a distance, or from either side, or from above: in other words, you can be yourself, or you can be someone else looking at you, and follow the action – from a variety of different angles. And of course you can, and most players do, switch between these perspectives as and when you/they like. As well, all of the characters – both you and your enemies – can morph into other characters and can shape-shift in a mind-numbing variety of ways (shrinking, expanding, flying, disappearing). The constant technological innovations in this industry, of course, are produced by the intense competition among the video game companies and the huge multi-million-dollar stakes involved. Each company is constantly searching for the newest technological wrinkle, the next concept in design – more perspectives, bigger guns, more secrets, better graphics. 'The one constant in video games,' one gaming executive claims, 'is that nothing ever stays the same for long'.[4] And this, too, is why many media/pop culture observers claim that it is the video game industry that is in the vanguard of techno-pop development.

Intensities, Antinomies, Dystopia and the New World Order

I want now to return to some of the interpretive questions raised above – why are these games so violent? Why does the violence take the form it does? And why are so many kids playing these games? – and to suggest a reading that situates such play/games within the fractured political-economic landscape of the late twentieth and early twenty-first centuries and within the sorts of cultural imaginaries that theorists of late capitalism and postmodernity suggest are produced in and by such a world.[5] I should note that those teens I know spoke only indirectly about the games in the terms that I will suggest below. I am thus attempting to explore here an interpretation that gives coherence to an otherwise inchoate and only partially articulated set of player responses.

Theorists of late capitalism/postmodernity have argued that the crises of post–1960s 'Fordist' capitalism produced a dispersed, more globalized capitalism ('post-Fordism') characterized by corporate strategies of production and accumulation that are more flexible (small batch production, subcontracting, outsourcing) than those under Fordism. The new global reach of corporations – and the 'time-space compression' that has resulted from the quicker turnover and delivery of commodities – are also hitched to a new localism, for the greater flexibility of corporations enables them to eliminate high-volume Fordist inventories and to cater to the particularized needs and tastes of ever-smaller populations ('niche marketing'). These new global/local configurations are accompanied by the seemingly contradictory processes of increasing centralization (the creation of monopolies and corporate mergers) and increasing decentralization (an increase in small businesses). They are also accompanied by vast new financial networks and markets – paper entrepreneurialism, 'stateless' money, hedge funds that can topple national currencies and lead to global recession – and by unimaginably large quantities of recycled and deferred debt.[6]

This vast new global political economy is accompanied as well, these scholars suggest, by a new cultural topography. The fragmentation, ephemerality and chaotic flux of post-Fordist capital markets, and bourgeois society's increasing reliance on the manufacture of imaginary appetites, have produced a culture which celebrates spectacle, fantasy, fashion, ephemerality, difference, and the commodification of cultural form.[7] In postmodern culture, image reigns supreme, and there is a preoccupation with surface and style (producing a 'depthlessness' that is manifest, Jameson suggests,[8] not only in popular culture but also in academic theorizing – hence the calls for the end of grand (depth-model) narratives). A postmodern aesthetic also flattens history, so that the past is experienced less as referent and more as image – as in the glut of nostalgia films that have paraded across the movie screen in recent years.[9] So, too, in this world of the simulacrum – in which life imitates art, and the copy replaces the original – image is piled upon image in a newly-fashioned logic of the everyday wherein the world of *Pulp Fiction* films splices almost seamlessly into nightly news images of random murder, ethnic genocide, Kosovo and Gulf War missile strikes – the latter, a video war if ever there was one[10] – and indeed into the world of the shopping mall arcade itself. Or think of the recent US invasion of Iraq (by soldiers raised and trained on video games) that was transmitted to us digitally – as if in a video game – and placed the viewer (at home in her living room) in a tank, behind a gun, chasing an Iraqi – again, as if in a video game. The double interpellation here is of bourgeois subject/citizen as soldier and of soldier as everyday video gamer (and thus as citizen-saviour of the world). Finally, these theorists argue, this is a world of fragmented, multiple and reconstituted subjectivities – an age no longer of 'alienated' selves but rather of 'schizophrenic' ones, a time when ADD (attention deficit disorder) in children and manic depression in adults are coming to be seen as functional rather than dysfunctional.[11] Asking any longer whether the economic drives the cultural – in Jameson's terms, whether postmodernism is the 'cultural logic of late capitalism' – or vice versa, may be beside the point. Clearly the two fit together and feed off one another in a relationship of mutuality that makes it difficult to separate the one from the other.

I want to suggest that the sorts of violent video games with which I am concerned are signature late twentieth- and early twenty-first-century cultural texts which mirror, reproduce and refract the post-Fordist, postnational, boundary-shattering world we inhabit today. As such they enable today's youth to explore emergent forms of subjectivity that are keyed into that world.

One of the things I find most striking in these games is the contrast between the prosaic nature of the plots and story-lines, and the extravagance of the spectacle, the violence and the action. In all of the videos I know, a minimalist narrative – almost an anti-narrative or a carica-ture of a narrative, albeit one that references mythic themes (like saving the earth from invading aliens) – is swallowed up by the intensities of image and color – by the graphic excess that dominates the medium. As the creator of blockbuster game *Doom* recently stated: 'Story in a game is like story in a porn movie. It's expected to be there but it's not that important'.[12] [. . .] But isn't this cannibalizing of narrative by spectacle precisely modernity's crisis in the postmodern[13] – the rerouting of linear histories in spectacles of con-sumption and in spectacles that – like the video game of the mall in the arcade in the mall – are totally self-referencing? History, if one can call it that – the way in which the games move from and obliquely reference the prehistoric, the historic, the future and so on – becomes fantasized and fetishized and flattened, in a way that is not unlike the histories of nostalgia and the nostalgic histories in recent Hollywood films that Jameson writes about in his famous article on the postmodern present.[14] Is this not, too, why the settings for these video games, while identifiable and (often) every-day – a mall, a city, a desert – are non-locatable and non-specific? They could be anywhere or everywhere, and they have no history.

Another feature of these texts that stands out – and that I think clearly points to the world beyond the text – is the way in which they tropically represent the ruptured landscape of today's end-of-the-millennium, deter-ritorialized, post-Fordist world. Today's new world order is one in which borders of every stripe – bodily, national, continental – are being refigured and re(con)textualized.[15] It is such a world, I suggest, that provides the referent for these video worlds, for they too are worlds without borders – both national and bodily – and indeed without clearly defined anywheres. They play out mythic plots (which are at once the loftiest and the most prosaic of story-lines – and which bear uncanny resemblance to new world order political and military rhetoric) in deterritorialized landscapes strewn with body parts and split subjectivities. Moreover, the radical disjunctions that occur in these games as players move from level to level – from the desert to the North Pole to a lava pool, or from a post-industrial city to medieval ruins to a prehistoric dinosaur park – are not unlike those of a deterritorialized post-Fordist world, one in which the isomorphism and interconnectedness of the disjunctive and incommensurable – first world/ third world sites of production and distribution; the radically distinct images/stories (Iraq–Congo–Detroit) that are sutured together on the evening news – has become one of its defining features.

 And it is here that I would locate the violence that characterizes these games. Such violence is not reducible, I would suggest, to some lack or some plenitude within the self, nor does it produce real-world violence (any more, say, than television nature documentaries or pictures on the evening news). To repeat, if one in ten million players becomes a Littleton/Springfield/Paducah/Jonesboro killer, this is surely weak evidence of a causal link between video game play and real-world violence. [. . .] Rather I see the violence as symptomatic of today's new world order of boundary violation – of the assault on the nation-state, of the reconfiguring of global and local, of the dissolution, deterritorialization and remapping of the subject and of corporeality. It is also expressive of the paranoia, dystopia and conspiracy rhetoric that characterize such a world (and that proliferate in popular culture today – for instance in television shows such as X Files). With the dissolution of national boundaries, violence has become ubiquitous to the point of arbitrariness, not only from the standpoint of the 'other' but now also from the standpoint of the 'self'.[16] It is the violence of these ruptures, I would suggest, that is reflected in these video texts.

But it would be a mistake – a fallacy of misplaced concreteness – to take the violence as only, and too literally, attached to the form of its appearance on the screen. Like the Freudian fetish, it both reveals and conceals its referent, often in transmogrified, grotesque form; and in a postmodern world – in which mutual metaphorization and translatability between cultural forms (the slippage between copy and original, between fantasy and reality, between the evening news and the video arcade) have become a dominant cultural and psycho-social aesthetic – the violence on the video screen, I would suggest, simultaneously slips between multiple signifieds, between a shattering of the borders not only of the body but also of the body politic. As mentioned above, these are not the terms in which those teens I interviewed spoke about the games. What they *do* talk about repeatedly are the special effects, the backgrounds/landscapes, the gore, the weapons, the game action, and the innovations that appear in a given game. Teens are, not surprisingly, often recalcitrant informants. They are also, sometimes intentionally, not particularly articulate about what draws them to these games. A typical response: 'I like the action', or, 'I dunno, man; they're just fun'. I found that the most interesting comments came while they were playing – and reacting to – a game itself (especially a new game). Still, the everyday world of teens is as much a part of the media-saturated, post-Fordist world of today – and as shaped by its cultural topography – as any other.

Bodies and Agency

It is the way in which video games play with and on the body – rather than the body politic – that my teen informants appear drawn to more than anything else. When body parts bounce across the screen before vanishing (and then sometimes regenerating/reappearing), when guns and machines replace bodies or body parts (and vice versa, as in the martial arts-inflected games, where the body itself becomes a weapon), when characters grow tall and shrink – or become invisible, turn into flying machines, appear as hologram doubles – those teens I know gush with excitement. 'Look at what Duke can do, and how he took apart that monster'. 'He doesn't have arms, but can still kick ass!' 'That dude [a half-human, half-animal hybrid] lost his leg!' In this sense, these games seem to provide, and indeed incite, ways of re-imagining bodies and selves.[17] Here the body is experienced as detachable/combinatory and porous rather than bounded and whole, and the self as 'intensity'[18] – and site of intense action – rather than as 'emotion'. Living in an increasingly technologized cyborg culture where the boundary between human and machine becomes ever more blurred,[19] these games play with the border not only between self and other but also between one type of self and another. In so doing, they offer players an opportunity to explore new subjectivities they find exciting and enhancing and they enable a re-imagining of human possibility and action in a post-contemporary world.[20]

[. . .]

By way of conclusion, I want to leave the new world (dis)order and return to the shopping mall. When I enter the arcade in the mall that is five minutes from my house, I am struck by the disjuncture I feel between the space and feel of the mall itself and the dystopic violent worlds that the teens who crowd into the arcade are imaginatively engaged in. If there is anywhere in the US an interpellating experience for the millennial bourgeois subject, it is here in the shopping mall – here where such a subject constitutes itself through consumption and dresses itself, both literally and figuratively, for the workaday world beyond. What does it mean, then, that the sons (and increasingly daughters) of these shoppers are blowing up bodies and revelling in gore in the room next door? Is it not a type of refusal of the world of the bourgeois subject – a world whose other (non-consumptive) half is the world of work, the world for which these teens are being prepared and into which they are being disciplined in school? This is the great wrenching antinomy I see in many of those teens I know: their world revolves around the twin and opposed experiences of pleasure and discipline. They bridle at the discipline of school and live for the pleasures of the after-school and the weekend. And yet they know (some of them at least) that it is only through the harsh disciplining of body and mind that those pleasures – the pleasures of the mall – may one day be theirs. A refusal, then, whose realization will no doubt be subverted, but a refusal nonetheless.

It is nevertheless also true, however, that the distinction between mall and arcade is less real than it seems. For the mall beyond the arcade projects its own version of fragmented subjectivity and indeed of body parts detached from whole and from context. The bourgeois subject typically visits one store for underwear, another for running shoes, a third for shirts and dress pants: body parts redux. And, with rare exception, this subject shops alone and with specific needs/body parts in mind. Moreover, the commodity form – as Marx taught us long ago for his own era of industrial capital, and as many have recently shown for the contemporary transnational post-Fordist moment – depends on, and thus inscribes, alienation, violence and exclusion. Put more directly, the commodity *is* embodied violence, and the shopping mall, *ipso facto*, a product – and veiled act of consumption – of that violence. Perhaps, then, we might see the video arcade as rule rather than exception, as spectacle/performance that embodies the logic and rule of the mall itself.

Notes

1. David Sheff, *Video Games: A Guide for Savvy Parents*, New York: Random House, 1994, pp 40–43.
2. Craig Wessel, *Quake Authorized Strategy Guide*, Indianapolis: GAC/Shaphard Poorman, 1998, p 5.
3. *Duke Nukem Instruction Manual* (distributed with the video game), 1993.
4. *Next Generation* 1998, p 12.
5. Fredric Jameson, 'Postmodernism, or the Cultural Logic of Late Capitalism', *New Left Review* 146, pp 53–92; David Harvey, *The Condition of Postmodernity: An Enquiry into the Origins of Cultural Change*, Cambridge, MA: Blackwell, 1989; Scott Lash, *Sociology of Postmodernism*, New York: Routledge, 1990; Kenneth Surin, 'On Producing the Concept of a Global Culture', *South Atlantic Quarterly* 94(4), pp 1179–1199.
6. Richard Barnet and John Cavanagh, *Global Dreams: Imperial Corporations and the New World Order*, New York: Simon and Schuster, 1994, pp 359–418.
7. Harvey, *Condition of Postmodernity*, p 156.
8. Jameson, 'Postmodernism'.
9. Jameson, 'Postmodernism', p 69.
10. A video war in more ways than one. I recall an interview Tom Brokaw did with a US flight commander during the Gulf War during which Brokaw asked how it

was that US pilots were able to fire their missiles with precision while in the middle of steep bank turns and while flying at the speed of sound. The commander said his pilots had developed their reflexes and their ability to shoot accurately through extended video game play.

11. Emily Martin, 'Flexible Survivors', *Anthropology News* 40(6), p 5–7.

12. *Game Informer* 2003 (121), p 46.

13. Jameson, 'Postmodernism'.

14. Jameson, 'Postmodernism'.

15. Arjun Appadurai, *Modernity at Large: Cultural Dimensions of Globalization*, Minneapolis: University of Minnesota Press, 1996; M. Hardt and A. Negri, *Empire*, Cambridge, MA: Harvard University Press.

16. Jonathan Beller, 'Desiring the Involuntary: Machinic Assemblage and Transnationalism in Deleuze and *Robocop 2*', in *Global/Local: Cultural Production and the Transnational Imaginary*, ed. Rob Wilson and Wimal Dissanayake, Durham: Duke University Press, 1996, pp 193–218, p 202.

17. Anne Allison, 'Cyborg Violence: Bursting Bodies and Borders with Queer Machines', *Cultural Anthropology* 16(2), 2001.

18. Jameson, 'Postmodernism'.

19. Donna Haraway, *Simians, Cyborgs and Women: The Reinvention of Nature*, New York: Routledge, 1991; Donna Haraway, *Modest Witness@Second Millenium: FemaleMan meets OncoMouse*, New York: Routledge, 1997; Carol Clover, *Men, Women, and Chain Saws: Gender in the Modern Horror Film*, Princeton: Princeton University Press, 1992; Angela McRobbie, *Postmodernism and Popular Culture*, New York: Routledge, 1994; Anne Balsamo, *Technologies of the Gendered Body: Reading Cyborg Women*, Durham, NC: Duke University Press, 1996.

20. Allison, 'Cyborg Violence'.

ZERO TOLERANCE

23

PUBLIC RESPONSES TO A FEMINIST ANTI-SEXUAL VIOLENCE ADVERTISING CAMPAIGN

Jenny Kitzinger

[. . .]

The Zero Tolerance campaign was launched in 1992 by the local government in Edinburgh (the capital of Scotland). It was the first major advertising initiative in Britain designed to challenge social attitudes towards assaults against women and girls.[1] The campaign addressed the view expressed by many professionals, activists and researchers in this field that: 'the real battle lies in making fundamental changes in a society that allows and even encourages child sexual abuse' (DeYoung 1988: 111). It attempted to address the gap highlighted by Conte and his colleagues that:

> While many prevention professionals recognise that fundamental change in power relationships in families and in society from a sexist to egalitarian distribution will be necessary to prevent sexual victimisation, not enough has been done to link political and cultural life and sexual victimisation. (cited in Tharinger *et al.* 1988)

The Zero Tolerance [ZT] campaign was explicitly informed by feminist analysis and attempted to reframe the issue in these terms. It highlighted the fact that most perpetrators of sexual assault are male and suggested that there are links between the social construction of male sexuality and the potential for abusive behaviour (Dominelli 1986; Finkelhor 1982; Hearn 1988; Hollway 1981; Kelly 1988, Smart 1989). The campaign drew links between the various abuses perpetrated against women and girls throughout their lives, and it linked rape, battering, murder and abuse. Rather than present rape as an isolated aberration, the campaign designers wanted to draw attention to the continuum of sexual intimidation that children, especially girls, experience while they are growing up. Abuse was defined as everything 'from flashing to rape'.

The ZT campaign was deliberately high-profile and provocative. A central strand of the campaign was the display of huge advertisements on the city's buses and on prominent placards in Edinburgh's prestigious main shopping street. The advertisements showed simple white on black stark statements such as: '85% of rapists are men known to the victim', 'Male abuse of Power is a Crime' and 'No Man has the Right'. This attracted intensive media attention. Edinburgh District Council also involved local communities in a series of related events, and distributed leaflets, postcards and little 'Z' badges that people could wear to show their support for the campaign.

The campaign materials were designed to counter some persistent stereotypes in the media about where, and by whom, children are likely to be abused and to challenge the idea that you would automatically know if a child was being victimised. [. . .] The designers deliberately chose to locate their images indoors (focusing on violence in the home rather than on the streets/ wilderness etc.) and the posters were designed to challenge class stereotypes. The women and girls in the pictures were shown in 'posh' surroundings, with evocations of the Victorian era (e.g. china dolls). In addition, no visible signs of physical or mental damage were displayed. This was both because ZT designers did not want to produce more images of women as victims and because they wanted to make the point that abuse was often hidden. It was also a response to research which showed that people might turn away from upsetting images rather than engage with them. [For example, one campaign poster featured a photograph of two young girls playing with dolls and other toys on a rug in a wooden floored room. A doll's house, soft toys and a doll on an upholstered chair, and small chest of draws are in the background. Above the photograph it is stated 'By the time they reach eighteen', and below the photograph 'one of them will have been subjected to sexual violence'. The bottom of the poster features the capitalised words 'FROM FLASHING TO RAPE MALE ABUSE OF POWER IS A CRIME'.]

Researching People's Responses

A two-stranded approach was adopted to evaluating the campaign. Along with colleague, Kate Hunt, we conducted a street survey in Edinburgh of 228 people. In addition I used ZT materials as discussion prompts in 55 focus groups in order to access more in-depth data about people's responses. Thirty of these focus groups discussions discussed the whole ZT campaign, 25 of the groups simply discussed one poster [that featuring the two young girls described above] alongside a broader discussion of the issue of child sexual abuse in general.

[. . .]

The survey gives a basic idea of people's awareness of the campaign and their reactions to it. Sixty-four per cent were already aware of the campaign prior to being questioned about it, 76 per cent were positively in favour of it (only 6 per cent had a negative reaction to it). The campaign had also provoked a lot of discussion. Over one in three (39%) of those who were already aware of the campaign had talked about it with someone else. The survey also highlighted some differences in responses between men and women (12% of men but only 2% of woman disliked the campaign) and between younger and older respondents (people over fifty were twice as likely to be critical as those under 50).

The focus group research was designed to allow more in-depth exploration of reception processes and to unpick some of the reasons why different people might react differently. In all of the 30 groups which discussed the campaign in general a similar format was followed. I started by asking people what (if anything) they remembered about the campaign and what they thought about it. They were then shown the poster images, without their captions, and invited to reconstruct the strap-lines. Finally, the actual caption was revealed and their comments sought. Such methods are designed to tell us more about reactions than effect *per se*. However, they can give us some insight into the latter, especially where research participants had already been exposed to the ZT campaign in natural settings and could talk about their reactions at the time and memories of the materials.

General Comments and Reactions

The discussion in focus groups reflects the overall positive responses evident in the street survey. People make comments such as: 'I think it's eye-catching and terrific', 'they got people talking', 'it made me think'. Some men felt the message was very thought-provoking and many woman saw the campaign as empowering: 'It lets you know you don't have to put up with it' (Group 51); 'It gives women strength [. . .] It's making you aware of your rights' (Group 12); 'It's like some injection of power, that brings you courage and you just feel great' (Group 59). Some women reflect on the importance such a campaign from a very personal perspective.

> To me that was the most vivid one [No Man Has the Right]. Simple
> and straight to the point – 'No man has the right' [. . .] Years ago
> someone said something similar to that to me and that really changed
> . . . it didn't change my life overnight but it changed the way I thought
> [. . .] It was like a realisation. I'm not meaning to be dramatic, but I
> remember thinking 'that's right'. It suddenly sunk in. (Group 65, f)

Some women who had been sexually abused express a strong sense of
identification with the campaign:

> You know that sort of prickly feeling, like when you see something and
> think . . . oooooooh! It was when all the posters were up [. . .] right
> along Princes Street [. . .] I couldn't believe it. I was going along in the
> bus and I thought: 'There's one, there! There's another one. They
> haven't got them all along Princes Street [have they]? . . . YES! They
> have! It was very good. [I felt] 'Yes, this is what I want. I want people to
> see this [. . .] Next month it will be on the buses. They'll go by and
> you'll go: 'Yes, I'll get on that one. Look at that!' (Group 16)

In contrast to one police officer who worried that the campaign might be
'scare-mongering' or 'upsetting', the survivors were very positive about the
campaign. They welcomed the way in which ZT placed the issue in
the public domain, relieving them of the main burden of placing it on the
agenda.

> It lets you know it's there. It is not because somebody is standing there
> saying 'I was raped as a child' that it's there [. . .] The council definitely
> deserve a round of applause for that, because they're relieving the
> burden of bringing it up into everyday life from the people who are
> affected by it.

They also felt the campaign could be important for children currently
growing up in abusive situations: 'It's because of the absence of posters like
that when we were little that we had to keep it down – we had to deny it –
bury it deeper and deeper.'

Common Readings and Reported Positive Impact

The focus group discussions reveal a high degree of consensus about the
main meaning of the images and shows the level of sophistication people
bring to their readings of such representations. The picture of the two
children playing with their dolls is identified as 'nostalgic', like 'a Father

Christmas card picture' (Group 15, f), and 'old fashioned' (because of the black and white print and the type of clothing and toys). It is also identified as having the sort of aspirational qualities associated with advertisements. [. . .] People make comments such as:

It's like the Dulux shade cards. (Group 9, f)

An insurance advertisement: 'secure yourself and your child' . . . safe little ideal, happy, playing environment. (Group 2, f)

Research participants were usually clear that the image was 'middle-class' and (until they saw the caption) thought that it projected the suggestion of happiness and security:

f: . . . nice wooden floor, nice middle-class, very comfortable.

f: Lots of toys, very expensive dolls house. (Group 5)

A happy home, isn't it? You can imagine mum down the stairs, just about to shout up 'Tea's ready!' (Group 4, f)

People often comment that the campaign imagery is not what they expected – saying they were more used to images of frightened, poor or despairing children (the type of image often used to advertise children's charities). [. . .]

When shown the actual caption: 'By the time they reach 18 one of them will have been abused', those who had not already seen the poster on public display express considerable surprise. It sometimes takes a few moments to 'digest' the messages but then, once again, a high consensus is clear in how most people interpret the meaning of the advertisement. The combination of traditional image and disturbing words is identified as particularly powerful:

Well, it seems like little, idyllic, naive, two happy little girls playing and the idea of abuse seems all that more sort of negative and oppressive and bad. (Group 20, m)

The picture on its own doesn't tell the story, [but . . .] when you then wrap it with all the other phrases on there, it completely turns it around. (Group 19, m)

Some people comment that it was important that the images themselves were attractive. As one young man remarks: 'It lures you in' (Group 20). Some say that when they had seen the posters up in Edinburgh this had caused them to read a message they would normally have avoided.

These posters with the pictures – talking about the violence and with the non-violent pictures there. In a way they made me think. Even today they made me think more about it. If it had been a sort of violent

picture I would just have sort of dismissed it because I don't like violence, you know, I don't like dwelling on it particularly. (Group 58, f).
f: These visual images are quite peaceful but the words are frightening. [. . .] Personally, for me, you need a peaceful, domestic scene but what the writing gives you is the horror.

[. . .]

Many research participants also read the advertisement as conveying the message you can't tell by looking whether someone is being abused. '[It's] Implying that every child looks safe, but they aren't' (Group 19, f); 'Things might seem normal' (Group 17, f); 'You never know what goes on in anybody else's life' (Group 58, f).

[. . .]

Research participants also recognise that the focus is on including abuse by known men: 'It explodes the myth, that rapists are guys who jump out of a dark alleyway' (Group 50, m). One man talks quite specifically about the concerns the caption generated for him:

> That bit at the bottom – 'husband, father, stranger' . . . That makes me feel uneasy, and anything that makes me feel uneasy, makes me think. That's what's really good about it. I go to work and put my bairns [children] in the nursery, what's going on in the nursery? What's going on with my bairns? (Group 53, m)

Some research participants draw attention to the contrast between these posters and routine mass media coverage: 'The stranger gets publicised, if it's the husband or the father it gets swept under the carpet' (Group 51, f). Some also contrast the information in the poster with the sort of advice they had been given at school or from parents. One sixteen year old, abused by her mother's boyfriend, explains:

> Kids need to know. We did stuff on strangers at school – it made you more scared of strangers [. . .] but it wasn't strangers that were doing it to me. (Group 48, f)

Another woman, sexually assaulted by her father, comments that the message on this poster was:

> . . . the opposite of what I was told. I was told 'Don't get in a car with strange men'. That was the only time you would ever get harmed, if you did something like that. (Group 6, f)

Most research participants were also clear that the advertisement emphasised that abuse did not only happen in chaotic working-class families. The advert, they say, conveys the message that: 'it's not just like deprived kids and deprived families' (Group 22, f); [. . .] 'It could be someone living in a mansion, it could be someone living in a hovel' (Group 53, m).

The above discussion shows a close correlation between the intended message of the producers and the understanding of that message by audiences. It also shows how a particular strategy (using attractive images to draw viewers in) had been effective in reaching some people. Some research participants report that the campaign had influenced them to change their minds, that it had raised their awareness and made them think and talk more about the issue. One man, for example, says that the advertisements made him think about how he used power over his children: 'Every time I've shouted at my kids I've sat back and thought "how could I have done that better?"' (Group 53, m). Others describe ways in which the campaign generated conversations, or encouraged women and children to seek help.

'Effect' in Action

In addition to people reporting that the advertisements had had an impact on them, this was also sometimes evident in the focus group themselves. Some of the transcripts show how the discussion of materials (albeit in the artificially focussed setting of a focus group) could shift ideas and lead people to change their minds. For example, research participants often puzzled over the suggestion that one out of every two girls would encounter some form of abuse by the time the time they were eighteen. Much criticism focused on the statement 'from flashing to rape' in the advert [. . .]. Individually people often criticise this caption for either 'hyping up' or 'diluting' abuse statistics ('you think, oh well, they're only talking about flashing'). However, in the focus groups this statement frequently generates discussion between people about their own experiences of being flashed at – a process which often leads participants to state that it should not simply be dismissed as a joke. The caption also led to the gradual exchange of information previously excluded from common knowledge. This process was vividly illustrated in one group of friends in their early twenties. They initially dismissed the poster's suggestion that 50 per cent of girls would encounter some form of abuse. They saw this as an exaggeration, until, that is, they tentatively began to reflect on their own experiences when they were between the ages of 13 and 16. This culminated in the following exchange:

f2: . . . all these years I'd just thought: 'Oh, that was the night I lost my virginity'. I hadn't even took the time to think about what actually happened [. . .] He forced me. Now I'm thinking, for fuck's sake, when I lost my virginity I was raped. I remember actually thumping him to get him off me and he wouldn't get off. [. . .] He said: 'If you don't do it now, you'll never do it.' [. . .] I was too young, I didn't want to do it [. . .] I couldn't physically get him off me. I was beating him and I couldn't get him off. It was all over.

f1: The first time I got drunk, I lost my virginity. I didn't want to do it either. I was pretty young as well.

f3: You see, I'm the exact same. I was steaming [drunk] and in retrospect I wish it had never happened [. . .] So that's every single person in this room.

In fact, at that stage it was not 'every single person' in the room. The only man present had not commented. However, later in the session he remarked:

m4: One thing, which I have never ever told anyone about [. . .] I was at a party when I was sixteen [. . .] I was staying overnight [. . .] and I woke up and there was somebody in bed beside me, groping me. [. . .] It frightened the absolute life out of me. (Group 4)

The young women's descriptions of 'losing their virginity' and the young man's account of being groped had not previously been discussed among this group of friends. The research participants' willingness to share these experiences at this point was partly facilitated by the focus group discussion. However, it was actually triggered by the controversial caption – 'from flashing to rape . . .'. This caption seemed to give permission for a continuum of experiences to be explored and taken seriously. It had this sort of effect on dynamics within several groups, and often came to be positively evaluated by participants during the course of the discussion, precisely because they began to reflect on, and exchange, their own experiences.

The next [section] looks more closely at how people identify (or not) with the posters, how some 'misread' the message, and explores some people's ideological opposition to the campaign.

Identification with the Images: Class and Ethnic Identity

If people only identify with images which closely reflect their own lives you might expect the middle-class imagery to alienate working-class people. [. . .] If questioned closely some research participants agree that the images show homes far more wealthy than their own ('It would take a week's wages to buy a dolls house like that'). However, they seem to identify closely with the scene. One man (a manual worker on the railways) responds to the picture of the old woman and young girl by saying:

> That's my wean [pointing at the child] [. . .] I've just left my weans in the house with their grandmother [. . .] That's my house, there's my horrible mother-in-law and there's one of my weans. (Group 53, m)

[. . .]

Some also felt that the campaign's middle-class imagery effectively redressed stereotypes in the media, making comments such as: 'If it could happen to them, it could happen to anyone.' (Group 18, m); and '[it's] showing it's universal' (Group 58, f).

Thus initial concerns by some commentators on the ZT campaign, that the images were too 'middle-class' and would not 'speak to' working-class people, were not borne out by the audience research. Such concerns underestimate the sophistication with which people read the images and ignore the ZT campaign's exaggerated play on advertising conventions.

Different issues arose around the 'whiteness' of the images and some non-white research participants were clear that they could not see the images as universal. (I use the term 'non-white' or 'ethnic minorities' to include research participants who identified as British Asians and/or Black). Research participants from ethnic minorities were more likely to scrutinise the ZT materials to see whether or not they included 'black imagery' and to comment on this aspect. Whereas some white people did not seem to notice that one of the children in the 'from flashing to rape' poster was non-white, this was often noted by research participants from ethnic minorities. These participants were often concerned about stereotyping non-white men as abusers or further problematising black/Asian families. At the same time some felt that it was vital to explicitly include non-white people in the images. One black woman, for example, comments that abuse is such a 'silent issue amongst the black community. They keep it right under the carpet' and is concerned that 'maybe [. . .] that [the campaign] had just sealed that' (Group 59, f). In this sense, the 'whiteness' of the images appears to be more of a problem than their middle-class emphasis (this 'whiteness' was not just about the nature of the models, but also the surroundings, décor, the white doll etc.). The nostalgic, almost Victorian, look of the posters could also be alienating. As one woman comments: 'I wouldn't associate that with my own home or my mother's [. . .] they are very whitey, whitey'.

[. . .]

The western feminist emphasis on male abuse of power was also not always seen as appropriate by women from different cultures:

> We are Asian or whatever, there is a hierarchy within the house and if you happen to be the top female [. . .] For white people, yes, it is legitimate maybe just to relegate it to males' abuse of power [. . .] but for people like us it is not true, it is not reality. I live with my aunts and uncles and whatever and my husband could be the last person meting out the abuse (Group 59, f)

Over and above issues of identification, some people's responses to ZT varied in other ways. Whereas, most people quoted above apparently understood the main thrust of the ZT campaign, some of the group discussions revealed some 'misinterpretation', resistance and more outright opposition. [. . .]

Polysemy and 'Misreadings'

[. . .]

The above discussion shows congruence between the producer's intentions and most people's interpretation of the campaign. However, some research participants responded quite differently.

One example of a misreading was evident when three different working-class respondents, at first glance, thought that the bare floorboards shown in [one] advert in [. . .] indicated that the family were too poor to afford a carpet. It was only when they look at the rest of the picture that they correct themselves. This is an interesting example of how the same symbol: stripped floor boards – may be read differently by people from different socio-economic backgrounds. Their ability to then re-read the advert in ways more congruent with the intentions of the producers, however, shows a level of cultural bi-lingualism.

A second and more sustained example which suggests the polysemy of an image was evident in some people's insistence on looking for symptoms of abuse in the pictures of the two girls. When they were shown the picture without the caption some people thought the girls in [the poster] looked happy. Once they had seen the caption, however, they sometimes revised their opinion, saying the children looked sad or lonely. Several even decide which of the two children is the obvious victim. This is partly a function of what people expect to see. For example some people expect a child who has been sexually abused to be 'withdrawn' and limp, sitting in the corner with her head down (rather like the images used on the television news and in some children's charity advertisements). Indeed some people try very hard to read the Zero Tolerance photographs in this way – looking for signs of abuse:

> The little girl doesn't look secure to me – sucking her thumb and the way she's sitting. (Group 2, m)
>
> *That's* the one who's been abused – She's very withdrawn. (Group 51, f)
>
> I think it's *that* one, she's got her legs crossed. (Group 17, f)
>
> [. . .]

Invariably the 'dark-skinned' child was selected as the victim, although no one who selected her made reference to this fact. Indeed few of the white groups explicitly identify her as black or Asian and a few white people even assumed the children were twins.

Re-Negotiating the Statistics

In addition to circumnavigating the photographer's efforts to show children without visible signs of abuse, some people re-negotiate the statistics through reinterpreting the images. They cannot believe the implication that one in every two girls would encounter some form of abuse and try to interpret the poster accordingly. A few people recall the picture from memory as having shown three or four (or even ten) children rather than two. When shown the actual picture they try to find more children than are actually there. One man, for example, peers closely at the image and asks: 'Is there a baby in the chair or is it a doll?' (Group 19, m).

People also resist the message by complaining that 'flashing' should not be included as a form of abuse. Such a broad definition of abuse is, they say, ridiculous and misleading:

> Maybe a father will take a wee lassie in the bath with him and wash her. Is that going to be classed as sexual abuse, because she's seen you naked? You know, from the ridiculous to the sublime! (Group 53, f)

Others feel that the poster is obviously biased and that: 'statistics can be used to prove almost anything' (Group 57, m). Even if they accept the statistic, some people object to them being publicised. As one man asks, what can you do about it?

> What are you going to tell women? Simply don't know any men? Just

forget about them? [. . .] Just keep away from men? Don't have any-thing to do with them? (Group 53, m)

Others acknowledge that the figures might be true but are quite clear that, in one woman's words, 'the men I know aren't going to behave like that' (Group 50, f). Research participants also sometimes interpret the stat-istics presented in the campaign in ways which distance the information from their own lives. For example, one retired woman, reacting to a campaign statement that almost 50% of female murder victims are killed 'by their partner or ex-partner', suggests that these are mainly prostitutes murdered by their clients. The figures are therefore, she explains, not applic-able to 'ordinary people'. In addition there are some suggestions that the statistics displayed by the Zero Tolerance campaign are not as bad as they might seem because the figures included 'bogus' cases such as 'date rapes' which should not really count. People relate this back to stories they recall from the mass media:

[. . .]

Well there was a case in the paper just about a fortnight ago [. . .] about a young lady lawyer and a male lawyer and she allowed him to stay the night in her apartment [. . .] she undressed in front of him and so he assumed that was an invitation and so he tried it on and she sued him for rape. [. . .] I'm sorry for the woman that is genuinely raped [. . .] but by the same token, if [. . .] the situation grows and grows and grows and he's getting the come on, I think that girl's got everything she deserves. (Group 54, f)

In this way many people manage to keep rape and assault as the preserve of 'stranger danger' or misfortunes that only happen to women who 'ask for it'.

Ideological Questioning and Opposition

The above discussion addresses forms of negotiation with the campaign material. Some of this is informed by ideological opposition but is not always explicitly presented in this way. But there were also examples of outright opposition and rejection. The strongest and most focused area of opposition concerned the gender-politics of the presentation. Indeed, this was the subject of extensive press attention: the *Sunday Times*, for example, lambasted the campaign for being 'anti-male', a 'poisonous' 'grotesque libel' and a 'Goebbels-style exercise in hate propaganda' (*Sunday Times*,

9 October 1994). Within the focus groups some were concerned about the focus on girls 'at the expense' of boys. This was a complaint not simply from men and was a perspective which came from a variety of different positions. One woman who had herself been abused says she knew how important public recognition was and therefore: 'I felt sorry for the boys who were left out of that' (Group 6). Another survivor of abuse stresses the importance of recognising that some perpetrators are female (Group 16, f). Focusing on child sexual abuse as a problem for girl-children is also seen by some as undermining the 'dignity' of the problem:

> It's kind of making abuse a little girlies' thing. You know, there is something in that that is kind of denying it the dignity it deserves. It is something that happens to people and is perpetrated by people. (Group 6, f)

For some this is a question of strategy:

> f: We're not disagreeing at all that there are problems, or saying that it's not the true state of affairs but you don't solve it by this antagonistic . . .
> f: You don't help these men to sort themselves out by alienating them further.
> f: Or help the women help themselves either. [. . .]
> f: This is just anti-male, it's nothing more. (Group 58)
> [. . .]

A few men did indeed say they felt excluded, attacked and insulted by the posters. One man angrily asserts:

> It could be *my* little girl, it could be *my* mother, it could be *my* sister's that's raped or attacked or whatever. [But] I'm rejected on the same side as the rapist [. . .]. But let me tell you that my aggression toward that male is probably greater because it's *my* little girl, *my* wife, *my* mother, *my* sister and I've seen what can happen to them and how they might then be nervous of me. So I want to get back to sorting out the males, that not only would attack my mother, my little girl etc., but they would attack *me* as well. What I'm saying is that I'm also a victim of this male abuse of power. (Group 53, m)

The explicit feminist emphasis of the campaign is clearly rejected by some people. Presenting sexual violence and abuse in this way was seen as 'sexist' and 'old-fashioned':

[. . .]

It's the 'male abuse of power' that is offensive [. . .] It's too limited, it's restrictive and it's way too sexist. [. . .] It pisses me off right now just looking at it, it really does. And it pisses me off in that sort of really aggressive feminist butch 'I hate men' way, you know, and I just think that's a non-starter as a position these days. (Group 58, f)

The pendulum, according to some respondents, has swung too far against men and their side of the story is no longer heard:

f1: The man's position [is] being rubbished, I think we women have done a lot of harm.
f2: We've done ourselves more harm than good. (Group 54)

Conclusion

This [reading] has looked at how people relate to a campaign [about sexual violence] that tr[ied] to counter many of the stereotypes in the mainstream media and [was] attempting to introduce a feminist perspective on the issue. The campaign clearly attracted attention, was thought-provoking and generated conversations. In some groups it was evident that the campaign changed people's thinking, even shifting their assessment of their own experiences. Some women felt supported in resisting abuse in their own lives, some men felt challenged positively to reflect on their own behaviour and attitudes towards women and children. However, it is also evident that the campaign met misunderstanding, criticism, resistance and outright opposition. Clearly the potential for one campaign to influence people is limited in the face not only of its own qualities or flaws but also the context in which it is operating. The ZT campaign was trying to introduce a frame of understanding sexual violence which was alien to many people. It also had to compete with pervasive mainstream imagery. The degree of positive support for the campaign and the extent to which it engaged people are testimony to its success. A well-designed campaign can provide important alternatives, offering symbolic support and provoking some people to rethink some of their assumptions. However, the impact of a single campaign can never compare to the power of the mass media. Any individual message will be read in its broader social and cultural context and may be overwhelmed by more pervasive representations. This research showed that sometimes it is hard for individual alternative messages to be understood or even 'seen'.

Note

1. It has subsequently been taken up and adapted for use across the UK, however it is the initial Edinburgh campaign [. . .] which will be addressed here. The initial ZT materials were developed by Edinburgh District Council Women's Committee in consultation with groups working with victims/survivors of domestic violence and sexual assault.

References

DeYoung, M. 1988. The Good Touch/Bad Touch Dilemma. *Child Welfare* LXVII(1), pp. 61–68.

Dominelli, L. 1986. Father-Daughter Incest: Patriarchy's Shameful Secret. *Critical Social Policy* 16, pp. 8–22.

Finkelhor, D. 1982. Sexual Abuse: a Sociological Perspective. *Child Abuse and Neglect* 6(1), pp. 95–110.

Hearn, J. 1988. Commentary. Child abuse: Violences and Sexualities Towards Young People. *Sociology* 22(4), pp. 531–544.

Hollway, W. 1981. 'I Just Wanted to Kill a Woman' Why? The Ripper and Male Sexuality. *Feminist Review* 9, pp. 33–41.

Kelly, L. 1988. *Surviving Sexual Violence*. London: Polity.

Smart, C. 1989. *Feminism and the Power of Law*. London: Routledge.

Tharinger, D. et al. 1988. Prevention of Child Sexual Abuse: an Analysis of Issues, Educational Programs and Research Findings. *School Psychology Review* 17(4), pp. 614–634.

Warner, G. (1994) Time to Give Zero Tolerance to the Sex Warriors. *Sunday Times*. October 9.

24

GLOBAL DISCOURSES OF COMPASSION
AUDIENCE REACTIONS TO NEWS REPORTS OF HUMAN SUFFERING

Birgitta Höijer

[. . .]

Global Compassion

According to Nussbaum (2001: 301) compassion is 'a painful emotion occa-sioned by the awareness of another person's undeserved misfortune'. She regards compassion as a complex emotion including such cognitive beliefs as that the suffering of the other is serious, and that the suffering person does not deserve the pain (2001: 306 ff.). This makes the suffering person an innocent victim of some gruesome acts or circumstances. Following Nuss-baum we may conclude that compassion is both an affective and a cognitive reaction. Following Tester (2001: 18) the concept of compassion will here be reserved for compassion for the suffering of others in the public sphere. [. . .] In the following, compassion has to do with perceiving the suffering and needs of distant others through media images and reports. Global compassion is then a moral sensibility or concern for remote strangers from different continents, cultures and societies.

[. . .]

Through extensive media coverage, images of distant suffering have become part of ordinary citizens' perceptions of conflicts and crises in the world. Further, **humanitarian** non-governmental organizations (NGOs) have been growing in number and membership, and they have attained more prominent positions in the West (Tvedt, 1993). The latest trend within marketing is humanitarian sponsoring, in which big companies give money and other resources to social and humanitarian aid. Companies want to win goodwill by being seen as benefactors, and human sponsoring is a fastgrowing form of marketing today. Of course, it may be discussed whether this is a cynical exploitation of human suffering or an expression of true compassion. Here, however, it is enough to draw attention to the phenomenon as part of a humanitarian trend in the West, the defence of human rights, which is to be seen as one aspect of the globalization process (cf. Beck, 2000; Sassen, 1998).

Fostering by Television

It is hard to find the chicken and the egg in the development of global compassion because there is a complex interplay of factors behind it rather than a linear causal chain of relationships. Anyway, media coverage seems to be something of a driving force in the development influencing both the public and the politicians. [. . .]

The relationship between media coverage and political reactions and measures is by no means given, however. As Natsios (1996) shows, many factors, such as domestic politics, geopolitical interests and other coincidental foreign policy crises, influence the process. And the media reporting often becomes part of propaganda strategies (Höijer et al., 2002). In the recent Afghanistan War, American authorities put pressure on the media to refrain from reporting civilian casualties and suffering so as not to adversely affect public support for the bombings. The chairman of CNN instructed the staff that if such news was going to be broadcast, they should balance the reporting of victims in Afghanistan with reminders to the audience of the victims of the terror attack on World Trade Center and the Pentagon (Ottosen, 2002).

However strong or weak, politically determined or not, the media effect may be in relation to different humanitarian crises, it seems quite obvious that it is primarily through the media that we, citizens and politicians alike, meet depictions of the suffering of distant strangers.

Television especially, with its reach and visual impact, may therefore play a key role in the fostering of a collective global compassion. Photographic pictures are often perceived as truthful depictions of reality. As audience, the experience is that we are seeing the innocent victims of the violence with our own eyes, and the pictures become evidence of the suffering. Through the media, and especially through the moving images of television, people have become aware of the sufferings of remote others and are challenged to include strangers in their moral conscience. Although there are, as we shall see, different ways of responding to distant suffering, no one can deny the existence of large-scale humanitarian disasters.

On the whole, news media focus more on civilian populations as victims of conflicts and wars than before. According to the BBC war reporter Martin Bell (1998: 15–16) the reporting 'has changed fundamentally' from mainly reporting military aspects, such as strategies and weapon systems, to reporting with a greater focus on people – 'the people who provoke them, the people who fight them and the people who suffer from them'.

[. . .]

And quantitative content analysis studies show an increased exposure of pictures of human suffering among civilian populations in television news, and that the visual presentations have become more lurid (Cronström, 2000; Höijer, 1994, 1996). The camera explores faces twisted in pain, or lingers on wounds and bloody bandages, it zooms in on broken and mutilated limbs, or pools of blood, and the injured are not soldiers but ordinary people.

Photographers and journalists may, like Martin Bell, be seriously committed to humanitarian reporting. [. . .] But media reporting on distant suffering may also be part of more cynical commercial interests, in which the media sell human tragedies in a global market place. In the pursuit of attention, news producers follow the logic of increasingly dramatic coverage, and journalists become desensitized and blasé (Moeller, 1999).

The Ideal Victim

[. . .]

According to the moral ideals of the humanitarian organizations there should be no social boundaries for qualifying as a victim worthy of help. However, in international politics as well as in the media, many victims never qualify as worthy victims. The hundreds of thousands of victims of the civil wars in Liberia and Sudan in the middle of the 1990s are two 'forgotten' examples discussed by Minear et al. (1996). Chomsky (1999) asks why the Western powers do not pay attention to Kurdish victims, and there are many more examples, such as Sierra Leone, Burundi, Ethiopia and Eritrea.

Further, some victims within an area picked out by the West are worthier; that is, they are perceived to deserve our empathy better than others. According to Herman and Chomsky (1988: 38) people abused in what are regarded as enemy states are portrayed 'as worthy victims, whereas those treated with equal or greater severity by its own government or clients will be unworthy'. Worthy and unworthy relates to the extent and character of political and mass media attention and indignation.

If we leave the macro-political level and turn to a more general socio-cultural level we may also discriminate between ideal and less ideal victims. Children, women and elderly people are often seen as helpless in a violent situation, and therefore they are more suitable as ideal victims than males in their prime (Christie, 1996). 'Mothers and children make ideal victims', writes Moeller (1999: 107) in her critical discussion of the television coverage of famine; she continues:

> . . . men associated with violent political factions can starve by the thousands without creating a flutter of interest in their victim status. The men are culpable, it is assumed, in not only their own deaths, but in the deaths of the truly blameless. Only when victims have been identified as 'bona fide' are they candidates for compassion.

That the ideal victim is a cultural construction becomes apparent if we consider historical and cultural variations in the victim status of women. Women who are assaulted by men are not always seen as victims, in some cultures not at all. Without any feelings of compassion from people an elderly woman could be burned to death in a witch trial some hundred years ago in Scandinavia. And it is only recently that male soldiers' systematic rape of civilian women from the enemy side have been condemned. During the Second World War it was more or less accepted that Russian soldiers, for instance, committed massive rapes of German women immediately after the capture of Berlin.

The Media and Humanitarian Organizations

Television not only pays attention to victims in newscasts but also in entertainment programmes. In broadcast gala shows artists perform for charitable purposes and the audience is urged to donate money to humanitarian organizations. [. . .] In Great Britain charity programmes – so-called telethons, for example, Live Aid, Children in Need and Comic Relief – are successful and they appeal to both those who can give a lot and those who can give only a little (Tester, 2001).

Campaigns and televised gala shows may be most directly related to activity in the form of economic support for aid, but it is the informative programmes that create the necessary conditions for their success via their depictions of distant suffering. The media often present different views of issues, but when it comes to compassion with the victims, hegemonic unity prevails. Minear et al. (1996: ix) conclude that the news media have 'become a major humanitarian actor in their own right, helping to frame the context within which government policy is formulated and humanitarian action is mounted'.

[. . .]

It is not the purpose of this article to go [. . .] into the intricate relationship between humanitarian organizations, the media and international politics. Instead a fourth part, and a part that all three institutions are dependent on in their social practices will be brought up, namely the public.

The humanitarian organizations are dependent on the public as citizens giving money gifts, the media are dependent on the public as audiences paying attention to their texts and programmes, and policy makers are dependent on the public as opinion. Given the mediating role of the media, on the one hand between humanitarian organizations and the public, and on the other hand between politics and public opinion, makes it especially important to focus on the public as the audience for humanitarian reporting in the media. How do people react to the emotional engagement media offers by focusing on innocent victims for political conflicts, war and other violence?

Audience Reactions

In the following, the discussion will be based on two sets of empirical studies of audience reactions. One set of studies focused on violent news in general and combined brief telephone interviews carried out with a representative sample of Swedes (in total 500 interviews) with in-depth personal interviews with a variety of individuals (Höijer, 1994, 1996). The other set of studies consisted of focus group interviews about the **Kosovo War** with different groups of citizens in Norway and in Sweden (Höijer and Olausson, 2002). Thirteen groups were run in Norway and 11 in Sweden, and the female and male informants were recruited from different occupational sectors and age levels. Kosovo-Albanian and Serb immigrants were also interviewed.

Extent of compassion

Although it is a risky and uncertain task to determine the extent of compassion for victims of distant suffering among the audience in general, I shall here present some figures indicating a division of the audience into those who express some type of compassion and those who are more or less indifferent. Further, there are different reactions among different segments of the audience.

The results in Table 1 are based on telephone interviews in which the public answered open-ended questions about their reactions to pictures of victims for violence (conflicts, war and so on) in news reports. Table 1 shows that half of the respondents (51 per cent) said that they often or quite often do react to the pictures of distant suffering. About a quarter of the public (23 per cent) said they were totally indifferent and do not react at all, and 14 per cent said they react sometimes but very seldom. Some (7 per cent) gave unclear answers that could not be categorized. The table also shows gendered differences and differences among age groups. Women react with compassion more often than men, and elderly people much more often than younger people. Feelings of pity, sadness and anger were reported, and women especially also said that they sometimes cried, had to close their eyes or look away, because the pictures touched them emotionally.

I shall return to gender differences later, and here only comment on the difference between age groups. It is, of course, possible that younger people are more desensitized and blasé because they are more used to seeing fictitious violence and blood, injured victims and dead bodies. But there are other plausible reasons. Young people are often occupied by their own development and identity formation, and in this process it may be hard to engage in the suffering of distant others. Distancing oneself from global suffering may also be a way of warding off an all too pessimistic life view. 'I am not unpleasantly affected', as a young man said, 'reality is terrible and so are human beings.' Elderly people are not symbolically threatened in their own identities by suffering others in the world, and they have a deeper knowledge of the world and greater life experience. Therefore they may be more open to both their own feelings and to global suffering.

Table 1 Audience's reactions to pictures of suffering on television news (%)

	Gender			Age in years					
	Total	M	W	5–19	20–29	30–39	40–49	50–64	65–99
React often or quite often	51	41	59	28	37	49	49	54	68
React only sometimes	14	17	12	22	14	16	17	13	9
Do not react at all	23	32	16	41	31	22	19	25	14
Other answers or do not know	7	6	8	4	6	7	12	7	5

Notes:
Number of respondents: 554.
Source: From Höijer (1994).

Compassion is dependent on visuals

The compassion that the audience expresses is often directly related to the documentary pictures they have seen on television. When asked about their spontaneous impressions of the Kosovo War most of the audience groups interviewed started to talk about the television pictures of streams of refugees or pictures of crying people in refugee camps, especially pictures of children and elderly people:

> 'It was what I saw of live pictures on television that made the strongest impression, all the innocent people, all those who cried.'
>
> 'I have terrible memories of children stepping on board buses and sitting by the windows crying.'
>
> 'I remember that I saw crying people on television. They had lost someone in their family and they could not find them again. There were a lot of people and it was very crowded on the gravel roads along which they were walking.'

Pictures, or more precisely our interpretations of pictures, can make indelible impressions on our minds, and as a distant audience we become bearers of inner pictures of human suffering. [. . .]

The impact of photographic pictures is not least due to the truth-claim connected with them. They are perceived as truthful eye-witness reports of reality. The audience very rarely questions the reality status of documentary pictures, or sees them as constructions of situations or events (an exception from this is discussed under the heading 'distantiation'). Documentary pictures are instead experienced as if they give direct access to reality and they therefore insist upon being taken seriously.

[. . .]

Compassion is dependent on ideal victim images

The audience accept the dominant victim code of the media and regard children, women and the elderly as ideal victims deserving compassion. When describing their emotional reactions the groups interviewed about the Kosovo War unanimously talked about these categories of civilian people:

> 'It makes a really strong impression to see children and elderly people, and women, infirmly wandering about. You start thinking about how it is for them.'
>
> 'I felt so terribly sorry for them. [. . .] Seeing all the elderly people and the children. They are so tired that they can hardly walk.'

'I saw a news item from an empty village and there was an old, old woman left there. She could not go on any longer. I thought it was so terrible for her.'

A condition for being moved is that we as audience can regard the victim as helpless and innocent, and this was sometimes also explicitly pointed out by participants in the study: 'I was most affected by the fact that innocent people were stricken.'

A news item about a crying middle-aged man in a refugee camp in Macedonia who, in front of the television camera, begged to be brought to Norway challenged this cultural conceptualization of a worthy victim. In most of the interviewed groups they considered the man distasteful and selfish and they charged him with bad behaviour. They also thought he was not behaving in a manly way:

I thought it was a shame to behave as he did when you think about all the pregnant women and sick people. They need to be helped and he should have begged for them. He should have said: 'Please help them!'

A man in his prime is not worthy of our compassion since we do not regard him as helpless and innocent enough. Instead he should be active in fighting the enemy or helping the helpless ones. Elderly men are conceptualized differently since they are considered weak and have a right to be cared for. In one of the groups this was underlined by an utterance about the middle-aged man who begged to be taken to Norway: 'If he had been an old man over seventy'.

[. . .]

Forms of compassion

Boltanski (1999) distinguishes between three forms of emotional commitment in relation to distant suffering: the mode of denunciation, the mode of sentiment, and the aesthetic mode. The first refers to a perspective in which compassion (pity in Boltanski's terminology) is combined with indignation and anger and turned into an accusation of the perpetrator. The suffering is considered as unjust. In the mode of sentiment [. . .] [t]he suffering is experienced as touching and compassion is tender-hearted and sympathizes with the victim's gratitude at receiving help from a doctor, a nurse or humanitarian workers. The aesthetic mode is described by Boltanski (1999: 115) as a third possibility, which 'emerges from the criticism of the first two. It consists in considering the unfortunate's suffering as neither unjust nor as touching, but as sublime.' As examples he discusses paintings, for instance those by Goya, in which the horrible and the grotesque sides of the unfortunate's suffering is revealed.

Looking at audiences' responses to televised distant suffering we may quite clearly recognize the mode of denunciation and the mode of sentiment. It is harder to identify the aesthetic mode as a form of compassionate reading. There are, however, two other forms of compassion, which may be identified. In one, compassion is combined with feelings of shame and in the other with feelings of powerlessness. This gives us four forms of compassion identified in audience reactions. Below they are named tender-hearted compassion, blame-filled compassion, shame-filled compassion and powerlessness-filled compassion:

Tender-hearted compassion focuses on the suffering of the victims and the responses of pity and empathy it gives rise to in oneself as a spectator:

> 'It breaks my heart when I see refugees. They are coming in thousands and they tell what they have been through. It's so terrible'; 'I felt pity for them when they stood there in the mud and the cold weather. They had very little food and you could see the fear in their eyes.'

Blame-filled compassion brings up the suffering of the victims in combination with indignation and anger: 'I became angry when I saw the many innocent people and civilians who died and were stricken by the conflict.' The indignation may be directed towards someone seen as responsible for the excesses. In political conflicts it is often a person in power more than the specific perpetrator who executed the violent act. In the Kosovo Conflict Milošević was an ideal enemy to accuse. He was conceived of as having an evil disposition, of being dangerous, powerful and inhuman both by the media and by the audience (Höijer et al., 2002): 'He is evil, manipulative, and stark mad'; 'He is a terrible man, a psychopath.'

Shame-filled compassion brings in the ambivalence connected with witnessing the suffering of others in our own comfortable lives and the cosiness of our living room. Shame is 'an emotional state produced by the awareness that one has acted dishonourably or ridiculously' and 'knowledge of the transgression by others' is part of the emotional state (Reber, 1985: 313, 695). Concerning distant suffering you know that you have transgressed the moral obligation to help suffering others. 'I had such a bad conscience and I almost did not manage to watch any more terrible scenes on television. And they weren't just scenes, it was reality.' In the feelings of shame there may also be a component of anger or denunciation directed at oneself for being passive and not engaging in the destinies of the remote victims [. . .]

Powerlessness-filled compassion arises from a subjective awareness of the limits of the media spectator's possibilities to alleviate the suffering of the victims. It brings forth sentiments of impotence and powerlessness: 'You feel so helpless and there is so little you can do. You can of course give some money but that will not stop the war'; 'I got a feeling that it would never stop and I experienced so much impotency.'

The various forms of compassion may take different forms in the individual spectator, and they may also be represented simultaneously in the same person. A spectator may for instance feel tender-hearted compassion, blame a perpetrator *and* experience powerlessness in relation to the same news story or reported encroachment. [. . .]

Distantiation from compassion

Far from everyone in the audience feels compassion with the victims of war and other conflicts. There are also different ways of turning one's back on the suffering of distant others. [. . .]

Mostly people interpret the news referentially, that is, the reports are regarded as truthful descriptions of reality. To see pictures of streams of refugees and to hear a reporter talk about them is to believe that people are forced, by others or by circumstances, to flee from their homes in order to escape terror or other disasters. In political conflicts and wars such news pictures are also part of the propaganda war between the parties involved. People may be aware of that but still be overpowered by the impact of the photographic pictures of the suffering. Sometimes, however, a critical propaganda perspective may be strong and take over. This was the case when the interviewed Serbian immigrants, especially the male groups, saw the news about Kosovo-Albanian refugee streams. The news pictures were regarded as have been staged for propaganda purposes:

> On television all pictures may be arranged. They show the same strong pictures over and over again. They showed dreadful pictures, for instance they broadcast the same family on a horse-drawn cart several times. And they said that thousands of Kosovo-Albanians were hiding in the forest. But to me the pictures seemed incredible, arranged.

A more common critical perspective, which creates a distance from the human suffering, is to criticize the news in general for commercialism and sensationalism. News media give a distorted picture, according to this view, by paying too much attention to violence and human misery:

> The news reporting is focusing more and more on dead bodies and acts of violence. It seems to be the only thing of news value, and that can be quite disturbing. Especially when they are reporting from hotbeds

of war. If nobody has been shot or blown to pieces there are no reports. It makes you quite critical of the media.

Another way to form a distance is to apply an us–them perspective in which the culture, mentality and way of living and behaving of the others, that is, the suffering people, are dehumanized. With stereotyped thought figures such as 'In the Balkans they think only of vendetta', 'It is a totally different culture from ours', 'It is something about their temperament', empathy is turned away and the lack of involvement is rationalized and legitimized. Why bother about people who are primitive and uncivilized and not like us, civilized citizens in democracies? [. . .]

Just becoming numb or immune to the pictures and reports about human suffering on a large scale is also quite a common reaction: 'I cannot engage in it any longer. A dead body no longer touches me.' Being fed with news about suffering may in the end lead to feelings of satiation and numbness. [. . .]

Gendered compassion

As shown in Table 1, women react with compassion more often than men. Gender differences were also very evident in the in-depth interview studies. Distantiated and repudiating interpretations were more common among male audience groups than among female. [. . .] [M]en more often said that the documentary pictures of children in need, or of mutilated or dead persons, did not move them. 'Seeing a dead body doesn't affect me particularly, I guess I've become blasé' is a more typical reaction among men than among women.

To a greater degree than men, women focus on the humanitarian aspects of disasters, conflicts and wars, and make empathic interpretations:

'I feel so deeply sorry for the refugees.'

'It breaks my heart to see them. It was cold and they had almost nothing to eat. You could see the fear in their eyes.'

'I was moved by the children and the elderly people, the women who infirmly wandered about. It was summer, it was hot and I thought about how things were for them.'

Sometimes female viewers identify with the situation of the victims, going so far as to imagine themselves as distressed in the same ways: 'Imagine that someone came and put a gun to your head telling you to leave. Otherwise you will get shot. You have to leave your own home, the house you have bought and built yourself.'

There may be many factors contributing to gendered differences. Obvious social reasons for the difference are that women are fostered to show more feelings and mostly have the caring role in family life. Further, war is historically and culturally an extremely male domain in which glory, violence and manliness are called forth. To feel solidarity with victims simply does not accord with male ideals about heroic warfare and violence.

Men also mainly conduct other outrages, and the story about male violence is told again and again in the media. [. . .] When men hear and see documentary depictions of the victims of violence, they meet a story about themselves through the hidden myth of violence and manliness. This is an unacceptable idea, a painful experience, and the violence-imbued self-conception is something one tries to keep at arm's length. This is achieved by not allowing oneself to react very strongly to images of death and suffering. Men shield and defend themselves by looking at the pictures without showing any outer signs of emotion. Women are not threatened in their identities at all in the same way when confronted with documentary depictions of the human suffering caused by some kind of violence. On the contrary, women may even be confirmed in their more positive self-conception, assured that violence is not part of feminine culture. Since women do not experience any threat to their self-conception, they can afford to remain more open to the depictions of suffering and have greater leeway for emotional reactions [. . .]

I will also bring up a difference in an inner moral voice between women and men, which gives different frames of references for interpreting a political and violent conflict. As suggested by Gilligan (1982) women's moral judgement focuses on care while men's moral judgement focuses on justice. Women construct the moral problem for human action in conflicts and choice situations as a problem of care and responsibility. Hurting someone is considered selfish and immoral. A female perspective thus calls attention to hurt, pain or suffering as something wrong and morally problematic. This is also often the case, as we have seen, when the female audience creates meaning out of the media reports on violent conflicts, wars and other catastrophes.

According to Gilligan (1982), men construct the moral problem as one of rights and rules and they reason about justice more than about care. From a justice point of view, violence could even be accepted under certain conditions, namely when it is used to rectify or to avenge a previous injustice. In such a perspective, questions of the suffering of human beings may be put in the background. This was done when a majority of the male population in the West supported the NATO bombings of Kosovo and Serbia. For instance, in March 1999, 65 per cent of Norwegian men supported the bombings but only 44 per cent of Norwegian women (Opinion, 1999).

We find the same gender patterns in relation to the military attack by the United States and Britain on Afghanistan following the terrorist attack of September 11th on World Trade Center and the Pentagon. At the beginning of October 2001, 80 per cent of the male population in Britain supported military actions compared to 68 per cent of females. By the end of October 2001, public support among British women for the bombing had decreased to 51 per cent. Swedish opinion data from the beginning of November 2001 shows an even larger difference between the sexes. While 59 per cent of the male population in Sweden supported the bombings only, 27 per cent of the female population did so.

From a justice perspective, it is morally right to bomb in order to rout the enemy and take vengeance for violent or unrighteous acts conducted by the enemy. From a care perspective, bombings are morally wrong because they will hurt and kill people and they will inevitably lead to new suffering among innocent victims.

Conclusion

In the critical media debate it is a quite common view that suffering is commodified by the media and the audience become passive spectators of distant death and pain without any moral commitment. Žižek (2001) emphasizes the narcissistic traits of what he calls the capitalistic subjectivity in which we are superficially touched and give money for charity just in order to keep the distant other at arm's length. Moeller (1999) almost takes it for granted that the American audience she discusses does not care about the human suffering it is fed with by the media.

[. . .]

Compassion fatigue may be another reason for the distantiation from the media pictures of innocent victims for war, conflicts and terror. According to Tester (2001: 13):

> Compassion fatigue is becoming so used to the spectacle of dreadful events, misery or suffering that we stop noticing them. We are bored when we see one more tortured corpse on the television screen and we are left unmoved [. . .] Compassion fatigue means being left exhausted and tired by those reports and ceasing to think that anything at all can be done to help.

The concept 'compassion fatigue' seems to imply an earlier stage with some compassion. The large number of reports on suffering and the repetitive and stereotyped character of the depictions may tire the audience out. [. . .] A subsequent new human catastrophe somewhere else in the world may, however, evoke their compassion again.

When discussing the impact of the growing television exposure of human suffering on the audience it is important not to simplify the discussion. We should not idealize the audience, believing that all we need to do in order to awake compassion and engagement is to expose people to pictures of humanitarian disasters. Nor should we believe the opposite, that the audience mainly turns away in cynicism and compassion fatigue, fed up with reports of expulsions, massacres, genocide, and terrorist and bomb attacks. And the media are not good Samaritans wanting to help the world, nor are they totally corrupted cynical and commercial agents who exploit and sell human suffering. There are different media systems, different news policies and different news journalists.

There are many questions that we need to address with systematic empirical research: questions of how different media report on different human catastrophes, questions of changes over time in media reporting, questions of how different audience groups react to different humanitarian disasters reported in the media, and questions of changes in audience reactions over time.

References

Beck, U. (2000) *What is Globalization?* Cambridge: Polity Press.

Bell, M. (1998) 'The Journalism of Attachment', pp. 15–22 in M. Kieran (ed.) *Media Ethics*. London: Routledge.

Boltanski, L. (1999) *Distant Suffering: Morality, Media and Politics*. Cambridge: Cambridge University Press.

Chomsky, N. (1999) *The New Military Humanism: Lessons from Kosovo*. Monroe, ME: Common Courage Press.

Christie, N. (1996) 'The Ideal Victim', pp. 17–30 in E.A. Fattah (ed.) *From Crime Policy to Victim Policy*. London: Macmillan.

Cronström, J. (2000) *Gränslöst II: om det symboliska TV-våldets inflytande på individer, medier och samhälle*. Stockholm: Institutionen för journalistik, medier och kommunikation (licentiatuppsats).

Gilligan, C. (1982) *In a Different Voice: Psychological Theory and Women's Development*. Cambridge, MA: Harvard University Press.

Herman, E.S. and N. Chomsky (1988) *Manufacturing Consent: The Political Economy of the Mass Media*. New York: Pantheon Books.

Höijer, B. (1994) *Våldsskildringar i TV-nyheterna. Produktion, utbud, publik.*

Stockholm University: Department of Journalism, Media and Communication, No. 5.

Höijer, B. (1996) 'The Dilemmas of Documentary Violence in Television', *Nordicom Review* 1: 53–61.

Höijer, B., S.A. Nohrstedt and R. Ottosen (2002) 'The Kosovo War in the Media – Analysis of a Global Discursive Order', *Conflict & Communication Online* 1(2): www.cco.regener-online.de

Höijer, B. and U. Olausson (2002) *Medborgare om medierna och Kosovokonflikten.* Örebro University: Studies in Media and Communication, No. 23.

Minear, L., C. Scott and T.G. Weiss (1996) *The News Media, Civil War, and Humanitarian Action.* Boulder, CO: Lynne Rienner Publishers.

Moeller, S.D. (1999) *Compassion Fatigue: How the Media Sell Disease, Famine, War and Death.* New York: Routledge.

Natsios, A. (1996) 'Illusions of Influence: The CNN Effect in Complex Emergencies', pp. 149–69 in R.I. Rotberg and T.G. Weiss (eds) *From Massacres to Genocide: The Media, Public Policy, and Humanitarian Crises.* Cambridge, MA: The World Peace Foundation.

Nussbaum, M.C. (2001) *Upheavals of Thought: The Intelligence of Emotion.* Cambridge: Cambridge University Press.

Opinion. (1999) *Landsomfattende meningsmäling 25 mars.* Bergen, Norway: Opinion AS.

Ottosen, R. (2002) 'Pressfriheten under press efter 11. September', in S. Finslo (ed.) *Norsk Redakørførenings Arbok 2001.* Kristiansand, Norway: Høyskoleforlaget.

Reber, A.S. (1985) *The Penguin Dictionary of Psychology.* London: Penguin Books.

Sassen, S. (1998) *Globalization and Its Discontents: Essays on the New Mobility of People and Money.* New York: The New Press.

Tester, K. (2001) *Compassion, Morality and the Media.* Buckingham: Open University Press.

Tvedt, T. (1993) *En studie av frivillige organisasjoner i norsk bistand.* Universitetet ÖÖi Bergen, Senter for utviklingsstudier.

Žižek, S. (2001) 'Njutning förbjuden', *Dagens Nyheter* 22 August.

GLOSSARY

agenda setting: the establishment of, or attempt to establish, an issue as a matter of social concern. The mass media are seen as important vehicles through which priorities for social concern are set.

appearance as a social problem: the notion that peoples' attitudes and proclivity to anti-social, abnormal or even violent behaviour are reflected in how they dress and adorn themselves.

attitudinal effect: a change in attitude as a consequence of witnessing, experiencing, reading, or being informed about something (see also **ideological effect**).

audience reception: how media audiences make sense of and interpret media texts. Audience reception research examines how audiences interpret media content. It is generally theorized that audiences' social positions and identities are reflected in their interpretations.

BBC Producer Guidelines: now called the BBC Editorial Guidelines, these comprise the British Broadcasting Corporation's code of ethics which guide programme-makers on how to uphold standards of taste and decency, accuracy, impartiality, and fairness in both factual and fiction programme content. The guidelines provide specific advice on how to treat the representation of violence, criminal and anti-social behaviour.

behavioural effects research: in media violence research, the term used for psychological studies of how audience behaviour is affected by engaging with violent media content. Research of this kind has often been conducted in laboratory settings where immediate short-terms effects are observed.

Bobo doll: a large inflatable doll used in Bandura, Ross and Ross's behavioural effects research studies. In a laboratory setting, children watched a short film or video of an adult physically and verbally abusing (punching, kicking, and hitting with a mallet) the doll. Researchers then observed the child to see if they imitated the adult's behaviour toward the doll.

British Board of Film Classification (BBFC): the advisory body that oversees the certification of films for exhibition in the UK.

censorship: process involving the suppression, deletion or blocking of material from public expression on the grounds that it is offensive, unsafe or illegal.

citizen journalism: also known as 'participatory journalism', is the act of citizens 'playing an active role in the process of collecting, reporting, analyzing and disseminating news and information', according to the seminal 2003 report *We Media: How Audiences are Shaping the Future of News and Information*, by Shayne Bowman and Chris Willis. They say, 'The intent of this participation is to provide independent, reliable, accurate, wide-ranging and relevant information that a democracy requires'.

Columbine High School shootings: in 1999 in Littleton, Colorado, Eric Harris, 18, and Dylan Klebold, 17, shot and killed 12 of their fellow high school students and one teacher and wounded 23 others. After the hour-long rampage, the teenagers killed themselves. It was suggested that violent media content, and especially computer games, influenced their actions.

compassion fatigue: the notion that as a consequence of experiencing or witnessing suffering to such a degree that we eventually stop noticing that suffering, we are unmoved or even bored by it, and feel unable to do anything to help victims of suffering.

content analysis: the quantitative measurement of media content according to the amount of page space, screen time, or frequency of occurrence of certain issues, events, images, types of people, etc.

critical theory: an approach to analysing social phenomena originally developed in the early twentieth century by the Frankfurt School of social theorists and which remains highly influential in sociology, media and cultural studies. Critical theory aims to generate positive social change through the analysis and critique of social structures of power.

Cullen Report, 1996: the public inquiry led by the Honourable Lord Cullen set up to investigate the circumstances that led up to the shootings at Dunblane Primary School in Scotland in 1996.

cultivation analysis/cultivation theory: see **Cultural Indicators Project.**

Cultural Indicators project: the project initiated and developed by George Gerbner and his colleagues that theorizes the consequences of living in a mass-mediated cultural and symbolic world. It is argued that over time the violence encountered in fictional television programming, including films, cultivates conceptions of social reality and understandings of those who have and who do not have power in that reality.

cultural studies: an interdisciplinary research tradition that grew out of Marxist theory and leftist politics that is primarily concerned with investigating relations of power within institutions, in textual representation, and in audience interpretation of texts.

cyberstalk/cyberstalking: the act of gathering private information about a person for the purpose of pursuing them and/or using computer-mediated communication systems such as e-mail or the internet to communicate with a person with the intention of threatening them or making them feel afraid.

desensitizing: the notion that the more someone views or experiences a phenomenon, such as violence or death, the less they are emotionally affected by it.

discourse: language expression (speaking, writing and representation) that produces particular understandings of the object referred to. Michel Foucault theorized discourse as the means by which knowledges, as well as subjectivities and power relations, are constituted. For Foucault, discourses are used to legitimate the exercise of power by nations, states, institutions, corporations, individuals, etc. over others.

dreadfuls: dreadfuls, or penny dreadfuls, were low-priced books for sale in the UK during the nineteenth and early twentieth centuries. They were referred to by this term because readers paid one penny to purchase them. Most contained melodramatic tales of vice and virtue, often with strong elements of horror and cruelty. Their main audience consisted of young and/or poorly educated readers, primarily male.

Dunblane Primary School: in March 1996 an unemployed former shopkeeper, Thomas Hamilton, walked into the school in Dunblane, Scotland, armed with two pistols and two revolvers and opened fire on a class in the school gym hall. He killed 16 children of between 4 and 6 years old, and one teacher, and then killed himself.

effects theory: in the media violence debate, the term 'effect' is generally used to refer to claims that violent media content will affect audiences either in terms of encouraging them to behave violently, or think that committing violent acts against others is acceptable. Effects are variously analysed as behavioural, emotional, attitudinal and/or ideological in nature.

emotional effect: engagement with media representations of violence is often said to have emotional effects on audiences. Depending on the context of the representation, it is suggested that fear, empathy, compassion, lack of compassion, happiness, etc. can be variously evoked by mediated violence.

ethnographic/ethnography: the qualitative, analytical description of human social phenomena based on spending considerable periods of time with the subject of study. For example, in media research, ethnography has been used to explore journalistic, decision-making in the production of television news, and audience interaction with television programmes, films and video games.

eve-teasing: the euphemistic term used in India for the sexual harassment or molestation of women by men.

factual media violence: the reporting and/or showing of actual incidents of violence caused by intentional or accidental human actions, including written, photographic, video, audio, digital or film documentation of such violence.

fascists: those who advocate the rights, authority and interests of the nation state over and above the rights of the individual. Associated with extreme right-wing totalitarian dictatorships, a key feature of fascism is its suppression of working-class organization, politics and representation.

fictional representations of violence: the dramatization of fictitious incidents of violence caused by intentional or accidental human actions in, for example, fictional feature films, plays, television dramas (such as soap operas and serials), and video and computer games.

Fordist: the model of mass production and consumption named after Henry Ford (1863–1947) involving highly differentiated divisions of labour and assembly-line production. The model is critiqued as involving the exploitation of workers in the pursuit of capitalist profit.

framing: the institutionalized way in which media texts are encoded and which may be influential in how audiences interpret those texts. Frames, which tend to be unconsciously created rather than consciously imposed on data, enable us to cognitively perceive, organize, and make sense of information.

gangsta-rap: rap music commonly critiqued as advocating violence, especially gun violence. Often contains explicit language and misogynist lyrics.

the gaze: the concept used to theorize how the visual media create a point of view for the audience to look at what is presented. Feminist theory has identified how the gaze is most usually a masculine one that objectifies women and encourages audiences to look upon them as sex objects.

globalization: the organization of activities, networks and economies across national, geographic and cultural borders and boundaries. Involves local markets and cultures becoming increasingly dominated and determined by transnational markets and culture.

happy violence: the depiction of violence as painless, funny (such as in the context of cartoons), thrilling and leading to a happy ending.

hate crimes: criminal acts committed against people on the basis of their gender, ethnic, sexual, religious and/or cultural identity.

hegemonic power: see **hegemony**.

hegemony: Italian political theorist Antonio Gramsci's (1971) notion of 'hegemony' suggests that the 'dominant' classes in society have to constantly renegotiate their position with the 'subjugated' classes. To maintain power, they must rule by winning people's consent to the economic system that privileges those already in positions of power, rather than through coercion or repression.

Hillsborough Disaster: in 1989, during the Football Association semi-cup final between Liverpool and Nottingham Forest at Hillsborough Stadium in Sheffield, England, 96 people died and 766 were injured when police mismanagement of the crowd caused overfilling of parts of the stadium. Fans at the front of the stadium, unable to escape due to chain link fencing installed to keep 'hooligans' off the pitch, were caught in a deadly crush. Live graphic footage of the disaster was shown on British television as cameras and commentators switched their attention from the very early stages of the football match to the horror of fans dying in front of their eyes.

homophobia: aversion to, or prejudice against, homosexuals and homosexuality.

humanitarian: devoted to human welfare and the view that all people should be treated with equal dignity and respect.

hypermasculinity: the exaggeration of those stereotyped male attitudes and behaviours that tend to emphasize virility, physical strength, aggression and anti-femininity.

ideological effect: it is sometimes claimed that how the media represent violence can have an ideological effect on audiences by way of conditioning beliefs that certain forms or acts of violence are justified when committed by one person, group of people, or nation, upon another person, group or nation.

ideology: a concept associated with Marxist theorizing that conceives of the dominant social classes' worldview as conditioning the meanings through which all classes and groups understand the world in which they live.

imitative learning/imitative aggression: behaviour that is an outcome of one individual observing another's behaviour and replicating that behaviour.

interpretivist: a research approach concerned with investigating how people understand, define and interpret social and cultural phenomena.

James Bulger: the 2-year-old child killed by two 10-year-olds in Bootle, near Liverpool, UK, in 1993. At the boys' trial, the judge speculated as to whether the killers' actions had been prompted by their watching the video *Child's Play 3* in which a possessed child/mannequin terrorizes children. No evidence of the offenders having seen the film was ever found.

Kosovo War: this refers to two periods of armed conflict that occurred in Kosovo, the southern province of Serbia and former part of the Federal Republic of Yugoslavia. In 1996–99 this comprised the conflict between Albanian national liberation separatists and the Serbian and Yugoslavian armed forces, and in March to June 1999 the war between the North Atlantic Treaty Organization (NATO), which was seeking to defend the stability of the southern Balkan states and the European Union amid the Albanian and Serbian/Yugoslav conflict, and Yugoslavia.

longitudinal studies: studies in which data are collected from the same group of individuals at regular intervals over a period of time – usually months or years.

lynching: putting people to death, usually by mob action, without due legal process. Victims are usually members of marginalized social groups.

mean world syndrome: the idea that because the media represent violence to a much greater extent than it actually occurs in society, audiences develop a belief that the world is far more dangerous than it actually is and live in fear of becoming the victims of violence.

media dependency: a theory that we depend on the media for information about our social environment, important social issues, cultural values and entertainment. The more the media performs these functions for a person, the more that person is open to media influence.

media effects: see **effects theory**.

media literacy: the ability to actively read, analyse, and critically evaluate media content, the format in which content is presented, and potential influences of media content.

message system analysis: the term used by George Gerbner and his colleagues for the annual content analysis of all fictional television programmes in terms of number of violent acts portrayed, as well as the analysis of the gender, ethnicity, age, mental and physical ability/disability, occupation, etc. of victims and perpetrators.

misogyny/misogynist: a hatred of women/a woman hater.

moral panic theory: a theory that the media fuel fears about imaginary threats posed by particular groups of people and/or activities through sensationalist reporting and that the escalation of fear results in calls for state intervention in the form of direct action or policy legislation to counteract the imagined threat.

National Viewers and Listeners Association (NVALA): founded in 1965 by activist Mary Whitehouse, this UK pressure group sought to reduce what it regarded as the harmful portrayal of violence, sex, bad language, blasphemy and homosexuality in the British broadcast media. In 2001 the organization changed its name to 'Mediawatch-uk'.

neoliberalism: economic doctrine advocating market-led growth and the privatization of state-owned enterprises.

no causal effects: the term used to argue that the media have no direct influence on viewers' attitudes or behaviour. It is commonly used in the media violence debate in countering of the arguments of **effects theory**.

Orientalism: the discourse through which the West subordinates Asian cultures by constructing them as 'other' and which provides the intellectual justification for the political and economic exploitation and domination of Asian peoples and countries by Western nations and corporations.

paedophiles: people who are sexually attracted to children. Paedophilia is the condition of being sexually attracted to children.

Payne Fund Studies: an extensive set of research studies investigating the effects of film viewing upon youth audiences in the USA in the late 1920s and early 1930s. The studies remain to this day the largest audience research investigation of film effects, and included the study of the effects of watching depictions of crime and violence. The studies were largely discredited because of the simplistic cause-effect assertions drawn between film viewing and subsequent violent and criminal behaviour.

pornographic representation: see **pornography**.

pornography: the depiction of people, often in sexual acts or poses, that is designed to sexually arouse.

Port Arthur: in April 1996 in the town of Port Arthur in southeastern Tasmania, 29-year-old Martin Bryant used a semi-automatic rifle to kill 35 people and injure 37 others. Commonly known as the Port Arthur Massacre, it was initially speculated that Bryant's actions may have been influenced by his viewing of violent videos. No evidence to support this assertion was found.

positivist science: a research approach that believes that both the physical world and society can be studied objectively and that the biases of human judgement do not impact on our ability to observe and identify truthful facts about phenomena.

post-modern/post-modernism: in media and cultural studies, this term is predominantly used to refer to the post-industrial period marked by the ascendancy of consumer culture in which grand narratives of liberal, modernist theory of truth have been rejected.

post-structuralist: an analytical approach concerned with identifying and challenging hierarchies and discourses of power in society, and which regards those hierarchies and discourses as influential in determining human subjectivity and the meanings and opportunities associated with those subjectivities.

Press Complaints Commission (PCC): the independent UK body set up in 1991 to deal with complaints from members of the public about the editorial content of newspapers and magazines.

rhetorical/rhetoric: the use of language in a way that is intended to persuade.

semiotics: the study of the social production of meaning through signs which emphasizes the examination of how cultural context affects the meaning of texts.

September 11, 2001: the date on which al-Qa'ida carried out a series of terrorist attacks against the USA through the hijacking of four commercial passenger airliners. Two of these were crashed into the two towers of the World Trade Center in New York, which both collapsed. A third was crashed into the US Department of Defense headquarters in the Pentagon in Arlington, Virginia. The fourth plane crashed into a field in Pennsylvania. The attacks resulted in 2986 fatalities.

sexual harassment: the act of making sexual advances, such as touching or grabbing, and/or offensive sexual comments that are neither welcomed or appropriate.

sexual violence: the degradation or harming of an individual in a sexual manner.

social constructivist approach to media violence: an approach that emphasizes the analysis of how violence is subjectively represented, described, and explained by the media, and which does not accept that there is necessarily any objective reality behind that description.

social learning theory: the theory that learning occurs as a result of observing and imitating behaviour in others.

social reformers: people who advocate the need for social change (often coming from the middle classes), primarily through government intervention. Usually associated with the desire to change social practice in accordance with the reformer's own moral and ethical standards. Those social reform organizations that have campaigned about media content have tended to reflect highly conservative ideologies.

stereotypes: simplistic and generalized representations of groups of people based on, for example, their gender, ethnicity or sexuality, that fail to take into account individual differences and which often perpetuate false and negative characterizations.

structural violence: violence that is the result of social inequalities of power and which is manifested in, for example, poverty, suffering, and/or lack of opportunity.

subjective identities: identities adopted by a person as part of their internal state of perceiving and interacting in the social world.

terrorism: the unlawful use or threat to use violent force against people or property to achieve political, religious or ideological objectives.

video nasty: term used by the UK tabloid press to refer to uncertified horror films available on video cassette released in Britain during the early 1980s, and which the Director of Public Prosecutions considered potentially obscene.

voyeurism: the practice in which an individual finds gratification, usually sexual, from watching or otherwise engaging with the private details of other peoples lives. Can also generally refer to the use of an image as spectacle which is intended to gratify the viewer.

war on terrorism: the term used by George W. Bush's US government and its principal allies to describe the campaign to kill and destroy individuals and groups deemed 'terrorist', as well as nations identified as supporting terrorism, following the September 11, 2001 attacks on the World Trade Center and Pentagon.

white separatism: political movement to keep white people separate from people of colour, usually motivated by the ambition to maintain the 'purity' of, and social supremacy for, whites.

INDEX

Related books from Open University Press
Purchase from www.openup.co.uk or order through your local bookseller

---

VIOLENCE AND THE MEDIA
Cynthia Carter and C. Kay Weaver

- Why is there so much violence portrayed in the media?
- What meanings are attached to representations of violence in the media?
- Can media violence encourage violent behaviour and desensitize audiences to real violence?
- Does the 'everydayness' of media violence lead to the 'normalization' of violence in society?

Violence and the Media is a lively and indispensable introduction to current thinking about media violence and its potential influence on audiences. Adopting a fresh perspective on the 'media effects' debate, Carter and Weaver engage with a host of pressing issues around violence in different media contexts – including news, film, television, pornography, advertising and cyberspace.

The book offers a compelling argument that the daily repetition of media violence helps to normalize and legitimize the acts being portrayed. Most crucially, the influence of media violence needs to be understood in relation to the structural inequalities of everyday life. Using a wide range of examples of media violence primarily drawn from the American and British media to illustrate these points, *Violence and the Media* is a distinctive and revealing exploration of one of the most important and controversial subjects in cultural and media studies today.

224pp   0 335 20505 4 (EAN: 9 780335 205059) Paperback

Critical Readings
MEDIA AND GENDER
Cynthia Carter and Linda Steiner (eds)

- How is gender constructed in the media?
- To what extent do portrayals of gender influence everyday perceptions of ourselves and our actions?
- In what ways do the media reinforce and sometimes challenge gender inequalities?

Critical Readings: Media and Gender provides a lively and engaging introduction to the field of media and gender research, drawing from a wide range of important international scholarship. A variety of conceptual and methodological approaches are used to explore subjects such as: entertainment; news; grassroots communication; new media texts; institutions; audiences. Topics include:

- Gender identity and television talk shows
- Historical portrayals of women in advertising
- The sexualization of the popular press
- The representation of lesbians on television
- The cult of femininity in women's magazines
- Images of African American women and Latinas in Hollywood cinema
- Sexual violence in the media
- Women in popular music
- Pornography and masculine power
- Women's relationship to the Internet.

This book is ideal for undergraduate courses in cultural and media studies, gender studies, the sociology of the media, mass communication, journalism, communication studies and politics.

Essays by: John Beynon, Mary Ellen Brown, Helen Davies, Elizabeth Hadley Freydberg, Margaret Gallagher, Heather Gilmour, Patricia Holland, Sherrie A. Inness, Robert Jensen, Myra Macdonald, Marguerite Moritz, Carmen Ruíz, Anne Scott, Lesley Semmens, Jane Shattuc, Saraswati Sunindyo, Lynette Willoughby.

384pp   0 335 21097 X (EAN: 9 780335 210978) Paperback
0 335 21098 8 (EAN: 9 780335 210985) Hardback

Critical Readings
MORAL PANICS AND THE MEDIA
Chas Critcher (ed)

First developed by Stanley Cohen in 1972, 'moral panic' is a key term in media studies, used to refer to sudden eruptions of indignant concern about social issues. An occurrence of moral panic is characterized by stylized and stereotypical representation by the mass media and a tendency for those in power to claim the moral high ground and pronounce judgement. In this important book, Chas Critcher brings together essential readings on moral panics, which he locates in contemporary debates through an editor's introduction and concise section introductions.

The first section discusses moral panic models and includes contributions on the history and intellectual background of the concept. Differences in thinking between British and American moral panic scholarship are also examined. A second section features important case studies, including AIDS, Satanism, drugs, paedophilia and asylum seekers. This is followed by readings that look at themes such as the importance of language, rhetoric and discourse; the dynamics of media reporting and how it affects public opinion; and the idea of the 'risk society'. Finally, readings critique and debate the use and relevance of moral panic models.

Critical Readings: Moral Panics and the Media is a valuable resource for students and researchers in media studies, criminology and sociology.

Essays by: David L. Altheide, Nachman Ben-Yehuda, Joel Best, Theodore Chiricos, John Clarke, Stan Cohen, Chas Critcher, Mary deYoung, Julie Dickinson, Erich Goode, Johanna Habermeier, Stuart Hall, Sean P. Hier, Tony Jefferson, Philip Jenkins, Hans Mathias Kepplinger, Jennifer Kitzinger, Daniel Maier-Katkin, Angela McRobbie, Peter Meylakhs, Suzanne Ost, Bryan Roberts, Liza Schuster, Stephen Stockwell, Kenneth Thompson, Sarah L. Thornton, Sheldon Ungar, Simon Watney, Jeffrey Weeks, Michael Welch, Paul Williams.

352pp   0 335 21807 5 (9 780335 218073) Paperback
        0 335 21808 3 (EAN: 9 780335 218080) Hardback